The Medical Metropolis

AMERICAN BUSINESS,
POLITICS, AND SOCIETY

Series editors
Andrew Wender Cohen, Shane Hamilton,
Kim Phillips-Fein, and Elizabeth Tandy Shermer

Books in the series American Business, Politics, and Society
explore the relationships over time between politics, society,
and the creation and performance of markets, firms, and
industries large and small. The central theme of this series is
that culture, law, and public policy have been fundamental
to the evolution of American business from the colonial
era to the present. The series aims to explore, in particular,
developments that have enduring consequences.

A complete list of books in the series
is available from the publisher.

The Medical
Metropolis

Health Care
and Economic Transformation
in Pittsburgh and Houston

Andrew T. Simpson

PENN

UNIVERSITY OF PENNSYLVANIA PRESS

PHILADELPHIA

Copyright © 2019 University of Pennsylvania Press

Published by
University of Pennsylvania Press
Philadelphia, Pennsylvania 19104-4112
www.upenn.edu/pennpress

Printed in the United States of America
on acid-free paper
1 3 5 7 9 10 8 6 4 2

A catalogue record is available from the Library of Congress
ISBN 978-0-8122-5167-8

Contents

Introduction

Making the Medical Metropolis

In 2008, the University of Pittsburgh Medical Center (UPMC) hoisted its logo atop the U.S. Steel Building, symbolically declaring that the era of big medicine had replaced the era of big steel in Pittsburgh. Since its creation in 1990, UPMC has become the largest private employer in the Commonwealth of Pennsylvania, with more than eighty thousand employees and steadily growing revenue—now well over $15 billion per year. The transition between an industrial economy and a service economy strongly grounded in health care is now central to how Pittsburghers see the identity of their city for the next century.[1]

More than 1,200 miles to the south, in Houston, Texas, health care is also playing a critical role in that city's ability to navigate changes in the global economy and in its plans for the future. In April 2008, Forbes.com named Houston one of the ten "recession-proof" cities in the United States.[2] While this glowing projection did not come to pass, Houston was able to better weather the most recent economic downturn, actually gaining more jobs by 2010 than it lost in the Great Recession. Oil and natural gas remain important, but the health care and the service sectors also play a critical role in Houston's economy.[3] Since 2007, health care employment has risen by more than 20 percent, and the Texas Medical Center, located only a few miles from downtown, is touted as the "largest medical complex in the world." In 2018, information released by its management organization, TMC Inc., claimed the medical center alone had in excess of 106,000 employees and more than "$3 billion in medical construction projects underway." They also claimed that medical center hospitals had ten million "patient encounters per year, 180,000 + annual surgeries," and three-quarters of a million emergency room visits a year. Like in Pittsburgh, a booming health care sector is critical for how Houstonians see their city's future.[4]

Both Pittsburgh and Houston have emerged as national models for how to build an economy for the postindustrial era. According to pundits and scholars, their "formula" for success is easy and replicable: focus on economic diversification by building strong medical, educational, and applied research sectors through links with hospitals and universities; make older core industries more efficient through automation; attract and retain a young, educated, upwardly mobile workforce by investing in quality-of-life amenities; and draw civic leadership from a new generation of young, hip politicians who can relate to this new "creative class."[5]

Other cities, like Evansville, Indiana, are paying attention. Evansville is located roughly eight hundred miles down the Ohio River from Pittsburgh, and over the last several decades, this city of around 120,000 people has lost longtime manufacturing employers like Whirlpool and experienced the boom and bust of the extraction economy (coal). However, it has many of the same features as Pittsburgh and Houston, including multiple universities, an established community college system, and, since 2014, an extension campus of the Indiana University School of Medicine. Leaders are promoting these assets by using a civic reinvention narrative that echoes the rallying cry shouted by civic elites in larger cities, claiming that by becoming a regional center for health care delivery and medical education, along with other investments in higher education, finance, and new housing, Evansville will be able to attract and retain a younger population and finally share in the seeming prosperity of the health care–oriented postindustrial city.[6]

This reinvention narrative relies on a flattening of history. In it, hospitals and universities are treated as bit players who suddenly step into a starring role when the lead actors suffer an untimely demise. Its heroes—the elected officials, leaders of not-for-profit health care organizations, and educated in-migrants affiliated with local universities and health care systems—are "visionaries" who make the bold and uncontroversial choice to prioritize the development of advanced research and health care as the new engines of economic development. Reinvention is a foregone conclusion. While this story contains essential elements of truth, it also obscures as much as it illuminates. Almost no attention is given either to the long-term development of not-for-profit hospitals or universities, their changing relationship to American capitalism, or the public policy choices that shaped their development before the moment of economic reshuffling.[7]

This book traces how health care helped to build the postindustrial city into what I call the "medical metropolis," which is a city where health care plays a dominant role in its economy and identity. From the 1940s to the present, civic elites, including civic development groups, elected officials, not-for-profit health care administrators, and individual physicians, have worked to build a new identity for each city as a site for cutting-edge biomedical and clinical research, medical and health professional education, a home for innovative health care business practices, and centers for quality patient care. The transformation of both Pittsburgh and Houston into medical metropolises is rooted in the changing business environment. Not-for-profit health care emerged as a multi-billion-dollar business at the very moment when the postindustrial turn was reshaping the broader U.S. economy. The medical metropolis is not an accident. At the heart of the process of making it is a set of choices with consequences, both intentional and accidental. Choice matters not only for understanding the actions that built the medical metropolis, but also for understanding how and why these actions often ignored or fell short of creating an economy and city that fully served all residents.

The Medical Metropolis is the first comparative historical study of the evolution of academic medical centers, the business of not-for-profit health care, and the effect of using hospitals as a cornerstone of urban economic development across multiple cities from 1945 to the present. Urban historians have been more attentive to the ways that health care shapes the city than historians of medicine, but within both fields, there is more work to be done.[8] One important new direction is to examine the synergistic relationship between the business of not-for-profit health care and urban development. Doing so reminds us that both private markets and public policy matter for understanding why change occurs over time.

Examining the intersection between private markets and public policy also requires exploring the dynamic relationship between health care payment and health care policy—a nexus which has been a particularly fruitful area of study for several generations of historians of medicine, but that only recently has been examined in the 1980s and beyond in sufficient detail.[9] By detailing the growth of specialty medical services such as cardiovascular surgery and transplantation medicine, this book shows how these not only contributed to the civic identity of Pittsburgh and Houston, but also how specialty medicine became a lucrative business that imported patients into each city and exported the clinical knowledge and business acumen of not-for-profit health care institutions and their famous physicians.

It also examines the relationship between not-for-profit health care and efforts to use biomedical research to help reinvent the postindustrial city. Biotechnology became a way to bring together civic elites, elected officials, and not-for-profit health care into a conversation about what the future of the medical metropolis should look like and how to share the responsibility to achieve this vision. While biotechnology has failed to meet its lofty expectations in both communities, nevertheless it has played an essential role in rebranding each city as a global center of innovation, which has attracted a wide range of other technologically focused investments.

The Medical Metropolis contributes to an emerging debate about the growing role of not-for-profit institutions in modern American communities, though less attention has been paid to their history in the post–World War II era.[10] This book examines these institutions in two critical ways. The first is by showing why large not-for-profit health systems are created and how they grew in the 1980s and beyond, including building affiliation networks, showing why large health systems sought merger partners, and illustrating how some grew through acquisition. This provides context for the book's second contribution to the debate about not-for-profit community responsibility—examining demands by elected officials on not-for-profit health systems to provide more reduced-cost patient care, as was the case in Houston, or make payments in lieu of taxes to cash-strapped cities, as was the case in Pittsburgh. Each of these stories shows the tension that occurs when health care institutions, seen as "a once charitable enterprise," grow to become a foundational part of the modern urban economy.[11]

At the heart of this story is what I term the hospital-civic relationship. This idea is shorthand for the theoretical and practical interconnection between civic elites, not-for-profit health care administrators, physicians, elected officials, and ordinary citizens with not-for-profit health care institutions. This is a dynamic relationship that evolves from a model where hospitals and health care supported the growth of the industrial city in the early postwar years to a more market-oriented vision by the end of the century. It is also a relationship that is deeply contested and reflects the goals, priorities, and values of each party.

I use "hospital" in this formulation because not-for-profit hospitals are the most visible way that most residents of the medical metropolis relate to health care. Academic medical centers have emerged as a triumph of modernity and a symbol of what the American health care system can accomplish. They are often a focal point of community identity and a potent symbol of modernity. At the same time, to urban residents displaced by their expansion, used willingly or unwillingly as clinical material, or denied their services because of an inability to pay, they are symbols of the excesses of capitalism and the persistent racism and injustice that still scar the face of the American city.[12] Not-for-profit health care also includes medical schools, insurance companies, and physician practices. Not all of these have received sufficient attention from historians, and this book touches on the contributions of each. *The Medical Metropolis* draws from existing literature in the history of medicine and business history, as well as a robust and growing literature about the history of community medicine, to examine how business decisions and social justice concerns intersected around issues of health.[13]

Why Pittsburgh and Houston?

Today, not-for-profit health care is a major employer in several major American cities besides Pittsburgh and Houston, including Cleveland, Baltimore, Atlanta, and Chicago.[14] Health care has also helped to provide these cities with a new way to market their postindustrial identity. Simply fly into their airports and the traveler is confronted with an eye-popping number of advertisements linking health care, innovation, and future urban growth. So, if the health care economy is now touted as part of the solution for postindustrial inequality, then the lack of attention paid by historians to its development is an oversight which should be corrected if we want to plan for a just and sustainable economic future. By using a case study approach that focuses more deeply on two cities, I hope to provide insight that historians, policymakers, and citizens can apply to conversations about their own city's past and present.

Even as the medical metropolis is marketed as the future, their deep roots in the older industrial economy are still strong. Pittsburgh's nickname remains the "Steel City"—branding which still appears frequently on everything from T-shirts to the names of numerous businesses. Even the three "diamonds" in the logo of the city's professional football team, the Steelers, represent the three critical elements of steel-making (coal, iron ore, and scrap steel), and help to tie that team to the region's past.[15] In Houston, while

the Oilers may have given way to the Texans, the extraction economy and
the city are still synonymous.

There are, however, a number of reasons why these cities work as units
of analysis. Perhaps the most important is that they are broadly representative of the historical and geographical trends that converged in other cities
to help make the medical metropolis. I didn't always assume this was the
case. In fact, when I began this project, I assumed that each city had a
widely different story. Pittsburgh, after all, is a fading industrial city located
in the heart of the Rust Belt, whose recent history is marked by decline,
population loss, and much-touted, but still uneven and incomplete, Renaissance. Houston is a growing Sun Belt city that, since World War II, has
struggled more often with managing the problems of growth than those of
decline.[16] Instead, what I found was that while local differences do matter,
broad national forces such as medical reimbursement streams, federal biomedical research monies, and individual decisions made in the private
medical market by physicians, hospitals, and consumers played a homoge-
nizing role in making the medical metropolis.[17] A focus on health care also
helps to enrich a growing literature on the rise of service sector jobs over
manufacturing ones and high technology over heavy industry as part of the
development of a broader neoliberal project.[18]

Access to archival and other primary sources also played a central role
in determining my choice of cases. In both cities, there is a rich array of
archival sources that help to tell the story of making the medical metropolis.
With a bit of searching, it is possible to access at least some records of
large not-for-profit health care organizations, as well as the papers of the
individual physicians and administrators who provided these organizations
with leadership. Access is, of course, easier for the more distant past than
the present. However, as new collections of personal and institutional
papers are being added to area archives at a rapid pace, the documentary
record continues to grow and will enable future generations of historians
with more evidence to continue to tell the story of the medical metropolis
as it evolves in the twenty-first century and beyond.[19] Finally, I was the
beneficiary of the generosity of numerous individuals and organizations,
many of whom are named in the acknowledgments, who shared their time
and their personal and organizational records.

An examination of both Pittsburgh and Houston also helps the reader
to understand how national definitions of urban health and civic identity
have changed over the course of the last seventy-odd years.[20] Even though

the way that an individual city's leaders and citizens choose to present it to the world is a deeply local choice, the decision to highlight certain sectors, like health care, as part of Pittsburgh's and Houston's national and international images reflects broader national values about social justice, economic competition, and the distribution of power. As more historians embrace the comparative case study approach, this question of the construction of civic identity in the post–World War II era is being engaged in more detail, which can help civic leaders and individuals committed to urban development to go beyond the platitudes of health care's civic contribution and think critically about how the business model for this sector can be reformed to build vibrant, just, and sustainable communities for the future.

The medical metropolis is not a product of chance or luck, nor did it suddenly emerge with the collapse of the industrial economy. For more than half a century, efforts to think critically about the role of health care and its relationship to the economic and physical health of the American city have played an important role in how civic elites, leaders of not-for-profit health care institutions and universities, and ordinary citizens have planned for the future.[21] While these plans have often focused on the narrowly defined interest of each group, the consequences of their shared efforts, both intentional and unintentional, built the medical metropolis.

Chapter 1

Building Cities of Health

Medical Centers in Pittsburgh and Houston Before 1965

In 1959, leaders in Pittsburgh's health insurance and not-for-profit hospital sectors distributed a promotional booklet titled "Pittsburgh's Fortresses of Health: 200 Years of Hospital Progress," which was meant to showcase the vital role that not-for-profit health care institutions played in protecting the health of the city and the region. The booklet argued that hospitals, and by extension a larger tradition of not-for-profit health care, were "built and maintained by the people of the community" and thus represented the way that health care supported the growth and stability of the industrial city.

Even though this was a marketing scheme, its use of the phrase "city of health" reflected that after World War II the fate of cities and health care was interwined.[1] Since the 1920s, not-for-profit hospitals, medical schools, and universities claimed that their threefold work in patient care, medical education, and biomedical research, or what the Houston Chamber of Commerce called the "eternal triangle," gave these institutions a special place within the industrial city as a guarantor of a broadly defined notion of health that encompassed both physical health and economic health, or what might be termed civic health.[2] This understanding of the relationship between not-for-profit health care institutions and civic health was prioritized as part of efforts to expand the New Deal state by Harry Truman and his successors after World War II by improving health care delivery system and by making large amounts of funding available for biomedical research.

Legislation like the Hospital Survey and Construction Act of 1946, more popularly known as Hill-Burton, made money available from state and federal governments and helped to build new general hospitals and academic medical centers. While Hill-Burton disproportionally benefited smaller communities, large academic medical centers still took advantage of the program.[3] Local governments also demonstrated their commitment to hospital construction. In some localities, like Allegheny County, Pennsylvania, where Pittsburgh is located, hospital development authorities were created, which issued tax-exempt bonds to support the growth of not-for-profit health care institutions.[4]

The dramatic expansion of federal funding for biomedical research through the growth of the National Institutes of Health after World War II also demonstrated a broad commitment to the idea of civic health. Not-for-profit health care institutions, such as university medical schools and their affiliated hospitals, were important beneficiaries of a philosophy that linked scientific research with social and economic progress. Moreover, the increasing ability of disease advocacy groups to influence the direction of federal health research spending also played a critical role in helping to build a biomedical research economy.[5] In addition to governmental support, private dollars, which had been an important part of medicine before World War II, remained an essential, if somewhat less visible, part of the overall health care funding mix, especially given the tendency of capital, as well as a concentration of medical specialists, to agglomerate in urban areas.[6]

Exemption from most federal, state, and local taxes was another way that some health care institutions enjoyed a special status. This privilege was not without obligation. To qualify for their not-for-profit status, hospitals were required to provide some degree of care for patients unable to pay. What this care looked like varied over time from an almshouse model that linked treatment to service in the hospital to a model that, by the early twentieth century, often had an explicit expectation that charity patients were clinical material for scientists, physicians, and medical students.[7]

Hospitals and other not-for-profit health care institutions like medical schools were the physical spaces where this vision of civic health was articulated. As such, these institutions were expected to serve primarily as locational assets rather than be seen as important economic actors in their own right.[8] This idealistic understanding existed in tension with the reality of the urban economy. As these institutions grew, questions emerged about the most efficient way to manage their resources. The answers helped to create new management and planning structures that prioritized efficiency and fiscal probity, and, in doing so, deemphasized efforts by civic elites to promote them as locational assets. It also prioritized an understanding that not-for-profit health care was part of a market-oriented vision for how the American city should remake itself for the postindustrial future.

This is not to argue that one model simply replaced the other, or that change was sudden and clear-cut. In fact, not-for-profit health care institutions always operated within a set of financial constraints that required careful attention to budgets and expenditures, as well as a cautious outlook on what amenities and services were needed to attract patients and donors. Over the course of the twentieth century, however, the narrative that civic elites, not-for-profit health care leaders, and even everyday citizens promoted—about the value of hospitals and not-for-profit health care institutions in the industrial city as locational assets rather than centers of economic activities themselves—gradually, but decisively, changed to emphasize the latter over the former. Throughout this book, I use the term "hospital-civic relationship" as a shorthand for this changing and complex relationship between not-for-profit health care and cities.[9]

A Medical Center for Pittsburgh

Before Pittsburgh was known as either the Steel City or the medical metropolis, it was the gateway to the West. The point of land where the Allegheny, Monongahela, and Ohio Rivers intersect played a key role in the battle for the territorial rights of North America.[10] During the first decades of the nineteenth century, it became a manufacturing center, claiming several glass mills as well as potteries, breweries, and iron works.[11] The city's primary metals industry remained the provenance of numerous small-scale operators until the discovery of a large seam of low-sulfur coal nearby, which was ideal fuel for a new technology, the Bessemer furnace.[12] A ready source of fuel, a growing immigrant workforce, and abundant local capital combined in the later part of the nineteenth century to help rationalize the primary metals industry. As mills sprang up all along its river valleys, the companies that employed these workers pursued a brutal form of vertical and horizontal integration.[13]

In Pittsburgh, and across the United States, the profits from industrialization poured into a wave of institution building. Universities and medical schools were important beneficiaries. Here, private dollars intersected with larger professionalization efforts in medicine to create new organizational forms like the academic medical center. This concept linked hospitals and medical education into a shared space under the control of a university. It remained a relative rarity, if not a fairly common aspiration, during the first decades of the twentieth century. In fact, most medical education was conducted by proprietary medical colleges that had little uniformity in their curriculum and lax requirements for admission. The Flexner Report of 1910, commissioned by the Carnegie Foundation for the Advancement of Teaching, has traditionally been hailed as the watershed moment that sounded the clarion call to move from the proprietary model to the university-based model. Over the next several decades, as medical education moved, at least in theory, closer to the Flexnerian ideal of being provided by a full-time teaching faculty with training in the basic sciences and clinical opportunities at a closely affiliated modern hospital, the academic medical center emerged as the crown jewel of the American health care system.[14]

Translating community support for better health into creating an academic medical center took time. During the early 1920s, several not-for-profit hospitals provided teaching services to the University of Pittsburgh's medical school. However, these hospitals, as well as several of the university's professional schools, were scattered throughout the city. While both the Flexner Report and the American Medical Association initially cited the University of Pittsburgh as an excellent example of what a modern medical school should be, funding issues, combined with the lack of a medical center, quickly created challenges for retaining this accolade.[15] Decentralization presented a particularly difficult situation for medical school administrators; not only did it make them dependent on a cadre of part-time faculty, but as other medical schools across the country started to consolidate operations, it raised questions about how committed the medical school was to fully embracing the Flexnerian model. By 1921, the problem had gotten so bad that the Pennsylvania State Board of Medical Licensure threatened to downgrade the school's ranking, effectively undercutting the ability of its graduates to practice in the commonwealth.[16]

In the fall of 1920, John Gabbert Bowman, then the director of the American College of Surgeons, visited the city to talk about the organization's hospital standardization and reform programs. Two days later, Bowman left with a job offer—to become the next chancellor of the University of Pittsburgh. On his way back to Chicago, Bowman stopped in Rochester, Minnesota, to visit with his friend Dr. William Mayo. Bowman mentioned the job offer to Mayo, who gave him the following advice: "If you were my son, I would make you go to Pittsburgh. Do you realize that Pittsburgh is the last place in the United States where there is not a great university and where there could be one? The people, the wealth, the stability—everything is there. You could build one of the great universities of the world. God made you for the job. You must go."[17]

Whether or not it was divine intervention, Bowman's arrival ushered in a new era for the University of Pittsburgh and the idea of an academic medical center in the city. With the support of the city's powerful industrialists, Bowman and his staff, particularly medical school dean Raleigh R. Huggins, promoted the idea of building a medical center in Pittsburgh.[18] At the heart of this campaign was an attempt to lay the groundwork for the powerful linkage between civic modernity and modern medicine that structures the hospital-civic relationship up to the present. A promotional pamphlet published during the late 1920s or early 1930s quoted prominent figures like famous neurosurgeon Dr. Harvey Cushing, Surgeon General Dr. Hugh S. Cumming, and Dr. John T. Finney, a pupil of William Osler and first president of the American College of Surgeons. All spoke about the general value of medical centers to improving health, but Cushing spoke to the anxiety that many in Pittsburgh's industrial elite and emerging middle class felt about the city's reputation as a social and cultural backwater. Cushing said, "All I can say is, from a distant standpoint, that Pittsburgh is practically unknown, medically speaking, to the country at large. A great medical center could well enough be established in Pittsburgh; but a medical center amounts to nothing and will remain negligible unless you can capture the proper men to conduct it and to put it on the map."[19] In fact, backers hoped that the presence of an academic medical center would send a powerful message about the city's modernity and economic success; after all, only a city that was both modern and wealthy would be able to marshal the public and private resources necessary to fund an academic medical center's construction, upkeep, and continued expansion.

While recruiting nationally recognized personnel remained a perennial issue, construction began in the 1920s and 1930s. Ground was broken for a children's hospital in 1926, an eye and ear hospital opened in 1934, and, finally, a general hospital, Presbyterian Hospital, opened in 1938. An outpatient clinic, the Falk Clinic, opened in 1931. Elizabeth Steele Magee Hospital, which primarily focused on labor and delivery, retained its independence and nearby location, but entered into a teaching agreement

Figure 1. Aerial view of Pittsburgh's Oakland neighborhood including the University of Pittsburgh's Medical Center, circa 1949–1950.

OAKLD01.UA University of Pittsburgh Archives Photograph Collection, 1810–2006, UA.Photos, University Archives, Archives and Special Collections, University of Pittsburgh Library System.

with the university in 1931.[20] The number of general hospital beds in the surrounding fifteen-county region also continued to grow. Between 1931 and 1941, the ratio of general hospital beds per one thousand people grew by 11 percent in Pittsburgh. When all fifteen counties in the Southwestern Pennsylvania region were added together, there was a more than 50 percent growth in general hospital beds from 1931 to 1956.[21]

During these same years, civic leaders and elected officials created a public-private partnership tasked with reinventing the city for the next half-century to address persistent fears about the city's industrial and physical decline. Named the Allegheny Conference on Community Development, it was formed in 1943 and worked as a formal body supplemented by a network of informal partnerships, often hashed out at the corporate board level. Especially in its early years, one feature that made it unusual was its clearly demarcated lines of authority. Philanthropist and corporate titan Richard King Mellon was the driving force behind the Conference's creation and had a great deal of say over its actions and priorities. Mellon, and his brother-in-law Alan Magee Scaife, who died in 1958, were major patrons of the university and its medical center during the postwar years.[22]

Aggressive marketing campaigns by elite-led development organizations were an important way to inform the public and potential regional investors, not just about what type of health facilities a region boasted, but how engaged they were with civic improvement and providing health for current and future industrial workers. For example, in a series of cartoons drawn to commemorate the seventy-fifth anniversary of the Pittsburgh Chamber of Commerce in 1948, one prominently featured drawings of the medical center and surgeons standing over an operating table above the organization's tagline, "Pittsburgh's Prosperity is Your Security."[23] Large local companies also reinforced the link between the provision of patient care by not-for-profit hospitals and local economic stability in their marketing materials. In April 1956, local electric utility Duquesne Light placed an advertisement in the *Wall Street Journal* designed to show current residents and potential migrants how Pittsburgh area hospitals supported a new, healthful image for the once smoky city. The ad featured large aerial photos of the University of Pittsburgh health center, complete with a helpful key to the hospitals and outpatient clinics. Just below one of these photos was a drawing of a happy middle-class couple with the tagline, "The New Pittsburgh . . . building to improve the HEALTH of its PEOPLE."[24]

The service lines offered by not-for-profit hospitals reflected the overlap between patient care responsibilities and the protection of the industrial workforce highlighted by these advertisements. The decision by the University of Pittsburgh to invest in industrial medicine, the forerunner to today's occupational health, illustrates this point.[25] In 1929, medical school dean Raleigh R. Huggins was able to convince local steel executive Edward Bindley to fund lectures in industrial medicine, and by 1937 more money was donated by Westinghouse Electric to expand the medical school's curriculum in this area.[26] By 1952, the university was promoting its industrial medical program as part of the broader services it provided to the community

Figure 2. As part of the locational asset model, civic organizations like the Pittsburgh Chamber of Commerce argued that hospitals helped to contribute to overall economic stability of the city and region, rather than focusing on their role as economic actors in their own right. Originally drawn in 1948 for a newspaper advertisement campaign by Ralph Reichhold, and reproduced in 1949 in "A Cartoonist Looks at Pittsburgh," a commemoration of the chamber's seventy-fifth anniversary.

and region through its role as a locational asset. For example, a promotional brochure for the medical center reminded the local community, "No less than machines, men are becoming the employers' 24 hour-a-day concern by reason of economic evolution and growing necessity," and "Losses incurred by curtailment of production as the result of nonoccupational sickness, for example, are mounting into the billions of dollars annually." Research included the standard teaching and research but, perhaps even more important, "consulting services to all types of industrial organizations." In addition, the university worked with the Industrial Hygiene Foundation to help "slash the enormous wastage involved in the cost of absenteeism. It is keeping employees on the job."[27] Other service lines that supported both workers and their families, like emergency medicine and obstetrics, were also areas of focus by the region's hospitals.[28] While it is not clear if the gospel of industrial medicine in Pittsburgh had much support among the workers who were supposed to benefit from its paternalist outreach, the creation and subsequent support for the program does highlight a critical part of the locational asset model—that industrial leaders and medical philanthropy understood that the primary reason to support a city's health care assets was to protect its industrial workforce and, in doing so, protect its economic security.

Patient care and the physical expansion of hospitals supported the locational asset model in a very present-oriented fashion by helping industrial workers and their families remain healthy and productive. The relationship of the other two legs of the triangle to the locational asset model was more complex and also helped civic elites see not-for-profit health care as a set of institutions that could strengthen the city's present competitiveness in relation to other growing industrial centers and, in doing so, perhaps help to shape the city's future. In this respect, biomedical research was essential for helping to create a reputation for each city as a center of scientific and technical innovation. On a day-to-day level, biomedical research brought in federal and private dollars to institutions, helping to fuel their physical growth.[29] However, for civic boosters, the real value of biomedical research, at least within the locational asset model, was for promoting a narrative of civic progress.

Pittsburgh's role as a center for polio research serves as an instructive example. In September 1952, officials from the medical center distributed a glossy three-color brochure titled "War on Polio: A Progress Report of the University of Pittsburgh Medical Center"; it featured stories about the "polio fighters from the University of Pittsburgh and other research centers" traveling all over the country to conduct experiments and field trials (including a gamma globulin trial in Houston) designed to stop the disease, as well as the progress being made on a vaccine in the school's virology laboratories.[30] Pitt researchers were not simply participants in the fight against polio; the gamma globulin field trials conducted between 1951 and 1953 were led by a member of the university's faculty, Dr. William McDowell Hammon from the Graduate School of Public Health. In the battle to beat back polio, however, it was a virology researcher named Dr. Jonas Salk who gained the most national attention with the success of his killed-virus vaccine in 1955. Salk soon became the face of medical innovation in Pittsburgh and his success became an important way that civic elites marketed Pittsburgh.[31]

Expanding hospitals and service lines to meet the needs of the industrial city cost money. The creation of the Hospital Service Association of Pittsburgh, or what later become Blue Cross of Western Pennsylvania, played a powerful role in providing that capital from the 1930s onward. The Blues were autonomous not-for-profit organizations tied together by a central office in Chicago. Plans existed for regions, states, or even multistate areas. Typically, because of their not-for-profit orientation and the fact that Blue Cross plans used a concept called community rating that pooled risk across a wide range of groups in the community, they were tax-exempt, unlike their commercial competitors.[32]

Blue Cross played a particularly central role in Pittsburgh. Part of the grand bargain for labor stability during World War II was extending fringe benefits to workers, like employer-sponsored health insurance.[33] In the early 1950s, it started to offer coverage across the nation to members of the United Steelworkers, helping to serve as a model for how corporations could provide health insurance coverage for their workers.[34] Blue Cross guaranteed a steady stream of clinical income and, in many cases, removed the uncertainty of collections and the possibility of unpaid bills, which, during the Depression, had been a persistent struggle for hospitals nationwide. In 1943, for example, Blue Cross payments to hospitals in Western Pennsylvania totaled $2,987,767; by 1945, that number had risen to $4,378,756; and the following year, enrollment in the plan topped 1 million people. The numbers of enrolled continued to grow throughout the 1950s, reaching over 1.7 million by 1952. By 1958, Blue Cross payments to hospitals totaled $50,339,169 for that year alone.[35]

Blue Cross reimbursement provides an example of how a private market for health care was also operating to build hospitals, alongside the efforts of philanthropists and universities. Many hospitals from the late nineteenth and early twentieth centuries were originally built with a large number of ward beds, which made sense in an era when most working people paid for their hospitalization costs out of pocket or received charity care. Ward beds were cheap, they allowed for easy teaching, and their lack of privacy discouraged long stays. And, while a move to more semiprivate rooms was under way in the early decades of the twentieth century, in Pittsburgh, Blue Cross helped to perhaps speed up this process by guaranteeing many of its members semiprivate accommodations.[36] For example, in 1946, 79.4 percent of Blue Cross–sponsored hospital admissions to the state-aided hospitals in western Pennsylvania received semiprivate accommodations, with only 20.6 percent receiving ward accommodations. Contrast this with non–Blue Cross admissions at the same hospitals, of which 58.6 percent of admissions received ward accommodations, and semiprivate accommodations were given to only 41.4 percent. As a report sponsored by the Hospital Council noted, "People with more money go to the hospital and purchase better accommodations."[37] Even though market capitalism and hospital administration had long coexisted, by the 1960s, the pressure on these institution hospitals to be more responsive to the needs of the private market was gaining steam. This was also the case in Houston and would, by the end of the decade, have a profound effect on how the hospital-civic relationship evolved, despite the protestations by not-for-profit health care administrators and civic elites that hospitals should continue to primarily exist as a locational asset supporting the industrial economy.

The Creation of the Texas Medical Center

The story of the Texas Medical Center starts in Pittsburgh. Eighteen years after John Bowman was first invited to Pittsburgh, a young Texas dentist named Frederick C. Elliott arrived in the city on business. Elliott had just been appointed as the dean of the Texas Dental College, and he was visiting to speak with his counterpart at the University of Pittsburgh's Dental School. "When I was leaving," Elliott recalled, "I asked the dean about the beautiful building across the street. He said it was the university. I asked him about what college of the university needed such a large building. He smiled and told me that all of the colleges of the university except medicine and dentistry were in this building. . . . As I thought about this building on my way back to Houston, an idea came to me. Why not house all educational disciplines related to health in one building?"[38] His observation of the University of Pittsburgh's Cathedral of Learning provided the intellectual seed for the Texas Medical Center—so much so that Elliott provided free dental services to a young architecture student at Rice University in exchange for renderings of the proposed Houston medical center. Later, he had the renderings made into a plaster model that featured a working Torch of Eternal Health made from a Bunsen burner, a pan of water (to create steam), and a flashlight.[39] Translating the hope of creating a medical center into the reality of building one was a difficult and lengthy process. It required cultivating strong links among local philanthropists, industries, and the health care community.

In 1836, Augustus and John Allen purchased the land that became modern-day Houston and started building a city, which they named in honor of Sam Houston.[40] The city soon began to grow rapidly, reaching over two thousand people only three years later and serving for a short time as the first capital of the Republic of Texas. Even after Houston failed to become the permanent capital due in part to a perception that its swampy location was incompatible with health, its links to a broader southern commodity market proved essential for future economic success.[41] Its role as a commodity center was helped by persistent efforts to make it into a port city, which came to fruition with the completion of the Houston Ship Channel in 1914, allowing the city, especially in the wake of the 1900 hurricane that destroyed the Port of Galveston, to emerge as the leading port city in the entire state.[42]

In the popular imagination, the oil industry is Houston's defining economic sector.[43] While the early wildcatters may represent the stereotypical Texas oil men, the period of corporate consolidation starting in the early decades of the twentieth century and the intervention of the Texas Railroad Commission brought relative stability to a still-volatile industry and helped to increase and consolidate the revenue from oil production and refining. Moreover, as the oil industry matured, it served as the base for a global oil services industry, petrochemicals, as well as a strong finance and legal sector in which Houstonians also played an outsized role.[44]

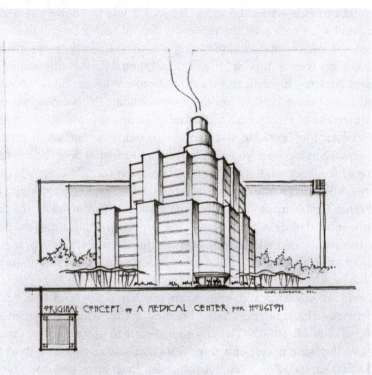

ORIGINAL CONCEPT of A MEDICAL CENTER for HOUSTON

Figure 3. Original concept drawing of the proposed Texas Medical Center by Karl Kamrath, commissioned by Frederick Elliott, circa 1940s.

MS071 Frederick Elliott, DDS, Series IV, Box 9, folder 6, John P. McGovern Historical Collections and Research Center, Houston Academy of Medicine–Texas Medical Center Library, Houston, Texas.

The financial seeds for the Texas Medical Center (TMC) were planted during the transitional years between the decline of the cotton economy and the rise of the extraction economy. In the 1930s, the Houston cotton firm of Anderson, Clayton & Co. faced a situation that threatened to destroy it from within. The firm was founded in 1904 as a partnership between two brothers, Frank and Monroe Dunaway Anderson, and their brother-in-law, Will Clayton. By the 1930s, this small partnership had grown to become one of the most successful cotton exporting firms in the world.[45] As the partners aged and their health declined, a combination of internal partnership agreements and federal tax laws forced each of them to start thinking about how to divest their stakes in the company. M. D.

Anderson, who was a bachelor, decided that the best way to handle his divestment was not to force his partners to pay $20 million for his shares, but rather to endow a foundation as his primary beneficiary.[46]

The M.D. Anderson Foundation had a four-part mission: to improve working conditions for laborers; to establish and support the construction of hospitals and other health-related facilities; to seek to generally improve the quality of life; and to promote "health, science, education, and advancement and diffusion of knowledge and understanding among people."[47] When Anderson died in 1939, the bulk of his assets were transferred to the foundation, leaving his trustees Colonel William Bates, John H. Freeman, and Horace Wilkins to decide on the specifics of how to fulfill its mission. None of these men was in a hurry to spend the Anderson Foundation's money. They waited until the right opportunity presented itself, which finally came in 1941, when the state of Texas passed legislation allowing for the creation of a state hospital for cancer treatment and research.

Bates, Freeman, and Wilkins saw the cancer hospital as a starting point for an entire medical center to be built from the ground up in Houston. They were also active in helping the Texas Dental College affiliate with the University of Texas system to become the University of Texas Dental Branch. These two institutions formed the nucleus of the TMC. To secure the cancer hospital for Houston, the M. D. Anderson Foundation approached the legislature and promised a matching donation of $500,000 if money was allocated for the Houston site. Always looking to save money, the legislature agreed to the Anderson Foundation's offer, essentially allowing the state to build a new hospital at half the price. The Anderson Foundation's grant was even more generous since the foundation agreed, over and above the initial investment, to provide both temporary quarters and a permanent building site for the new hospital, further helping to pass the cost of the project along to private donors.[48]

In 1942, the M. D. Anderson Cancer Hospital acquired the former estate of Captain James A. Baker, located on Baldwin Street, as a temporary headquarters.[49] The next challenge came in selecting a permanent site for the cancer hospital. The Anderson Foundation had two key criteria: it had to have room for expansion and it had to be affordable. They found the perfect site just south of downtown, bordering Hermann Park. It also had one additional advantage—there was a preexisting hospital, Hermann Hospital, located on a corner of the proposed medical center site. By including Hermann, the Anderson trustees solved the problem of enticing a general hospital to relocate by simply building the medical center around an existing one. On December 14, 1943, the voters of Harris County approved the sale of the Texas Medical Center site to the foundation.[50]

Foundation trustees also hoped to bring undergraduate medical education to Houston. The University of Texas Medical Branch was located in nearby Galveston, and it was unlikely that the foundation would be able to convince the legislature to build a new undergraduate medical school with an existing one already nearby. As a concession, they were able to negotiate for the creation of a new University of Texas Postgraduate School of Medical Education housed at the state cancer hospital.[51] Having an undergraduate school of medicine, however, was far more prestigious and gave the TMC a legitimate claim to the missing leg of the eternal triangle—medical education.

While they were considering their options, in Dallas, the private Baylor College of Medicine was embroiled in a fight with Baylor University and the Southwestern Medical Foundation over control of that school's destiny. The school was founded in 1900 as the University of Dallas Medical Department. The lack of a real University of Dallas didn't appear to dissuade the entrepreneurial physicians who were determined to bring medical education to north central Texas. Affiliation with Baylor University came in 1903, but it wasn't until 1909 that the university assumed financial control over the medical school.[52] The marriage between the medical school and the university was not a happy one, and in the late 1930s, the Southwestern Medical Foundation was chartered in an attempt to help provide a solid revenue stream for the school and to also help it build better clinical facilities for its students. The new foundation seemed like a winning solution for all parties, but as plans for a medical center in Dallas started to take shape, it became clear that the new foundation, rather than Baylor, would own the physical plant at the proposed medical center. This added one more layer of unnecessary governance to an already tense situation.[53] Southwestern officials made it clear that they were going to build a new medical center in Dallas with or without Baylor's participation, and they started to make plans to create a new medical school if the deal with Baylor fell through. When Baylor canceled its affiliation with the Southwestern Medical Foundation, both Baylor and the Anderson Foundation sensed an opportunity to bring undergraduate medical education to Houston.

The collapse of the proposed affiliation came at precisely the right time for the Texas Medical Center. Baylor was already a name in the state—

many of the Houston area doctors who hadn't attended the University of Texas Medical Branch had graduated from there. Moreover, attracting a preexisting school promised substantial cost savings, since they already had equipment, faculty, and students that would make the move to Houston. Not surprisingly, the move was lubricated with private dollars. The Anderson Foundation promised an initial infusion of $1 million in cash to pay for the construction of a new medical school and $100,000 a year for ten years to help pay for operational costs. The Houston Chamber of Commerce pledged $50,000 a year for ten years to also help defray operating expenses.[54] Baylor moved into an old Sears and Roebuck building in Houston in the summer of 1943 until its permanent facilities were completed in 1947. Hospital facilities for teaching were another priority for the school, and in the fall of 1946, the Department of the Navy built a hospital just to the east of the medical center site. Soon after the opening, ownership of this hospital was transferred to the Department of Veterans Affairs, and in 1949 a formal affiliation agreement was signed with Baylor.[55]

Even though the Anderson Foundation was the public face of the future medical center, just as in Pittsburgh, civic elites saw its growth as good for the region's civic health. The most powerful were the 8F crowd, named after the suite at Houston's Lamar Hotel where they met. This group "had a three-fold powerbase: substantial wealth founded on corporate development, general support of the local business community, and intimate ties to major officials in local and national politics."[56] Major players included Jesse H. Jones, James A. Elkins Sr., George and Herman Brown, Jim Abercrombie, and Gus Wortham. In later years, Leon Jaworski, William and Oveta Culp Hobby, R. E. Smith, and Walter Mischler were also a part of 8F.[57] Many of the members were involved with the Texas Medical Center or its component hospitals as either board members or major donors.[58] Also, like their counterparts at the Allegheny Conference, these (mostly) men were not focused on hospitals as a potential growth sector for Houston. Instead, they envisioned a city with an economy dominated by industries in which they had experience—construction, manufacturing, energy and petrochemicals, banking, and legal services. The Chamber of Commerce, on which 8F members held leadership positions, implemented policy decisions and promoted the city in the national and international press.[59]

The growth of the medical center was remarkable. "The people of Houston, as they read their daily newspapers," mused Elliott, "may have thought

that groundbreakings and dedications were daily occurrences in the Medical Center."[60] The early postwar years also saw the expansion of Hermann
Hospital and the construction of a variety of new general and specialty
hospitals within the corporate boundaries of the TMC. As the only general
hospital existing within the site at the time of its chartering, Hermann was
fortunate that it didn't have to start from scratch. However, Hermann did
need substantial upgrades, especially since it was slated to serve as the primary teaching hospital for Baylor. In 1949, the hospital grew to 625 beds
with the opening of a new air-conditioned pavilion (a major marketing
advantage in postwar Houston) that also contained "fourteen operating
rooms and a blood bank."[61] These new beds helped to transform Hermann
into a major player in the Houston hospital market and a major institution
within the TMC. The hospital also opened a professional building across
the street.

While Hermann's expansion helped the medical center grow, the relocation of existing hospitals and the creation of new hospitals within the
TMC truly signaled its ascendency as a major medical center. One of the
first hospitals to be built anew was The Methodist Hospital. Its roots date
back to the Spanish influenza epidemic of 1918–1919, when Dr. Oscar Nor-
sworthy offered to sell his private hospital located on the corner of Rosalie
and San Jacinto to the Texas Conference of the Methodist Episcopal Church.
In 1951, a new Methodist Hospital opened its doors.[62] It was immediately
celebrated as a triumph of modernity and an example of the best of what
the industrial city could offer in the way of modern health care. In a 1952
edition of *Modern Hospital*, The Methodist Hospital was featured as "The
Modern Hospital of the Month." Its internal organization was described in
painstaking detail—the article extolled the hospital's lobby and corridors
featuring live plants, its well laid-out emergency entrance, and the distribution of services by floor. It provided a guide to service locations—obstetrics
on three, the Blue Bird pediatric clinic on four, psychiatry on seven, and so
on. Even more attention was lavished on the new hospital's ancillary spaces
like the beauty shop, the doctors' coffee bar, and dining and waiting areas.
For all the praise, three hundred beds proved to be too small for the rapidly
growing hospital, and by 1956 more than thirty patients a day were turned
away for lack of space. The hospital broke ground on a major new expansion
in 1960 to try to solve this issue. High occupancy rates persisted even after
this addition, with fifty to seventy-five patients still being turned away daily

by the middle of 1965. Baylor's affiliation with The Methodist Hospital in 1950 meant capital equipment upgrades, since medical school physicians wanted access to the latest equipment for research and patient care.[63]

Two other hospitals were added: St. Luke's Episcopal Hospital and Texas Children's Hospital. Other institutions, including the Institute of Religion, The University of Texas Speech and Hearing Institute, Texas Women's University's School of Nursing, and the Houston State Psychiatric Research Institute also moved to the medical center.[64] One of the most important was the Texas Institute for Rehabilitation and Research, later simply The Institute for Rehabilitation and Research, or TIRR, which played a key role in working with NASA to build space medicine programs during the 1960s and beyond.[65]

Houston also aggressively embraced biomedical research as a part of building a new community identity. The success of M. D. Anderson and cancer research was an early talking point for civic elites to show that Houston was entering the ranks of modern cities, complete with strong institutions and brilliant scientists. Promoting the hospital's research successes was done in a myriad of ways, from articles explaining how the hospital's architecture promoted discovery and the exchange of ideas, to parts of larger articles in Chamber of Commerce-sponsored publications like *Houston Magazine* discussing specific examples of research conducted by M. D. Anderson scientists and clinicians.[66] Other institutions, like Baylor College of Medicine and the Methodist Hospital, also featured heavily in promotional campaigns linking innovative research to civic pride, with one 1961 article headline claiming "Baylor's Research Put Houston in Forefront in War on Disease."[67]

Decentering the Locational Asset Model

The spectacular growth of individual hospitals and medical schools, as well as the steady stream of biomedical innovations that poured out of laboratories in both cities after World War II, seemed to confirm the value of not-for-profit health care institutions as locational assets.[68] But not everybody agreed. In fact, by the late 1950s and early 1960s, there was a growing articulation within the health care sector that its value to individual cities and the nation as a whole transcended the supporting role assigned to it by the locational asset model. While the growth of private insurance like Blue

Cross provided one way to see how markets and not-for-profit health care institutions interacted in the postwar city, a growing emphasis on the economic value that they brought to the city as employers and consumers also helped to decenter the locational asset model. Arnold A. Rivin, the managing editor for the American Hospital Association's trade publication *Hospitals*, captured this sense in 1960 when he argued, "If someone were to ask you to name the biggest industry in the country, you would probably think of steel, of automobiles, of petroleum, of railroads, perhaps of some others. Yet there is still another 'industry,' which in terms of investment and assets is greater than our six largest railroads combined, greater than the combined assets of General Motors, Ford, and Chrysler. This is the vast hospital industry that employs one out of every 44 working persons in the United States and costs more than $12,000 a minute to operate."[69]

Rivin hit on the limitations of thinking of hospitals primarily as locational assets. While longtime not-for-profit health care administrators were loath to think of their institutions as entirely transcending the traditional bounds of the locational asset model, their growing physical and economic footprints were impossible to ignore. Thus, many who thought deeply about this relationship blended a celebration of the market with more traditional language that also highlighted civic contribution. For example, Rivin argued, "bigness itself is no excuse for being. It is what this giant does that counts: The human lives that are placed in hospital hands, the people who occupy our hospital beds, and the other human beings whose health is protected by hospitals that they don't have to become patients."[70] Historian Rosemary Stevens has argued that this represents a "constructive ambiguity," which allows the mission of the hospital and the agenda of its administrators, trustees, physicians, and patients to shift to meet changing community and financial needs. Stevens reminds readers that the need to generate revenue and efficiently manage hospital resources has always been important and should not be seen as absent in a locational asset model.[71]

Organizational and Employment Challenges in Pittsburgh

The Pittsburgh region's hospitals were scattered across several counties. Moreover, they more often than not competed against each other for a similar patient population, resulting in the underutilization of hospital beds. In 1959, the Pennsylvania Economy League, an affiliate of the Allegheny Conference, produced a report on hospital planning in the United States. Out of this report, and other work being done by the American Hospital Association, came new types of voluntary hospital planning bodies. The new body in Pittsburgh was the Hospital Planning Association of Allegheny County and was led by C. Rufus Rorem. Rorem's experience with health planning dated back to his work with the Committee on the Costs of Medical Care in the 1920s and 1930s. His move to Pittsburgh from Philadelphia (where he had previously directed that city's hospital council) was a great coup for organized health planning in the city.[72]

Figures like Rorem and Robert Sigmund, director of the Hospital Council of Western Pennsylvania, advanced a narrative that better hospital planning could protect the public interest. For example, a 1960 document laying out the organization's planning principles clearly states that "hospitals are basically public service institutions, constructed through taxation and philanthropy," and "the public which constructs, uses, and supports hospitals deserves maximum and effective use of the capital investment and personnel. This requires conscious effort by responsible community leaders." Yet the Hospital Planning Association became a forum for a range of not-for-profit hospitals to come together under the auspices of market rationalization and cost control to carve out defined geographic and service-oriented market niches. Meeting minutes over these decades show the tension between expanding access to care and the realities of working together to divide up the region's hospital market to limit competition and ensure sufficient revenue for individual institutions.[73]

Pittsburgh's Mercy Hospital provides an example of how hospital planning worked to encourage hospitals to increasingly think of themselves as businesses. The Catholic hospital was founded in 1847 by the Sisters of Mercy and became a teaching hospital the following year.[74] The hospital continued to grow and developed links with the University of Pittsburgh Medical Center under the leadership of its administrator, Sister M. Ferdinand. By the 1960s, she and others led a move to keep the hospital in its urban location adjacent to downtown Pittsburgh and the increasingly African American Hill District. This meant that the hospital could no longer just rely on its reputation as a quality Catholic hospital but instead needed to invest in modernizing its mission and its facilities. To do this, both Mercy and the Hospital Planning Association, as part of working groups of similar hospitals, compiled and analyzed a range of data, including admission rates for competitor hospitals, the percentage of specialty-service-line beds, and, in at least one case, information about general practice physicians with specialty (obstetrical) admitting privileges.[75] At the University of Pittsburgh's medical center, a new organizational body, the University Health Center of Pittsburgh, was created in 1965. In the press release announcing its formation, Harold S. Overholt, the new chairman of the organization, claimed that even though UHCP "demonstrates a concord of intent and direction in those activities relating to teaching, research, patient care and service, it also preserves the essential independence of each institution to operate and develop toward the achievement of its own goals."[76]

One of the most potent ways that these new coordinating and promotional bodies helped to subtly, and perhaps even unintentionally, decenter the locational asset model as the measure of a health care institution's value was by highlighting the growing role of each hospital or medical school as major employers and regional consumers. For example, a report commissioned by the Hospital Council noted that in the region surrounding Pittsburgh in 1956, "there were 184 full time personnel per 100 patients per day" in its general hospitals. While this was lower than the national average of 208 personnel per 100 patients, it still made up a significant portion, around 60 percent, of the $76 million in total expenditures made by regional hospitals.[77] The University of Pittsburgh and its medical center also made up an important part of western Pennsylvania's health employment. This was made clear in a set of 1963 notes written in preparation for a city council meeting by the university's chancellor, Edward H. Litchfield. Handwritten on a piece of yellow legal paper (later transcribed and presumably circulated to the Pittsburgh City Council), it read, "Pitt has 4400 employees and a payroll of $26,000,000. We hired 406 faculty and employees in September, we have passed up J. & L. [Jones and Laughlin Steel, the only major steel company with plants left in the city by the early 1960s] as the city's largest private employer. . . . Oakland hospitals—1963—3837 employees—$16,665,000." The paper ended with a note that health center hospitals (Presbyterian, Eye and Ear, and Montefiore) had "construction underway exceeding $15,000,000."[78]

Their large size and rationalized organizational charts allowed not-for-profits to focus on deepening their talent pool by hiring more full-time medical school faculty, often with more impressive academic qualifications than the existing local medical doctors that had provided part-time teaching service. This thinking was in line with contemporary trends in medical education that held that only full-time faculty would have the time to fully stay abreast of rapid technological changes in medicine.[79] In fact, at many medical schools, administrators saw the creation of a full-time medical faculty as one additional step in the process of moving toward a higher set of educational standards that would vault them into a national, rather than regional, marketplace for students and faculty talent. These efforts strained town-gown relationships. In the late 1950s, the American Medical Association found that in Pittsburgh, the "relations are good between the medical school and the medical profession locally and in the state," but throughout the 1960s, fights over how committed the medical school was to supporting non-university-affiliated hospitals and local medical doctors led to charges that the school was "empire building." Writing in the *Pittsburgh Post-Gazette* in 1966, medical writer Henry W. Pierce reminded readers that the debate over faculty hiring wasn't merely "an intra-mural academic squabble" and that "the University of Pittsburgh is here to serve the people. It has a responsibility to train doctors—good doctors—who will stay in this area. It has a responsibility to promote local talent. It has a responsibility to build an atmosphere in which this local talent will want to stay and work."[80]

The fight over full-time faculty sucked up oxygen in the press and it obscured the growing importance of nonphysician staff to the overall health care employment picture in the medical metropolis. Hospitals required more maintenance, housekeeping, dietary, accounting, and public relations staff to function. These positions often paid very little, offered few opportunities for professional advancement, and were reserved for African Americans. A 1959 report for the Pittsburgh Commission on Human Relations noted: "Some Negroes could be found in almost every category of hospital employment. However, the more skilled the position and the more training it required, the smaller the proportion of Negroes holding it. Thus, one in three workers employed in maintenance, food service, laundry and housekeeping service, and practical nursing were Negro. In comparison, only one in 10 technical and clerical workers were Negro; while only two of each 100 persons of the medical and nursing staff were Negro."[81] Racial disparities around issues of employment are confirmed by census records, which show that between 1950 and 1960, the ranking of black women working as "attendants" at "hospitals and other institutions" rose from the sixth most common job category to the fourth most common job category.[82] As demands on staff time grew, wages, especially for lower-paid minority non-clinical staff, often failed to keep pace, further souring the relationship between hospital labor and management, which helped to illuminate cracks in the locational asset narrative and sow the seeds of future inequality in health care employment. This tension boiled over by the late 1960s, when a Pittsburgh branch of the New York–based Local 1199 union sought to represent workers in area hospitals. Local 1199's roots were in the Retail Drug Employees Union, which by the late 1950s was planning to unionize New York City hospitals. Smaller and more militant than other unions, leaders of 1199 like Leon Davis and Elliott Godoff chose Montefiore as a target both for its liberal social outlook and for the fact that it was having trouble adjusting this outlook to a changing hospital-civic relationship that required a more businesslike administration. By the end of 1958, the union had forced a recognition vote and won. Efforts to unionize other New York City hospitals soon followed.[83]

The decision by Local 1199 to come to Pittsburgh in 1969 was part of a larger effort to expand its reach. It also built on deep concerns about the continuing gap between the rhetoric of the hospital-civic relationship and its reality for workers.[84] Presbyterian-University Hospital, as well as Mercy Hospital, which were both actively reaching out to include minority communities in administrative and patient care decisions, were important targets for this union. In a flyer titled "Help Us Avoid a Hospital Crisis," members of 1199P (the Pittsburgh local) called for the community to support social justice for hospital workers:

We are nurses aids, orderlies, dietary, housekeeping and maintenance workers at Presbyterian-University Hospital. We take temperatures, scrub floors, serve patients, prepare food and maintain the building. We do the hundreds of other tasks that are absolutely necessary to keep the hospital running and assure good patient care. But we cannot continue to provide health services to the community while we are making $1.75 an hour, with very few benefits and poor working conditions. We work long hours, all shifts, holidays and week-ends and we still take home poverty wages. *The plain truth is that hospital workers cannot afford to get sick and become patients in the very hospitals they do so much to keep running.*[85]

Not-for-profit hospital leaders largely resisted calls for unionization. Presbyterian-University Hospital's executive director Edward Norian argued that conflicting claims as to what union represented workers meant that 1199's call for an election "would be obviously unsatisfactory to a substantial minority of our employees" and the hospital, with no clear legal mandate to call an election, would not "enforce such exclusive representation on our employees." Norian also countered that the hospital had raised wages 24 percent in the three years before 1969, and an additional 9 percent that year. He argued that the hospital was acting on the results of a report commissioned by the Hospital Council that recommended increased pay for front-line workers.[86] In a letter sent to workers in October 1969, Norian claimed, "We will work with you to the best of our ability to continue to improve this hospital as a fine place to work. In the meantime, we ask that you do not support any organization who's [sic] major tactic is violence and disruption." He closed by alluding to the special role of hospitals in the urban economy and the supposed shared sacrifice of health care employment, saying, "Before you support this union, ask yourself who is behind it. Find out if outside organizations from this New York union are the type of people you want to lead you. Ask yourself if you really need this kind of union to protect you at this hospital. Ask yourself if any union, particularly this union, would be a solution to any of your problems, or would it be just another big problem for all of us?"[87]

Union leaders were not persuaded and ramped up pressure on Presbyterian-University Hospital to hold elections. Accusing Norian and the hospital's board of "dictatorship," one flyer from the union's organizing committee claimed that they were "afraid of majority rule," and believed that "Presbyterian workers are SECOND CLASS CITIZENS." "We say to Norian," the flyer continued, "THIS IS NOT YOUR PLANTATION! WE ARE NEITHER YOUR SLAVES NOR YOUR CHILDREN."[88] The union also turned to Coretta Scott King, the widow of slain civil rights leader Dr. Martin Luther King. She had emerged as a national advocate for 1199 in 1969 in Charleston, South Carolina, where she marched with striking hospital workers. Later that year, she also supported hospital unionization efforts at Johns Hopkins.[89] Her visit to Pittsburgh came on March 19, 1970. Speaking to a large crowd, she argued, "The truth is that the large majority of hospital workers are black, most of them women. Their campaign for a union is part-and-parcel of the struggle going on everywhere for dignity. . . . Soul power plus union power equals victory."[90] While 1199P's efforts were frustrated, the issues of health care employment, living wages, and social justice would continue to call into doubt central elements of the locational asset narrative well into the twenty-first century.[91]

Organizational and Employment Challenges in Houston

Building a medical center in Houston also required new ways to think
about coordinating hospitals to maximize efficiency. To do this, Texas Medical Center Inc. was chartered as a Texas nonprofit corporation in November 1945. The new corporation had a mandate to "promote and provide
for or assist" the establishment, maintenance, and development of dental
and medical facilities, and to help provide "a general health program for
the State of Texas, as well as special health programs."[92] The idea of creating
a management umbrella was essential to the success of the new medical
center, since there was not a single dominant institution that could act as
a coordinating body for medical center development. TMC Inc.'s board
originally had nine members, with Dr. Ernst W. Bertner overseeing much
of the early coordination. This number would grow in later years.

One of the first actions of TMC Inc. was to make sure that its vision of
building a $100 million medical center had a realistic chance of succeed-
ing.[93] In 1946, they commissioned James Hamilton and Associates, a
Chicago-based hospital consulting firm, to conduct a market analysis of the
Houston region. Among the wide variety of recommendations that made
their way into the four-hundred-plus-page report was a sense that the
Houston area's rapid growth meant that demand for inpatient hospitalization would continue to grow in the coming decades.[94] The report also recommended that hospitals within the medical center attempt to coordinate
services as a way to hold down costs. Writing to Bertner in 1948, R. Lee
Clark, then director and surgeon-in-chief of M. D. Anderson, echoed the
suggestions made by the consultants, saying, "We are attempting to build
here in Houston a unique Medical Center in that we are endeavoring to
operate the various functions by finances secured from divergent sources.
This can at once be our strength and our weakness."[95]

Clark's nuanced understanding about the difficulties of sharing services
and binding divergent and competitor hospitals into a shared enterprise in
the name of good fiscal management highlighted some of the difficulties
of the project. For example, two years before Clark's letter, Bertner first floated
the idea of creating a stand-alone outpatient facility to serve all medical
center hospitals, a plan which never came to pass. The failure of the central
outpatient clinic left TMC Inc. to act primarily as a facilitator for member
institutions rather than a direct provider of patient care. It embraced this
new task, building the roads, bridges, and flood control structures that

made the medical center possible. TMC Inc. maintained a small management staff, preferring to work through several joint committees.[96]

Another critical function of TMC Inc. was public relations. Its press machine was able to leverage contacts in the local and national media to promote the medical center. It helped that two of the medical center trustees were Jesse Jones, who owned the *Houston Chronicle* as well as a range of other media outlets, and Oveta Culp Hobby, who, along with her husband, owned and managed the *Houston Post*.[97] This local and national outreach helped the medical center to build a narrative that it was a growing space for innovation and healing that owed its very conception to a combination of market forces and individual philanthropy rather than federal programs like Hill-Burton, Medicare, or the federal grant funding programs.[98]

Health care employment also became an important way that Houston's hospitals demonstrated their connection to the larger market economy. Just as in Pittsburgh in the 1950s, efforts to build a full-time medical staff at Baylor led to town-gown conflict. Here, the primary issue was admitting privileges at the city's public versus private hospitals.[99] The roots of this argument date to a 1953 decision to establish a professional service plan designed to help compensate Baylor physicians and other health professionals for the work they provided at the city's public hospital, which claimed that since it absorbed the costs for teaching, the professional service fund was simply designed to help compensate individual staff members rather than the school.[100] This claim did little to mollify local medical doctors, who continued to grumble that the presence of Baylor in a public hospital was a violation of the separation between church and state.[101] Local medical doctors and academic physicians did coexist, if not always peacefully, in the city's not-for-profit hospitals. At The Methodist Hospital, physicians with admitting privileges were also appointed to Baylor as part-time faculty. Despite this, competition for patient revenue led to friction. However, in an era of rapid growth, these disputes were typically settled quickly as patient volumes continued to grow.[102]

Total hospital employment was also an important metric to measure the success of the not-for-profit health care sector in Houston. For example, an August 1957 article in *Houston Magazine* noted: "One out of every 113 metropolitan Houstonians is employed in a hospital."[103] Another article, this one also appearing in *Houston Magazine* in 1964 and titled "Houston's Hospitals: Focus of a Nation's Eyes," used the example of payroll costs to "show what a big business care of the sick can be." The article claimed that 1963 "payroll expenses for the 28 hospitals reporting [which included Medical Center hospitals as well as a smattering of suburban general hospitals] amounted to $43,469,000."[104]

The Bayou City also struggled to reconcile the reality of hospital labor with the narrative of hospitals as a locational asset. Data collected in a 1964 Southwest Research Institute report shows the reality of wage disparities by race and gender. Of thirteen TMC institutions that provided employment data, the vast majority of employees made under $250 per month, with the next largest group for men making between $350 to $399 per month, and $250 to $299 per month for women.[105] Nine institutions further broke this down by gender and race. Of these men earning under $250 per month, 82 percent were African American. Of the eighty-seven white men reported in this salary category, forty-nine were married and thirty-eight were not. These categories were not reported for African American men.[106] Women fared even worse: 670 women earned between $1 and $199 per month, and 343 women earned between $200 and $249 per month. Here again, most of the lowest wage earners were African American at 75.8 percent versus 24.2 percent. However, the slightly higher category had more white women (64.8 percent) than African American women (31.7 percent). Only one African American woman earned between $500 and $599 per month, compared to 111 white women.[107] In short, the numbers showed that large pay gaps existed around gender and race, but there is little evidence that this reporting did much to change pay scales. In fact, the employment numbers were not collected because of issues of equality but rather as part of a market analysis for a proposed apartment building adjacent to the TMC.[108]

There was little room in Houston to contest wage issues. In the private sector, employers were notoriously hostile to unionization, and in the public sector, Texas law prohibited strikes.[109] However, in 1968, thirty-four African American patient care staff at Ben Taub General Hospital walked out of work to protest what they felt was discriminatory treatment. This was one of several "sickouts" that occurred over the next several years to protest working conditions in the Harris County Hospital District.[110] Despite the press coverage of sickouts and of worker concerns over discrimination in the hospital district, since Texas was a right-to-work state, health care unionization proved elusive in Houston's hospitals during the late 1960s and early 1970s.

Using employment numbers and wages could call attention to labor unrest, but citing the total value of capital invested in medical centers helped to show the commitment of the community to these institutions. Throughout the 1950s, local newspapers and hospital trade publications alike cited the total value of the medical center's facilities, a number that ranged from $75 million to $100 million and always seemed to be growing. The constant move to quantify construction value was very visibly linked with a defense of free enterprise and private philanthropy.[111] By the 1970s, while the total value of each hospital or clinic was still emphasized, newspapers and TMC promoters were also paying attention to the dollar value of medical construction as medical center institutions continued to build new facilities, demolish or renovate old ones, and add more parking—a perennial issue for all TMC patrons. In 1974, the *Houston Post* informed readers that more than $100 million in planned expansions were slated for the medical center, which included multimillion-dollar projects by M. D. Anderson, the University of Texas Health Science Center schools, and TMC Inc. Each of these projects linked the city's construction sector with its medical sector, helping to further illuminate the ways that not-for-profit health care supported the overall economy.[112]

Construction costs were not the only way that not-for-profit health care made a case for its growing economic power. Individual institutions also focused more heavily on new metrics to demonstrate their worth in the urban economy, such as quantifying the dollar value of their economic footprint and highlighting the multiplier effect of their spending in the local and regional economies. This reflected a growing national movement to rethink how not-for-profit health care discussed its civic contributions. In the minutes of the 1950 annual meeting of the American Association of Medical Colleges, Dr. Franklin Murphy warned of internal resistance by medical professionals toward promoting institutions as critical to local development, noting, "Candidly, I think part of our membership regard it as a little undignified to approach the public with facts that are related to things which the public is called upon to support. There seems to be a rather medieval point of view about the right of the public to concern itself with the products that is asked about." Murphy continued:

It is the strong conviction of your chairman that until we tell our story in a way in which the public can understand and appreciate,

we have little hope of getting continuing and expanding public sym-
pathy . . . many of the things we debate and discuss, dream, hope,
and plan to do will, in effect, remain strictly academic unless we can
bring along with us to help us implement these problems the people
on whom we depend not only for our financial but our moral and
psychological support. . . . In short, we must now recognize an elementary fact of American life, namely, the necessity of not only
producing a salable product of high quality, but, just as importantly,
packaging it and merchandising it in a vigorous though honest and
dignified way. I purposely use those terms which are normally
restricted to manufactured products such as rice crispies in order to
point out that in the last analysis we are dealing with the same public, namely, the great American public on who we depend for the
fulfillment of our dreams and aspirations.[113]

Baylor embraced Murphy's call. For example, a 1967 article titled
"Baylor—A Catalyst in Houston's Growth" highlighted the school's traditional role as a supplier of physicians for the city and the state, but it also
noted that much of Baylor's research budget "was spent locally" and that
"Baylor pays for water and electric bills; buys food for its students, staff,
and faculty; buys chemicals and laboratory apparatus in vast quantities;
and pays its faculty and staff." Its students, the article said, were powerful
consumers and shapers of Houston's civic image: "They buy toothpaste,
groceries, automobiles, houses, property, drugs, toys, televisions, refrigerators, services, keep bank accounts and have insurance policies—the things
that keep Houstonians in business. They also give to Houston that abstract,
immeasurable quality called an image. To grow, a city must attract new
people, good people. It must be, not simply known, but renowned. Baylor
has helped Houston accomplish this feat in fewer years than many other
'medical' cities."[114] By the mid- to late 1960s, when issues of staffing, medical construction, and spillover effects were taken together, civic elites and
their allies in not-for-profit health care were beginning to make a clear
argument that the old idea that hospitals and medical schools were primarily a locational asset, whose primary purpose was to support industry,
needed to be replaced with a new understanding of civic health that valued
these institutions as emerging economic actors in their own right.

* * *

While unique local circumstances shaped the development of the not-for-profit health care infrastructure in both cities, the idea of hospitals as a locational asset was a critical way that civic elites, health care administrators and workers, and ordinary citizens understood the hospital-civic relationship in the decades following World War II. In the locational asset model, not-for-profit hospitals and medical schools, with their laboratories, teaching wards, and specialized spaces like emergency rooms, helped to guarantee the health of industrial workforces through their "eternal triangle" of teaching, research, and patient care. As part of this bargain, the growth of these institutions was underwritten with public and private dollars.

Both not-for-profit hospitals and urban residents increasingly came to understand that this vision of the hospital-civic relationship was incomplete. By the end of the 1950s, the role of health care institutions as major economic factors became more visible. Whether it was touting employment numbers, construction projects, or the ripple effect of not-for-profit hospitals and medical student's consumption on the broader regional economy, these institutions started to make a clear case that health care was more than just a locational asset.

At the same time, when it came to health employment, the reality differed sharply from the mythology that more health care employment meant better physical and economic health, which seemed to be emerging from the mid-1960s onward. Pay disparities and limited mobility characterized the sector for most nonphysician employees and varied across genders and races. Efforts to unionize in both cities also met with limited success.

As the next chapter will show, the rising tensions outside of hospital walls due to the civil rights movement, the Great Society, and an unfolding urban crisis helped to reshape the expectations for administrators, providers, and patients about what the hospital-civic relationship should look like in the decades ahead. This helped to pave the way for an expanded definition of "civic health" in the 1960s and 1970s that included issues of social justice as they related to access to medical care and employment.

Chapter 2

The Hospital-Civic Relationship in the Shadow of the Great Society

In 1972, the *Pittsburgher Magazine* ran an article by Jeff Krieger that attempted to define what the relationship between hospitals and communities should look like in the shadow of the Great Society. Krieger argued, "Hospitals can no longer be content with catering only to those people who can afford medical care, but must widen their horizons to include the treatment of all people, regardless of their socio-economic status. This involves a new concept in health care, oriented toward the individual patient and his needs. This new system of health care calls for comprehensive community-oriented treatment, in which a patient is offered prevention, cure, and rehabilitation of his social as well as his physical illness." He concluded by saying, "the hospital can best function as a provider of comprehensive health care, and as a social institution."[1] What is particularly noteworthy is that Krieger was not a high-powered health care administrator, a powerful physician, or government bureaucrat—he was most likely a high school student. The *Pittsburgher* was not a mainstream economic development or promotional publication—it was the student-run magazine of one of the city's prestigious private schools, Shady Side Academy.

By the early 1970s, the idea that not-for-profit health care institutions should exist primarily to support the growth and stability of the industrial economy did not seem to capture the complexity of their role in the urban economy or their potential as agents of future change. Due in part to the success of their marketing campaigns, as well as the rapid flight of population and capital from American cities, not-for-profit health care institutions became more visible in the urban landscape. This rising visibility, combined with the energy from the social changes of the 1960s, offered a potential new direction for the hospital-civic relationship in which social justice issues like health and economic disparities assumed a prominent role in a conversation about what the hospital-civic relationship should look like moving forward. Here, the responsibility of not-for-profit health care institutions went beyond the eternal triangle of research, education, and patient care that underpinned the locational asset model. Instead, it encouraged hospitals and medical schools to continue their traditional contribution to urban economies, but to also think beyond these prescribed roles and reach out across racial and class lines to address concerns that members of a perceived "underclass," who had been either excluded from gainful employment or held at the bottom of the employment ladder by systemic discrimination, threatened the future of the metropolis.[2]

The loudest voices promoting this new potential vision of the hospital-civic relationship were activists—both within minority and low-income communities and inside not-for-profit institutions themselves. This activism came in many degrees. For some, like Mercy Hospital's administrator Sister M. Ferdinand, social justice issues were central to the vows she took as a nun. For others, like Dr. Carlos Vallbona, the chairman of Baylor's Department of Community Medicine, and Dr. Peter Safar, the Pittsburgh anesthesiologist who acted as the founding medical director for Freedom House Ambulance Services, social justice concerns may have been secondary to their professional responsibilities as academic physicians to find new ways to improve health care delivery. Whatever the motivations, each group did more than just talk about how the hospital-civic relationship could change. Working together, they built clinical and health care employment programs, attempted to open institutional doors to more inclusive governance, and envisioned the future of the medical metropolis as one in which civic health was defined as more than physical health or the economic health of industrial corporations, but also included economic equity, social mobility, and political inclusion for all citizens. Their positions were strengthened by a partnership, albeit sometimes a rocky one, with federal and local governments, whose own efforts to launch and maintain a Great Society reflected many of the same goals, if not always the same understanding of what these goals might look like, for the future of the medical metropolis.

A word of caution is in order about how far this potential vision of the hospital-civic relationship penetrated into the popular consciousness. Despite the hopeful tone of Krieger's article, the contemporaneous commercialization of medicine was not subservient to the emerging emphasis on social justice. Instead, the two ideas were often promoted and executed alongside each other. Indeed, the intersection of these ideas with not-for-profit health care institutions provides yet another opportunity to explore the varying ways that the tension between margin and mission defines the hospital-civic relationship.[3]

A New Definition of Civic Health in Pittsburgh

Efforts to redefine civic health in the late 1960s and early 1970s had their roots in concerns over the rising cost of medical care. Free and reduced cost medical care, or charity care, was one opening for a broader conversation about what civic health meant for the present and future.[4] From the 1930s onward, thanks largely to the growth of private health insurance, the percentage of charity care that institutions provided decreased, even though costs for that care increased. For example, in 1933, 54 percent of patient days in Allegheny County were "free" or "part-pay," but by 1960 that number had fallen to 14.2 percent, largely related to the expansion of private health insurance like Blue Cross.[5] In 1962, at a meeting of area hospital leaders, University of Pittsburgh Chancellor Edward Litchfield noted that, countywide, the cost of "'free care' exceeded $10,000,000" in the previous year and that each of the nine major hospitals in the county had delivered about $7.5 million of the total figure.[6] Of course, this discussion reflected a great deal of self-interest. Those responsible for hospital balance sheets wanted to minimize their financial exposure while maximizing the sense that their charity care contributions continued to help justify their special status in the community. This balancing act was not always natural. However, by making the cost of charity care an issue, not-for-profit health care institutions started a conversation about what a new definition of health should look like for all residents of the medical metropolis.

This conversation was helped by the passage of Medicare and Medicaid in 1965. Medicare covered patients sixty-five and over and provided a cost-plus reimbursement across states and providers. Medicaid covered the "categorically needy," typically those receiving welfare as well those covered by previous indigent medical programs like the "categorially related needy"; the "categorically related medically needy," who were people who might be eligible for welfare under federal guidelines but could not get it under state rules but nevertheless had medical needs; and those who had conditions that might allow them to get welfare but whose income remained too high (but still low enough not to be able to afford medical services) known as the "noncategorically related medically needy."[7] It retained the vestiges of older public assistance programs by allowing states to set their eligibility and coverage requirements beyond these groups and required that each state's programs meet a minimum threshold of "providing physician services, skilled nursing home services, inpatient hospital services, outpatient hospital services, and other laboratory or x-ray services."[8] Their passage, against the vigorous lobbying of stalwart medical groups like the American Medical Association, was a triumph of political compromise for House Ways and Means Chair Wilbur Mills, and sent a strong message about the social priorities of postwar liberalism as they related to health.[9] Both programs profoundly reshaped the way that health care institutions interacted with their clinical services. No longer were groups like the poor and the elderly automatically treated as a burden; instead, by receiving a payment stream for their care, medical centers were able to treat those at the margins of the social contract while still increasing the revenue they were able to bring into both medical schools and teaching hospitals.[10]

A second way that health, urban policy, and cost control intersected with efforts to redefine civic health was around urban renewal. If the cheapest medical care is none at all, then thinking among some urban planners was that slum clearance programs could eliminate health disparities and reduce the need for charity care by physically changing the urban environment. For example, rodent and weed control programs as well as efforts to reduce infectious diseases were part of the larger justification for razing "slums" in many American cities after World War II.[11] This is not to argue that the traditional drivers of urban renewal, including increasing property values or making space for expanded hospitals and universities, were not important, but simply to point out that urban renewal itself was a complex process.[12] Even after public support for urban renewal waned during the 1960s, the idea that the state had a responsibly to improve health outcomes in low-income and underserved communities led to new types of programs, such as addiction prevention and management, in many of the same neighborhoods scarred by slum clearance.[13]

Despite efforts to address divergent health outcomes, both in Pittsburgh and nationally, low-income and African American communities still lagged behind those of affluent and white Americans. For example, the city's 1969 application to the Model Cities program noted that the neighborhoods targeted for federal assistance had higher than average rates of syphilis and tuberculosis deaths, as well as lower rates of childhood immunizations. High rates of mental illness also were reported.[14] Higher infant and overall mortality rates, often linked to substandard housing conditions, poor treatment by white medical professionals at area hospitals, the city's noxious environmental conditions, and difficulties in finding and retaining employment, were also long-standing areas of concern.[15]

Health disparities provided an opening for activist groups like the National Welfare Rights Organization and the Black Panthers to advance a critique of the American health care system as discriminatory, both in the care it provided to patients and in the employment that it provided to low-income communities and communities of color.[16] The story of John Williams is illustrative of how health and activism intersected. Through an interview with his mother, the *New Pittsburgh Courier* profiled Williams in the fall of 1971 as he was recovering from injuries he sustained after being shot by the police. Apparently, he had a formative experience growing up next to a vacant and overgrown lot owned by the Pennsylvania Railroad in the city's Homewood-Brushton neighborhood. The weeds and pollen from the lot exacerbated his sibling's asthma. When the family attempted to clear the space to address the family's respiratory issues and also to make it into a playground, what the paper called "slaying the weeded dragon," the company intervened and posted no trespassing signs. Continued illness drove them from the neighborhood—Williams and his family moved eight times over the next several years—before finally settling into public housing. The forced move, corporate indifference, and poor health showed John Williams how race, class, and health disparities came together in the United States to reinforce poverty.[17]

This linkage was also gaining national attention through the Poor People's Campaign, which planned another March on Washington in 1968 to call attention to issues of poverty, health, and economic exclusion. Only a few weeks before the march was set to commence, civil rights leader and advocate for the poor Dr. Martin Luther King was assassinated in Memphis, Tennessee, while supporting striking sanitation workers. In the wake of his murder, riots occurred in several major American cities, including Pittsburgh. The evening of Dr. King's assassination, administrators at Mercy Hospital were already meeting with area residents about creating a new type of committee that would serve as a bridge between the hospital and the surrounding neighborhoods.[18] The Neighborhood Committee on

Health Care (NCHC) was formed by hospital administrator Sister M. Ferdinand and other Mercy executives to repair a strained relationship with the surrounding neighborhood. Sister Ferdinand noted one telling comment about the hospital's relationship to the community: "'You treated us at Mercy. But you have never accepted us.'"[19] This comment shocked Sister Ferdinand and helped her to realize that the hospital could do more than just provide care for the poor, it needed to be a part of the solution to poverty and health disparities; she wrote: "We recognized immediately that inadequate health care presently compounds the evils of poor housekeeping and high unemployment which already deny black people their rightful place in society. Hastily-put-together health care programs are not enough to do the job that is needed to be done."[20]

The NCHC had no real power to influence policy. Instead, it was an advisory body to the hospital's human relations committee. By drawing membership from surrounding neighborhoods, it was supposed to allow residents a voice in what service lines the hospital offered, give them a say in helping to expand minority hiring programs, and allow the community to help shape future plans for the hospital's physical expansion. The thirty-member body represented a cross-section of interests, including the Hill and Uptown neighborhoods, and the hospital's immediate neighbor, the Spiritan Catholic Duquesne University. The full committee was slated to meet nine times a year, and a smaller executive committee was to meet quarterly. Subcommittees were added later to address personnel, medical services, legislation, community relations, and services provided to the community.[21]

One of the primary concerns of Sister Ferdinand and the NCHC was providing more accessible primary care services. In 1969, Mercy opened three Primary Care Stations in locations like public housing and a men's homeless shelter.[22] Along with another space next to the hospital's ER, these were supposed to act as triage points to determine where ill patients should go—the emergency room, where treatment costs were more expensive, or a new multi-million-dollar ambulatory care facility that the hospital completed in 1976, where a range of allied health personnel, rather than physicians, could see patients. In theory, the triage strategy helped to reduce medical bills and shorten wait times, making for happier patients. By 1971, the Primary Care Stations had nearly six thousand visits.[23] Tied to these stations was a van-based Caremobile, designed to expand nonemergency ambulatory treatment and provide some preventive care.[24]

By the mid- to late 1970s, frustration with the limited authority of the NCHC and the slow pace of change within the hospital boiled over with some committee members. In his resignation letter from the NCHC, Reverend Dr. J. Van Alfred Winsett of the Ebenezer Baptist Church, located on Wylie Avenue in the Hill District's social and cultural heart, claimed, "I feel that my time is being wasted each month as we meet and are unable to bring about some meaningful changes which should take place, especially as it relates to positions being filled by minorities." Reverend Winsett further noted, "I have listened attentively to the presentations made by officials in charge of administering the hospital and, whereas they give explanations for things being as they are, they seem to be against instituting methods which will bring about change. . . . I feel that my time is too valuable to play games as some seem to be doing at Mercy Hospital."[25] Despite the frustrations of some members such as Winsett, the NCHC provided a pathway for engagement with the community and in doing so offered to rewrite a potential model for how citizens and institutions could come together to discuss what civic health could mean in a more inclusive and participatory fashion.

Other hospitals also sought to deepen their relationship with low-income and minority communities in the hope that better health outcomes might bring stability to the city. Since the mid-1950s, the Jewish Montefiore Hospital had operated one of the only home care programs in Western Pennsylvania.[26] At first, the program was only open to indigent residents of the Hill District, but by the early 1960s, it expanded to cover patients with Blue Cross coverage.[27] In 1971, Montefiore opened a dental clinic for low-income residents of the Hill District with the help of $350,000 in Model Cities money. Its director, Dr. Wilvor C. Waller, was an assistant professor at the University of Pittsburgh Dental School.[28] Later that year, Montefiore agreed to provide medical direction for the Hazelwood-Glenwood Neighborhood Health Center.[29] The University of Pittsburgh also increased its commitment to extending care to low-income neighborhoods. In 1970, board members at the University of Pittsburgh–affiliated Presbyterian-University Hospital were notified that it had increased its outreach programs by joining other area hospitals in providing medical services to the Terrace Village public housing project. This decision was spurred on in part by "the Health Center's belief that those people who 'live in the shadow of the Health Center' can be cared for in a comprehensive manner."[30]

Suspicion ran deep among some community activists of the motivations behind efforts by the university and not-for-profit hospitals to suddenly become interested in expanding care in low-income and minority communities. In Homewood-Brushton, the same neighborhood the Williams family was forced to leave, the neighborhood health center actively worked to keep the University of Pittsburgh's medical school out of the facility. For example, when representatives from the Department of Health, Education, and Welfare traveled to the city in the summer of 1967 to hold a meeting about the future of the neighborhood health center program, community groups from Homewood-Brushton picketed the meeting, holding signs bearing statements like "medical students belong in school, not in our medical center," reflecting an always-present tension between efforts to expand health care and concerns over what was really driving institutional behavior.[31] Despite this, by the early 1970s it seemed that an emerging consensus was taking hold, that not-for-profit health care institutions could play a role in promoting social justice in the rapidly changing city. This changing definition of civic-health was also emerging in Houston.

Redefining Civic Health in Houston

Concerns over charity care also opened up a debate about what the hospital-civic relationship should look like in Houston. Unlike Pittsburgh, Houston had a public hospital. It was founded in the 1920s and named for former Confederate president Jefferson Davis; however, by the 1950s, the hospital was regularly in the news for its dangerous conditions, including a series of infant deaths from *Staphylococcus* infections in 1957–1958. Appalling conditions at Jefferson Davis even provided inspiration for *The Hospital* by Dutch playwright Jan de Hartog, which offered a scathing critique of care in the nation's public hospitals. In response to the failure of Jefferson Davis to provide adequate care, and the bad publicity that came with it, a new charity hospital opened in 1963 which was named after Ben Taub, a philanthropist who was deeply involved in the city's public hospitals.[32] In 1965, voters in Harris County finally passed a referendum to create a special taxing district, the Harris County Hospital District, to help fund the cost of indigent care, which made substantially more local resources available by the end of the decade.[33]

From the moment that the doors to Ben Taub opened, it, too, presented problems for Houston's poor. For some, it was long lines, and for others it was finding affordable and reliable transportation to the hospital. The solution was to find a way to bring nonemergency ambulatory care to the people who needed it, similar to Mercy Hospital's primary care centers in Pittsburgh. In 1967, representatives from Settegast, a primarily African American neighborhood in the far north of the city, approached the Hospital District and Baylor College of Medicine about creating a site in the neighborhood to provide poor residents with outpatient services. Even though the residents had developed a plan for developing a clinic and won a planning grant from the Office of Economic Opportunity, Baylor declined to participate in the venture, citing insufficient faculty manpower as the justification for its decision.[34] The residents then continued their discussions with the Hospital District and also reached out to the Houston Medical Forum for help with staffing their clinic. By 1969, however, internal changes at Baylor, along with the rising sense of community responsibility that the leadership of not-for-profit health care institutions seemed to manifest nationwide, meant that the medical school was now clamoring to participate in the Settegast project.[35]

What was really driving the about-face was the creation of a new Department of Community Medicine. The genesis of this department came in April 1969 when, in response to student pressure, a joint faculty-student curriculum committee recommended the establishment of a new department. Moreover, the curriculum committee also recommended that classes and a rotation in the Department of Community Medicine be integrated into the school's core curriculum and that the department offer additional rotations for students with a deeper interest in this new type of medicine.[36] The department saw itself as the vanguard of the patient-centered medical care revolution in the city. One of its early annual reports argued that "medicine is in the midst of a social revolution focusing on the health services and health care delivery."[37] At the heart of this revolutionary agenda was an embrace of the concept of "comprehensive care." Seven major components structured this ideology: health education, preventive care, episodic care for acute illnesses and injuries, management of chronic illness, physical and mental rehabilitation services, "life adjustment services," and environmental health.[38] This new strategy of comprehensive care aligned with federal efforts through the neighborhood health center movement to think more holistically about the relationship between health and poverty.

The neighborhood health center movement was formally launched in 1965 by the Office of Economic Opportunity (OEO). OEO represented a new philosophy for federal antipoverty programs that had its roots in the "discovery" of the structural causation of poverty during the mid- to late 1960s by policymakers and academics.[39] Combating poverty as a structural rather than an individual problem opened the door for the federal government to build administrative programs with the goal of fostering conditions of greater opportunity as part of Kennedy and Johnson's famous War on Poverty. A difference that set OEO apart from other existing agencies within the federal antipoverty orbit was its embrace of the concept of "maximum feasible participation," which mandated the involvement of the community groups in creating and administering antipoverty programs.[40]

At the heart of the idea of using health care to help address urban poverty was a new care delivery model. Hospital emergency departments or private physician practices typically used a fee-for-service payment model that incentivized frequent repeat visits. Fee-for-service was very costly, not just for patients, but also for the larger health care system. While Medicaid reimbursements varied by state, Medicare allowed hospitals to bill at cost plus 2 percent, and physicians to bill at "customary, prevailing, and reasonable" rates.[41] Neighborhood health centers, by contrast, drew their inspiration from the settlement houses and prepaid group practice that was more prevalent in American medicine during the earlier decades of the century. At the heart of each of these traditions was an emphasis on providing preventive care and paying attention to the importance of environmental factors in shaping health, rather than simply trying to maximize the number of visits made by each patient.[42] The resulting "comprehensive care" ideology that emerged in neighborhood health centers dovetailed with new ways that medical students and some older faculty, especially in community medicine departments, were increasingly seeing the future of American medical care.[43]

Another way that OEO-sponsored neighborhood health centers differed from traditional hospital outpatient departments involved the issue of control. Neighborhood health centers were grant funded, meaning that their creation needed to be initiated by community actors rather than by local government or not-for-profit health care systems. What this meant was that, at least in theory, neighborhood health centers were a more democratic space to deliver care since all three actors would be partners. However, what often happened in practice was that whichever entity was the grantee was able to set policy. Despite this, citizen-administered neighborhood health councils also had a voice in the operations of neighborhood health centers and in selecting residents to receive job training.[44]

At Baylor College of Medicine, Dr. Carlos Vallbona, the chair of the Community Medicine Department, was the interface between the medical school, the Hospital District, and the community. The Spanish-born Vall-bona arrived in Houston in April 1955 after completing his internship in pediatrics at the University of Louisville School of Medicine. From 1959 to 1969, Vallbona worked in rehabilitation medicine at the Texas Institute for Rehabilitation and Research.[45] At some point during 1969, a grant for $117,718 was approved by OEO to plan a more extensive network of neighborhood health centers in Houston.[46] Exactly how much contact there was between Vallbona and the Hospital District prior to the establishment of the Department of Community Medicine is unclear. According to an article in the *Houston Post*, Vallbona had been acting as a consultant to its board of managers for some time; in 1969 he was appointed chief of its community medicine service.[47]

One of his early challenges was to repair the strained relationships with the African American community that came out of Baylor's initial refusal to participate in the Settegast project. "Why now?" asked one African American woman at a community meeting about Baylor and the Hospital District's plans. "Just what's the hurry?" she continued, "these community folk have been suffering here a long time without the concern of Baylor . . . unless they wanted them for some experiment." Other residents were blunter in their criticism of the school's newfound desire to reach out. "We want absolutely nothing to do with Baylor, is that clear—nothing," noted one Settegast resident.[48] Vallbona recognized the challenges he faced in convincing residents and community health councils that the school did, indeed, have good intentions.[49] The department's first annual report described the difficulties between the medical school and Houston's black community. "We have encountered overwhelming difficulties in working to establish comprehensive care facilities for teaching purposes," claimed the report. "Community support is necessary for a medical school involvement in the planning and operation of a comprehensive care facility, but in our case we have encountered much opposition from both consumers and providers. This opposition and frank hostility have prevented ready access to existing clinic facilities that could have evolved into model comprehensive care centers."[50]

Despite tension between the school and the community, the number of neighborhood clinics, which gradually became more comprehensive neighborhood health centers, continued to grow as Baylor and the Hospital District worked with other area health care providers, OEO, and Model Cities to find additional funding to coordinate community health services.[51] Until the summer of 1970, existing clinics, Settegast and Baytown, were the only sites in operation. In July, an independently operating clinic at Casa de Amigos was brought under Hospital District control. The following spring, in May 1971, a new site at Acres Homes was opened, and in 1972 another site in the Sunnyside neighborhood was opened. Finally, in 1973, Ripley House joined the network.[52] In each of these sites, the clinical and the administrative duties were split between Baylor and the Hospital District. The medical school provided medical staffing, while the Hospital District assumed administrative responsibilities.[53]

Casa de Amigos provides an example of how the comprehensive care ideology interacted with patient expectations. In the late 1960s, Casa de Amigos operated in a Methodist church that, like the surrounding neighborhood, had shifted from white to Hispanic. The church's minister was looking for a way to assist its new congregants, and he and a local internist named Dr. Carlos Speck started to offer health services in the evening in the church's basement. Demand soon outstripped Speck's capacity, and he and the minister approached Vallbona about Baylor becoming involved.[54]

Casa de Amigos became a central research node for the department's efforts to examine how to provide services for low-income populations. Much of the funding for this came from a three-year, $160,000 per year grant from the Robert Wood Johnson Foundation and the Commonwealth Foundation to conduct a range of studies and community health programs for Mexican Americans, including a sociological study focusing on the relationship between Mexican Americans and health led by Julius Rivera from the University of Texas El Paso.[55] Rivera's studies provide a window into how community care functioned in Houston, and how the community related to the caregivers and the clinic environment. At Casa de Amigos, the majority of the patients were women and children. Most men, Rivera noted, "neither attend the clinic nor take much part in making health decisions. . . . This contention is supported by the fact that as a rule men do not succumb to sickness. They do not have time, and cannot afford to accommodate sickness. This is not a matter of machismo. It is a matter, first but not least significantly, of having some medical assistance in their job, as most of our respondents reported. Secondly, and more importantly, men's attitude toward health is far less sympathetic because they see less illness."[56] Also, in contrast to prevailing discourses about the emergency room and community hospital acting as a first step in the illness cycle,

Rivera noted that a visit to Casa de Amigos was often the last attempt to cure disease. "It is a common practice to visit the clinic only after an initial home remedy has been tried. People do not utilize the clinic services unless the case has moved beyond the normal limits of home control. People do not run for medical attention at the first signal of physiological discomfort; not even when this attention is available within walking distance. In fact, they do the opposite. Only when the situation gets to be unmanageable do they go to the clinic."[57] Thus, most day-to-day health issues in the neighborhood surrounding the clinic were regulated by a complex relationship among traditional folk remedies, over-the-counter remedies, and academic medicine. In his reports on Casa de Amigos, Rivera describes the use of *yerbas*, or herbal teas brewed at home to prevent or quickly cure illness. When *yerbas* failed, potential clinic patients then sought out over-the-counter remedies and patent medicines. Rivera also noted that Mexicans and Mexican-Americans were acutely sensitive to the role of diet as a determinant of health.[58]

Rivera's research encouraged Baylor to expand its services. For example, evidence of nutritional deficiencies validated the decision to create a community nutrition program at both Casa de Amigos and Ripley House.[59] Language barriers at Casa de Amigos also prompted Baylor to launch a medical Spanish program to train students and residents to communicate with non-English-speaking patients. In 1973 to 1974, plans were put into place to design a training program for young Chicano mothers to recognize the signs of stress, dubbed "*nerviosidad*," in their friends and families, and to connect them with appropriate health resources.[60] Finally, the clinic served as a test site for research in medical informatics. Grant monies were secured to build a computerized patient records management system at Casa de Amigos in the hopes that, if it were successful, it could be expanded district-wide.[61]

Rivera and his team conducted 119 interviews with residents in the neighborhoods surrounding Casa de Amigos and Ripley House to determine who visited the clinics.[62] A very small sample of these raw questionnaires reveals the following about the patients:

1. All were women and most were in their twenties, married with multiple children.
2. None worked, but most had husbands that did work. The husband's occupations were largely working class and included laborer positions as well as some lower white-collar clerk positions.

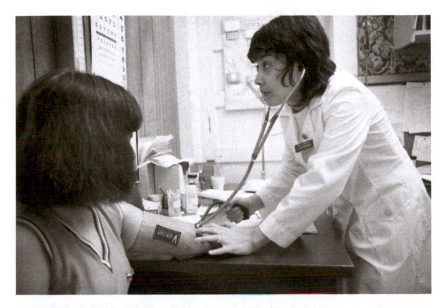

Figure 4. Casa de Amigos clinic manager Alicia Reyes examines a patient at the clinic in April 1973.
Courtesy of Baylor College of Medicine Archives.

3. Overall income varied from around $1,800 per year to $13,000 per year, with most in the $5,000–$7,000 range.
4. Residential tenure varied from several months to several years, indicating some stability.
5. Most appeared to be reasonably happy with their clinic experience.[63]

In other work, drawn from surveys of patients at Casa de Amigos rather than residents at large, Rivera noted that "the image of the clinic looms large among the families visited as a clear blessing in their lives," and "the instances of misinterpretations and misunderstandings between family members and clinic workers are few and far between. Family members often made positive remarks without solicitation."[64] "Some even said that they did not mind waiting in long lines" (a common gripe at other clinics like Baytown and Settegast) and that families often compared the services and environment offered by the clinics favorably with the services provided by private physicians and hospitals.[65] Increased patient volumes at all the clinics confirmed this preference, rising from 11,763 visits in 1969 to 72,139 by 1972. For 1973, Baylor projected that the total number of visits would rise above 100,000.[66]

Market-Based Attempts to Care for Low-Income
Patients in Pittsburgh

While social justice concerns may have seemed to dominate the neighborhood health center movement, the strengthening relationship between the private market and not-for-profit health care that became more visible in the postwar years continued to put pressure on institutions to think about how to monetize indigent care beyond chasing Medicaid dollars. In fact, traditional spaces for care, like hospital emergency departments and private physician offices, still remained places where the poor could access care. Several of Rivera's surveys noted that patients who were dissatisfied with neighborhood health centers often visited the emergency room at the public Ben Taub. Other patients headed to not-for-profit hospitals elsewhere in the city if the lines at the hospital or the neighborhood health center were too long, if the commute for them was too onerous, or for any other variety of personal reasons, including negative interactions with staff.[67] These patients put pressure on the financial bottom lines of these institutions and raised the question whether more market-based solutions might be able to create a more efficient solution to problems of community health.

This was the concern on the minds of administrators at the University of Pittsburgh's hospitals and health professional schools when they conducted a comprehensive assessment of their ambulatory care programs in May 1970 and found them too scattered and serving too many groupings of income levels. Two years later, as a way to potently standardize care across the range of ambulatory programs, the University Health Center of Pittsburgh (UHCP) proposed the creation of a health maintenance organization.[68] The term "health maintenance organization," or HMO, entered the lexicon in the early 1970s. Coined by Dr. Paul Ellwood, a physician from Minnesota, the idea had its roots in an older model of prepaid group practice that had been roundly condemned for years by groups like the American Medical Association. At the heart of Ellwood's thinking was that this new model of care would "encourage prevention, timely primary care, and the economical use of resources."[69] Federal support for HMOs reached a high-water mark in 1973 with the passage of the HMO Act. Most early

HMOs were often not-for-profit organizations that attempted to blend serious efforts to improve care with well-intentioned efforts to address cost issues through capitation, or set payments to physicians and hospitals, rather than billing on a fee-for-service basis.

Even in these not-for-profit plans, there was an understanding that the rules of the market, like supply and demand and attention to revenue and expenses, applied if these organizations were to succeed. For example, UHCP representatives projected that their not-for-profit HMO could serve up to thirty thousand people but would need to have a diverse client base, including the University of Pittsburgh, to create a deep enough risk pool to offset potential losses in poorer neighborhoods.[70] In order to create this diverse risk pool, several "packages" were proposed, including a "preferred package," which provided total care to individuals and families, as well as more limited packages covering specialty services like dental or vision care.[71]

While this hybrid not-for-profit/market-based plan seemed like a possible way to drive patient volume to university hospitals and sidestep the substantial commitment that participating in the neighborhood health center movement required, it is not clear that the university really took it seriously. Evidently, staff at UHCP were responding to an invitation to develop an HMO and didn't want to leave potential grant money on the table; thus, they rushed the application process and ended up confusing area health-planning agencies that weren't aware of the university's plans to radically revamp its ambulatory care programs.[72] There was also internal doubt about its viability. In a letter to Steven Sieverts, the executive director of the Hospital Planning Association of Allegheny County, the university's vice chancellor for the health professions, Dr. Francis Cheever, noted, "I am not yet convinced as yet [sic] that active participation in the development of a regionwide HMO umbrella agency is the course of wisdom for the University Health Center of Pittsburgh."[73] In the end, the plan failed to gain traction and was soon forgotten.

While UHCP's plan never took off, there were other attempts to blend the power of the market with the social justice–oriented goal of expanding care to low-income communities. The same year that UHCP was planning its HMO, a group of Pittsburgh physicians partnered with the Metropolitan Life Insurance Company to build the for-profit Central Medical Pavilion close to Mercy Hospital in the Uptown neighborhood. Backers of the new hospital promised a "one door" model of medicine where patients could receive all the care they needed at one facility and where their records could be easily maintained to prevent medical errors or overtreatment.[74] Driving this new model of health care was an increased focus on preventive care and a payment structure that was supposed to gradually trend from fee-for-service to a hospital-sponsored (and Metropolitan Life–backed) HMO, projected to enroll up to fifty thousand people.[75]

The plan ran into immediate skepticism. Liberal critics like Monsignor Charles Owen Rice, Pittsburgh's famous "labor priest," worried that the hospital was a profit-making wolf in sheep's clothing.[76] Rice denounced the project as a scam designed to " 'cream off' profitable cases while making no contribution to the health facilities of our city."[77] Despite the promise of backers, like former boxer turned community activist Larry Huff, that the facility would offer some health care job training programs, area residents raised concerns that the jobs promised to area residents by hospital backers might not materialize or, if they did, they would be menial.[78] Speaking to the *New Pittsburgh Courier*, Harold K. Swindell noted: "It should be built if it has provisions for the black community, such as training programs—a career ladder." He also noted, "If there are going to be insurance programs, there should be some sort of financial consideration given to residents of the Hill, especially in the Emergency Department." Other black Pittsburghers also expressed a guarded skepticism about the project's ability to create jobs for the neighborhood, as well as a sense of resignation about another large-scale urban clearance project coming to the Hill District.[79] The NAACP's initial response to the project was "completely negative," with Executive Secretary Timothy Stevens claiming that "homes" and not more hospital beds needed to be the focus of efforts to revive the neighborhood.[80] Local physician groups and the county medical society raised a different set of concerns. They worried that the hospital was too ambitious, that the fifty thousand subscribers projected by HMO backers would never materialize, and, frankly, that a massive HMO which required patients to go to a single hospital might take income from their pockets.[81]

The community concerns about exclusion seemed well founded—during the construction process, the general contractor, the Dick Company, and one subcontractor were charged with racism by the NAACP, which argued that the companies failed to hire enough black construction workers on the project.[82] The bad news continued even after the hospital's doors opened. By 1977, only 5,100 people had enrolled, which was "considerably below both the 25,000 member break-even point and the 50,000 member goal."[83] With such a low number of subscribers, there was an insufficient ability to pool revenue to offer sharp discounts to the low-income neighborhoods surrounding the new facility. Eventually, Central Medical Pavilion was absorbed by the St. Francis Health System, and the issue of how to use free markets to extend care into underserved communities was left unsettled.

Health Care Employment in Pittsburgh

The second part of reconfiguring the hospital-civic relationship in both cities along both social justice and market-oriented lines during the 1960s and 1970s was explicitly linking health care employment with social and economic mobility. This built on efforts by not-for-profit health care institutions to use health care employment to show their emerging role in the postindustrial economy, and efforts by unions and activists to show how poor working conditions and low wages undermined the idea that not-for-profit health care should be seen as different from the industrial workplace. Certainly, these efforts continued, but what differed from the way that community activists saw health care employment was that, despite the wage and mobility issues, it could nevertheless also be a targeted solution to combat racial and economic inequality. This is not to say that elite civic development organizations were totally uninterested in the possibilities of health care employment as a potential pathway for economic diversification; in fact, overlapping membership between these organizations and not-for-profit hospital boards surely meant that each organization was aware of the growing importance of the health care sector as an employer. But, during the 1960s and 1970s, these organizations viewed it as less of a priority for their efforts than strengthening the industrial and white-collar service sectors.[84]

This left activists, not-for-profit health care institutions, and smaller philanthropies as the primary drivers of efforts to link health care employment and social and economic justice. This push benefited from the sustained investments in academic medicine that followed World War II. Cold War tensions empowered groups interested in medical education to also push for increased federal funding to produce more physicians, a problem that was already gaining traction with the appointment of the President's Commission on the Health Needs of the Nation by Harry Truman in 1952, and perhaps more forcefully with the publication of the Bane Report in 1959.[85] This report "shocked the public by projecting a nationwide shortfall of nearly 40,000 physicians by 1975" and helped to drive the passage of a series of bills at the federal level providing more money to fund medical and other health professional education legislation, at first through matching grants and later through capitation payments.[86]

In the wake of the Bane Report, the federal government implemented a variety of programs designed to increase the total number of workers in the health field, such as the Manpower Development and Training Act of 1962, Vocational Training Act of 1963, Health Professions Educational Assistance Act of 1963, Nurse Training Act of 1964, Allied Health Professional Personnel Training Act of 1966, and Health Manpower Act of 1968.[87] Each of these acts brought more monies to medical schools and encouraged the creation of a wide variety of new educational programs. Moreover, increasing manpower through job training dovetailed nicely with national goals to create an "opportunity society" as an end to traditional welfare programs.[88]

Activists and not-for-profit health care institutions in Pittsburgh focused on creating programs designed to provide health care employment to address immediate issues of underemployment in low-income communities. This likely had to do with the city's more visible transition to a service-oriented economy than Houston's, as well as the concentration of its African American population into several defined neighborhoods.[89] Agencies like OEO, as well as private foundations, helped to provide the capital for programs that raised the possibility that health care employment could actually provide a pathway out of poverty for low-income urban residents.[90] At the same time, motives for supporting these programs varied and just as often were grounded in the personal and academic agendas of participants.

Freedom House Ambulance Service provides an example of how these forces shaped program development. It grew out of a partnership among University of Pittsburgh anesthesiologist Dr. Peter Safar, Presbyterian-University Hospital, the University of Pittsburgh's Graduate School of Social Work, the Maurice Falk Medical Fund, and Freedom House Enterprises, an OEO-sponsored not-for-profit corporation designed to promote the development of black-owned and -operated businesses.[91] The program also received financial support from a range of local foundations like the Maurice Falk Medical Fund, the Richard King Mellon Foundation, the Sarah Mellon Scaife Foundation, the Pittsburgh Foundation, the Allegheny

County Medical Society Foundation, and private organizations and governmental sources like the Allegheny Conference and Model Cities as well
as generating revenue through fees for providing ambulance services.[92]
According to an article published by Safar and his medical coworkers, its
goals were as follows:

> Working in conjunction with Freedom House Enterprise, Inc.
> (FHE) whose primary goal is to develop businesses in the ghetto
> districts of Pittsburgh, the authors undertook a project which
> attempted: (a) to offer dignified, rewarding employment to ghetto
> residents; (b) to improve emergency ambulance service in one of
> Pittsburgh's slums; (c) to demonstrate prehospital life-support in
> the community by mobile intensive care units (MICU's), with the
> hope of eventually establishing MICU service area-wide; (d) to test
> curricula for training emergency medical technicians in hospital-
> based programs as a pilot project for national recommendations;
> and (e) to test the feasibility of newly-defined ambulance design and
> equipment recommendations.[93]

Less than half of the initial class of trainees had completed high school, and
many had never held steady employment.[94] In the first training cohort, the
trainees' age range spanned from twenty to fifty, with three age clusters at
twenty-two to twenty-three, twenty-six to twenty-seven, and thirty-two to
thirty-five.[95] Overall, the job training goals reflected the broader OEO philosophy of building skills and work histories to enable residents of impover-
ished neighborhoods to function in the private job market. The training
was remarkably successful—twenty-five of the thirty-four total graduates
from the 1967 and 1969 classes remained employed by Freedom House in
1971.[96] Most trainees felt that the training program was useful. When surveyed in 1971, 72 percent indicated that in five years' time "they would
like to be performing the same job or be the manager of an ambulance
service."[97]

Each partner, however, approached the program by prioritizing different goals. Model Cities administrators and civic activists saw it as an
employment program—an extension of a perceived responsibility of the
medical center to provide opportunities for poor residents through medically oriented career training.[98] Safar was mainly concerned with using the
program as a test bed for other research he was conducting as part of the
National Academies of Science-National Research Council's Committee on

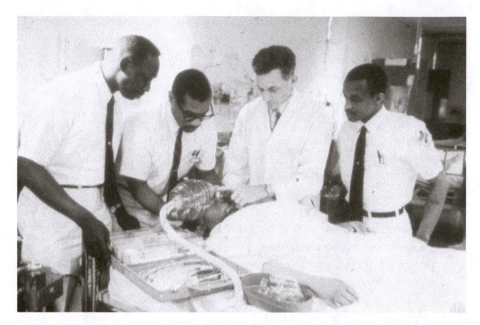

Figure 5. Dr. Peter Safar with Freedom House trainees, probably in the late
1960s.

Photographer unknown. Peter Safar Papers, 1950–2003, UA.90.F102, University Archives, Archives
and Special Collections, University of Pittsburgh Library System.

Emergency Medical Services to develop a standardized training program
for paramedical personnel and a standardized design for the ambulance.[99]
The competing agendas that led to the program's development did, at
times, have a corrosive effect on employee morale. Mitchell Brown, a
trainee who later had a long career in emergency medical services and public safety in Ohio, remembered, "I watched people use that project Freedom
House as a guinea pig. . . . I don't mean that in a positive sense," he
added.[100] Regardless, Freedom House provided ambulance service that was
highly regarded by medical professionals, patients, and the community.
One patient, a prominent African American politician, wrote to thank Freedom House for "the efficiency with which they worked and their concern
for my welfare." Another patient expressed her "heartfelt thanks" to Freedom House: "Seeing my only son graduate from Penn State," she wrote, "is
a day I will always remember with gratefulness in my heart for you and
friends like you who made it all possible."[101]

Another program to use medical careers to create a path out of poverty was the Medical Career Orientation Program (MCOP). The goal of MCOP was to expose high school students to health careers and potentially create an interested and prepared pipeline to a future health care workforce.[102] Between June and August 1968, MCOP admitted fourteen students. The program attempted to pair each student with a mentor and provide practical and theoretical experience with a variety of health care careers, which meant that students were exposed to a wide range of activities. Other activities included participating in clinical rounds, viewing films about health careers, and attending "seminars on careers in medicine and medical research" with current medical students. In an attempt to "preserve the students' identification with the Black community," they were also introduced to black physicians and health professionals, attended a guest lecture on the history and future of black medical professionals, and participated in a meeting where sponsors, students, and members of the community interacted. This meeting appeared to generate support for the program and provided community members and parents with a chance to offer suggestions for program development.[103]

The language of urban crisis and fear of civil unrest loomed large in the program's founding DNA, reminding urban residents of the potentially dangerous consequences of ignoring economic mobility for all urban residents. The program's first director, Dr. Raymond L. Hayes, noted, "Now is a time of concern for all Americans. Our country is torn by civil disorder, crimes of violence, racial strife and urban decay. In this atmosphere of unrest, it is consoling to contribute to and participate in a purposeful endeavor as occurred [sic] at the University of Pittsburgh School of Medicine this summer, the Medical Career Orientation Program (MCOP)."[104] In 1969, additional funding from the Maurice Falk Medical Fund allowed it to expand from a summer program to a year-round schedule.[105] As one student noted, MCOP was eye-opening: "Before I entered into this program I didn't even know that this building (Scaife Hall) existed. I used to think that if you were Black you could only go to certain colleges, but after I entered this program I learned of all kinds of opportunities offered to Black students."[106]

Mercy Hospital was also actively building a job training program for area residents. First announced in the summer of 1968, this program hoped to place area residents into health jobs as part of the hospital's broader outreach to the community.[107] That July, twenty-two teens were enrolled in a career development program partially funded by the Mayor's Committee on Human Relations, which also sought to expose them to a variety of health careers. Mercy's program also seemed successful. Hospital administrators were happy, and as the chairs of the hospital's Human Relations Committee and Neighborhood Advisory Committee on Health Care, Regis Bobonis and Jacob Williams, put it in a letter to a member of the Pittsburgh Board of Education, "As one youngster put it . . . 'Leaving here is like shutting a door on part of your life.' "[108] The program continued, but without as much acclaim, at least through the following year.[109]

Health Care Employment in Houston

While Houston did not see the same visible deindustrialization as Pittsburgh in the late 1960s and early 1970s, health activists also drew a direct line between the economic future of the region and its health care labor force. Producing more medical professionals quickly became one way to ensure a sufficient supply for the region's health care economy. In 1971, Baylor College of Medicine shortened the MD course of study to three years and also began to standardize the process of allied health professional training with the opening of the Center for Allied Health Manpower Development. This center was supposed to coordinate disparate programs in the medical center as well as offer an institutional home for the physician's assistant program started by the college.[110] The University of Texas also grew in Houston, opening a medical school in the Texas Medical Center in 1970. By 1973, it had been renamed the University of Texas Health Science Center at Houston, reflecting the addition of the Dental Branch, a new School of Public Health, the Medical School, a Speech and Hearing Institute, a Graduate School of Biomedical Sciences, a Division of Continuing Education, and a newly created School of Allied Health Sciences, which started by offering certificates in X-ray technology but soon expanded to include other areas of allied health care.[111]

The expansion of medical schools and the shortening of physician training programs did not necessarily translate into more health care jobs for low-income Houstonians, although certainly the dramatic expansion of facilities must have meant more health care employment overall. Instead, the clearest way that not-for-profit health care institutions worked to build health care employment for poorer residents was through neighborhood health centers, which employed community health workers drawn largely from surrounding neighborhoods. They acted primarily as patient advocates in the neighborhood health centers and also conducted home visits.[112] However, according to Carlos Vallbona, the community health worker program was largely ineffective. He felt that the community health workers were more interested in a paycheck than a career in health services. There was also the issue of training—community health workers were thrown into their jobs with little formal training and were expected to pick up skills "through osmosis." Consequently, they often made suggestions to patients that were "not medically orthodox."[113] Vallbona admitted that the visits were "rather perfunctory" and didn't always seem to follow the goals of monitoring medication compliance or providing useful health education. It is also unclear how much emphasis was put on the program. He recalled that employment programs were instituted primarily as an attempt to meet the guidelines of OEO grants and that the program withered away when the Public Health Service took a more active role in providing funding for Houston's neighborhood health centers.[114] Left out of this analysis was an acknowledgment of the struggle between community health advocates and orthodox medicine over who controlled what medical care looked like and what constituted appropriate approaches for comprehensively treating low-income patients.[115]

While the community health worker idea may not have been a success in the eyes of Vallbona, the creation of a public high school in Houston with a focus on training health professionals did offer not-for-profit health care institutions an alternative way to bring low-income Houstonians into the health care economy. In his deeply researched history of Baylor College of Medicine, Chancellor Emeritus Dr. William T. Butler recalled that the school had a long-standing commitment to developing interest in health care and medicine among high school students.[116] Just as with MCOP in Pittsburgh, the impetus was twofold: helping to promote a broad definition of "community health" that included the economic health of underserved or minority communities, and helping to provide a stable workforce for a growing medical economy in the region.[117]

Using the existing public school system to build a feeder workforce for the city's not-for-profit health care institutions was not unique to Houston. In the summer of 1972, LeGrande Elebash, the assistant for Baylor executive vice president Dr. Joseph Merrill, as well as Robert Roush, the director of the Center for Allied Health Manpower Development, both examined ways to forge stronger links between Baylor College of Medicine and the Houston Independent School District. According to Roush, Elebash looked at a model of medical school/community engagement that Johns Hopkins had developed in Baltimore. This model, called the Health Sciences Career Program, was a combination of programs that shared an explicit goal of health employment and training for underserved youth.[118] Elebash was interested in a partnership that Johns Hopkins had built with Dunbar High School, providing after-school training opportunities in laboratory work, child care, and clerical work.[119] Roush, however, envisioned a more comprehensive program. In the summer of 1972, he convened a group to brainstorm. With approval from Merrill, the idea to create a high school dedicated to the health professions was presented to the Houston Independent School District via telegram and accepted by mid-August.[120] Baylor's support was essential to the school's success. In addition to the involvement of Merrill, Roush, and Vallbona, Baylor's chancellor, Dr. Michael E. DeBakey, used his personal connections as a member of the Texas Advisory Council for Vocational Education to secure funding. Baylor provided the physical space in the Cullen Building for the initial class of around forty students.[121] Baylor continued to provide support and, over the years, has continued its partnerships with the school (since renamed for DeBakey) and now works with universities like the University of Texas–Pan American to develop career preparation programs for minority students interested in medical school and the health professions.[122]

By the middle of the 1970s, however, the idea that social justice should play a role in structuring the hospital-civic relationship was fading. Rising concerns over the cost of medical care, a sense within health care and government policy circles that a perceived shortage of health care employees was not as great as might have been originally anticipated and thus required less financial support, and growing conservative backlash against government spending and the social justice outlook of American liberalism came together to reshape how many urban residents defined civic health. Moreover, expressing a faith in free markets, which had long been part of the American health system, became more permissible in American political life, and commensurately, within the halls and executive suites of not-for-profit health care institutions.[123]

*　*　*

In both cities, health employment programs were often the first to wind down. Freedom House Ambulance service closed in 1975, falling victim to a changing political climate and tightening municipal budgets.[124] Declining financial support by the Maurice Falk Medical Fund helped eventually shutter MCOP sometime in the 1970s, although the philanthropy continued to give money throughout the rest of the decade to promote training for black high schoolers in the sciences, support for minority graduate students in psychology, and for the creation and expansion of an urban mental health program.[125] It is not clear how much longer Mercy Hospital's employment program survived after the cessation of Model Cities and OEO by the Nixon administration. The Neighborhood Committee on Health Care continued until the early 1980s, despite Sister Ferdinand's retirement in 1978, and in Houston, the High School for the Health Professions continues to grow.[126] In 2017, the high school moved into a new $67 million building featuring "state-of-the-art medical training equipment with teaching labs for dentistry, rehabilitation, and patient care," as well as "mock hospital rooms and science labs that mimic real-world research and labs and provide hands-on experience."[127]

A more lasting success came out of efforts to expand care. Neighborhood health centers like Casa de Amigos and Ripley House remain open to this day as part of the Harris County Health System, the new name for the Hospital District. The Homewood-Brushton Neighborhood Health Center also still operates as the Alma Illery Medical Center, named for the civil rights activist, and today anchors a network of primary care services.[128]

A new definition of civic health encompassing both physical and economic health had major consequences for both cities. It also shows the power of intended and unintended consequences for shaping the development of the medical metropolis. In Houston, the creation of a Department of Community Medicine at Baylor meant that the medical school had a committed group of individuals to advance a narrative that linked physical and economic health. Through the creation of neighborhood health centers, physicians in the medical school worked with community members to try to expand care to underserved communities and individuals to make this goal a reality. Moreover, with the Harris County Hospital District as a partner, entities like Baylor and, later, the University of Texas Health Science Center at Houston could become committed partners in community health, because after a transitional period in the mid-1970s, they were no longer solely responsible for seeking funding in an increasingly hostile environment. In this sense, they had the best of both worlds. They could repair damaged images in the community, respond constructively to student demands for more community involvement, and go about the business of training without having to be too invested in the financial future of the neighborhood clinics. Moreover, the creation of the Center for Allied Health Manpower Development and the High School for Health Professions also helped to link the needs of the market for more health care employment with a narrative of social justice that sought to target this employment to groups and individuals that could use it as a step on the ladder of social and economic mobility.

In Pittsburgh, the intentional and unintentional consequences of the decision to expand care and link health employment with social justice helped to transform the hospital-civic relationship. The immediate needs of the urban crisis encouraged not-for-profit health care, the foundation community, and the government to form partnerships to support community health efforts. Mercy Hospital's extension of care into underserved neighborhoods and efforts to bring ordinary people into hospital decision-making through the Neighborhood Committee on Health Care offered real possibilities for change. Moreover, other efforts, such as Montefiore Hospital's efforts to promote better dental care and the University of Pittsburgh's support of community-based health care at Terrace Village, showed a commitment to the linkage of health and social justice. Through programs like Freedom House, not-for-profits, governments, and individuals sought to find a way to build lasting pathways for economic advancement in a changing society for underserved adults. Programs like the Medical Career Orientation Program sought to achieve a similar goal for underserved youths. In the end, however, the lack of federal support for the continuation of Great Society medicine led to a drying up of federal funds and the inauguration of a period of retrenchment. At the same time, concerns over suitability and cost led some of these same actors to turn to the market to try to find a way to offset some of their future responsibility for the health of the most vulnerable in the medical metropolis, which they did through failed efforts to build HMOs at the University of Pittsburgh and Central Medical Pavilion.

As the funds supporting this social justice vision dried up, many not-for-profit health care institutions turned toward new areas of revenue generation and prestige—including cardiac care and transplantation medicine. These high-dollar, high-publicity service lines became the new face of the medical metropolis and helped to normalize a more market-oriented vision of the hospital civic relationship from the mid- to late 1970s onward.

Chapter 3

City of Hearts, City of Livers

Specialty Medicine and the Creation of New Civic Identities

On a balmy Good Friday in 1969, Houston heart surgeon Dr. Denton Cooley implanted the world's first total artificial heart in a patient named Haskell Karp. The heart was intended as a bridge to a cardiac transplantation, which occurred three days after the first surgery. Despite Cooley's efforts, Karp died two days later—only living five days from his first operation. The implantation of the total artificial heart was a watershed moment and was hailed as a triumph of modern technology and quickly became a symbol of the possibilities of modern scientific medicine. It also provided Cooley with global publicity and elevated Houston's reputation as a center for advanced specialty medicine.[1]

Pittsburgh's emergence as a "city of livers" came more than a decade later. In late 1980, Dr. Thomas Starzl, a kidney and liver transplantation pioneer, was recruited to the University of Pittsburgh. He quickly became the face of medical progress in the city and helped rebuild Pittsburgh's reputation for biomedical innovation. Starzl's transplantation program rocketed the University of Pittsburgh to global prominence and gave the city a new identity at a time when the steel mills were closing and the future seemed bleak.[2]

The growing prominence of specialty medicine in both cities helped to transform the hospital-civic relationship into one that embraced the power of private markets and the ability of entrepreneurs to transform the medical metropolis for the postindustrial future. In this model, the social justice possibilities of medicine became overshadowed by its role as a social good—saving individual lives and giving struggling communities a new identity for the postindustrial future. At the same time, the new version of the hospital-civic relationship that arose as specialty service lines grew emerged gradually and built off from all three legs of the "eternal triangle," like full-time medical school faculty members conducting basic and clinical research, medical students and residents assisting with clinical services, and patients willing to use new technology like the artificial heart and undergo experimental procedures like liver transplantation. Specialty medicine also contributed financial support for the model of the hospital-civic relationship that it helped to eventually overshadow.

The push to develop specialty service lines owed much to the long-standing trend to prioritize medical specialization as a marker of technical prowess and economic power.[3] It also relied on a growing acceptance of a more commercialized business model within the not-for-profit health care sector and the application of principles from the corporate sector such as process efficiency, statistical modeling, and the need to find new markets.[4] A final factor was the growing national and international scope of the medical marketplace from the 1970s onward that provided new patients and new locations for prominent physicians to spread their clinical and financial knowledge.[5]

Specialty medicine helped build the medical metropolis in two critical ways. First, it contributed to ongoing efforts to create new identities for both Pittsburgh and Houston as centers of postindustrial innovation. These efforts both predated and occurred alongside the broader efforts to build economies around biotechnology and advanced manufacturing, which are discussed later. Second, the rise of specialty medicine created a new import-export economy for clinical and business knowledge. While it may have seemed very different from the primary metals or extraction economy, the specialty medical import-export economy was nevertheless deeply embedded in modern capitalism and in an increasingly international medical marketplace.

Civic elites and elected officials had little to do with building specialty medicine in the medical metropolis beyond it being part of a new technologically focused urban future, helping with the physical expansion of not-for-profit hospitals and medical schools when possible through favorable zoning decisions and financing opportunities, and occasionally providing in-kind donations for special services like organ procurement. However, even in the absence of a coherent plan to market specialty medicine as economic development, its very growth changed the way that the nation and the world saw the medical metropolis.[6] Thus, the increasing prominence of specialty medicine helped to normalize a more market-oriented and outward-looking vision of the hospital-civic relationship that emerged by the 1980s and 1990s and helped to promote the investments in biotechnology and in building large health systems, which are discussed in more detail later. While this chapter will talk about two particular service lines, cardiovascular surgery and transplantation medicine, and will focus on three figures, Dr. Denton Cooley, Dr. Michael E. DeBakey, and Dr. Thomas Starzl, many not-for-profit hospitals and many other physicians developed a variety of specialty service lines that also helped to build the medical metropolis.[7]

Houston Becomes a City of Hearts

While Cooley's operation on Haskell Karp kicked off a media firestorm, he was not the first Houston surgeon whose exploits in the operating room generated headlines. During the early to mid-1950s, Dr. Michael E. DeBakey, often working alongside Cooley, was the face of medical progress in the city. DeBakey, who first came to Houston in 1948 from Tulane University, was often in the news for his dramatic surgical firsts and inventions, including the use of the artificial material Dacron as an arterial patch to repair aneurysms.[8] Media attention brought him global prominence, which he parlayed into a reputation as a medical statesman, and in 1964 he performed an abdominal aneurysm surgery on the Duke of Windsor. When the duke informed the world that he was "very glad to give this brief New Year's message from the Methodist Hospital here in Houston, Texas," where he was "now convalescing from vascular surgery performed by Dr. Michael DeBakey, the greatest expert in the field today," the city's reputation as a center for advanced specialty care was solidified, helping to draw even more prominent patients to Houston.[9]

After vascular surgery, the next great frontier was open heart surgery. Its success rested on the ability to mechanically circulate oxygenated blood by creating a machine that could replace the heart and lungs during surgery. At medical centers throughout the United States, including in Houston, physicians engaged in a range of experiments to create this type of machine, often visiting one another and sharing ideas.[10] In 1957, drawing from the work of Dr. John Kirkland and Dr. Walt Lillehei, Cooley created a blood oxygenator he dubbed the "Cooley coffeepot," since parts of it came from

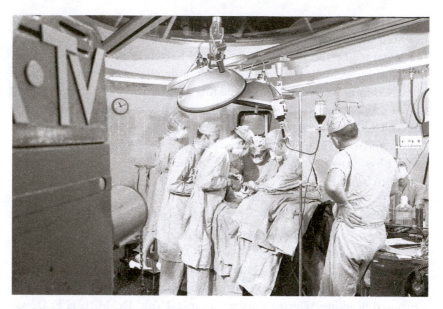

Figure 6. On May 2, 1965, at The Methodist Hospital in Houston, Dr. Michael DeBakey performed an open-heart surgery that was transmitted live to the Geneva University Medical School via the Early Bird Satellite. Houston's KTRK-TV (see camera on the left) filmed the procedure.

Photograph by Gene Davis, courtesy of Baylor College of Medicine Archives.

a commercial kitchen supplier.[11] Cooley soon had several more manufactured by a medical supply company, which, when combined with a pump to circulate the oxygenated blood, allowed him to expand his practice volume from a few open heart procedures a day to a " 'production-line' basis."[12] In fact, by 1968, nearly 10 percent of all open heart surgeries in the United States were performed at hospitals affiliated with DeBakey or Cooley.[13]

In the mid-1950s, this increase in volume necessitated that Cooley move his surgical operations to the conjoined St. Luke's Episcopal Hospital and Texas Children's. In addition to putting space between him and DeBakey, with whom his personal and professional relationship was rapidly deteriorating, the move also allowed Cooley to define his clinical practice and carve out a niche in an increasingly competitive cardiovascular surgical market in the city.[14] The result was the Texas Heart Institute (THI), which was chartered in 1962. This new not-for-profit institute was a product of

Cooley's Johns Hopkins education and his deep connections to the city's elite as a born and bred Houstonian. He envisioned the THI as a research institute linked to Texas Children's Hospital and St. Luke's Episcopal Hospital that would be supported primarily through surgical fees and private-sector donations. In the five years between chartering and groundbreaking, he enlisted the help of prominent Houstonians like Robert Herring, the CEO of the Houston Natural Gas Company, as fund-raisers. Herring was particularly important because he was the head of the Roy C. Fish Foundation, which, among other things, had a mission of supporting cardiovascular research. Herring and Cooley also had quite a bit of common social ground. Both men were residents of River Oaks, a prominent Houston neighborhood, and they traveled in the same social circles.[15]

Two other innovations also helped to make Houston into a city of hearts during the 1960s and 1970s—cardiac transplantation and the development of the artificial heart. Throughout the 1950s and into the early 1960s, a range of experiments related to transplantation were conducted, including experiments in Mississippi that involved implanting a chimpanzee heart in a human patient.[16] Then, in December 1967, word came from South Africa that Dr. Christiaan Barnard had conducted the world's first successful human organ to human patient cardiac transplant. Barnard followed his first surgery with another successful transplant on January 2, 1968, and kicked off a race among surgeons in Houston, California, London, and numerous other academic medical centers across the globe to be the next surgeon to successfully complete the procedure. That same month, it looked like Dr. Norman Shumway at Stanford would become the first American surgeon to complete a successful cardiac transplant, but Shumway's transplant patient died fourteen days after receiving a new heart. Dr. Richard Lower, a colleague who moved from Stanford to the Medical College of Virginia, also encountered patient fatalities after transplantation.[17]

In May, Denton Cooley tried his first cardiac transplantation. Cooley's patient was a forty-seven-year-old accountant from Phoenix named Everett Thomas, into whom he transplanted the heart of a fifteen-year-old suicide victim. Thomas survived for 204 days and became the first successful heart transplant with long-term survival in the United States.[18] Soon after operating on Thomas, Cooley performed two more heart transplants, and by September of that year, Cooley had performed a total of ten transplants, including a pediatric heart-lung transplant.[19] Attempting to dethrone Cooley as Houston's transplant leader, DeBakey built the first multiple organ transplant program in the city. In August, he led a surgical team of sixty people and completed the world's first combined heart, lung, and kidney transplant. The race continued, with Cooley completing an astounding twenty-two heart transplants in 1968 and 1969.[20] By March 1971, 170 total heart transplants had been performed across the globe—yet only twenty-four patients were still alive.[21] The problem of tissue rejection was primarily to blame, along with an organ procurement system that lurched from crisis to crisis, rather than providing hearts on a regular or as-needed basis. Organ transplantation was costly and uncertain, especially when the cost of the operation including surgical time, a private jet service to retrieve a donor organ, the strain that a transplant placed on hospital resources in terms of added security, public relations, and maintaining a sterile recovery were tallied.

These problems raised an interesting possibility. What about creating a mechanical organ to do the same thing as a human one? In 1964, DeBakey won a grant from the National Heart Institute to develop mechanical assist devices, including a total artificial heart. He recruited an Argentina-born physician named Dr. Domingo Liotta away from the Cleveland Clinic to form the nucleus of Baylor's program. Liotta, who had already been working on building a total artificial heart, was tasked primarily with perfecting the left ventricular assist device (LVAD), which was a partial cardiac assist device, and told to work on the total artificial heart as a secondary project. DeBakey was partial to the left ventricular assist device, believing that a total artificial heart required too much work to be practical in the near term. Liotta and Cooley hoped that the total artificial heart, rather than the LVAD, would be a more effective bridge to transplant.[22]

On April 5, 1969, they decided to implant their artificial heart to save the life of Haskell Karp. Both maintained that it was purely a last-ditch effort and was always conceived of as a bridge to transplant.[23] DeBakey, who was out of town at the time, was livid and viewed the entire episode as a betrayal of him personally as well as of Baylor College of Medicine. To this day, barrels of ink have been spilled about the suspected origins of the Cooley/Liotta artificial heart and whether it was stolen, or if it was indeed a new design paid for with private dollars.[24] The irony of the whole situation was that it didn't really matter where the artificial heart came from; what mattered was that it had been implanted in the first place, and that the Texas Medical Center was the only place in the world that had the technology and the people to make implanting a total artificial heart possible—a fact amplified by the Houston press and distributed to wire services across the United States by the public relations staffs at various hospitals, thereby confirming the value of specialty medicine for helping to create a unique reputation for Houston as a city of hearts.[25]

Importing Patients and Exporting Clinical and Financial Knowledge in Houston

Another critical way that DeBakey and Cooley established their reputation (and, by extension, Houston's global reputation as a medical metropolis) was by importing patients and exporting clinical and financial knowledge through their academic writing and surgical training programs.[26] Houston-trained medical students and surgical fellows spread out all over the United States and the globe. Dr. Edward Diethrich was one example of a cardiovascular surgeon who parlayed the reputation of his mentors (DeBakey) into a successful cardiovascular practice elsewhere. In 1971, Diethrich opened the Arizona Heart Institute in Phoenix. He gained national fame in a 1972 *Life* magazine profile where he was dubbed "Ted Terrific" and cast as a swashbuckling evangelist for the evolving business of coronary artery bypass grafting (CABG).[27]

Since the 1960s, CABG has become the financial foundation on which cardiovascular surgery rests. The idea behind it is deceptively simple: the goal is to use a section of an existing artery from elsewhere in the body to create a new path for blood to reach the heart—effectively bypassing an existing arterial connection that is damaged or blocked.[28] The rising popularity of the operation came in the late 1960s after Dr. René Favaloro at the Cleveland Clinic reported successful outcomes. Earlier in the decade, DeBakey had experimented with arterial grafting but his patient died of a "perioperative infarction."[29] CABG has a number of advantages over other cardiac surgeries. First, the survival rates are high. Second, while the operation requires dexterity and clear vision, it is ideally suited to a team approach—fellows and residents can open the patient's chest and remove needed arteries from elsewhere in the body, then the senior surgeon can swoop in and connect the bypass grafts, and leave the junior members of the team to close. CABG was also not treated as experimental surgery by private insurance companies or Medicare, which meant that there was a steady stream of money associated with performing the operation. This procedure helped Cooley to build the Texas Heart Institute into a volume

Figure 7. Dr. Denton Cooley operating at Texas Children's Hospital in 1977.
Photo by Kleesiek in MS043 Denton Cooley, box 50, folder "1977," John P. McGovern Historical
Collections and Research Center, Houston Academy of Medicine–Texas Medical Center Library,
Houston, Texas.

leader in heart surgery. The nearby Shamrock Hilton was filled with so
many patients waiting for the procedure that it was known as the "Cooley
Hilton."[30]

Surgical volume required efficacy. Cooley did this by organizing his
surgical space in a honeycomb-shaped suite of eight operating rooms,
arranged around a central supply room. This allowed him to quickly move
between operating rooms and for supplies to always be close at hand. He
also managed his own time effectively. Each operating room was connected
to cameras that fed into monitors in Cooley's private office, which allowed
Cooley to quickly monitor surgical patients while tending to administrative
tasks.[31] What made this model work were two things: first, that more and
more of the actual surgery could be handled by surgeons other than Cooley,
and second, that the cardiac surgery itself was becoming more standardized.
According to the *New York Times*, this efficiency paid off handsomely for

Cooley. By the early 1980s, "his annual medical income passed $9 million a year." Cooley also grew his fortune by investing in real estate, until the oil bust of the late 1980s forced him to a substantial bankruptcy when the city's commercial property values collapsed.[32]

The growing reputation of the THI as a model for cost-effective, high-volume surgery attracted international attention. In the mid-1970s, Cooley and the Dutch government undertook an innovative program to provide heart surgery for patients who were unable to access it in a timely fashion in the Netherlands. Called either the Dutch Air Bridge or Dutch Airlift, it was the brainchild of a dissatisfied cardiac patient named Henk Fievet, who created an advocacy organization for Dutch cardiac patients named Nederlandse hartpatiënten Vereniging, or Dutch Heart Patients Association. *Dagblad de Telegraaf* journalist Frits Gonggrijp lionized Fievet as "a man from the people, somewhat of a Ralph Nader of the heart patients of the Netherlands. He is a crusader, a man who decided to fight 'city hall' behind the dikes."[33] Whether or not Fievet, who died in 1977, lived up to this billing is unclear. What he did do, along with Dutch surgeon Dr. P. J. van der Scharr, was to convince the Dutch government and the social insurance system that it was more cost-effective to outsource the backlog (estimated to be in the thousands) to Denton Cooley for an estimated fee of around $8,000 to $10,000 per patient, including travel expenses.[34] On July 23, 1976, an initial group of seven patients came to Houston.[35] Over the next five years, around 1,500 Dutch patients arrived in Houston for surgery.[36] They underwent a similar set of procedures to American patients, including cardiac catheterization if needed (this was typically done before the patient arrived), additional testing to confirm the referring physician's diagnosis and to confirm that surgical intervention was warranted, and operative and postoperative care.[37] Cooley's outcomes compared favorably against other heart centers accepting Dutch patients; in fact, Houston had lower death rates for most patients over the age of thirty-five after one year.[38]

The Dutch were not the only foreign patients flocking to Houston. In 1981, the *Houston Business Journal* ran a large article about the links between Saudi Arabia and the Bayou City. While most of the article focused on the extraction economy, some sharp-eyed readers may have seen a smaller section claiming that the city had emerged as an important destination for medical care, stating that "The Medical Center, in fact, has been the attraction for the free-spending princes that have made headlines in

London in the past. The story still abounds throughout the Medical Center of one prince who arrived for a checkup last year in his own Boeing 707 filled with family, friends and servants. The entourage took over the entire fifth floor of The Warwick, favored not just for its location but for its European-style service and tight-lipped staff."[39]

The rich foreign playboy, buying the best medical treatment that the American health system had to offer, held an unmistakable allure for providers of specialty care, who were struggling to find adequate reimbursement models for domestic patients as they attempted to understand the emerging managed care market, which is discussed in more detail later. Foreign patients were cash payers, and often at full sticker price.[40] By the late 1980s and 1990s, many TMC hospitals created robust international outreach programs, including physician exchange programs, and participated in travel packages "with annual checkups provided in the tours" to capture this market.[41] International offices also provided services for the patient's families while in Houston.[42] The Methodist Hospital, for example, started to make a strong play for more international patients through an international referral program they created called the "Friends of The Methodist Hospital." This program reached out to foreign physicians who had trained at the hospital and left the United States to create a pathway to Houston for their current patients. It also sent out newsletters, offered a consultation telephone line, sponsored symposia in foreign countries, and even created continuing medical education programs in Houston for "friends."[43]

Both DeBakey's and Cooley's growing reputations meant that they were also asked to export their clinical and financial knowledge to build programs overseas. In 1975, the Saudi government completed the King Faisal Specialist Hospital and Research Centre in Riyadh. According to the hospital's medical director, Dr. Russell Scott Jr., the goal was "to create a hospital and research institute that would take a position among the outstanding medical centers in the world."[44] The Hospital Corporation of America (HCA) was contracted through its international division to manage the hospital, which included providing staffing and developing capacity. The company's roots go back to a fraternity house at Vanderbilt University in the late 1950s, where Thomas F. Frist Jr. met Spence Wilson. Wilson's father, Kemmons, was a cofounder of the Holiday Inn hotel chain, which pioneered a new model for the hotel industry. Kemmons Wilson's willingness to buck tradition appealed to the entrepreneurial Frist.[45] After leaving

Vanderbilt, Frist attended medical school at Washington University in St. Louis and then served as an Air Force flight surgeon at Robins Air Force Base in Georgia. Frist realized that hospitals could follow a retail-oriented model by consolidating resources and operating as chains.[46] He reached out to his father, Dr. Thomas F. Frist Sr., a prominent Nashville cardiologist who already had hospital ownership experience, and two other investors with roots in the fried chicken industry—a former pharmacist and surgical supply company owner named Jack Massey, whose investment in Kentucky Fried Chicken made him millions, and Henry Hooker from Minnie Pearl's Chicken.[47]

In order to build the hospital's reputation and specialty medical capacity quickly, representatives from the Saudi government and the company sought out expertise from academic physicians and administrators.[48] In January 1976, shortly after the new hospital opened, representatives from all three groups convened in Houston for a two-day conference. The medical equipment, training, and staffing the new hospital needed to build out its specialty services were also discussed.[49] Later that year, both HCA and the Saudi government approached DeBakey about helping to build an open-heart surgery unit at the new facility.[50] As part of this agreement, Baylor sent teams on an overlapping three-month rotation, which included "a senior surgeon, an associate surgeon, an anesthesiologist, two cardiopulmonary perfusionists, two operating room nurses, and four intensive care nurses" and an administrative assistant. In the first year, they treated 225 cases, with a mortality rate that "compare[d] favorably with those reported at most major cardiovascular centers in the United States."[51] The strong results also continued into the second year, with a low mortality rate, a growing number of surgical cases, and strong cooperation between the Saudi and HCA staff and the Baylor team. As a report for the second-year activities noted, "The teams from Baylor and the personnel of the Hospital continue to work harmoniously as one team, and many Baylor personnel are now returning to Riyadh for a second three month rotation." Moreover, Saudi residents came to Houston to train.[52]

This new unit seemed to represent a win-win-win. The Saudis fulfilled a critical goal of their health care modernization plan by introducing cardiovascular surgery to the country, training their own physicians over a five-year period to eventually provide it, and building the specialized spaces needed to house these procedures. HCA was able to offer lucrative specialty service lines, including cardiovascular surgery and oncology, which, just as at U.S. hospitals, helped to drive revenue. The money made in Saudi Arabia then allowed HCA to invest in other overseas operations in Central and Latin America, Western Europe, and Australia.[53] Baylor gained access to a patient population with the types of medical conditions that allowed its trainees to sufficiently hone their skills, as the senior surgeons experienced. In a 1977 article in *American Medical News* highlighting the creation of the program, Baylor surgeon Dr. Arthur C. Beall Jr. noted, "there are a large number of people with congenital heart defects, like the backlog of patients in the U.S. in the 1950s when we started doing open-heart work."[54] A year later, Beall reaffirmed the altruistic nature of Baylor's involvement, saying to the *Houston Chronicle*, "We've gone to Saudi Arabia because we were asked for medical help. . . . We wanted to be of service. If somebody asked for help to fix a flat tire, you would try to help. Our motivation has been the same."[55]

Whatever the motivations of each party, the arrangement was not without controversy. In 1982, two anesthesiologists, Dr. Lawrence Abrams and Dr. Stewart Linde, alleged that Baylor would not allow them to participate in the exchange with Saudi Arabia because they were Jewish. The pair filed a suit, citing both diminished earning potential and professional harm for career advancement since, as Beall noted, King Faisal presented a unique opportunity to train on a volume of conditions not always seen in the United States. The question of compensation was particularly interesting— court filings show that Baylor physicians could stand to make substantially more money in any given year by spending three months in Saudi Arabia. Internal budget documents from Baylor also express concerns over the high salary rate paid to participants in the program, which by 1982 had a total budget of over $4 million.[56] For its part, Baylor contended (incorrectly) that since the Kingdom of Saudi Arabia banned the entry of Jews into the country, regardless of salary or opportunity, they were unable to offer Abrams and Linde a position on the rotation. After four years of litigation, Baylor was found to have discriminated against the two physicians based on religion.[57] Baylor's contract with the HCA/Saudi program appears to have ended by late 1984 or early 1985.[58]

Throughout the rest of the 1980s and 1990s, DeBakey continued to export clinical and financial knowledge from Houston. In the United States, he lent his expertise and name to the construction of DeBakey-branded Cardiovascular Centers at community hospitals in Kenosha, Wisconsin, and Hays, Kansas. The chief surgeon at the Kenosha facility was a long-time member of DeBakey's surgical team.[59] DeBakey also formalized his international consulting efforts by creating or affiliating with at least two firms. One was the DeBakey Consulting Group. Created in 1989, the company claimed in promotional materials that it allowed DeBakey to "formalize his commitment to advisory services" by allowing him to "combine his experience and leadership with the capabilities of a team of renowned medical professionals—who in turn are supported by the resources of several of the world's leading professional service firms."[60] The firm drew expertise from Baylor physicians and used the Office of the Chancellor as its official mailing address. Links to the private sector included health care planning firms like the Douglass Group of Deloitte & Touche, and health care architects like Watkins Carter Hamilton. DeBakey Consulting Group was particularly active in Turkey, working with President Turgut Özal to plan a new teaching hospital in Malatya that was later named for Özal after his death. The firm's services included assisting with the architectural design of the hospital and working with the client to create a plan to "recruit, train and certify key staff for this tertiary hospital, which now serves as a referral center for many Middle Eastern and Mediterranean nations."[61] It is not clear what the financial arrangements looked like for Baylor or DeBakey, but it appears that DeBakey Consulting Group tried to merge the mission of the school to spread knowledge with the efficiency of corporate America to create new medical facilities overseas.

In the late 1990s, DeBakey affiliated with another consulting group, DeBakey-Pechersky Partners, LLC. This was a partnership between DeBakey, Lebanese engineer and entrepreneur George S. Zakhem, and Anna Pechersky, a Kazakhstan-born former running champion turned international business facilitator. The goal of this company was to seek out opportunities in developing countries to create specialized cardiovascular care facilities. The services that the company would provide included construction, helping to match projects and financing, government relations with the United States to help secure foreign aid, contract negotiation services, and on-site physician and staff training after the facility was built. It seems that the company's primary project was pitching to the government of the former Soviet Republic of Georgia to create a stand-alone cardiovascular care center. Existing records don't fully indicate if this project was ever successful or what role the company played in its development beyond the proposal stage.[62]

There was one more way that specialist physicians "exported" knowledge from the medical metropolis—in this case, knowledge about the business of cardiovascular care. In the early 1980s, a combination of changes in reimbursement for surgical procedures as a consequence of managed care, rising competition from other surgical centers, and the introduction of new, less invasive procedures like balloon angioplasty that were conducted by interventional cardiologists rather than surgeons led to a decline in the THI's revenue. To offset this, Cooley diversified the staff and found new ways to capture more of the market for CABG. One critical way he did this was by drawing from the Dutch Air Bridge experience and offering volume discounts on cardiac procedures for large employer groups. Cooley called this new service, which the THI introduced in 1984, CardioVascular Care Providers (CVCP).[63] The idea for the program came about at a Houston cocktail party where the CEO of Tenneco, a large self-insured energy company, approached Cooley with his concerns about understanding the financial exposure the company had with providing care for cardiac patients. Cigna Insurance Company also approached Cooley around the same time.[64] Cooley applied many of the principles used by large managed care organizations, such as data analytics and packaged pricing, to build a volume-based program that could generate revenue for the THI while saving everybody money on a per-procedure basis. CVCP created a database of cardiac patient outcomes and used risk pooling among physicians to set fees for sixteen different diagnoses that were lower than the sum of individual charges, but still high enough to make a profit on most cases and spread out risk on those that were a financial loss. This wealth of information allowed CVCP to build risk models to manage costs. This deep data dive helped CVCP to determine what operations to cover and how to price each operation.[65] For example, the plan billed $13,800 to insurance providers for a CABG, "in contrast to the average Medicare payment of $24,588."[66] By 1985, Texas state practice laws forced the modification of CVCP's organizational structure in two key ways: one, the organization became a stand-alone, not-for-profit corporation that was "physician-directed," and two, physician services and facility charges were separated into two separate contracts as a way to better manage risk for the organization.[67] In 1993, St. Luke's started to accept flat-fee Medicare patients for cardiovascular care.[68]

The THI's focus on volume led some in the Texas Medical Center to view Cooley as "a mass marketer of second rate-medicine." In article in the *New York Times* in 1994, DeBakey claimed: "He is interested in doing large volumes of surgery at cheap prices. There are many community hospitals doing the same thing and just as cheaply."[69] The implication was that Cooley's approach was antithetical to the values of an academic medical center. However, in reality, DeBakey's comment reflected instead a certain ambiguity about the place of specialty medicine in the medical metropolis. While DeBakey saw it primarily as a social good that lengthened the lives of individual patients, he also recognized that it helped bring economic stability to medical centers and to the cities in which they were located. The question was one of balance between these two aims.

Cooley, on the other hand, viewed specialty medicine as business and a social good. While he was proud of the lives he saved, he was also proud of his business acumen. In fact, Cooley and CVCP administrators wrote and spoke frequently about this new business model for cardiovascular care, helping to assure its national visibility. He even called it the "first . . . that may have the greatest impact on health care."[70] The lessons learned from this program about data management, cost control, and efficiency helped to reshape the business of cardiovascular surgery.[71] In one retrospective on the history of the THI, Cooley made this view of specialty medicine clear, saying, "Indeed, much of our reputation is based on the volume of patients we can handle. As an admirer of Sam Walton, the founder of Wal-Mart, I am happy to be dubbed the Sam Walton of heart surgery."[72]

Making Pittsburgh into a City of Livers

Specialty medicine, in this case transplantation medicine, also helped to transform Pittsburgh's version of the hospital-civic relationship. Just like their counterparts in Houston, surgeons at the University of Pittsburgh greeted the transplant era with excitement, and then watched it slip away in frustration when they were unable to control organ and tissue rejection. As early as 1964, Dr. Bernard Fisher started a kidney transplantation program and, in 1968, surgeon Dr. Henry Bahnson performed the first cardiac transplantation in Pennsylvania on a boxing promoter from Pittsburgh's Squirrel Hill neighborhood. However, with the inability to control organ and tissue rejection, the university's transplantation programs languished throughout the 1970s.[73] The arrival of Dr. Thomas Starzl in late 1980 revitalized transplantation medicine in Pittsburgh.

Most surgeons regarded livers as too difficult to transplant, largely because of the sheer volume of blood that flowed through them. Some limited work had been done in the middle of the 1950s that involved transplanting an extra liver in dogs, in the hope that the new liver would gradually replace the damaged one, but this procedure received little attention from the broader medical community.[74] Starzl, in fact, wasn't even aware of these experiments until 1957, when he heard a lecture on it.[75] This lecture sparked a change in his own research methodologies, including the creation of the technique of blood bypass during replacement surgery and the injection of the donor liver with cold solutions to prevent ischemic injury.[76] In early 1963, while at the University of Colorado, he attempted a series of human liver transplantation trials on five patients, all of whom died within a month. These deaths, when combined with others at Peter Bent Brigham Hospital in Boston and in Paris, spelled the end of active human liver transplantation for several years. Then, in 1967, Starzl and several others tried liver transplantation again, but its low success rate (more than half of liver recipients died within a year) meant that it was an operation that was performed sparingly for the next decade or so.

This left kidney transplantation as the primary avenue for surgeons to continue to refine their techniques and to test antirejection regimens in human patients.[77] It was an alluring area of medicine because of evidence that when kidneys from identical twins or members of the same family were transplanted, the procedure was successful. This proved that the single greatest problem was rejection and not surgical complexity. During the 1970s, kidney transplantation also received another push—the passage of the End Stage Renal Disease Act of 1972 (ESRD), which helped to create a new industry around dialysis and transplantation.[78] This act declared that people with ESRD were "disabled" and made Medicare monies available, regardless of age, to pay for dialysis and kidney transplantation. Most ESRD monies were spent on dialysis, but transplantation surgeons were also now guaranteed reimbursement for a procedure that heretofore had been considered experimental by most government and private insurers.[79]

The standard antirejection regimen for kidney transplantation was a combination of the drug Imuran and the steroid prednisone throughout the 1960s and 1970s. Starzl had access to a new antirejection option, cyclosporine, which changed the face of transplantation medicine. Cyclosporine is derived from a naturally occurring fungus that was discovered in Norwegian soil in 1969–1970 by workers from the Sandoz Corporation, a Swiss pharmaceutical firm, who were looking for antibiotics.[80] Laboratory testing showed the compound was not an antibiotic, but it did help to weaken the immune system, a key finding for combating tissue and organ rejection. However, human clinical trials also revealed that, while the drug helped manage rejection, it had a problematic side effect—it caused damage to the kidneys. Thus, transplantation surgeons were faced with a quandary. Their best hope for making transplantation a viable procedure damaged the very organ that most of them transplanted. Starzl decided to try a new approach derived from his old antirejection methodologies. Instead of treating transplantation recipients only with cyclosporine, he diluted the drug with steroids, and, despite a great deal of trepidation and even outrage from some quarters of the medical community, Starzl's gamble worked.[81] Shortly after that, Sandoz launched two additional trials, including one at the University of Texas Health Science Center in Houston, through which Denton Cooley gained the cyclosporine he needed to resume heart transplantation.[82] By the time Starzl came to the University of Pittsburgh, it was clear that the cyclosporine-steroid combination would revolutionize transplantation medicine. The drug was still undergoing testing, which meant that those who had access to it also had a near monopoly on successful transplantations. By 1986, Starzl was experimenting in animals with a new antirejection drug, FK 506, which was more potent than cyclosporine and could be given in smaller doses. He moved to human trials in 1989. Success with FK 506 further established the Pittsburgh program as a world transplantation leader, helping to drive more and more very ill patients to the city.[83] Starzl, like DeBakey and Cooley, was also a prolific author, and his publications, and the fellows he trained, exported clinical and scientific knowledge from Pittsburgh about transplantation surgery and antirejection drugs.[84]

Like the artificial heart, organ transplantation was a technically complex and dramatic procedure that generated a great deal of public interest. And like Cooley and DeBakey, Starzl and his colleagues at the University of Pittsburgh understood its public relations value, even if surgical outcomes remained uncertain. In fact, Starzl's first four liver transplantation patients in Pittsburgh died within the first twenty-two days after their operations. But his fifth operation was a success, and the face of a happy pediatric patient rescued from the brink of death on the television news paid public relations dividends.[85] Good publicity begat corporate support, which came as a result of a growing sense that transplantation medicine represented another way that universities and not-for-profit health care were contributing to a high-technology vision for Pittsburgh's economic future. Major local corporations like U.S. Steel, Rockwell International, Alcoa, and Westinghouse donated corporate jet service to assist with organ procurement,

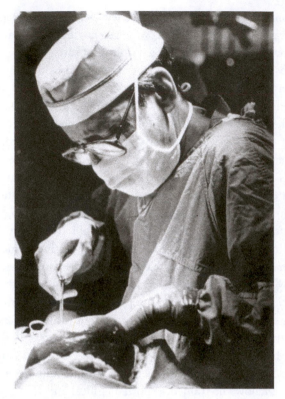

Figure 8.
Dr. Thomas Starzl
performing surgery,
circa 1980s.

Photographer unknown.
Box 374, Folder 25, Dr.
Thomas E. Starzl M.D.
Papers, 1908–2017, UA.90.
F56, Archives and Special
Collections, University of
Pittsburgh Library System.

an effort that became known as "the University of Pittsburgh Air Force,"
which helped to save on organ procurement costs.[86]

The publicity around organ transplantation also made Starzl into a
celebrity. In 1984, he received what many sports-obsessed Pittsburghers
might call his highest honor by throwing out the first pitch when the Pittsburgh Pirates played the Los Angeles Dodgers at Three Rivers Stadium. The
following year, the *New York Times* discussed Starzl and the city's rising
medical prominence in an article titled, "Center for Transplants Aids Pittsburgh Ascent." The article noted that Starzl and his team performed 166
liver transplantations in 1984, half the total number performed nationally,
and 210 kidney transplants. The University of Pittsburgh's medical center
also performed 60 heart transplants (15 percent of the U.S. total), 12 heart-
lung transplants, and 6 pancreas transplants. It dubbed the transplantation
program "the biggest lift since Dr. Jonas Salk developed the polio vaccine
at the school in the 1950s."[87]

Importing Patients and Exporting Clinical and Financial Knowledge in Pittsburgh

Transplantation medicine, especially liver transplantation, was on far shakier financial ground than cardiovascular surgery. One of the things that made Houston into a volume leader in specialty medicine was clear reimbursement pathways that didn't force medical centers to take losses on the procedures when patients couldn't pay. Take kidney transplantation as an example. Even with ESRD, Medicare paid providers $1,876 for renal transplantation during the early 1980s, or about 80 percent of what it deemed a total allowable cost for the operation. University Surgical Associates, the faculty practice plan for the University of Pittsburgh's Department of Surgery, priced the operation higher than what Medicare allowed, at about $3,600, which left the difference to be paid by patients out of pocket, by health insurance (when it covered the procedure), or written off as charity care.[88] However, the fees charged by University Surgical Associates represented only a fraction of the total cost of the procedure. Not included in this figure was the cost of organ procurement, which Starzl estimated at about $8,000 per kidney at the University of Pittsburgh, as well as additional charges for presurgical consultation, pre- and postoperative hospitalization, and the cost to maintain an immunosuppression regimen.[89] Starzl lobbied hard to gain insurance coverage for transplantation medicine, something that was more widespread by the mid-1980s.[90]

This helped the bottom line of the medical center. In 1987, Bahnson noted, "transplanted patients of various types have filled the cracks in Presby's occupancy, 20–25 percent of the total beds."[91] He also noted that, as more difficult patients were transplanted, the program would be competing for increasingly scarce bed space due to longer length of stays in intensive care units. Full beds and covered procedures meant revenue—by the early 1990s, Starzl recalled that the medical center was transplanting around six hundred livers a year at the cost of roughly $250,000–300,000 per case. As he remembered it, transplants were an essential part of the clinical revenue stream that Dr. Thomas Detre, then the senior vice chancellor for Health Sciences and first president of University of Pittsburgh Medical Center (UPMC), used to build the medical center during the 1980s and 1990s.[92]

International patients also played a role in building transplantation specialty medical services in Pittsburgh. There were, however, some critical differences to what was happening in Houston. One of the biggest was that transplantation medicine raised a different set of ethical issues than coronary artery bypass grafting, which was relatively quick and used the patient's own body as a donor for the arteries needed for bypass. Because of the relative scarcity of organs and the long waiting list, when foreign patients were transplanted in Pittsburgh, it created a popular perception that their procedure came at the expense of an American patient. This was amplified by the local media. On May 12, 1985, the *Pittsburgh Press* published an article titled "Favoritism Shrouds Presby Transplants," which claimed that foreign nationals, Saudi Arabians in particular, were leapfrogging Americans waiting for kidneys by virtue of their wealth and political connections.[93] Interestingly, the *Pittsburgh Post-Gazette* found that Americans tended to receive more livers than foreign patients, but the outcry over kidney transplantation illustrates the problems that accepting international patients could bring a domestic not-for-profit institution.[94] This article, as well a number of follow-up pieces, made several charges against the transplant program regarding foreign patients, including that Starzl favored foreign patients over American patients when it came to transplantation; foreign patients were regarded as a prime revenue source for physicians and hospitals, and subsequently were charged much higher fees for similar procedures than American patients; and later that summer, the *Press* added an additional charge that foreign patients may have been transplanted with inferior organs.[95]

Throughout the spring, summer, and fall of 1985, these stories were front and center of the news cycle. The university remained silent about the *Press*'s charges, saying only that it denied the charges and would be preparing a statement on organ transplantation policies.[96] In a document titled "Background Information and Recommendations Concerning Organ Transplantation in Foreign Nationals at the University Health Center of Pittsburgh," Bahnson and the transplant program argued that "articles in the Pittsburgh Press, we believe, have inappropriately overplayed several aspects of the matter of foreign nationals. This has seemed to those impugned to reflect an effort to dissemble and discredit."[97] The document then went on to address the criticisms raised by the *Press*. For example, it noted that there was a 9 to 1 ratio (550 to 61) of U.S. to foreign renal transplants and that "what was done was to go to the extra effort to make it possible to transplant foreigners."[98]

The position paper also claimed that Starzl's reputation as a leader in the field made him a target for international referrals, which he often could not turn down due to broader diplomatic considerations. Moreover, because of the international nature of transplant research, physicians at the University of Pittsburgh felt that they owed a debt to foreign countries which had assisted with its research, either through financial contributions, by sharing of their own knowledge (like Switzerland and Sandoz's work on cyclosporine), or who had provided fellows who were trained in Pittsburgh. Finally, Bahnson argued that maintaining a strong international presence through transplantation on foreign patients was essential if the University of Pittsburgh program wanted to retain its leadership role in the field, especially as more and more transplant centers opened across the United States and the world during the middle of the 1980s.[99]

Perhaps the most important part of the document was its refutation of the *Press*'s allegations that the Pittsburgh transplant program treated foreign patients simply to pad its bottom line. According to a 1985 article in the *Press*, foreign patients were forced to pay an average of $7,000 in surgical fees per kidney transplant, versus the average fee of around $3,600 that was billed to domestic patients for the same procedure. Moreover, the *Press* claimed that foreign patients tended to generate more ancillary revenue, since they often had longer postoperative inpatient stays and often chose costly "Gold Coast" accommodations designed for VIPs.[100] Bahnson acknowledged the higher fees and pledged to even out the pay scale among recipients; however, he maintained that the differential fee structure was a consequence of the earlier ambiguity over transplant payment structures and not an intentional plan by the transplant program to profit from foreign national patients. He even spelled out a defined policy for allocating organs for foreign nationals based on a percentage system that a committee of transplantation surgeons from the university recommended to help combat the perception of favoritism while still allowing for some transplantation in international patients.[101]

Increased volume was a double-edged sword because, while it brought revenue to the University of Pittsburgh, it also encouraged other academic medical centers to create their own transplantation programs, often staffed by surgeons trained by Starzl. This raised some issues when local hospitals, such as Presbyterian-University's competitor Allegheny General Hospital, wanted to expand their transplant programs, but also opened up opportunities to forge partnerships that could help to create a better geographical distribution for new transplantation programs, such as Baylor University Hospital in Dallas, Texas.[102]

The Baylor University Hospital–Pittsburgh program grew out of a personal connection between Starzl and another physician, Dr. John Fordtran. Starzl had first met Fordtran in 1971 when Fordtran's son came to the University of Colorado for a kidney transplant. In a rare success at the time, Starzl was able to transplant a cadaveric kidney that worked long after the operation.[103] After his success with cyclosporine, Starzl, at Fordtran's invitation, gave a grand rounds at Baylor University Hospital in Dallas in the fall of 1983. By early 1984, discussions were under way about Starzl helping to create a liver and kidney transplantation program at the hospital. Because Baylor University Hospital was the primary teaching hospital for the Southwestern Medical School (the entity that had replaced Baylor College of Medicine after its move to Houston in the 1940s), this affiliation would be a joint venture between two academic medical centers.[104]

Once the leadership from the various departments and medical schools were on board with the affiliation, the details were quickly put into a written agreement. Fellows would receive training in Pittsburgh and then rotate to Dallas for practical experience. Baylor University Hospital physicians associated with the transplant program were given faculty appointments in the University of Pittsburgh Medical School. Any professional fees collected by both organizations above their costs were held in a joint fund, which would be split equally at the termination of the affiliation agreement.[105] The relationship was, according to Starzl, "a model of altruism."[106]

The linkage was intended as a test run for establishing a hub-and-spoke model of knowledge diffusion, whereby the Pittsburgh program would serve as a hub for transplant surgeon training and would then send fellows to connected "spokes" to get new transplantation programs (especially liver-focused programs) up and running. A Starzl-trained transplant surgeon, Dr. Göran Klintmalm, took a leading role in setting up the program, and fellows from Pittsburgh were also recruited to Dallas. With Starzl's assistance, the program performed its first transplant in April 1985 and, by the end of the year, had completed forty-two liver transplants. After the announcement of the Pittsburgh–Baylor University Hospital tie-up, several other academic medical centers, including Georgetown University Medical Center in Washington, D.C., approached Starzl about establishing an affiliation.[107]

One particular request to become a "spoke," however, flummoxed administrators at the medical center, because it came not from a university or not-for-profit hospital but from corporate America. In 1985, a Nashville-based surgeon named Dr. Jefferson Pennington approached the University of Pittsburgh about establishing an affiliation with the for-profit Hospital Corporation of America to help the company create what it called a "Center of Excellence" in transplantation medicine.[108] HCA's rapid ascent led many in academic medicine to view it with fear, as this book will discuss in more detail later, and its interest in entering transplantation medicine almost certainly caused concern for medical center leaders in Pittsburgh, such as the senior vice chancellor for the Health Sciences, Dr. Thomas Detre, and his vice chancellor, Jeffrey Romoff.[109] However, there were also some major advantages to a partnership with HCA that a patchwork affiliation with several not-for-profit academic medical centers would not yield. The first was that HCA had very deep pockets. In fact, one of the first things that representatives from the University of Pittsburgh insisted on was that, if the deal was consummated, HCA would be required to provide substantial funding from clinical revenues, as well as assisting with obtaining grant funding for a new center for transplantation research located at the University of Pittsburgh.[110] A new research center would give Starzl and his team the budget to pursue almost any type of research they wanted and for any duration—in effect, this would have consolidated Pitt's position as the transplantation research capital of the world. This was a big request. What would HCA get in return? Immediate access to Pittsburgh's transplantation fellows and the promise of a talent pipeline for the future.[111]

Initially, the program would be centered at HCA's founding facility, Park View Hospital in Nashville, and that hospital would serve as the sole transplantation facility for the entire HCA system.[112] In a meeting in Pittsburgh on April 4, 1986, Detre and representatives from HCA sketched out a much more ambitious plan. In addition to the Park View facility, they also planned to create a network of four regional transplantation centers at HCA hospitals to absorb what they felt was a substantial demand for transplantation services throughout the HCA system. Staff for these regional transplant centers would be trained at a central training institute located at the University of Pittsburgh, and would first hone their skills in university-affiliated hospitals before gaining additional experience in HCA facilities. HCA would pay the cost of education as a stipend, with a years-of-service-or-payback provision built into the contract. Another plus of the central training institute was that it "would provide regional continuing education opportunities for its graduates centrally and at all regional sites" and offer "a much appreciated opportunity for our practicing medical specialists and a great boost to the quality of care we deliver in the system."[113] Detre also noted that this network of domestic regional centers provided a wedge for clinical expansion. "In the future," he claimed, "one could imagine a European and Middle Eastern connection."[114]

At the same time, while a series of transplant centers could export knowledge from Pittsburgh, it could also threaten the ability of the medical center to import patients and generate revenue from transplantation medicine. Attorneys warned university administrators that "20% of PUH and Children's Hospital business results directly or indirectly from transplant services (i.e. pre and post hospitalization and testing, as well as the transplant admission itself)" and that, given the national push to reduce hospitalization as part of managed care, it was unwise to steer patients away from the medical center "by creating additional competition elsewhere."[115]

Where organs came from for HCA's transplant centers was another issue. The complicated history of organ procurement in the United States is outside the scope of this book, but before 1984, there were few limitations on how local organ procurement agencies could distribute organs.[116] Administrators at Pitt, however, worried that the plan to rely on HCA's network of community hospitals as organ donation centers for the regional transplant centers would look too much like organs were not being justly allocated, and might run afoul of ethical organ allocation practices.[117]

Another of the University of Pittsburgh's concerns with the affiliation was protecting its investment—Starzl. HCA even wrote to Jeffrey Romoff in June 1986 confirming that "there is no attempt being made to subversively remove Dr. Starzl from his environment at the University," and reminding him that "HCA is interested in pursuing an affiliation with the University of Pittsburgh which will allow us to select, prepare, and open three or four liver transplantation centers within the HCA system, wherein the Pittsburgh located program continues to be the hub and the HCA facilities are the spokes."[118]

The affiliation with HCA never materialized, but it did raise questions about what the primary goal of developing specialty medical services was for physicians and institutions. A letter sent to Pennington from Starzl in the middle of the attempt to create the University of Pittsburgh/HCA affiliation reinforces this point. Starzl described how he saw his own relationship to building profitable specialty service lines: "I hope you will respect the ethical and academic framework which I have proscribed for myself and my colleagues. We would like to be instruments of society, rather than entrepreneurs. And, if given the chance, I think we can be of real assistance."[119]

Nevertheless, Starzl still received inquiries about helping to set up new transplant programs, including from overseas. In a letter to Bahnson in the summer of 1985, Starzl noted, "We have had persistent inquiries from Saudi Arabia about the possibility of setting up an Arabian states (possibly even including Israel) network so that countries not now providing extensive cadaveric organ transplant services could develop these." While Starzl was "unwilling to do this as an individual," he believed that "the University of Pittsburgh, which has other educational interests in the Middle East, could be a very effective instrument," and "various members of our faculty, while not wanting to live in Middle Eastern countries, would be willing to contribute on a smaller scale." Finally, he argued, "If we want to carry our foreign national position to its logical conclusion of using services rendered here as an entree to increasing services there, we should try to do something."[120] Collaboration was further strengthened in the fall of 1989, when Starzl and Detre visited Saudi Arabia to discuss building stronger links as part of a conscious plan of internationalization being pursued by the medical center.[121] The Saudi visit resulted in at least a draft memorandum of understanding between the University and the Saudi government about working together to build a joint transplantation and transplantation research program.[122]

By the late 1990s, the medical center, now UPMC, dramatically expanded its international presence. The reason was that it made good business sense in a health care marketplace that now privileged large scale expansion and diversified investments, a subject which will be discussed later. Charles Bogosta, president of UMPC's International Service Division, described the health system's approach for building capacity as arriving with "a SWAT team" of knowledgeable professionals so the health system could hit the ground running in new areas of the globe.[123]

The Mediterranean Institute for Transplantation and Highly Specialized Therapies, or ISMETT, was one of the first overseas ventures. ISMETT's roots were in a personal connection—in this case, a conversation between an Italian transplant surgeon in Pittsburgh and a colleague back home, as well as a demonstrated market need—with more than two thousand patients with liver disease at a cost of $170 million per year to the Sicilian government to pay for the travel elsewhere for transplantation.[124] What made ISMETT different was UPMC's commitment to building a lasting partnership with the Sicilian government, rather than simply training staff and leaving. Reflecting on the opposition in Pittsburgh to ISMETT, Jeffrey Romoff, now UPMC's chief executive officer, noted that "no one had made money doing this. No one had done it successfully . . . Dr. Starzl was against it."[125] Moreover, there were substantial logical challenges, including complaints within the local medical community, issues around construction and medical supplies, and skepticism from those in Pittsburgh, who worried about diverting resources away from the health system's primary transplantation program or even UPMC's motives for undertaking the venture.[126] According to UPMC, ISMETT laid the groundwork for expanded overseas operations in Italy and elsewhere in Europe, including Ireland.[127]

In Ireland, UPMC focused initially on expanding another specialty service line—oncology.[128] Working with the Irish government and the private Euro Care International, in 2005, UPMC signed an agreement to develop comprehensive cancer care service at the private Whitfield clinic. The agreement equally spilt the costs and revenue between UPMC and Euro Care International, which represented a dramatic international expansion in cancer care for the health system. Echoing the language used by HCA around transplantation program growth in the 1980s, UPMC hoped to use a "hub and spoke" model to expand care out from Pittsburgh, claimed Bogosta.[129] This model relied on UPMC's heavy investment in telemedicine, which the health system was later able to use to provide pathology consultations for operations in China, Latin America, and elsewhere in the United States.[130] UPMC also built partnerships in Qatar to expand that country's trauma care capacity; in Singapore to develop a private center for liver, kidney, and bone marrow transplantation and treatment; partnered with the government of Kazakhstan to increase that country's oncology services; and continued to invest in Italy and Ireland.[131] UPMC officials have used the import-export language of the industrial economy to justify overseas expansion. In 2008, Romoff stated, "The truth of the matter is, is what we are taking from Pittsburgh, or what we are exporting from Pittsburgh, is the brains of our physicians, and the talent of our management, exporting it and bringing back the wealth to enhance Pittsburgh."[132]

This expansion was controversial. While UPMC spent more than $90 million to acquire a majority ownership stake in Beacon Hospital located in suburban Dublin, Ireland, back in Western Pennsylvania, they were closing a more than one-hundred-year-old community hospital acquired only a decade before in the struggling former steel town of Braddock, Pennsylvania. Even though UPMC was adamant that the two decisions were not linked, some members of the suspicious public saw this as an attempt by the not-for-profit to avoid caring for costly indigent patients. Braddock's mayor, John Fetterman, summed up the public's reaction to the situation in an interview in the *Pittsburgh Post-Gazette*, where he noted, "health care for poor people is a guaranteed loser . . . but you have to ask, is health care a right or a privilege? Do some people deserve it and some people don't?"[133]

*   *   *

The rise of specialty medicine helped to prioritize an ongoing movement toward a more market-oriented vision of the hospital-civic relationship. As domestic and international patients flocked to hospitals in each city seeking the best care, and popular authors and the popular press touted the programs built by DeBakey, Cooley, and Starzl, examples of the promise of specialty medicine to reinvent the economy for the postindustrial future by importing patients and exporting clinical and scientific knowledge, it seemed that the locational asset model and the social justice model were fading into the background.

What also helped to make specialty medicine a compelling story was that the people who were performing its most compelling operations became the face of progress and hope in the medical metropolis. Even before their rift over the artificial heart, DeBakey and Cooley were household names. Their appearance on the cover of *Life Magazine* in 1970, which dramatized the feud over the artificial heart, only heighted their celebrity status. In fact, when the feud was eventually resolved in 2004 (when DeBakey was in his late nineties and Cooley in his mid-eighties), this, too, received an outpouring of media attention.[134] Starzl's impact was arguably even greater for Pittsburgh—he became a specific figure that could be held up as an exemplar of the power of not-for-profit health care to provide new ways to promote the medical metropolis.

In addition to the symbolic value of specialty medicine for the domestic economic future, it also helped to internationalize the growing medical metropolis. Foreign dollars helped to pay for those U.S. patients who could not afford access to specialty care because of issues with insurance coverage or a lack of financial resources. Moreover, as the story of the Duke of Windsor shows, their willingness to travel to receive this care helped to confer a sense of legitimacy on the surgeons and institutions who provided it to them. Thus, when the decision was made to export their clinical and financial knowledge overseas, even if it meant partnering with for-profit companies like HCA, the explanation given by physicians like Arthur Beall, that this was simply performing a public service like changing a tire, didn't seem to unduly strain credulity. However, these operations eventually shifted from providing a service to entrepreneurial consulting operations.

Building these service lines also helped to reshape the business of medicine domestically. This was perhaps the clearest for Denton Cooley, who, drawing inspiration from Sam Walton and Walmart, built CardioVascular Care Providers to maximize efficiency and to drive more volume and revenue through his practice. That this became a model for cardiovascular reimbursement was even more confirmation that the business of specialty care was part of a larger battle about the soul of not-for-profit health care and the meaning of the hospital-civic relationship. It was a relationship that increasingly reflected a more market-oriented interpretation. In the early 1980s, Arnold S. Relman, the longtime editor of the *New England Journal of Medicine*, discussed this fear in an influential article in which, drawing a parallel to Dwight Eisenhower's 1961 farewell address, he warned of the ascendency of a "new medical-industrial complex" that was "a large and growing network of private corporations engaged in the business of supplying health-care services to patients for a profit—services heretofore provided by private nonprofit institutions or individual practitioners."[135] The irony of Relman's warning is that for-profit companies never became the primary drivers of the fearsome medical-industrial complex; instead, the same not-for-profit actors that Relman lamented were losing their power and authority had embraced business models and values ripped from the private sector to grow and reshape themselves, the business of medicine, and the hospital-civic relationship. But first, these not-for-profits would have to find new ways to weather the storm of deindustrialization.

Chapter 4

"When the Fire Dies"

Biotechnology and the Quest for a New Economy

As a cold morning broke on the next to the last day of 1985, *Pittsburgh Post-Gazette* subscribers shoveled a layer of icy snow off their front stoops and reached down to grab a newspaper full of sobering news. In a special section titled "When the Fire Dies," the newspaper reported that 59 percent of workers laid off from area steel mills were still out of work. Of these idled workers, nearly 97 percent were male, and over half were older than forty. Forty-three percent of those unemployed had been out of work between thirteen and twenty-four months, and most had only a high school education. Moreover, the collapse of the industry had changed employment gender dynamics in the region—now more than half of the spouses of unemployed former steelworkers were part of the labor force.[1] It appeared, in the words of veteran labor journalist John Hoerr, that for Pittsburgh "the wolf finally came."[2]

The wolf also came knocking in Houston. The *New York Times* informed interested readers that the "pickups and Jaguars alike" sporting the pro-oil bumper stickers, which drew inspiration from the late 1970s folk song and read "Freeze a Yankee in the Dark," had vanished as the price of oil collapsed from a high of thirty-three dollars a barrel in 1982 to a low of ten dollars a barrel by 1986.[3] As the extraction economy weakened, the unemployment rate reached a previously inconceivable 9 percent by January 1983. "With 70 percent of the jobs in the Houston area depending directly or indirectly on the oil industry," claimed the *Houston Chronicle*, "the bust was in full flower."[4] By the end of the 1980s, the *Houston Post* claimed that "if Houston's last decade were a ride at Astroworld, it would be so wild that small children and pregnant women would not be allowed.

The peaks were so high and the valleys so low the decade has been unequaled in Houston's history."[5]

The creation of an import-export economy for patients and clinical and financial knowledge as well as the elevation of physician-researchers like Drs. DeBakey, Cooley, and Starzl into a role as symbols of a new economy showed the value specialty medicine had for helping to reinvent the industrial city as the medical metropolis. But this was not the only way that the health sciences intersected with economic development by the 1980s. High-technology and biomedical experimentation also became part of a new narrative of progress that marketed the medical metropolis and how its civic elites and ordinary citizens presented it to the world. This development strategy was guided, at least in part, by a growing recognition and acceptance that not-for-profit hospitals and universities were not only important physical and economic anchors but were important economic and social actors in their own right. By embracing a vision of the hospital-civic relationship that foregrounded technology-focused economic development, residents of the medical metropolis accepted a more market-oriented role for health care that linked success to amorphously defined notions of "innovation" and "growth."[6]

Understanding why biotechnology emerged as economic development policy in the medical metropolis allows us to see the successes and limitations of a more market-oriented vision of the hospital-civic relationship for community building. It also allows historians to examine the mechanics of regional economic development efforts, including the problems of technology transfer and venture capital financing. Finally, it highlights the limitations of creating a public-private partnership model with little real power to shape public policy or consumer demand. After all, the consequences for the medical metropolis have been profound and led policymakers and pundits to seek solutions that favor a rigid formula that flattens historical complexity by encouraging civic elites in other rusting industrial cities to focus on economic diversification by building strong medical, educational, and applied research sectors at the expense of other sectors. It has pushed older core industries to become more efficient through automation, leading to job losses for less skilled or less educated workers. It has encouraged political leadership to attempt to retain and develop a young, educated, upwardly mobile workforce by investing in quality-of-life amenities. Finally, appealing to this new "creative class" has created real issues about how to manage gentrification.[7] Look no further than University of Pittsburgh chancellor

Wesley W. Posvar's statement that "we hope someday to turn the Mon Valley into Biotech Valley and give this area the shot in the arm it needs" to see the weight assigned to biotechnology as a regional economic development strategy.[8]

Biotechnology and the New Economy in Pittsburgh

While using high-technology and cutting-edge medicine to promote a regional brand was an important part of the locational asset model, as the polio story has shown, there was still substantial skepticism within academic medicine that lifesaving discoveries should be subject to the vicissitudes of the marketplace, potentially driving up their cost and limiting their access. Here the famous words of Jonas Salk, when asked about patenting the polio vaccine, seemed to still apply; he said to journalist Edward R. Murrow, "There is no patent. Could you patent the sun?"[9]

Beyond whether biomedical technology represented a special public good, there were other reasons why, prior to the 1980s, the economic value of biomedical research was limited. Difficulty attracting and creating a skilled workforce, issues with patent protection and with technology transfer for technology created with federal funds, and a lack of financing for speculative biomedical ventures all limited its potential as tangible economic investments. By the 1980s, the depth of the economic changes that affected both cities, favorable regulatory changes which promoted the commercialization of federally funded research in the life sciences sector, and the growing acceptance of a market-oriented vision of the hospital-civic relationship helped to slowly wash away any residue of discomfort about promoting biomedical research as part of a larger business of health care.[10] This is not to say that biomedical research, including biotechnology, was immediately accepted as economic development policy, or to claim that it ever was the sole way in which the postindustrial city looked to rebuild its economy for the future. Then, as now, it was never clear that this sector would live up to the hype, and in both cities, it remained only a part of an overall technology-focused economic development strategy.[11]

Advanced technology also required new workers who could do everything from basic laboratory science to complex financial transactions and sales. They needed fluency in math and science, college and graduate

degrees, and a less rigid understanding of the employer-employee relation-
ship than employees in the heavily unionized manufacturing sector.[12]
Where this workforce might come from vexed the city's civic elites. A 1963
book titled *"This Is Pittsburgh and Southwestern Pennsylvania: We Live Here
. . . We Like It"* captured the dilemma in a humorous yet telling fashion.
Drawing from the regional legend of the mythical seven-foot-tall super-
human steelworker Joe Magarac, it introduced the world to Jon Magarac.
Depicted on a separate page from the working-class icon, the broad-
shouldered and slim Jon was wearing a tie and a white shirt with its front
pocket stuffed with pens and carrying a large slide rule. The caption next
to Jon read, "He gathered together the ore of the past He mixed in the
'newest,' the 'finest,' the 'latest' He adds education, the best he can get, And
squeezes out ATOMS and powers the jet. With slide rules, computers and
technical skill There's steel in his courage and iron in his will. . . . JON
MAGARAC is Pittsburgh, today!"[13] But Pittsburgh never seemed to produce
enough Jon Magaracs, which forced civic elites to market "post-industrial-
ism" to established middle-class professional and technical workers to convince them to come to the city. Elite-led promotional campaigns like
"Dynamic Pittsburgh," launched in 1987, along with positive articles in
glossy magazines, promoted the city's lifestyle amenities and services to
show the world that Pittsburgh had moved beyond its gritty industrial
past.[14]

Neither of these efforts really addressed the needs of industrial workers
already in the Pittsburgh region who were living through industrial collapse. Generally, they had three options to navigate economic change:
unemployment, relocation, or retraining. Each outcome had its own consequences, as the *Pittsburgh Post-Gazette* detailed in "When the Fire Dies."
Joseph Sudar, a thirty-five-year-old former mill worker, was an example of
the consequences of not preparing for the economic change and being
unable to successfully navigate the new economy. He told the *Pittsburgh
Post-Gazette*'s readers about his transition from steelworker to unemployment. "After Vietnam I just wanted to make money and relax. . . . I could
have gone back to school—I had 1½ years in before the service. . . . At the
time there was no pressure. I had everything I thought I wanted. I thought
J&L [Jones and Laughlin Steel] would be there forever. We made a lot of
money. Who would have thought everything would fold up all of a sudden." Asked what he did now, Sudar replied that, for a while, he held a
part-time job with K-Mart and helped to raise his children, but by 1985, he

was unemployed again. "I wake up every day and my wife [who, incidentally, worked in a physician's medical laboratory], says, 'You should look for a job,' and I do, but I don't find one. It's frustrating." Sudar also considered relocating, but as he noted, "But who's going to buy your house around here?" In the end, Sudar felt trapped, saying, "I can't get a degree because who will watch my kids and who will pay for it. I'm looking for a good job, or maybe I play the Lotto and get lucky."[15]

Sam Grese offered a lesson in the power of relocation to change lives. The twenty-nine-year-old Grese once worked at the Dorothy Six Blast Furnace in Duquesne, Pennsylvania. After reinventing himself as a computer specialist, he moved to Rockville, Maryland, just outside of Washington, D.C., where he kept a picture of the blast furnace on his desk at IBM. Contrasting his new town of Rockville with his old hometown of West Mifflin, an industrial borough just upriver from Pittsburgh, Grese said, "There everything is growing so fast, you can't keep up with it. Here is it depressed. . . . When I come home I come through McKeesport, I see Dorothy Six. It is resting and dormant. I think about how much it meant to so many people in the area. Eventually things will change here. But it will take a while. I was not willing to wait."[16]

Grese made his transition from the blast furnace to the office park because of education. He attended Robert Morris College after he was laid off. And, by the early 1980s, a variety of corporate and governmental programs existed to try to retrain workers for the new economy.[17] Yet, even those that took advantage of these programs were often aware that they were still caught up in the changing ways that neoliberal capitalism reshaped labor markets in the late twentieth century. Steve Laurer, a third-generation steelworker laid off in 1981, discussed his transition from steelworker to student, saying, "It is a different world completely." He continued, "Blue collar is traditional, things are planned out for you. Someone is taking care of you, rather than you taking care of yourself. Now it is more survival of the fittest. You need the tools to achieve your goals—school—and from yourself personal attitude and ambition."[18] Preparing for entry-level health careers was one way that educational programs helped to connect former steelworkers with the new economy, but even this process could seem daunting. Roger Morgan, another former steelworker, argued, "the work [nurse training] is hard, very trying. Sometimes overwhelming. Before, I went to work eight hours and picked up my paycheck. Education tends to make you think more, I never knew the world ran like this."[19]

Biotechnology provided an important middle ground for regional elites to focus on as a path forward, because it avoided substantively addressing questions of corporate behavior, labor unrest, and the larger structural economic issues embedded in neoliberal capitalism that actually caused the postindustrial turn.[20] Promoting an economic policy grounded in hope and optimism for reinvention empowered the very institutions like universities, hospitals, and medical schools that the locational asset model had kept in the background. One should not overstate this point—technology-focused development, including biotechnology, was never the entire solution to postindustrial malaise, and legacy industries, while diminished in power and standing, were still regarded by nearly every urban resident as important or, in the case of Houston with the extraction economy, still dominant parts of the new economy.[21]

While the collapse of steel might have seemed abrupt to workers like Sudar, concern about overreliance on the primary metals sector had actually been a long-standing worry for regional economic planning groups like the Allegheny Conference on Community Development.[22] In the late 1950s and early 1960s, Edward H. Litchfield, the chancellor of the University of Pittsburgh and a Allegheny Conference member, emerged as a leading evangelist for the potentially transformative power of applied or industrial research as a pathway for economic diversification. Litchfield argued that "the way to economic growth and prosperity for Western Pennsylvania lies through industrial research."[23] This statement reflected more than a small degree of self-interest—after all, he hoped to re-center the University of Pittsburgh as a space for contract and applied research, a position lost earlier in the century with the separation of the Mellon Institute from the university. Litchfield's vision, however, was larger than just a single university. He believed that what was good for the University of Pittsburgh when it came to promoting industrial research was good for the region. Not only would industrial and applied research bring new private and federal dollars to the region, it would also attract, and perhaps even one day create, the new, highly educated workforce that the private companies producing these new discoveries would need if they were to create viable spin-offs.

Litchfield's vision for how to spatially organize the academic and commercial laboratories, as well as the spin-off companies that an industrial research economy depended on, drew from Stanford's Research Park in Palo Alto, California; Route 128 in Massachusetts; and North Carolina's Research Triangle; as well his own experiences with corporate research and development. Litchfield came to the University of Pittsburgh from Cornell's School of Business and Public Administration, and he was a member of the board of directors for Smith Corona and the Avco Corporation, which was a diversified maker of airplanes, farm machinery, and consumer appliances.[24]

In 1963, Litchfield commissioned architect Max Abramovitz to create what was "the equivalent of a 150-story building on its side" in Junction/ Panther Hollow, the ravine between Pitt's and Carnegie Tech's campuses.[25] The Oakland Corporation, which he formed to build the proposed research park, had high hopes for the project. "On the basis of experience," a promotional pamphlet for the Panther Hollow project opined, "one could conclude that the ideal research park would have an urban setting because the advantages of a country background are often offset by the unparalleled advantages of the city." According to the project's backers, the project's urban advantages included an ability to draw better talent than suburban campuses because "the key scientists and research leaders are people who want—and need—to keep one foot firmly embedded in the academic life."[26] To be built over the Baltimore and Ohio Railroad's existing tracks, the proposed building had both auto and rail access while forming a seamless pedestrian connection between the two universities' campuses. Anchoring the project would have been a joint collaboration between the University of Pittsburgh and the National Aeronautics and Space Administration (NASA), and other government, university, and private sector tenants were to occupy the rest of the building. It was "the first step in the creation of a wholly new and unprecedented type of community in Oakland" and the opening salvo in "the second stage of the Pittsburgh Renaissance."[27] In short, the project was supposed to be the catalyst for promoting the creation of a spin-off economy in Pittsburgh. Despite promotional efforts, it proved too steep an investment because of the $250 million price tag, Litchfield's alienating personal style, and the investment in suburban research and development sites by many of Pittsburgh's blue-chip companies.[28] By March 1965, the project was dead, but the idea that industrial research was the region's economic future lived on.[29]

The viability of biomedical research, and specifically biotechnology, was deeply tied to the revolution in genetics that occurred in the 1970s. The idea that an organism could be modified by recombining its DNA with that from another organism moved from the realm of science fiction when researchers at Stanford used tumor viruses to create recombinant DNA.

This method was difficult and time-consuming, but in 1973, Stanley Cohn and Herbert Boyer created a quick and easily replicable process for creating recombinant DNA.[30] Initially, recombinant DNA was greeted with skepticism amid concerns about the creation of superbugs and dangerous viruses escaping from laboratories and infecting major population centers.[31] Despite these concerns, the potential of recombinant DNA to provide powerful therapeutics and new technological advances in medicine proved more powerful than voices calling for restraint. This drumbeat of genetics as the future of modern medicine has only increased, with new areas like personalized medicine becoming important areas of growth for not-for-profit health systems.[32]

It was hard to tell in these early years if the investment in basic science was a success. One way to do this was to find a universal metric that would demonstrate that specific universities and hospitals were emerging as leaders. This strategy was not entirely new. In the locational asset model, civic elites and not-for-profit health care administrators often quantified and publicized the value of the dollars, largely private, that supported biomedical research. This showed citizens and potential new migrants (individual and corporate) the relative strength of a community's foundations and its commitment to supporting the health of the public. What changed by the 1980s was that, while private dollars were still celebrated, the real metric of success was now how many public dollars, in particular from the National Institutes of Health (NIH), not-for-profit health care institutions brought into the city. The University of Pittsburgh provides an example of linking perceptions of success to grant funding. In fact, from the early 1970s to the late 1990s, the University of Pittsburgh's ranking rose from thirty-seventh to tenth in the total amount of NIH funding.[33] This metric mattered for two reasons. First, NIH funding helped to serve as a proxy for demonstrating interest in the types of research being conducted in the university's laboratories. The more funding that an institution received, went the argument, the better the quality and potential impact of the research. The second reason was more practical. NIH grants came with funding to pay indirect costs, which could cover administrative expenses as well as costs for facilities, helping to create a new pool of revenue for the health sciences and for health care institutions—a story which is discussed in more detail later.[34] Federal support for specific projects also helped to confer a sense of legitimacy on the entire research enterprise. After all, if biomedical research was worthy of hundreds of millions of dollars in federal support, then it must also have some commercial value. And if it had commercial value, then not-for-profits could benefit by creating for-profit spin-off companies to bring laboratory research to the market. This thinking echoed Litchfield's call to commercialize the results of university-created applied research a generation earlier as the path forward for regional economic development.[35]

Creating successful spin-offs in the 1980s, however, required two additional ingredients. The first was a change in American patent law that made it substantially easier for universities and individual faculty members to commercialize research discoveries made with federal dollars. Popularly known as the Bayh-Dole Act of 1980, the law making these changes spurred commercialization of research paid for with federal dollars.[36] Bayh-Dole was part of a larger concern in the late 1970s and early 1980s with a perceived decline in innovation within the United States, which some policymakers assumed was a consequence of regulation that was too stringent. By assigning clear title to universities and industry, Bayh-Dole, especially when combined with the decision by the Supreme Court to allow the patenting of microorganisms in *Diamond v. Chakrabarty*, helped to usher in what contemporary observers hoped would be a boom in biotechnology.[37]

The second ingredient was the ability of institutions to access the venture capital market. This market underwent dramatic changes during the 1970s and 1980s which, when coupled with changes in patent law, also helped to incentivize commercializing technologies in the life sciences. One critical change came in 1978, shortly before Bayh-Dole was passed, when the federal government did two things: first, it cut the maximum tax rate on capital gains from 49 percent to 28 percent, which encouraged investors to seek opportunity in venture capital funds; and second, it repealed the so-called prudent man rule as part of the Employee Retirement Income Security Act.[38] This was designed to limit pension fund managers from making risky investments with the fund's capital reserves. The rule held that fund managers "could be held personally liable for the performance of any investments riskier than those a hypothetical prudent man might make."[39] Since most venture capital investments were inherently risky, pension funds could not invest in them without violating this rule. Once this rule was repealed, pension funds became important players in the venture capital market.

Even with all of these changes, at least in Pittsburgh, investing in biotechnology was often deemphasized at the expense of the city's more established medical device sector. Medical device companies held a great deal of

appeal for elite civic-development organizations like the Allegheny Conference because they built on existing regional strengths in robotics, bioengineering, and manufacturing. Medrad was a favorite company for groups like
the Conference to highlight. It dated back to the mid-1960s, when Dr. Mar-
lin S. Heilman developed a power injector for angiographies. Using loans
from family and friends as start-up capital, Heilman commercialized this
product and continued to develop a range of medical products, including
magnetic resonance and computed tomography equipment. By 1985,
the company and its spin-off, Intec, had received FDA approval for an
implantable portable defibrillator. The next year, this became a Medicare-
reimbursable technology, yielding a substantial profit potential for Eli Lilly
and Company, which had recently purchased Intec for $45 million.[40] In its
promotional pamphlet, *Pittsburgh's New Dimension in Advanced Technology*,
the Conference-affiliated Regional Industrial Development Corporation gave
Medrad a glowing write-up in a short promotional piece titled "Medrad/
Intec, Inc.—Thriving on Affairs of the Heart."[41] It billed the company as the
ideal model—an established core company that spun off companies at a
profit while also helping to define the region's niche in the advanced technology economy. The Medrads were few and far between. Part of the problem
was that, while established private companies could fund and bring their
technology to market, the question of how to transfer technology from the
university science bench to the boardroom remained unclear, which ham-
pered the ability of newer, smaller start-up companies to thrive.

Between 1960 and 1980, the city's total unemployment rose by more
than 18 percent, and manufacturing as a share of regional employment
declined by 26 percent, costing the city 32,913 manufacturing jobs.[42] Also,
not only did the percentage of Pittsburghers employed in the service sector
grow by more than 100,000 jobs to nearly 30 percent of the regional workforce, regional hospitals and universities were gaining national stature.[43] By
1984, the Urban Redevelopment Authority (URA), which was created to
guide Pittsburgh's first renaissance, could say with confidence, "Clearly, the
city's major economic strengths are the very substantial health, educational
services and business services industries, a limited manufacturing base that
can be utilized to strengthen selected industries with expansion potential,
the location of headquarters administration in the City for major corporations, and the potential for the expanded development of retail, wholesale,
transportation, and other services needed by businesses concentrated in the
City, and the regional urban center."[44]

At the University of Pittsburgh, the Foundation for Applied Science and Technology (FAST) was created in 1982 to streamline the process of transferring the results of applied scientific research. The genesis of FAST was in the early 1980s, when Richard K. Olson presented a preliminary outline of a program for technology transfer to Chancellor Wesley Posvar.[45] With changes in patent law in the air after the passage of Bayh-Dole, Olson and others saw an opportunity for the university. Olson, whose own background before coming to the university in 1978 was in corporate R&D, argued that "the present is a uniquely propitious time for mounting the necessary effort to design and implement methods and techniques for enhancing the coupling between Universities and Industry." Citing efforts to relax patent policies on the federal level, changes in the conduct of corporate R&D which reflected a closer alignment with university values, and the "recognition [by universities] that decreasing enrollment requires reallocation of some of their resources," the time to link the university and industry through a new formalized structure seemed right.[46]

Olson argued that FAST should be a "wholly-owned, tax exempt subsidiary of the University of Pittsburgh" charged with soliciting corporate support for new and existing faculty research projects, supervising contract research for industry, and even potentially developing a "University Associates program," designed to collect a fee to connect industry and faculty around shared research interests.[47] After its approval, however, the purview of FAST appeared to expand to include a wide variety of programs that promotional literature classified as "entrepreneurial assistance," which assisted faculty with a range of practical features of technology transfer, including venture capital identification and business plan development; technology incubator programs; helping non-university-related small business with grant writing and finding university partners; and assisting with securing grants from the Commonwealth of Pennsylvania.[48]

FAST reflected the growing corporatization of R&D that was sweeping through universities and hospitals. This becomes clear when looking at the language used to sell the program, which was both apocalyptic and deeply civic. For example, Olson argued, "The FAST proposal originated out of awareness that our nation is in jeopardy of losing its technological preeminence . . . and the conviction that our great research universities might reverse that trend."[49] In the *Pitt News* in October 1982, Posvar was even blunter, arguing, "In other words, the University of Pittsburgh is now committing itself to linking basic and applied research in order to accelerate benefits to society."[50] For his internal audience of faculty and staff, he downplayed this language and attempted to minimize concerns that FAST was simply a giveaway to the corporate sector or a potential magnet to pull talented researchers away from the university and into the private sector. For example, an article in the *University Times*, which ran the day before he made his statement about the program's contribution to the region's economy, strongly implied that Posvar believed that the financial benefits of FAST to the university outweighed the potential downsides.[51]

Solving the Problem of Commercialization in Biotechnology

Establishing technology transfer infrastructure was only one hurdle. Another was coordinating individual efforts to promote an advanced technology economy. More than a decade earlier, financier and Allegheny Conference member Henry Hillman announced the formation of Penn's Southwest. This private nonprofit corporation was devoted to marketing Western Pennsylvania's advanced technology and service sectors as emerging areas for regional growth.[52] This organization also became an early partner with the Pittsburgh Hightechnology Council to try to create a new reputation for Western Pennsylvania.[53]

The growth of these types of organizations coincided with the rise of the entrepreneurial state in Pennsylvania.[54] During his first term, Governor Richard Thornburgh was forced to confront a statewide decline in manufacturing employment. Thornburgh was often critical of attempts by previous elected officials to chase manufacturing jobs through state tax breaks and subsidies, and instead argued that the way to improve the state's economy was to embrace new potential areas for growth.[55] The governor proposed the Ben Franklin Partnership, which was a program explicitly designed to bridge the gap between the academy and the private sector. Creating four "advanced technology centers" across the state, it offered 50 percent match funding for university and private sector projects (with a distinct preference for private sector companies spun off from university-sponsored research) that promised to develop new technologies with the potential of creating research or manufacturing jobs, provided job training in advanced technologies, provided assistance with technology transfer between universities and the private sector, developed a market for advanced technologies, and helped to create or sustain any number of high-technology councils or other promotional agencies.[56] It became effective in the summer of 1982.

Civic elites and elected officials attempted to position the region to take advantage of these economic development efforts. In 1981, the Allegheny Conference formed an Economic Development Committee as part of a larger plan to create "a unified economic development strategy backed by a broad consensus."[57] The committee published its findings in 1984 as part of a two-volume report titled *A Strategy for Growth: An Economic Development Program for the Region*, which included a general framework for growth as well as suggestions for specific projects and was premised on two critical ideas. The first was that the Conference and local governments must "recognize the inevitability of change" and move away from past efforts to focus on preserving or augmenting old industries. The second was an acknowledgment that "the strategy should provide for many advances on a broad economic front, rather than a single thrust"—here, biotechnology emerged as a crucial component of a broader strategy for promoting the development of a diversified advanced technology economy.[58]

After the publication of *A Strategy for Growth*, regional leaders moved quickly to try to bring a variety of stakeholders together to build an advanced technology economy in Western Pennsylvania. In 1985, at the request of then-state legislator Tom Murphy, the Conference brought together the city of Pittsburgh, Allegheny County, Carnegie Mellon University, and the University of Pittsburgh to devise a specific set of proposals. Known as "Strategy 21," this report was a grab bag of technology and infrastructure development ideas, including the creation of a Western Pennsylvania Biotechnology Manufacturing Center and a National Center for Robotics in Manufacturing. The hope was that, given their relatively proximate location to Pitt and the Health Center hospitals, both centers would be able to leverage existing biomedical research resources, including space, equipment, and a pool of talented faculty from multiple academic disciplines.[59]

In 1987, the Pittsburgh Foundation attempted to survey the state of the region's biotechnology industry. On October 6, the foundation held a lunchtime meeting at the exclusive Duquesne Club to "identify the issues which represent barriers to efficient integration in biomedical research planning and implementation, to identify ways in which biomedical research findings can be efficiently translated into clinical applications and industrial production, and to determine how to best maintain a coordinated biomedical research agenda for Pittsburgh."[60] Attending the meeting

were the city's movers and shakers in private industry, the foundation community, and in higher education and health care.[61] Vincent Sarni and
Marco Wismer, both of Pittsburgh Plate Glass, played an important role in
leading the wide-ranging conversation. At points, Sarni seemed to channel
the entrepreneurial spirit of Edward Litchfield, who died in a plane crash
in 1968, by explicitly looking to Silicon Valley and Boston as models for
building a technology economy in Pittsburgh and arguing, just like the
Panther Hollow pitch two decades earlier, that regional deficiencies including a lack of skilled workers and that not having a dedicated infrastructure
for technology transfer held Pittsburgh's progress back.[62]

The growing interest of a range of stakeholders was also reflected in two
reports released in 1988, which aimed to understand the potential role that
biotechnology could play in reshaping Pittsburgh's regional economy. The
first, a January report, grew out of the conversations held at the Duquesne
Club the previous year. Conducted by Charles Rial and Associates and
Arthur Young & Co., it surveyed the state of biotechnology in the region
and found that "over 75 biotech or biomedical related research projects"
were currently under way. The report also identified several areas to prioritize for the future, including "drug and protein design, biosensors, [and]
cancer therapy."[63] All was not rosy. Rial and Young & Co.'s report found
several factors that limited commercialization potential for companies in
the region, including a lack of information about the process of bringing
technology from the laboratory to the market; a culture that was academically, rather than commercially, oriented; and interinstitutional rivalries.
The primary takeaway was that a central clearinghouse for biotechnology
commercialization was needed.[64] A second report drew many of the same
conclusions.[65] While consultants may have provided clear strategies for how
to make biotechnology into a commercial reality, it is not clear how many
of their specific suggestions were actually implemented.[66]

Effective commercialization was critical for the future of the medical
metropolis because, just as in the industrial research model for the region's
future laid out by Litchfield decades earlier, this was where biotechnology
added value to the economy of the medical metropolis. The key was creating spin-off companies to manufacture and market new technologies,
which in turn would grow, hire more people, and continue to generate
innovations that brought visibility to Pittsburgh's life science sector and
the not-for-profit institutions where the original cutting-edge technology
started life, creating, backers hoped, a self-replicating cycle of growth. The

key to making this work was having access to capital to fund not only research and development, but also the commercialization process.

In fact, soon after the publication of *A Strategy for Growth*, the Allegheny Conference noted that the lack of established venture capital firms in Pittsburgh might have an adverse effect on the ability of start-up companies at the Western Pennsylvania Advanced Technology Center to meet the match requirement for Ben Franklin Partnership Funds. To fill this perceived gap, the Conference decided to act as an intermediary between investors and emerging technology companies and created the Pittsburgh Seed Fund to provide early-stage venture capital investments. Additional Conference-sponsored programs included some direct funding to promote better university-private sector technology transfer, the provision of technical advice about financial management to the CEOs of emerging technology companies, assistance with the procurement of federal contracts, the creation of an Office of Promotion, and support for a customized job training program to help match companies with skilled workers.[67] Moreover, individual Conference board members also continued to work on their own to bridge the gap between venture capital and an emerging high-technology industry, often through personal or corporate investments in emerging venture capital funds in the Pittsburgh region.[68]

Working through the URA, local government also attempted to address the problem of access to venture capital by creating two programs to provide early-stage funding for fledgling technology companies. One was a purchase order program, which was designed to "make short-term loans to firms that have developed and are marketing a product and are able to secure a purchase order for that product, but are unable to finance privately the costs of meeting the order because of a lack of credit history or collateral."[69] The second was a revenue participation program, which offered financing on a three-to-five-year term and provided companies with the option to pay this loan back with stock. Both programs capped loan amounts at $150,000.[70] However, as a public entity, the URA needed to be careful about the level of risk it assumed.[71]

Despite these programs, the problem of access to venture capital remained. David Hillman of Pittsburgh National Corporation's Venture Capital Group noted, "we admit we're not yet as sophisticated as Boston and the West Coast, but banks here didn't have appropriate models for lending to these [high-tech and biotech] firms in an intelligent manner. However," Hillman continued, "cutbacks in Pittsburgh's basic industries,

Figure 9. The opening of the University of Pittsburgh's Center for Biotechnology and Bioengineering at the Pittsburgh Technology Center on April 2, 1993. Pictured are University of Pittsburgh chancellor Dennis O'Connor, Pennsylvania governor Bob Casey, and Robert Kormos, the director of the Artificial Heart Program.

Photograph by Jim Krandel and published in the *University Times* 23, no. 16. University of Pittsburgh Archives Photograph Collection, 1810–2006, UA.Photos Box 1, Folder 12, University Archives, Archives and Special Collections, University of Pittsburgh Library System.

and the 1982 recession has shaken a lot of beliefs including those of the banking industry. You can no longer make a lot of money lending to a very credit-worthy borrower."[72] By the end of 1988, the number of venture capital firms making investments in the Pittsburgh market had grown to fourteen, with eleven based in Western Pennsylvania. Taken together, these firms had "nearly $613 million" of total capital under management nationwide.[73]

Throughout the 1980s and early 1990s, it seemed like the biotechnology economy in the city existed largely on paper. However, in 1993, ground was broken for the Pittsburgh Technology Center, which was located on the site of the former Jones and Laughlin steel mill. Local government played a critical role in acquiring and clearing the site.[74] An early tenant of this repurposed industrial space was the University of Pittsburgh's Center for Biotechnology and Bioengineering, which had been created in 1987 under the leadership of Jerome Schultz. This new center provided a way to harness new and existing "multidisciplinary endeavors among the broad-ranging research and clinical activities underway within the University."[75]

Even with this new physical space in which to engage in experimentation and potential commercialization, the future of the city's biotechnology sector remained uncertain. It would not be for another decade or so, until the creation of the Pittsburgh Life Science Greenhouse in 2000, that a dedicated organization for collaboratively promoting and developing this sector would help to usher in a sense that biotechnology had stabilized and matured, and could offer a definite boost to the city's economy and identity as part of a larger innovation-centered brand for Pittsburgh emerging around the life sciences and health care.[76] But what about biotechnology in a city whose postwar economic story was dominated by growth, rather than decline? What role did it play in helping Houstonians think about how they would make their version of the medical metropolis?

Biotechnology in Houston

Houston's economy was booming in the postwar years. During the mid-1970s, it was growing at a rate of about one thousand new people a week as a result of both generous annexation policies and migration from places like the Rust Belt.[77] A favorite marketing strategy for the Houston Chamber of Commerce to demonstrate the city's ascendancy as a major American metropolis was to interview a transplanted northerner about why they preferred life in Texas. In a 1976 interview in *Houston Magazine* titled "Can a Transplanted New Yorker Find Happiness in Houston," Mike Turner admitted that a decade before he had quit his job rather than move to Houston, which, he claimed, "at that time, I thought was the end of the world." Unhappy, Turner returned to his old job and was promptly dispatched to Houston. Nearly ten years later, Turner was a convert—he effusively praised the city's generous annexation policies, which kept his property taxes low by spreading out the cost of municipal services, and its free-enterprise culture that shunned government-provided welfare as reasons why he was so happy in Houston. When asked which he liked better, his life in New York or in Texas, Turner said: "I always feel as if I'm being asked which do I love better—my aging, ailing father—or my growing, healthy, child."[78]

The strong confidence in Houston's economic future displayed by new residents like Mike Turner was meant to be inspiring, but it helped to gloss over the fact that the same forces of neoliberal capitalism that were weathering the Rust Belt were also at play in the Sun Belt. Despite this, a blind faith in growth, or what property developer and civic leader Kenneth Schnitzer called "a drunken stupor of prosperity," remained the norm.[79] Even when the city experienced the oil bust in the early 1980s, little happened to temper this effusion. For example, in a 1983 article in the *Houston Business Journal*, Peter Bishop, then a professor of Future Studies at University of Houston Clear Lake, noted that despite the temporary setback, the city was in an enviable position when compared to its competitor cities in the Northeast and Midwest. "Most cities," Bishop claimed, "plan to avoid catastrophe, Houston can plan for the advantage of opportunity."[80] The role that biotechnology could play in Houston's economic future was clear—oil and gas, not microbes or genes, still reigned supreme despite the volatility of the extraction economy.[81] However, like their counterparts at the Allegheny Conference, Houston's civic elites like 8F also worried during the 1950s and 1960s that too much of a focus on a narrow range of economic sectors would have negative consequences for the city's future. Slowly, then, they also sought to find ways to diversify the city's economy.

Spaceflight was one intriguing possibly. On September 19, 1961, the National Aeronautics and Space Administration made an announcement that profoundly changed the region and set into motion decades of collaborative relationships among NASA, the Texas Medical Center, and area universities—the Houston area was going to be home to the agency's Manned Spacecraft Center (MSC).[82] The story of how NASA decided to locate MSC reads like one of those Texas-size tales of either ingenuity or influence peddling. In the early 1960s, Texas exerted an outsized influence in Washington with Lyndon Johnson as vice president, Sam Rayburn as the Speaker of the House, Albert L. Thomas (a Houston Democrat) chairing the House Appropriations Committee Subcommittee on Defense, and another U.S. representative, Olin E. Teague, as chairman of the Subcommittee on Manned Space Flight. The intervention of Albert Thomas was critical. Thomas used his influence to sway an 8F member and his former college roommate at Rice University, George R. Brown, to broker a land deal, whereby the Humble Oil Company donated one thousand acres of land from its corporate holdings in Clear Lake, just south of the city, to Rice University in 1961. Then, in order to secure the land needed by the MSC, 8F members encouraged Rice to give land to NASA.[83] This substantial cost savings, combined with political pressure in Washington, assured Houston's quick victory in the race to be the headquarters of America's space program.[84] Members of 8F recognized the important role that NASA could play in positioning Houston as a leader in aerospace, high-technology manufacturing, and other industries related to the space program. The Manned Spacecraft Center became a hub for regional diversification almost immediately.[85]

Perhaps even more important was MSC's effect on the city's educational sector. Not only did it spawn the creation of a Department of Space Science at Rice University, but it also helped to create the University of Houston Clear Lake as a standalone campus, designed to support and provide on-the-job training for the NASA personnel at the center. Institutions in the Texas Medical Center also benefited from NASA's presence. TMC Inc.'s 1963 annual report briefly mentioned that the Methodist Hospital, and presumably its medical school partner Baylor College of Medicine, was conducting neurophysiology research for NASA. At the same time, the Texas Institute for Rehabilitation and Research (TIRR) had inked a research contract to study the effects of immobilization on the human body.[86] By 1965, the Texas Medical Center Inc. reported that at Baylor, "significant progress was also made in space medicine research in several departments of the college."[87] Annual reports through the rest of the 1960s reference NASA's continuing relationship with TMC institutions.

Even though space was just one way to diversify Houston's economy, science in service of oil and natural gas still dominated.[88] However, when the Texas oil bust began in earnest in the 1980s, the issue of economic diversity assumed a more prominent role in the public discourse around economic development. Not only did it lead to higher than normal levels of unemployment (by January 1983, the unemployment rate reached 9.1 percent), more importantly, it led to the gutting of the city's property development sector, which had been another engine of regional economic growth for several decades.[89] Compounding the sense of decline, the city's private sector leadership, now led by the Houston Chamber of Commerce with the death of many members of 8F, appeared powerless as outsiders snapped up local assets at fire-sale prices.

In the fall of 1983, the Chamber's Human Resources Council, chaired by the president of Baylor College of Medicine Dr. William T. Butler, at least briefly discussed "special efforts being made in Austin to develop an effective business/education relationship in high technology." At that same meeting, Charles E. Bishop, chancellor of the University of Houston system, said that "Houston had real problems in this area, and that we need more people interested and trained in translating the scientific accomplishment into marketable technology and products." In the end, it appears that the Human Resources Council, working with other councils of the Chamber, resolved to study the matter.[90] By the spring of 1984, the Chamber had created a Committee on Economic Diversification. In a draft report generated that year, which was presumably later released to the public, the Committee on Economic Diversification spelled out its charge, writing that the "hope for Houston's future is a diversified economy, one based on favorable long-term trends in national and world economic structures." It also cautioned that "Houston's leadership should not make the mistake of trying to pick those industries that will be the region's financial winners of the year 2000. Free enterprise will take care of that. Instead, for diversification to occur successfully in Houston, we strongly state that the underlying economic conditions must be right. Emphasis must be placed on fundamental socio-economic-intellectual conditions, not on particular economic sectors."[91]

Technology Transfer, Venture Capital, and Spin-offs in Houston's Biotechnology Industry

It soon became clear that free enterprise alone wouldn't be enough to provide the type of quick growth for the city's advanced technology sectors that the Chamber's members hoped to see. Just as in Pittsburgh, new partnerships and organizations emerged to support and nurture a range of investments in biotechnology. One of the most important was the Houston Economic Development Council (HEDC). Led by Kenneth Schnitzer, this group represented an alternative to the more traditional Chamber of Commerce. Bill Schadewald, the editor of the *Houston Business Journal* and a onetime adversary of Schnitzer's, recalls that the launch of the HEDC was a press conference held to "criticize the Houston Chamber of Commerce for its lack of action in responding to the economic crisis."[92] Others have argued that the organization was "spun off" from the Chamber but still shared overlapping membership.[93] In a letter soliciting support for the organization's Economic Diversification Committee, Dr. Charles LeMaistre, the President of M. D. Anderson Cancer Center, noted the support for the organization by "the City of Houston and a 54-member Council representing a broad cross-section of the city's most influential business and civic leaders."[94] It described itself as "a business-to-business organization dedicated to a primary mission: creating jobs and investments for the Houston area by retaining existing businesses, stimulating the formation of new businesses, and attracting businesses from other areas."[95]

It promised to concentrate on the areas that it saw were the most in demand, including space-related technologies, medicine, chemicals, tourism, and the city's convention sector. At least in its early years, the HEDC had the support of the city's business and not-for-profit communities and its elected leaders. HEDC's separate funding, including public funding from the city, county, and the Port of Houston, eventually became a problem as the organization spent freely during its early years on consultants, salaries, and marketing.[96] The HEDC did not build new biotechnology companies. Rather, its role was to market the city to new firms at home and abroad and to create a climate that made private sector entrepreneurship in biotechnology viable.

In oilman and developer George Mitchell, the city's biotechnology industry found a powerful backer. Mitchell was born in 1919 to a family of poor Greek immigrants in Galveston, Texas, and made his fortune in the oil and gas businesses, founding Mitchell Energy, which was an early pioneer in shale gas removal by hydraulic fracturing techniques.[97] Mitchell was also a prominent member of several boards within the Texas Medical Center and a major donor to Baylor College of Medicine. He strongly believed that Houston had the potential to leverage its medical facilities to create new, high-paying jobs that would help to sustain the city's growth into the next century. In 1974, George Mitchell opened his planned community, The Woodlands, about twenty-five miles north of the corporate boundaries of Houston.[98] As part of the development of The Woodlands, Mitchell set aside 1,500 acres, which he dubbed the Research Forest, for laboratory spaces, with 150 of these acres to be donated to not-for-profit organizations. One of the first tenants of the Research Forest was Baylor, which built a $4.5 million laboratory facility.[99]

Mitchell wasn't just content to provide land for an emerging technology infrastructure. He also established one of the most active venture capital firms in Houston in the mid- to late 1980s—Woodlands Venture Capital Group. This decision was a direct response to a perception that, like Pittsburgh, Houston did not have enough venture capital to develop the type of spin-off companies that backers of biotechnology touted as critical for the city's future economic success.[100] Between 1985 and 1994, Woodlands Venture Capital Group, later renamed Woodlands Venture Partners, raised close to $200 million as well as investing "more than $15 million in eight Houston area biotech and medical device companies."[101] Finally, Mitchell also attempted to promote cross-institutional collaboration among the University of Houston, Rice University, the University of Texas at Austin, and Texas A&M by donating land and money for the Houston Advanced Research Center (HARC). While HARC was not geared explicitly toward biomedicine, its location in The Woodlands Research Forest alongside Baylor and a variety of other spin-off companies was part of a plan to generate, like the Pittsburgh Technology Center, a critical mass that would serve as a node for regional high-tech development.[102]

Even with creating a new space for research and development in The Woodlands, the HEDC and its partners still had to work out the problem of technology transfer. One of the ways that the earlier Chamber-led Committee on Economic Diversification suggested that the city could leverage its technology transfer assets was that "The Texas Medical Center, Inc. or some other group should *consider establishing either a non profit or for profit subsidiary medical development corporation.*"[103] The committee also recommended that "business and civic leaders should study the successful approaches taken by other cities in developing and promoting high-technology growth and where possible take the necessary steps to assist in the development of medical businesses in Houston."[104] The following year, under the more aggressive leadership of the HEDC, a "New Technologies Task Force" recommended that the organization create a new committee to support the particular needs of an emerging number of companies transferring their technology to the market.[105]

Just as in Pittsburgh, commercialization mattered, because it was the point that speculative ventures brought back return on investment. A report prepared for the HEDC in 1985 by Arthur D. Little, Inc., and the Rice Center suggested the city was in a good position to create a privately supported technology transfer infrastructure that could become a national model for a maturing biotechnology industry. Pitching the strength of TMC institutions in basic and clinical research, the report argued that pharmaceutical companies would be a potentially important source of private capital for university spin-offs in Houston. Little urged the organization to target small to medium firms that were potential targets for acquisition by larger, more established firms, and foreign firms that had no clear locational presence already in the United States.[106] The report also recommended a path similar to the one that cities like Pittsburgh ultimately chose—building on the existing collaboration between a major university (Rice) and nonprofit institutions (Baylor, NASA) to try to create a thriving medical device sector.[107] In fact, what was needed, claimed Little, was to market the TMC, Rice, and Houston's workforce better to tap into this potentially lucrative marketplace.

While there were plenty of ideas about how technology should be transferred from the laboratory to the marketplace, how did it really function in Houston? The answer is that, just as in Pittsburgh, there were numerous plans for coordination by groups of civic elites, but these plans appeared to never fully materialize. Instead, individual institutions took a leadership role in creating both marketable technologies and spin-off companies to produce and sell these technologies. Baylor had been an early adopter of the idea that technology should be transferred from the laboratory to the marketplace. From the 1950s to the late 1970s, patent policy was typically ad hoc. In 1978–1979, however, Butler moved to formalize technology transfer structures.[108] Over the next two years, the school issued a series of reports and met with organizations like Arthur D. Little about how to accomplish this goal.[109] By 1983, the school settled on developing capability internally and founded BCM Technologies, which was designed to more quickly bring discoveries to the market.[110] In 1988, Stephen Banks joined as CEO. Banks began his career in Pittsburgh with the Hillman Company, the private equality firm that managed the investments of Henry Hillman and members of his family.[111] In the first year after its founding, BCM Technologies spawned fifteen spin-off companies. BCM Technologies didn't make Baylor rich—by 1993, it had only generated between $4 and $6 million for the school in income. The total revenue numbers were, however, less important than the promise that perhaps it would become another revenue source for the institution.[112] In the meantime, BCM Technologies played an important symbolic role in the community, demonstrating that the school's leadership and board of trustees valued entrepreneurship among Baylor faculty members.

Houston Biotechnology is an interesting example of a company spun off from BCM Technologies. The company was founded the same year as BCM Technologies by two faculty members, Dominic Lam and Jared Emery. Traditionally, Baylor researchers might license their discoveries to established companies, which allowed them to collect royalties without the distraction of day-to-day corporate management. In the case of Lam and Emery, James Elkins Jr., a prominent Houston banker and a member of Baylor's board, strongly encouraged the men to form their own company. The men set up shop in The Woodlands, right next to Baylor's Center for Biotechnology, which Lam also happened to direct.[113]

Other health care institutions also started to jump into the biotechnology fray. In 1984, M. D. Anderson started to explore creating its own for-profit technology transfer partner named Andetech. The close linkage of public and private institutions around commercializing health technology did raise some internal concerns. In a February memorandum to M. D. Anderson's president, Dr. Charles LeMaistre, Anderson's associate vice president for research, Dr. Eugene McKelvey, laid out the pros and cons of a public-private partnership for technology transfer: "Indeed, the involvement of private capital and industry in medical research appears to offer a realistic alternative to limited government funding. It is a definitive trend in this decade." McKelvey continued, "I would personally support an expanded role for private capital in M. D. Anderson research. However, I urge caution, particularly in the beginning, since this relationship is new and probably involves ignorance and misconception on both sides."[114] These concerns appear to have won out and Andetech never made it off the ground.[115]

One area where Houston appeared more active than Pittsburgh was seeking out foreign partners and markets for biotechnology. This is likely due to the higher degree of international involvement in Houston's specialty medicine market during the 1980s, since many of the same people who were negotiating to expand specialty care overseas were also addressing issues of technology transfer and commercialization. In 1988, Houston hosted a Japanese trade mission for companies looking to invest in local biotechnology, which HEDC leaders appeared to play a large part in coordinating.[116] A year before, Houston Biotechnology signed an agreement with the Japanese company Santen Pharmaceutical to distribute a product to treat secondary cataracts.[117] However, just as in Pittsburgh, the problem of access to venture capital continued to constrain the growth of biotechnology in Houston. Things seemed to worsen with the arrival of the Clinton health care plan in the early 1990s, and venture capital became even more restricted as fear of major changes gripped the biomedical research and financing sectors.[118]

In 1991, Baylor College of Medicine was named one of six research sites for the Human Genome Project.[119] Baylor had been very active in genetic medicine before the announcement—in 1985, the school founded an Institute for Molecular Genetics.[120] The school also worked to strengthen its ties with NASA and created, along with several other medical schools and universities, the National Space Biomedical Research Institute in 1997.[121] At the same time that Baylor was betting big on genetics, M. D. Anderson was also working to capitalize on this emerging area. In 1994, the institution petitioned the University of Texas Board of Regents to approve licensing agreements with several companies, including RGene, Argus Pharmaceuticals, and Intron. All three agreements funneled royalties or stock options back to M. D. Anderson.[122] With the appointment of Dr. John Mendelson as president in 1997, the institution gained a leader with proven experience in translational research. Before coming to M. D. Anderson, Mendelson had invented Erbitux, "an epidermal growth factor receptor inhibitor developed by ImClone," and through this process had developed clear ideas about the importance of research and technology transfer to institutional growth.[123] Mendelson expanded the institution's research capability and created a new research plan of six interlocking areas, including molecular markers, proton therapy, imaging, targeted therapies, metastasis and tumor environment interaction, and immunology.[124]

As Houston's not-for-profit health care institutions continued to expand their biotechnology programs, the Greater Houston Partnership, which grew out of the merger of the Chamber of Commerce, HEDC, and the Houston World Trade Association in 1989, doubled down on its support of the sector. In a glossy press release in March 2000, it announced to the world that Houston, and its surrounding communities like Clear Lake, constituted a "'third coast' in bioscience."[125] It went on to highlight the TMC institutions as well as NASA, Rice, and the University of Houston as important centers of technological excellence in the region. Finally, the publication let its readers know about a large number of recently established biotechnology companies (167) and the relatively large number of support companies (63).[126] In 2002, Governor Rick Perry created a Council on Science and Biotechnology Development.[127] Two years later, the governor's office announced that it planned to make the "Biotechnology and the

Life Sciences Cluster" an economic development priority. From this effort came two other important ideas—the creation of Regional Centers of Innovation and Commercialization and the Texas Emerging Technology Fund.[128]

*   *   *

In both Pittsburgh and Houston, the path toward building a postindustrial knowledge economy was more complicated than merely replacing smokestack industries like steel or oil with blue sky industries like biotechnology. The emergence of biotechnology as an economic possibility was part of a larger strategy to rebrand cities as hubs of knowledge and nodes of competitiveness in a globalizing economy. It had as much to do with the location of critical facilities and talent as it did with timing—economic collapse occurred at the moment that medicine, American patent law, and academic culture were undergoing important shifts that introduced new technologies and new standards of practice. This process built on changes in the hospital-civic relationship brought forward by clinical services like specialty medicine that celebrated the relationship between not-for-profit health care and private markets in a more active way than either the locational asset model or the social justice model had done. But the private market was not the only way that a biotechnology infrastructure was created in the medical metropolis. It also relied on the emergence of an entrepreneurial state, which helped to create new types of opportunities for growth like the Ben Franklin Partnership, and the actions of elite civic development groups like the Allegheny Conference and the HEDC, as well as those of universities and medical schools themselves, which sought to create formal structures for the development of for-profit companies to commercialize the research that was seen as essential to the future economy and identity of the medical metropolis.

Yet, despite the celebration of the new economy, biotechnology has proved not to be the panacea that civic boosters claimed. It is certainly important to the medical metropolis—there is no question that biotechnology brings a wide variety of jobs to communities. In Pennsylvania, 77,000 people were employed in biosciences statewide—with most in either Philadelphia or Pittsburgh in 2014.[129] More than 5,700 workers are directly employed in some type of clinical capacity in biotech and related industries in Houston as of 2017.[130] Yet these numbers are difficult to really quantify, since how biotechnology, life sciences, or biosciences (all umbrella terms) are defined varies.

There are also real questions about what the relationship between biotechnology and social justice looks like in the medical metropolis. For executives, and even some lower level staff, biotechnology can provide good-paying jobs.[131] Moreover, the bench scientist, the lab tech, the janitor who sweeps the floors, and the construction worker who builds the physical space where biotechnology happens all benefit from a sustained investment in this sector. Yet in the long run, creating highly skilled and highly specialized jobs can leave the most vulnerable residents of the medical metropolis out in the cold if they can't access the type of educational opportunities and job training opportunities that helped Steve Laurer and Roger Morgan in the 1980s.[132] As one Houston journalist aptly put it: "Success in biotech is going to mean a lot for Houston's Mercedes dealers—not so much for the guys selling Chevrolets."[133]

The search for "innovation" and "disruptive models" of economic development wasn't limited to the laboratory. During the same years that biotechnology was emerging as one path forward for economic development, the same language was emerging in the business of delivering care. Unlike biotechnology, which remains a speculative venture, clinical services are a stable foundation for the postindustrial transformation of both Pittsburgh and Houston. Not-for-profit health care providers emerged as the largest employers in both cities and perhaps a stronger component of how each city marketed themselves to the world than biotechnology. It is to this story, the transformation of the business of providing and paying for patient care, that this book will now turn.

Chapter 5

The Coming of the System
Changing Health Care Delivery in the Medical Metropolis

In January 1993, Larry Mathis, the President and CEO of Houston's Methodist Hospital, was elected chairman of the American Hospital Association, a national trade group for hospitals. This was an important honor for Mathis and a recognition that the Bayou City's hospitals had truly gained a national reputation. Mathis marked the occasion with a speech to the association's members, in which he devoted at least a portion of his remarks to the topic that was at the tip of everybody's tongues that year—health care reform. For decades, rising costs to both patients and hospitals had portended a crisis in the American health care system. In the early 1990s, federal policymakers and elected officials set out to find a way to address these issues. At the time that Mathis spoke, Bill Clinton, who had made health care reform central to his presidential campaign, was just coming into office—raising hopes and fears among the AHA's membership about what the new American health care system might look like and what role they would play in shaping any changes in what was now a multi-billion-dollar-a-year industry.[1] What Mathis likely didn't say, but what many in the audience already knew, was that despite their concerns, most of America's large not-for-profit health care institutions actually entered the decade with a much greater ability to influence the contours of the nation's health care system and, by extension, the economy of the medical metropolis, than ever before.[2]

Too often health systems are treated as a black box that emerges to replace industry as the focal point of urban economies. The problem with this formulation is that it becomes easy to assume that growth of health systems either simply happened as a natural result of deindustrialization, or developed out of a civic necessity. In fact, from the early 1990s onward, total health care employment in the United States has grown steadily while other sectors have stagnated, reinforcing the importance of this sector to the overall economy all while strengthening the economic and political power of large health systems within the medical metropolis.[3] Large not-for-profit health systems first evolved from a coherent and planned response to the changing business of medicine. While a sense of civic responsibility may have shaped decision-making, the growing prominence of a market-based model for structuring the hospital-civic relationship meant that business was the primary driver of change. During the 1980s, 1990s, and 2000s, not-for-profit leaders not only drew organizational inspiration from the for-profit sector by pursuing a wave of mergers and acquisitions that resulted in large horizontally and vertically integrated health systems, but were also more willing to speak in a language that echoed their corporate counterparts.[4] And, while many not-for-profit health care leaders genuinely believed that this full-throated embrace of market-oriented principles was the only way that their institutions would survive, and therefore be able to continue to benefit the communities they served, others understood that the embrace of the market model was a way to build their bottom lines and increase their market share. Whatever their motivations, by helping to destroy the narrative at the heart of the locational asset model—that not-for-profit hospitals were a special type of community institution that existed in a world that was both part of and outside of the private market for health care—not-for-profit leaders launched a new era in American health care that finally shredded the already tattered old understandings of the hospital-civic relationship.

The Changes That Shaped Local Health Care Markets

By the time Mathis ascended to the chairmanship of the AHA, three fears shaped the behavior of not-for-profit health care executives across the United States. The first was that new payment structures, such as private managed care organizations and Medicare prospective payment, would reduce clinical revenue and change the character of American medicine for the worse. The next, which never fully came to pass, was that for-profit hospital chains would subsume not-for-profits as the predominant space for health care delivery. The final fear was that potential federal health care

reform would undermine the ability of not-for-profit health care institutions to manage their own growth and, by extension, undercut the more
visible role that these institutions were playing in the medical metropolis.
Depending on location, market conditions, and on the priorities of individual executives and boards of directors, how much each fear influenced
decision-making varied, but all operated at some level as large not-for-
profits tried to bend the business of medicine to meet their own needs and
those of the postindustrial city.

In most cases, the fear of new payment structures was the most omnipresent. The rise of managed care had real effects on how not-for-profit
health care institutions conducted business. In a traditional health care payment model, hospitals and physicians charged a variable fee for each service
that was rendered. Cost control came from the patient's ability to pay and
was, at least in theory, a natural extension of free market supply and
demand that could be found at work in a variety of other sectors of the
American economy. The proliferation of employer-sponsored health insurance during and after World War II helped to lay the groundwork for a
cost control crisis, since patients and providers were able to pass high levels
of utilization and the associated costs to third-party insurance companies,
which then passed their costs along to the businesses that purchased insurance coverage for their employees.[5] In fact, between 1960 and 1980,
national health expenditures rose from 5.0 to 8.9 percent of gross domestic
product, while the cost for employers grew by 700 percent between 1970
and 1982.[6]

Health maintenance organizations (HMOs), with their capitated payment model, were supposed to be a solution to cutting costs and providing
better health outcomes. However, as the example of Central Medical Pavilion shows, in their early years, they often failed to live up to the hype
surrounding their potential transformative power. What changed in the
1980s was a growing focus on linking HMO-style care with for-profit insurance delivery. The capitated care model of HMOs allowed for-profit insurance companies more leverage in negotiating prices with hospitals and
physicians by setting what price they were willing to pay for specific types
of procedures.[7] The public sector soon embraced a similar model of cost
control with the emergence of Medicare Diagnosis Related Groups (DRG)
in 1983. Like private HMOs, this model made a specific amount of money
available up front, in contrast to the traditional method of reimbursement
which not only paid "reasonable costs" on a per procedure basis after the

fact, but also, as a legacy of the fraught politics of Medicare and Medicaid passage, reimbursed hospitals an additional 2 percent and nursing homes an additional 7.5 percent. Another costly legacy of the program was a provision that allowed insurance companies like Blue Cross to act as "fiscal intermediaries," which paid them to process Medicare claims.[8]

While reimbursing by diagnosis may have sounded good in theory, it assumes that every case is similar. For example, two patients might be admitted for coronary artery bypass surgery but experience different surgical outcomes. Under a DRG model, hospitals in the same region would be paid the same for each patient, even though one might require considerably more care than the other. To save money, hospitals were incentivized to provide less postoperative care. Private insurers worried that DRGs would become an excuse for hospitals to raise rates on non-Medicare patients to keep hospital balance sheets in the black. While many of the fears about DRGs never came to pass—hospital administrators became adept at picking codes to maximize reimbursement and using them to lower length-of-stay metrics—they did inspire hospitals to focus even more acutely on revenue management as a general business strategy.[9]

A second fear was that national for-profit hospital chains would emerge as serious competitors to individual not-for-profit hospitals within local or regional markets. The Hospital Corporation of America (HCA) was one of the biggest potential threats, despite the fact that it had been a partner, or potential partner, for building specialty medical services overseas or in faraway domestic medical markets during the 1970s and 1980s. But when it came time to compete for the local patients who formed the bulk of the revenue for not-for-profit health systems, for-profit medicine emerged as the enemy. HCA's decision to challenge not-for-profit health systems in their local markets was not capricious. Prior to the 1980s and 1990s, there had been a clear division of the market between large not-for-profits like the University of Pittsburgh or The Methodist Hospital, whose primary focus was on drawing patients from urban or suburban markets to academically affiliated hospitals. HCA and its competitors, by contrast, typically grew by acquiring or building small community hospitals in rural and suburban areas that had no clear link to academic medicine, unless the patient needed to be transferred to a higher level of care that was provided by an urban academic medical center. This strategy conformed well with the dominant organizational paradigm of the American health care delivery system, which was based on the principle of hierarchical regionalism. This model worked well for both for-profit and not-for-profit hospitals because everybody was able to generate revenue at their particular step along the continuum of care. However, as population patterns shifted, the small rural hospitals that had been the backbone of HCA's growth strategy lost patients. Moreover, suburban community hospitals were also being forced to develop their own limited specialty lines (which had largely been the territory of urban academic medical centers) in a bid to retain their market share. Thus, for-profit companies like HCA needed to find new ways to continue to generate revenue to ensure that stock prices remained competitive.[10]

One solution that Thomas Frist and other HCA executives settled on was creating economies of scale through size (creating a large enough regional and national presence to be able to negotiate down costs for supplies and labor) and through more direct ownership of facilities, rather than managing them on a contract basis.[11] Another solution was to try to compete against academic medical centers directly, either by moving into the specialty medical market at their own flagship facilities, as the attempted University of Pittsburgh/HCA transplantation partnership illustrates, or by simply purchasing urban teaching hospitals so that the for-profit companies could offer high-value services in markets where they did not have their own existing facility that could support these service lines. While for-profit academic medical centers never became the norm in the United States, the purchase of Wesley Medical Center in Wichita, Kansas, and the subsequent affiliation agreement with another teaching hospital, Lovelace Medical Center in Albuquerque, New Mexico, indicated that all hospitals, regardless of tax status, were subject to acquisition by for-profit hospital chains.[12]

The final fear was that health care reform efforts would upend markets and rewrite the rules by which both not-for-profits and for-profits operated. Even though efforts to remake the U.S. health care system had long been stymied by interest group politics and the resistance of powerful actors like the American Medical Association, the death of Senator John Heinz (R-PA) in 1991 helped to push this fear into overdrive when health care reform emerged as a critical campaign issue in the special election to fill his vacant seat. Harris Wofford, a former college president and lawyer residing in the Philadelphia area, faced off against former governor and Pittsburgh native Richard Thornburgh. Wofford argued that health care was a fundamental right and that Americans deserved as much access as was financially possible. Even though this thinking about easier access ran headlong into the issues that Larry Mathis would later identify in his speech to the American Hospital Association about unlimited patient demands made on limited hospital resources, Pennsylvania voters loved it, propelling Wofford to an upset victory and making health care reform an important issue in the 1992 presidential campaign. Upon assuming the White House, Bill Clinton quickly put into place a task force chaired by the First Lady, Hillary Rodham Clinton, to start to draw up recommendations for how to reform the U.S. health care system.[13] The response to all three fears typically entailed emulating the for-profit sector and seeking out ways to increase efficiency while keeping as much revenue as possible within each organization's coffers all along the continuum of care. To do this, not-for-profit executives created their own vertically and horizontally integrated health systems.[14]

Building Health Care Systems—Texas Style

Patient referrals are the lifeblood of any academic medical center, but they can be fickle. Too much traffic, inadequate or expensive parking for loved ones, too much noise, and too few amenities are all reasons why patients might decline, despite a superior level of care, to seek treatment in a particular hospital. The key to successfully managing referrals is developing relationships with critical staff such as social workers and physicians who manage patient discharge planning and eliminate barriers so that the process of moving from one level of care to another is easy. Over the course of the twentieth century, successful academic medical centers and teaching hospitals worked hard to cultivate referral networks. By the 1980s, however, these informal referral networks were insufficient to generate the type of patient volume and revenue that academic medical centers felt they needed to remain competitive and, in doing so, continue to contribute to the growth of the medical metropolis.

The Methodist Hospital was an early leader in the drive to build more formal affiliation networks. At the behest of senior leaders like Larry Mathis, who had risen from administrative resident to a senior vice president in 1980, the hospital underwent a corporate reorganization, creating the Methodist Hospital Health Care System. Managed by veteran administrator Tom Fourquren, this was an umbrella for organizing new satellite hospital construction and managing relationships with affiliated hospitals.[15]

Figure 10. By the mid-1980s, the Texas Medical Center's rapid growth had
helped to form a second skyline. Note downtown Houston in the background
of this image.

Unknown photographer. IC002 Texas Medical Center, Box 11, Folder 16, 1985, John P. McGovern
Historical Collections and Research Center, Houston Academy of Medicine–Texas Medical Center
Library, Houston, Texas.

At its heart, the system was about meeting two critical goals—establishing
geographic coverage and managing the flow of medically complex
patients back to the main hospital. A clear referral network was particularly important, since Methodist refused to honor most managed care
products, deciding instead to become the fee-for-service hospital of
choice for the region. This meant that it needed as many patients and as
long a length of stay as possible to keep its books in the black.[16] Methodist's affiliation network grew rapidly. In 1988, Mathis boasted that the
hospital had 3,372 affiliated beds "within an approximate radius of 150
miles of Houston," giving it "dominance in our region."[17] The affiliation

model did not last. It eventually fell by the wayside as concerns over exposing the main hospital to malpractice lawsuits for potentially dangerous care in affiliated hospitals hastened the program's demise.[18]

Aside from liability issues, the major problem with affiliation networks was control. Unless a hospital pursued the formal merger option, both sides retained the ability to break the agreement. Moreover, individual physicians didn't always want to direct patients in the way that administrators had hoped; personal connections, personal preferences, and aggressive marketing by rival hospitals all could redirect patient flow. What was needed to ensure that patient dollars remained in the system was a way to encourage control of clinical and other services up and down the continuum of care, similar to the model used by HCA.

Across the Texas Medical Center, Hermann Hospital was also pursuing an affiliation strategy, creating Hermann Affiliated Hospital Systems in 1980. Hermann was founded as a "public charity hospital" in 1925 by a bequest from the estate of George Hermann, a bachelor cattleman and real estate speculator. The hospital was a cornerstone of the TMC and, since 1971, the primary teaching hospital for the University of Texas Health Science Center at Houston. Over the years, the hospital emerged as a formidable competitor to other not-for-profit institutions like The Methodist Hospital by developing expertise in liver transplantation, burn care, and emergency medicine.[19] In a question-and-answer piece in the Hermann-published magazine *Horizons*, the hospital's public relations staff emphasized that Hermann's affiliation model was built on partnerships rather than acquisitions. They also focused on the way that an affiliated hospital system could offer services to help individual hospitals negotiate complex state-level health planning policy, including certificate-of-need laws. Hermann sold Affiliated Hospital Systems in 1987.[20]

By 1993, the changing landscape of local and national health care forced Hermann executives and board members to reconsider their decision. Instead of choosing to simply rebuild their affiliations, they decided that the time was right to go further and build their own integrated delivery system.[21] Integrated delivery systems differed from affiliation agreements in that they allowed a single organization to consolidate a variety of services along the continuum of care. They did this by owning the facilities where this care was delivered and employing the physicians and health professionals who delivered this care. This latter part, directly employing physicians, ran counter to decades of typical business practice in which most nonacademic physicians were independent business people with hospital admitting and rounding privileges who acted as feeders for hospital beds.[22]

To start building its integrated delivery system, Hermann tapped Gerald Tresslar, a longtime health care executive who had most recently been president of the Louisiana-based Ochsner Health Plan, as the operational leader, and Dr. Terry K. Satterwhite, an infectious disease physician, as board chairman.[23] Tresslar's and Satterwhite's charge was to build a physician referral network named OneCare. Even though this seemed like only a small part of integrating care delivery, OneCare was especially critical. In its earliest iteration, the new entity was an umbrella organization that would allow all Hermann physicians, including those in private practice and those affiliated with the University of Texas Health Science Center at Houston, to accept managed care contracts.[24] The real goal, however, was to create a network of providers that could serve as the tip of the spear for efforts to capture a larger slice of the managed care market in Houston, a market that hospital officials estimated would grow from 11 percent in 1994 to roughly 40 percent (at the high end) by 1996. OneCare was also seen as a hedge against efforts by other health systems to build their own integrated delivery systems, helping the hospital to retain its market share.[25]

As OneCare's sole corporate member, Hermann was free to lend the new organization money and provide backing for debt incurred by the company to fund expansion; however, legal strictures prohibited the hospital from directly influencing the care given to patients by OneCare physicians. Physician management services for OneCare were provided through a separate organization named Peak Systems. The organization grew rapidly. By the summer of 1995, OneCare had a network of 312 primary care physicians with distinct strengths in areas like family practice, pediatrics, and internal medicine, as well as 258 specialist physicians. OneCare had also started to lease freestanding offices throughout the Houston metropolitan area and had developed three built-to-suit new locations for its network of employed physicians. These new OneCare facilities helped to manage patient flow by serving as a site for specialty care revenue collection while keeping nonemergent patients out of the acute hospital setting.[26] The expanded footprint that OneCare provided was especially crucial as Hermann's potential patient pool moved to the suburbs. In fact, the Houston-Sugar Land-Baytown Metropolitan Statistical Area grew by 19.6 percent between 1980 and 1990 and another 25.2 percent between 1990 and 2000.[27] Between 1990 and 2003, suburban counties such as Brazoria, Fort Bend, and Montgomery Counties, which were home to affluent communities like the Woodlands, Sugar Land, and Pearland, were growing the most rapidly. With higher incomes came higher percentages of privately insured households—a market that hospitals and physicians were desperately trying to capture.[28]

Hermann Seeks a Merger Partner to Grow Its Footprint

As important as the work that Tresslar and Satterwhite were doing with OneCare was to the hospital's future, CEO David Page and board chairwoman Melinda Perrin understood that if Hermann was really going to remain an essential part of the regional health care market and continue to thrive as an employer and community institution, more drastic steps were needed to expand its geographic footprint into these affluent suburban locations. First named to the board at thirty-eight, Perrin was the daughter of the legendary Texas politician John Hill.[29] Perrin brought with her more than a family political legacy, and she soon proved to be an effective organizer and savvy politician in her own right as she negotiated Houston's clubby world of hospital boards. Page and Perrin identified several potential merger candidates, including HCA, which itself had merged with its for-profit rival Columbia in 1994 to form Columbia/HCA as well as the not-for-profit Sisters of Charity Health System and the Memorial Health System.

Houston's not-for-profit health care administrators did not particularly love Columbia/HCA. In 1996, Dan Wilford, the chief executive officer of the Memorial Health System, expressed the sentiments of many of his contemporaries when he told *Texas Business*, "If they can't buy you, they'll bury you. If they can't buy you, then they build something and beat you up with it."[30] But it was not really that unusual that Hermann considered it as a potential partner. For-profit health care played a much larger role in the Houston market than it did in many other cities. By the 1990s, Columbia/HCA already controlled about 22 percent of the inpatient hospitalization market in the region.[31] Merging with Hermann could potentially give the company access to the Texas Medical Center while expanding Hermann's ability to draw patients from Columbia/HCA's network of community hospitals in the region and beyond. In fact, St. Luke's Episcopal Hospital, which was closely connected with Dr. Denton Cooley and the Texas Heart Institute, was also considering building a stronger relationship with Columbia/HCA.[32] While there were worries over how well the two organization's cultures might fit together, it appears that what largely sank the deal were concerns over how Columbia/HCA might value Hermann's assets during the process of combining.[33]

The not-for-profit Sisters of Charity (SCH) Health System was another intriguing possibility as a partner. The charitable missions of the two organizations were in better congruence, and it would present less of an issue with the Texas Medical Center, whose charter prevented for-profit enterprises on its grounds.[34] Merging with SCH would have created a new three-hospital system with a combined market share of about "11.5 percent of the total market, measured by admissions and about 18 percent of the not-for-profit market," making it roughly comparable in size to The Methodist Hospital and Memorial's networks.[35] Both sides also felt that a merger would yield an increase in private-pay and managed care business. It also would have given Hermann access to more outpatient clinics, physician networks, and insurance products. Like the potential Columbia/HCA deal, it would have given Hermann access to referral hospitals located outside of the TMC while giving SCH access to the medical center. However, it would also position the new health system as a primary provider of medical care to poor Houstonians. This high level of care for the poor raised concerns about the mission undercutting the margin, especially if paltry Medicaid reimbursements or demand for charity care outstripped expectations.[36]

Another concern was SCH's religious mission, which raised questions about how Catholic health directives would affect the medical education and research that was conducted at Hermann.[37] In fact, during the due diligence period, a group of University of Texas and Hermann physicians and administrators generated a list that was submitted to SCH that raised a series of clinical and ethical questions about what procedures and behaviors currently would be compatible with Catholic health directives.[38] The final sticking point to a merger had to do with how both parties understood the terms of the affiliation agreement and the balance of power between the two partners.[39] When all three issues were taken together, the obstacles to forming a workable partnership, while not insurmountable, meant that a merger between the two organizations did not occur.

Hermann was also tentatively engaging in merger talks with the Memorial Health System at the same time it was courting other suitors. Memorial was the partner the hospital was most comfortable with; in fact, during a conference call in January 1997, Perrin noted that Memorial had long been Hermann's "hospital partner of choice."[40] Memorial had a history as a quality provider of acute care services in the Houston region. The health system's roots stretched back to 1907, when Reverend D. R. Pevoto purchased the Rudisill Sanitarium and renamed it the Baptist Sanitarium. By 1910, Pevoto's sanitarium had affiliated with the Baptist General Convention of Texas and had added "hospital" to its name. The hospital continued to grow, becoming the Memorial Hospital on January 1, 1932. During the 1960s, the hospital became one of the first in the Houston region to embrace the city's demographic change. In 1969, in part because of the decision of the Baptist General Convention not to allow affiliates to accept federal aid—a prohibition that also caused Baylor College of Medicine to separate from its corporate parent—the hospital system separated from the Baptist Convention and became the Memorial Health System.[41]

By the late 1990s, Memorial had a network of eight community hospitals that had excellent geographic distribution throughout the Houston-Sugar Land-Baytown MSA. What Memorial lacked, however, was access to an academically affiliated tertiary hospital with highly specialized service lines. The case for merger, rather than sale, also became clearer in January 1997, when board members like Perrin and representatives of management like Page and Satterwhite learned that Morgan Stanley valued the sale of the hospital at between "six to eight times earnings before interest, depreciation, and taxes." Despite this somewhat high estimate of value, Hermann's leadership concluded that the value of a well-developed integrated delivery system "could be much greater than the System's current sales price," ensuring that the hospital would continue to fulfill its mission into the next century.[42] It was at this point that Memorial was formally elevated to preferred-partner status. Initial stipulations called for a merger of hospitals with OneCare and Peak Systems, as well as nonhospital assets being retained by individual members.[43] Throughout the spring and summer of 1997, both sides worked through legal counsel to draft initial merger documents.[44] They agreed that David Page would become the new organization's chief operating officer and Dan Wilford, Memorial's CEO, would become the president of the combined organization. Memorial's board chair, George R. Farris, would become the initial board chair of the new company with Hermann's board chair, Melinda Perrin, serving as vice-chair.[45]

When it came to the merger's timing, Hermann had a major problem—the hospital had to close the deal by November 5, 1997, or risk losing $25 million in Medicare recapture monies as a consequence of the enactment of the Balanced Budget Act of 1997.[46] This drive for closure meant that

Hermann officials often felt that Memorial was dragging its heels, especially in the early fall of 1997, when serious differences between the two parties over the corporate structure of the new entity started to emerge. Finally, on November 4, barely in time for the Medicare recapture deadline, the closing occurred, and the Memorial Hermann Healthcare System was created. This new system represented the largest not-for-profit health care system in the Houston marketplace and brought a new partner into the Texas Medical Center.

System Building Through Acquisition: The Case of UPMC

While Memorial Hermann chose to pursue a partnership model for expanding its footprint, in Pittsburgh, the University of Pittsburgh Medical Center (UPMC) chose an acquisition model. This choice was shaped both by the specific market conditions in Western Pennsylvania, with its large number of small not-for-profit community hospitals and single medical school, as well as the personalities of the organization's early leadership, Dr. Thomas Detre and Jeffrey Romoff.[47] In March 1973, Dr. Thomas Detre assumed the chairmanship of the Department of Psychiatry at the University of Pittsburgh and the responsibility of managing Western Psychiatric Institute and Clinic (WPIC). Detre was a new breed of psychiatrist. According to historian Mary Brignano, who has written the most comprehensive corporate history of UPMC, Detre "raised eyebrows [in his previous position] at Yale" as a pioneer of drug-based pharmacological therapy and as a proponent of deinstitutionalization. Brignano also notes that he continued to raise eyebrows in Pittsburgh for his habit of "chain-smoking Marlboros through an ebony [cigarette] holder" and his tendency to wear his topcoat around his shoulders, leading to "muttered jokes about [Detre as a modern-day] Count Dracula," a reputation some thought he later used to his advantage in building the organization.[48]

Detre's arrival coincided with the increasing visibility of rising hospital costs and a more competitive environment for federal biomedical research funding, especially from the National Institutes of Health (NIH).[49] In the growing medical metropolis, funding from the NIH became an important metric that medical schools and their affiliated hospitals used to increase their national prominence and prove to local civic development organizations their symbolic and real economic value.[50] By focusing on NIH monies,

Detre was able to do several things. First, he was able to diversify the medical school's research portfolio, which dovetailed well with the push for biotechnology as a form of economic development by regional leaders at the University of Pittsburgh, Carnegie Mellon University, and the Allegheny Conference on Community Development. Next, using NIH grant money as a metric gave him the ability to quantify the value of specific departments and to rank the medical school nationally among its peers.

Detre understood the real and symbolic value of clinical revenue and NIH grants for his ability to gain autonomy for his department and WPIC within the University of Pittsburgh's administrative structures. Working closely with Romoff, the two men started close to home by negotiating what Brignano calls "an unusual financial pact allowing the Department of Psychiatry, rather than the School of Medicine, to keep the clinical income generated in WPIC."[51] This new arrangement guaranteed a steady stream of money that Detre could reinvest in the department to hire nationally prominent faculty and to fund new research projects. Second, Detre was able to negotiate that the department "be allowed to retain an amount equal to the indirect costs of its researchers' federal research grants from the NIH."[52] Throughout the 1970s, Detre and his staff continued to generate more and more revenue through their plan to "drive the clinical machine," while they also sought more and more grant monies as a way of increasing WPIC's research profile and collecting more indirect grant costs.[53] His success garnered notice within the medical center and university hierarchies. In 1982 he was named associate senior vice chancellor for the Health Sciences, and senior vice chancellor for the Health Sciences two years later.[54]

One of Detre's first tasks was defining what the center's organizational structure should look like for the future. In the locational asset model, merely having a collection of hospitals to treat the ill and a medical school to train physicians and conduct biomedical research was enough—after all, these institutions were supposed to backstop the industrial economy. However, as the broader set of economic changes that accompanied the postindustrial turn intersected with the changing business of medicine, better coordination between institutions was needed to achieve the sort of economies of scale and market footprint that the creation of affiliation networks and integrated delivery systems required.

The University Health Center of Pittsburgh, which was an administrative attempt dating to 1965 with the goal of formally linking hospitals and the university together around some shared services and governance, was no longer sufficient to meet the administrative needs of a university that was, as its support of biotechnology showed, determined to use its medical center to help take a leading role in the region's economic development. In 1983, at Detre's request, University of Pittsburgh chancellor Wesley W. Posvar agreed to withdraw the university from UHCP. In the place of the university, Posvar substituted Detre and WPIC. According to Brignano, and confirmed by memoranda from Posvar's files, this apparent "retreat" was instead a brilliant tactical move—the university's administration was given cover from the various boards of hospital trustees, many of which were composed of major donors and university trustees, while simultaneously allowing Detre and his staff to destroy UHCP from the inside.[55]

The heart of the health center was its general hospital, Presbyterian-University. This hospital was home to Dr. Thomas Starzl's transplant program as well as serving as the critical space for medical education within the complex. In March 1982, Dan Stickler, the hospital's executive director, sent a draft report of a reorganization plan for the hospital to Posvar. Stickler proposed the formation of a separate holding corporation known as Presbyterian-University Health Systems, Inc., as a way to separate out core hospital functions and other areas of potential revenue generation, including health data services and contract health management services (similar to the affiliation model pursued elsewhere).[56] While it is not clear from the archival record what final form this entity took, newspapers reported that it was created in 1982, and by the 1990s, it was being used to acquire property close to the hospital.[57]

Stickler's efforts opened the door to more substantial attempts to rethink not only the organization of the health center but also how various components of its identity were branded and sold to the public. In a lengthy memo dated October 1982 to Nathan Stark, then senior vice chancellor for the Health Sciences, and Edison Montgomery, a longtime University administrator who filled in for Stark during his service with the Carter administration in the Department of Health and Human Services, Detre spelled out the direction that he felt would be most beneficial to Presbyterian-University Hospital and the health center as a whole. Detre argued, "The 'university hospital' has first and foremost an *academic mission*. It does what other hospitals do only on a scale large enough to assure the public that it is responsive to community needs. . . . Academic goals infuse every activity and are the highest priority for the deployment of resources and the development of new services." Generating clinical revenue, he claimed, was important but should not be an overriding goal. " 'Restructuring' for the sole purpose of generating income is laudable, but perhaps the only justification for enhanced revenue for university hospitals—particularly those which, like the PUH, stand without peers in a large population area—is that profits are used to fund future developments in the health sciences." Yet markets still mattered: "With competition from major teaching hospitals, such as Allegheny General Hospital locally, the academic innovation and excellence of the University Health Center of Pittsburgh is a unique and effective marketing tool," Detre wrote. Finally, he argued, "We who inhabit the university hospital bear a unique societal responsibility. Should we lose sight of our overriding academic mission in a maze of corporate anomalies and leadership voids, we surely will have failed."[58] This memorandum identified the tension that Detre faced between academic mission and revenue generation as he moved to reform antiquated organizational structures within the university health center and build "a confederation of hospitals with many interests in common, but each with its separate identity, responsibility, and authority," into an integrated health care system.[59]

Soon after gaining power within UHCP, Detre went to work consolidating the other parts of the health center, first taking back governance of the Falk Clinic, the freestanding building originally built as the medical center's ambulatory care clinic. In 1985, Detre convinced Eye and Ear Hospital to sell its assets to the University of Pittsburgh, and then, once the sale was completed, WPIC assumed management of Eye and Ear.[60] Detre's next target was Presbyterian-University itself, which he eventually brought into the fold later that same year.[61] The following year, a new administrative entity named the Medical and Health Care Division of the University of Pittsburgh, or MHCD, was created to manage "the financial and clinical aspects of Pitt's School of Medicine, WPIC, the Falk Clinic, and Presbyterian-University Hospital (into which Eye & Ear Hospital would be merged)."[62] MHCD not only allowed for better coordination between hospitals, but it also designed a mechanism to plow hundreds of millions of dollars of clinical revenue back into medical education and the expansion of new research and patient care programs such as cancer care and transplantation medicine. Detre led this new division.[63]

MHCD helped to solve some of the internal problems of medical center management, but Detre realized that if medical center hospitals wanted to

increase their external market share in Western Pennsylvania, they needed
to find ways to quickly build research and clinical capacity around specific
areas of potential growth. Cancer provided one early opportunity. While
he was working to consolidate MHCD, Detre approached the Richard King
Mellon Foundation with a request that the foundation provide an initial $3
million grant to create a cross-disciplinary and cross-institutional center of
excellence around cancer, which became the University of Pittsburgh Cancer Institute (UPCI).[64] Brignano has argued that UPCI is responsible for
"seeding UPMC," because the funding model that it and the other centers
of excellence utilized was at the heart of the health system's expansion. This
management structure allowed Detre to demand financial support from all
participants, thus setting a precedent for central taxation from the Vice
Chancellor's Office, which "pushed the various university and hospital fac-
tions and fiefdoms into a cooperative venture, and it guaranteed start-up
funds until the center could earn its own income."[65]

In 1990, MHCD became the University of Pittsburgh Medical Center
(UPMC).[66] Even though this seemed like a simple name change, the transition allowed the new entity more freedom than its predecessor, including
delegating "selectively to UPMC under the oversight of appropriate University officers," responsibility for "development and alumni affairs, public
relations, government relations, human resources, facilities management,
legal services and some business services. Of course, the President of the
University retains the authority to modify the delegation of these management responsibilities."[67]

UPMC underwent a leadership change when Detre suffered a heart
attack in 1992. While he had been pondering retirement already, the heart
attack hastened the need to think about succession. His duties were split
into two positions—the senior vice chancellor's position, focusing on the
academic needs of the medical center, which Detre retained until 1998, and
another focusing on the hospitals. Detre argued that these positions should
be 'interrelated but independent."[68] After some controversy about the way
that he was appointed, this second position, senior vice chancellor for
health administration and president of UPMC, went to Jeffrey Romoff.[69]
Romoff had long been a controversial figure around the medical center. A
brash and outspoken Bronx native, Romoff first came to Pittsburgh following his late wife, a nurse who had worked with Detre at Yale-New Haven
Hospital.[70] Unlike Detre, who was an academic clinician, Romoff's advanced degree was in political science. He was, however, a more than

capable health care administrator. Romoff deeply understood the changing national and local health care markets and was passionate about ensuring that the University of Pittsburgh remained at the forefront of change.[71]

UPMC Grows Through Acquisition

On November 15, 1995, Romoff stood before the faculty of the University of Pittsburgh School of Medicine and delivered a scathing lecture about the future of health care for the country and for the region. The lecture was entitled "The Transformation of the Academic Medical Center: The Managed Care Marketplace and the Future of the University of Pittsburgh Medical Center," and in it he laid bare an unspoken truth that most people in the region who were part of the health care industry already knew but didn't always want to articulate. Romoff declared to the quiet lecture hall, "at the heart of the matter is the conversion of health care from a social good to a commodity. This is being driven by market forces as much as it is being driven by federal inaction."[72] Over the next hour, Romoff sketched out what must have been a frighteningly dystopian vision for the future of the region's medical care for his audience of university-based physicians and health care administrators.

Romoff told his audience members that he had been meeting with representatives from the for-profit hospital company Columbia/HCA and that they were showing a strong interest in entering the Pittsburgh market. He then warned the medical faculty about the substance of his conversation, telling them that it was a meeting about price-earnings ratios, acquisitions, balance sheets, and revenue capture. To hammer home his point, Romoff attempted to draw an equivalency between changes in health care and the older industrial economy by saying, "I did not hear a single word about what you as the faculty of the school of medicine and I would remotely associate with what health care is. What I was listening to was modern corporate America. What I was listening to was the story of what happened in the auto industry, was the story of what happened in the steel industry, was the story of what happened in the banking industry, the story in the accounting industry. It is a simple and clear economic story driven by market forces not driven by social good any more than the difference between a Chevy and a Buick is driven by a social good."[73] This commercialized, rather entrepreneurial outlook, Romoff implied, was the future of academic medicine and, without embracing it on their own terms, organizations like UPMC might suffer the same fate as those legacy industries that once underpinned the economy of the industrial city and, like them, fail to maintain their economic viability, thus impacting UPMC's mission of patient care, teaching, and research as well as its larger ability to help the region's economy.[74]

The following year, in an update to Elsie Hillman, a local power broker and the wife of venture capitalist Henry Hillman, on a potential merger between UPMC and Shadyside Hospital, a local community hospital generously supported by the Hillman family, Romoff doubled down on his assessment of the corrosive role of for-profit health care by arguing, "The entry of this for-profit company [Columbia/HCA] in the Pittsburgh community would instantly and radically accelerate all the effects of the current marketplace and result in dramatic downsizing, the selling of SSH [Shadyside Hospital] to a national company, the loss of control by leaders of the Pittsburgh community and what would ultimately be aggressive competition with the UPMC. The history and tradition of SSH," continued Romoff, "would be submerged to the goals of an outside, for-profit company, and the UPMC, the most significant academic and economic force in western Pennsylvania, would need to focus on a difficult struggle with a company that has no academic aspirations or resources."[75]

However, on that evening in 1995 when Romoff stood before the faculty of the school of medicine, the merger with Shadyside was in the future, and cutting beds, not retaining them, was another subject Romoff turned to. He argued that massive cuts were needed and many hospitals, including academic hospitals, would probably have to go out of business to restore balance to the market.[76] According to Romoff, the six-county region that made up the Pittsburgh medical market had 13,783 inpatient acute care beds. By projecting HMO bed utilization data from California onto the regional market, UPMC concluded that only about 3,400 inpatient acute care beds were needed to meet demand, "of which the UPMC already commands about 1000 at an 80 percent occupancy." When you added in the hospitals affiliated with the health system, claimed Romoff, "you now have enough beds for the whole future of health care in the six-county region. If indeed we maintained our market share, and our six friends including Children's and Magee maintain their market share, theoretically every other hospital should close."[77] What Romoff meant was that the tertiary hospitals in Western Pennsylvania were, by necessity, locked in a battle for survival and that extraordinary measures were necessary to ensure that UPMC continued to thrive.

The problem of surplus beds ran headlong into two other interrelated problems. The first was the push by managed care organizations and Medicare toward shortening inpatient length of stay, and the second was accomplishing this goal by utilizing outpatient care whenever possible. For example, by 1995, UPMC's inpatient length of stay had declined more than 25 percent from what it had been in 1992, while its admissions had remained relatively stable.[78] Length-of-stay issues were critical for providers because they directly impacted reimbursement. In a fee-for-service model, insurers acted as conduits, funneling money to providers to pay for procedures and for days spent in the hospital. Thus, it behooved providers to keep patients as long as possible, and it behooved insurers to try to push for early discharges. Under a managed care model where providers were paid a set fee per patient, it now behooved providers to push patients out the door as quickly as possible to lower their exposure and to be able to keep as much of the per-patient fee as possible. With this changed set of incentives, both payers and providers looked to increased outpatient utilization to deliver care in a more cost-efficient manner than inpatient hospitalization. UPMC had seen a 35 percent increase in its outpatient visits since 1992, with an additional 15 percent increase projected in 1995 alone. Even with these dramatic numbers, this still was not enough to offset the loss of revenue from decreased inpatient utilization; to do this, Romoff argued, the number of outpatient visits would have to "more than double" from a projected 315,177 in 1995 to more than 600,000.[79] This meant that UPMC would have to fight for every patient.[80] The regional response to this problem, just as in Texas, was to manage clear flows of patients between community and tertiary hospitals.

As with many other hospital systems, UPMC's managed care strategy reflected some key commonalities with changes occurring elsewhere in the national health care market. This strategy entailed a focus on controlling the cost of care to maximize revenue and to develop surpluses for further investment; developing partnerships with local insurers to drive their patients to its facilities; building networks of affiliated physician practices; creating satellite clinical locations to deliver a range of medical services to suburban patients; using better information technology to link parts of the diverse health system; and, perhaps most important, building a strong network of community, tertiary, and specialty hospitals as a way to capture as much of the inpatient market share as possible.

Romoff's talk indicated the central tension embedded in the market-based model of the hospital-civic relationship. The changing business of medicine encouraged not-for-profits to draw inspiration from the private sector as a way, they argued, to protect their academic and community service mission. Left unaddressed was how this decision to look to the market to preserve their mission might actually change their broader relationship with the medical metropolis. Instead, just as in Houston, the focus became on building a geographically broad footprint and growing their market share as a way to hedge for the uncertain future.

In Pittsburgh, the era of rapid hospital consolidation started in 1990 with UPMC's acquisition of neighboring Montefiore Hospital for about $150 million in total costs, including a $75 million payment to create the Jewish Health Care Foundation.[81] The acquisition of Montefiore was just the beginning volley in the war for hospital acquisitions. By 1997, major hospital systems in the Pittsburgh market were operating at least four subsidiary firms to build networks among tertiary hospitals, community hospitals, and independent physician practices. UPMC had Tri-State Health System, AHERF had Pyramid Health System, the St. Francis Health System had Health Systems Alliance Inc., and even smaller community hospitals like the Western Pennsylvania Hospital and Mercy Hospital had a short-lived affiliation through Community Health Partners. Each operated under slightly different business models. For example, Tri-State tended to prefer merging with community hospitals and acquiring physician practices, whereas Pyramid tended to view "itself primarily as a managed care company, designed to win contracts with insurers for its five member hospitals and five physician organizations."[82]

Romoff and other UPMC leaders claimed that "in bringing community hospitals into the system, UPMC approached each hospital at three levels— (1) the governing board, (2) hospital management, and (3) medical staff."[83] At the board level, UPMC relied on the same shared governance model that had created MHCD. This model gave it a voice in setting policy without purchasing the facility outright; it helped UPMC to bring partner hospitals into large purchasing contracts; it allowed the medical center to install proprietary health information systems; and it helped to link billing resources across different care provision sites.

To placate the hospital medical staffs, UPMC did not install school of medicine faculty as clinical department chiefs.[84] The line of thinking here was also clear: first, community hospitals were not primarily teaching hospitals so there was no need for academically-oriented service chiefs, and second, under Romoff, UPMC was committed to restructuring the physician-hospital relationship as one where a value-added contribution was the primary measure of a physician's organizational worth. As part of his lecture to the medical faculty, Romoff boldly declared that UPMC would primarily employ scientists and clinicians, rather than the medical professor of the past, who taught, researched, and treated patients.[85]

UPMC also moved to acquire outpatient facilities to help feed its hospitals. In 1996, it purchased Specialists Health Care, a freestanding surgery center in nearby Monroeville, Pennsylvania. This deal was particularly controversial since it was a direct challenge to the Forbes Regional Health System's dominance in the lucrative eastern suburban market of Pittsburgh. As part of this deal, UPMC paid many millions more than the construction value of a similar facility so that it could also acquire staff and a roster of existing patients. The decision to challenge the Forbes Regional Health System led Dr. Arnold Broudy, a faculty member at the school of medicine, to declare, "UPMC is metastasizing into the community. They have money to burn and they are burning it."[86]

This set of decisions allowed UPMC to create stable and geographically diverse revenue sources that would help to offset revenue decline elsewhere in the system as reimbursement rates and patient preferences changed. As Romoff bluntly put it to that crowded lecture hall, "we need to capture that 'quote fortune' [in clinical revenue being generated by community hospitals and outpatient clinics] to bring it back to mother, to backfill, and to pay for the academic mission, to backfill in what is the inevitable decline of what has been the mother lode of our financial structure, which has been the inpatient tower."[87]

Nonhospital Care and the Medical Metropolis

Romoff's and the UPMC executive team's strategy of steady growth through the acquisition of regional community hospitals and outpatient sites appeared to have been validated in 1998 when UPMC's largest rival, the Allegheny Health, Education, and Research Foundation (AHERF), collapsed in a spectacular $1.3 billion dollar bankruptcy.[88] At the heart of AHERF's troubles were efforts by its CEO Sherif Abdelhak to leapfrog UPMC as the region's largest health system by investing in medical markets outside of Western Pennsylvania. In 1987, after being blocked from building a new medical school in Pittsburgh, he stunned the health care community by engineering the purchase of the financially troubled Philadelphia-based Medical College of Pennsylvania.[89] Shortly after that, he responded to inquiries from another Philadelphia-based school, Hahnemann University, about a possible merger. When this deal was completed in 1993, AHERF had control of two medical schools and several hospitals in the Philadelphia market.[90] Abdelhak paid for the health system's expansion with debt financing, and when AHERF was unable to pay back its loans, he was accused of and plead guilty to directing other executives to use charitable funds from the hospital's foundation to "cover operating expenses" shortly before the health system declared bankruptcy.[91]

Even with AHERF's market position diminished, UPMC faced another threat to its control of the regional health care market: the transition of the health insurance giant Blue Cross of Western Pennsylvania into a health care provider. Unlike the Houston market, which was fiercely competitive, in Western Pennsylvania Blue Cross maintained more than 60 percent of the market into the late 1980s.[92] However, that hold was starting to slip. The organization's corporate plan for 1985 contained the following admonition: "For years, Blue Cross has been able to rely on a close, mutually supportive relationship with providers. This relationship can no longer be taken for granted. Hospital relationships, once a source of certainty, are now subject to change. With hospitals themselves now facing enormous competitive pressures, the divergence of interests between the hospitals and Blue Cross will widen."[93] The 1985 annual report was even less sanguine about the new relationship between the provider and area hospitals, arguing, "We will remember 1985 as the year during which the transition of the health care system into an intensely competitive and cost-conscious business became apparent."[94] To offset this, Blue Cross started to diversify its business and created a wide range of for-profit and not-for-profit subsidiaries.[95] By 1991, Blue Cross was now selling life and casualty insurance, started processing out-of-state Medicare claims, and even changed its name to Veritus Inc.[96]

Insurance products were only a first step. In 1993, executives at Veritus were feeling the same pressures to find new ways to control patient flow and clinical revenue. Veritus decided to address this by moving into the role of being both a payer and a provider. It started by attempting to purchase networks of physicians.[97] What was the benefit for a health insurer in buying physician practices and building physician referral networks? They were threefold. First, by owning its own physician practices, Blue Cross could exert pressure on UPMC (Tri-State) or AHERF (Pyramid) to make sure that a range of its products was offered across the full health care spectrum, since these physicians (often primary care physicians) had some ability to direct inpatient referrals. Second, like Tri-State, Veritus had a management service organization business and saw physician practices, either owned or affiliated, as a potential client pool for this service. Third, by either owning or affiliating with large numbers of primary care physicians, the organization gained the leverage it needed to impose cost control measures across the entire regional health care marketplace.

All of these factors came together in 1994 and 1995 when the insurer started to plan for the development of a network of seven primary care centers throughout the suburban Pittsburgh region.[98] The push for primary care centers coincided with yet another organizational change for Blue Cross. In 1996, the state insurance department gave its official approval for the merger of Blue Cross of Western Pennsylvania and Pennsylvania Blue Shield. The newly merged entity was named Highmark.[99] From the start, however, Highmark's foray into physician practice purchase went poorly. In 1994, Blue Cross/Veritus created Alliance Ventures Inc. as a subsidiary corporation to manage its physician practice acquisitions and, after 1996, to also manage its primary care centers. Alliance Ventures was projected to lose money for the first four years of its operation, and Blue Cross/Highmark spent fairly freely, about $23 million, in 1995 and 1996 to acquire physician practices.[100] The problem wasn't simply that Alliance Ventures lost money; it was how much money the company lost. Between 1996 and 1999, it lost $40 million. Moreover, the primary care centers failed to attract enough physician groups to fill them, forcing Highmark to rent out space to nonaffiliated medical businesses, including several UPMC-affiliated physician practices.[101] In the end, Highmark was not only unable to acquire the six hundred physicians it needed to make its physician practice arm profitable, but it also ended up selling back some practices it owned and encouraged stronger physician ownership in others.[102] By 2006, Highmark had also divested itself of the five primary care center locations that it had built.[103]

Both UPMC and AHERF also heavily invested in physician practice purchase as a way to ensure a steady stream of referrals to their hospitals. Contemporary media accounts put the number of physicians that UPMC acquired in the mid to late 1990s between four hundred and six hundred, with an estimated cost of about $25 million. It is also not entirely clear how much UPMC lost on physician practice purchases. In April 1998, a UPMC spokesperson characterized the losses as "not substantial"; however, a *Pittsburgh Post-Gazette* article that ran in November of the same year stated that the University Services Organization, UPMC's physician practice subsidiary, was losing $50 million a year.[104]

There were some valuable lessons from the foray into physician practice purchasing. One lesson was that physicians needed to have an ownership stake in their practices as a way to make sure that they continued to focus on generating revenue after the merger. Another was that more diligence was needed before purchasing physician groups as a way to weed out marginal performers that would lose market share over time anyway. Finally, it became clear to health care executives that massive capital expenditures on satellite faculties were a gamble that could pay off or could quickly become a cash drain if they didn't live up to expectations.

While Highmark was the first in the Pittsburgh market to bridge the payer-provider divide, UPMC's efforts to do the same were, perhaps, more successful and had a lasting effect on the region's health care market. Before UPMC built its own commercial insurance division, both organizations collaborated to provide managed care products for the Medicare and Medicaid markets.[105] In fact, during the mid–1990s, Highmark sold 20 percent of Security Blue, a Medicare HMO, to UPMC.[106] Both organizations also collaborated in traditional commercial markets, including a push for preferred networking status, which allowed Highmark to hold down rates while guaranteeing UPMC patient volume.[107] In fact, after six months of negotiations, a draft proposal for an integrated delivery and financing network (IDFN) was produced by which Highmark was to create an insurance product "centered around UPMC hospitals" and both parties would share the financial risk for the creation, imposition, and marketing of this product.[108] For many in Western Pennsylvania, especially those employed by hospitals and physician practices outside of the UPMC system, a Highmark-UPMC IDFN spelled the end of independent health care in Western Pennsylvania. But less than a year after Highmark and UPMC proposed their IDFN, the project lay in the charred ruins of mutual recrimination and accusations of noncompetitive behavior.

At the same time as the two organizations were working to create an IDFN, UPMC was also laying the groundwork for its own health insurance division. Soon after winning an HMO license from the Commonwealth of Pennsylvania, UPMC created new vendors to provide care within the HMO and across the health spectrum. One of these new vendors was Community Care Behavioral Health Solutions. In the fall of 1997, Community Care won the behavioral health portion of Allegheny County's managed Medicaid contract, which helped to solidify its position as a serious player in this type of business.[109]

However, the rising cost of care in the commercial insurance market continued to strain the relationship between Highmark and UPMC. As the two sides sat down to negotiate a ten-year reimbursement contract, Highmark took to the press to express its concerns that care cost more in UPMC hospitals than it did elsewhere in the region.[110] However, as costs rose and Highmark started to lose more and more money on its commercial underwriting, the insurer responded by raising premiums and pushing for even more discounts from hospitals.[111] Feeling as though it were under attack from its onetime partner, UPMC decided that it needed some leverage in these talks and so it moved to transition its Medicaid HMO into a commercial insurer. This had two effects. First, new insurance plans could offer lower rates to area businesses than Highmark, chipping away at Highmark's market share and forcing it to come to an accommodation on rates with UPMC; second, for companies that left Highmark and chose to insure with UPMC, the insurance plan could steer patients into the health system's hospitals.[112] Romoff claimed that this move was primarily defensive, and he derided the insurance business as "ticket-scalping" rather than being part of the real work of patient care.[113]

One can, however, raise questions about how defensive UPMC's entry into the insurance market was. During his 1995 lecture, Romoff had noted that UPMC would have to move more aggressively into the managed care market if it were to continue to grow and maintain its market share.[114] Only a few years later, in a lecture to the Health Policy Institute in December 1998, Romoff was more aggressive about the payer-provider link when he issued a direct challenge to Highmark about the very nature of the insurance business. Responding to Highmark CEO John Brouse's argument that "independent insurers provide a bridge between employers and providers that protects consumers," Romoff said, "bridges don't protect anyone. They just stay there and convey. They pass our high costs on to you."[115] In October 1999, UPMC Insurance announced that it had won a coverage contract with U.S. Airwoys for about twelve thousand employees. This contract forced the organization to contract with hospitals outside of Tri-State, especially Heritage Valley Health System, and marked a significant expansion outward.[116]

The fight for market share wasn't the only factor complicating the Highmark-UPMC contract negotiations. Another important issue was Highmark's decision to provide a $125 million loan to help fund the creation of the West Penn Allegheny Health System (WPAHS) out of the ashes of the AHERF's 1998 bankruptcy. Not surprisingly, UPMC not only objected to the loan, which, according to health writer Pamela Gaynor, it viewed as "a backdoor through which Highmark could ultimately take control of the merged health system," but it also objected on the grounds that a $125 million investment would give Highmark a powerful incentive to steer business to WPAHS—an argument that would be borne out nearly twenty years later with the creation of the Allegheny Health Network in 2013.[117]

Where were local civic development organizations and local government in the process of building health systems? Both were largely absent. There were good reasons. First, local government had little to do with hospital expansion outside approving the physical expansion of facilities and helping to provide tax-exempt financing. The decision to merge and affiliate rested with the individual boards of directors of each organization and their administrative staffs. Elite civic development organizations were also in a similarly powerless position when it came to shaping health system growth. Even though there may have been overlapping membership between the boards of not-for-profit health systems and the boards of groups like the Greater Houston Partnership or the Allegheny Conference, the job of these organizations was not to get involved in the internal operations of not-for-profits beyond helping to support their growth through venture capital financing or public relations and promotional efforts. This is not to say that these organizations didn't have a stake in their growth—after all, when it came time to market the medical metropolis, the growth of not-for-profit health systems fit the larger narrative of white-collar or service-oriented growth that elite civic development organizations were trying to sell.[118] In the end, market forces, rather than efforts at civic improvement, were the primary driver of health system expansion.

*   *   *

The "coming of the system" in the 1990s seemed to finally represent the triumph of a market-based vision of the hospital-civic relationship. As Jeffrey Romoff noted, these were indeed the years when health care shifted from being a social good to being a commodity. Several goals shaped the health system's behavior, including translating cost savings into capital formation, creating new payment structures either by working with existing insurance companies or creating new insurance products, gaining the necessary geographic coverage to ensure adequate patient flow throughout the system, and integrating vertically. At the same time, the preexisting relationships forged by geography and shared history played a critical role in driving health system behavior. In Houston, the lack of total market dominance of any single actor has made for a more fluid medical marketplace. As a consequence, the shifting winds of competition have led to a range of solutions to manage clinical revenue. Some, like The Methodist Hospital's building of affiliation networks, work in a specific time and place and are unable to endure in a lasting fashion, while others, like the Memorial Hermann merger, have forever recast the entire regional health care market. Drive around Houston today and you will see nodes of competing satellite hospitals in outlying areas, all absorbing more and more suburban patients, while care of poorer, urban patients is increasingly left to the Harris County Hospital District.

In Pittsburgh, the battle for health care supremacy that occurred during the 1990s was unique to this market but still mirrors many national trends. UPMC, like other systems, first gained control of specialized facilities—a move that Detre and Romoff successfully accomplished with the creation of MHCD in the 1980s. Next, they decided to establish referral networks from community hospitals back to the academic medical center. Unlike efforts in Houston to build networks of equal partners, Detre and Romoff preferred acquisitions, allowing them greater control over referral streams and the ability to more directly manage costs at feeder hospitals. Finally, leaders in Pittsburgh realized early that control over the health care payment—which resulted in the creation of new insurance companies or the vast expansion of existing ones—was essential for survival.

In the 1990s and 2000s, large health systems like Memorial Hermann and UPMC grew to become large employers and essential parts of creating a postindustrial identity for Pittsburgh and Houston. This is especially true for Pittsburgh and its relationship with UPMC. From placing its logo on the top of the U.S. Steel Tower to the signs that tout the health system's global reputation that greets visitors at the airport, UPMC has made it clear that it is not only the bedrock of the current postindustrial medical and educational economy but also its future. This clear signal that size is power echoes the rallying cry of large industrial firms in both cities but also raises a new set of issues about how these organizations meet their charitable and community obligations, a subject to which the next chapter will now turn.

Chapter 6

A Charitable Mission or a Profitable Charity?

Redefining the Hospital-Civic Relationship

By the time that UPMC hoisted its logo to the top of the U.S. Steel Tower in 2008, it was clear that the transition from the industrial economy to a postindustrial one was complete.[1] Stories about biotechnology start-ups in both cities continued to appear in the newspaper, and the major health systems created out of the frenzy of mergers and acquisitions increasingly gained visibility as significant employers and engines of urban renaissance. UPMC's decision to make a mark on the city's skyline was far from accidental. The U.S. Steel Tower had been built in the late 1960s as a landmark space to celebrate the return of the steel giant's headquarters from New York City to Pittsburgh. The building, made of COR-TEN steel, was designed to weather to a pleasant rusty patina, and its support columns were filled with liquid to enhance fire protection. At 841 feet, it was, at the time of its construction, the tallest building between New York and Chicago. It was a bold statement of confidence in the future but, by the 2000s, the building had changed ownership several times—with U.S. Steel becoming a tenant in its signature building. Echoing the language of efforts to expand specialty medicine, Jeffrey Romoff claimed that the decision to lease space in the iconic building was "in keeping with our goal of becoming the new export engine for this region." Romoff also noted how it would allow UPMC to "create a corridor for economic renaissance stretching from Oakland and to downtown," referencing ongoing efforts to redevelop the adjacent Lower Hill neighborhood.[2]

Not all Pittsburghers celebrated UPMC's bold claim on the city's future. Over the previous decade, as not-for-profit health systems emulated the behavior of their for-profit competitors, as specialty medicine emerged as a business, and as biotechnology and the persistent talk of innovation and disruption laid bare the economic and social divides in the medical metropolis, concerns about UPMC's growth were rarely far from the surface. Moreover, by the late twentieth and early twenty-first centuries, concerns about working conditions in UPMC's hospitals, questions about the level of its contribution to communities relative to its size, and fear of its growing political and economic influence were increasingly articulated by elected officials and ordinary citizens.

These charges created a line of attack alleging that health systems put profit before people and behaved more like for-profit corporations than not-for-profit health care institutions. During the 1980s and 1990s, elected officials like Mayor Sophie Masloff used this popular dissatisfaction with the changing business of medicine to attempt to reset the balance of power in the hospital-civic relationship by lobbying, threatening, cajoling, and flattering UPMC and other large health systems to make additional monetary contributions to the city's nearly empty coffers. By the mid-2000s, a revitalized labor movement was offering its own critique of not-for-profit health care institutions and raising even more questions about how to understand the balance between revenue and responsibility.

In Houston, concerns about the shifting balance of power in the hospital-civic relationship also emerged. While elected officials in Pittsburgh pressed for financial contributions from not-for-profit health care institutions, their counterparts in Texas, like state attorney general Jim Mattox, urged these institutions to provide more charity care to low-income Texans. This fight was legally, if not always politically, settled in the middle of the 1990s. This is not to imply that not-for-profit health care institutions had lost all sense of the obligations that justified their not-for-profit status, but the question of how to balance the need to generate revenue to remain competitive and the ability to redirect that revenue to civic betterment appeared, to many, to have come down decidedly on the side of capitalism, and this sparked a debate that has helped to redefine the terms of the hospital-civic relationship up to the present.

The Methodist Hospital and the Politics of Charity Care

Understanding how to value the contribution of not-for-profits is a contested area in the modern medical metropolis. Employment and revenue

Figure 11. The decision by UPMC in 2008 to affix its letters on the side of the U.S. Steel building marked a visible confirmation of the transformation between the industrial economy and the postindustrial service economy in Pittsburgh.

Photograph by the author.

numbers are one way to measure economic impact.[3] The growing size of
health systems created by either affiliation networks or acquisitions provides another. Harder to value are the other types of tangible and intangible
benefits to the community (supporting community events, scholarship
contributions, spin-off businesses, etc.) that these large health care not-for-
profits return.

One way to do this is by attempting to put a dollar figure on the amount
of charity care (typically understood as free or reduced-cost care) that a
specific not-for-profit health care institution provides. Not-for-profit hospitals have long tried to minimize the amount of charity care they provided,
arguing that too much would threaten bottom lines and make it difficult
to have the resources they needed to provide for paying patients, as the
example with Edward Litchfield in the early 1960s showed.[4] By the 1980s,
as costs continued to rise and access to care continued to decrease, not-for-
profit hospitals worried they would be forced to accept more low-income
patients to make up for the inability of public hospitals to fully address the
needs of this patient population. Medicaid's inability to cover the costs of
indigent care fully exacerbated these fears—and Texas Medicaid was particularly parsimonious. For example, a 1989 report noted that "Medicaid is
the largest single source of federal money for the State, bringing in more
than $1.1 billion in 1987; yet, in per capita federal spending on Medicaid,
Texas ranks the lowest of all the states at $114.50."[5] Even within the state,
Medicaid dollars were not distributed evenly. Urban, rural, and public general hospitals often saw more Medicaid patients than hospitals located in
affluent suburbs or those that catered to a wealthier clientele. To address
this disparity, the federal government created disproportionate share hospital (DSH) payments as part of the Omnibus Budget Reconciliation Act of
1981. Texas implemented the DSH program in 1986, but according to the
General Accounting Office, it tended to privilege public hospitals over voluntary, not-for-profit hospitals.[6]

Questions about cost and appropriate levels of service also appeared
around emergency medical care. In 1986, the Emergency Medical Treatment and Active Labor Act, or EMTALA, was quietly slipped into a Budget
Reconciliation Act. EMTALA came on the heels of several high-profile stories of not-for-profit hospitals either dumping patients that could not pay
their bills on public hospitals or turning away potentially indigent patients
seeking emergency care. This new law mandated that hospitals that accept
Medicare funds must properly screen patients to determine if an emergency

situation existed, stabilize them before transfer, and assist women in labor. What EMTALA did not provide for were additional funds to cover the cost of this mandate.[7]

AIDS care presented another area of concern.[8] By 1984, the city had "the sixth highest number of confirmed Acquired Immune Deficiency Syndrome cases in the nation."[9] The uncertainty in the early 1980s about how the disease was transmitted; the potentially uncontrolled cost of AIDS care, especially as private insurers dropped AIDS patients; and homophobia led most area not-for-profits to refuse to treat AIDS patients.[10] In fact, in 1986, The Methodist Hospital's Larry Mathis warned readers of the *TMC News* that "right now it looks like, if the AIDS problem keeps on its current track, it could be even greater than cardiovascular disease in terms of cost to the people of this country in consumption of health care resources. So it's hard to tell what the situation is going to be even three, four, five years down the line."[11] One of the few places AIDS patients could seek treatment in Houston in the mid-1980s was M. D. Anderson. The institution's president, Dr. Charles LeMaistre, used the link between the disease and a rare form of cancer, Kaposi's sarcoma, to justify accepting AIDS patients, knowing that the city was facing a health crisis. The cost of treating these patients was always a concern and, by 1985, Anderson was working to find a way to reduce its exposure by entering into partnership with the for-profit hospital firm American Medical International (AMI) to build a short-lived, and controversial, for-profit AIDS hospital known as the Southwest Institute for Immunological Disorders, which operated between 1986 and 1987.[12] M. D. Anderson and AMI's partnership was a unique way to attempt to blend profit and medical necessity. While the idea of monetizing AIDS never caught on, it did show how a market mentality had infused not-for-profit health care at all levels.

On the other side of the market from indigent AIDS patients were well-insured affluent and upper-middle-class patients. Building specialty care lines and innovative payment programs like CardioVascular Care Providers was one way that individual hospitals and not-for-profits like the Methodist Hospital, the Texas Heart Institute, and UPMC could capture this revenue. Another way was by competing based on offering a luxury hospital experience. While this move into luxury health care might have made sense from a business perspective, it looked problematic when, at the same time, not-for-profit hospitals were complaining about the cost of providing charity care to low-income Houstonians. This practice raised questions about whether these hospitals had strayed from their charitable mission and were still worthy of their not-for-profit status.[13]

Downscaling Upscale: Luxury and Charity
at The Methodist Hospital

A few weeks before the 1985 Thanksgiving holiday, KHOU-TV ran the first of a four-part news story that helped to redefine the relationship between nonprofit hospitals and communities across the country.[14] The story started as an exposé and alleged that Methodist failed to provide enough charity care to justify its tax-exempt status. Methodist was a tempting target for investigation. Throughout the 1970s, the hospital that was built on Michael DeBakey's success with cardiovascular surgery emerged as one of the most affluent hospitals in the Houston region. In addition to the influx of patient care revenue, the generosity of extremely wealthy donors and board members allowed the hospital to upgrade its physical plant to appeal to an affluent customer base by offering specialty services in a luxury environment.

The Fondren and Brown Cardiovascular and Orthopedic Research Centers, built with money from Ella Fondren, the wife of Humble Oil cofounder Walter Fondren, and construction and oil services magnate George Brown is an example.[15] Not only did this center help to make The Methodist Hospital a leader in these high-value areas of medical research and care delivery, but at the top of the new building were rooms that helped to pioneer a new model of medicine for Houston—the luxury hospital room, catering to the high-end patient who desired comfort and privacy. Today, the floor is a favorite of celebrities such as former president George H. W. Bush because of the tight security it offers and the luxury it provides.[16]

Class segmentation of the American health care system was nothing new; one historian equates the hospital of the 1920s to "a multi-class hotel or ship offering different facilities for different prices."[17] However, the emergence of hyper-luxury hospital suites in the 1980s and 1990s, while harkening back to the era of fierce competition that defined the first decades of the modern hospital, were part of a new amenities arms race that was fueled by the need to attract private-pay and well-insured patients to offset the rise of managed care products—a need that arose as an unintended consequence of the inability of the market model to keep pace with the ability of many Americans to pay for their increasingly specialized health care.[18]

What did these high-end customers get for the hundreds or thousands of dollars they paid over standard rates? A 1990s-era brochure for Hermann Hospital's exclusive 5 West Jones floor offers a glimpse. The first photo in the brochure is a patient having her pulse taken in bed—with assorted pastries and coffee in a silver pot in the foreground of the photo. The narrative opens, "Established in the Hermann Hospital's tradition of excellence in patient care, 5 West Jones is designed to offer high quality medical and nursing care while providing added amenities for patients who desire and are willing to pay for them." On top of the personalized care, patients could expect "a host of hotel-style amenities including: daily delivery of the *Wall Street Journal, USA Today,* and other major newspapers, fax and Xerox services, Desks for conducting business, Tea service with freshly baked cookies, An expanded menu, Patient/family activity room equipped with educational and leisure materials, board games and a television." The floor featured "one, three, and five room suite combinations featuring hardwood floors, silk Chinese rugs, solid cherry furniture, crystal lamps and refrigerators." Massage services, terry cloth robes, and beauty services were "available upon request and for an extra charge." Special admitting criteria were needed to experience 5 West Jones. For example, patients needed to demonstrate that they were properly insured or, if they were international patients, had sufficient funds to cover admission.[19] This last part was not unusual, since high-end international patients typically covered the anticipated cost of care by way of a cash deposit. The success of high-end floors like 5 West Jones and Fondren 12 reaffirmed the idea that there was money to be made by offering a customer-focused experience to affluent patients. Under the leadership of Larry Mathis, a critical innovation was to move scaled-back versions of high-end services downstream to attract upper-middle-class patients—in effect, downscaling upscale.

One of the first ways that Mathis did this was to continue existing efforts by the hospital to become a leader in promoting preventative care. Disease prevention and management had been a critical part of DeBakey's thinking behind the regional medical programs and their focus on heart disease, cancer, and stroke.[20] However, under this model, prevention and management were emphasized as a way to lead to better, and hopefully less costly, health outcomes. Methodist embraced the idea that preventative care and disease management could save money by avoiding costly procedures like surgical intervention, but hospital leaders like Mathis and his predecessor Ted Bowen also understood that there was a way to monetize the process of disease prevention by creating a range of subsidiary businesses that focused on packaging the experience of healthy living for an active, and affluent, clientele.[21] Many of these services were offered in the hospital's Total Health Care Center, located in the Scurlock Tower across Fannin Street from the hospital's main campus. This building was conveniently outside of the TMC boundaries and thus not subject to deed restrictions governing the operations of for-profit businesses.[22]

The building's goal was to create a space that combined services such as outpatient and physician care with ancillary services like hotel space near the hospital for patient's families. Ground was broken on the building in December 1977. By the early 1980s, it included high-end amenities like a health club, a Marriott hotel, and a "heart-smart" restaurant named Chez Eddy, after Eddy Scurlock, a prominent Houston oilman, hospital trustee, and financial backer of the Total Health Care Center. Preventative services were provided at the Sid W. Richardson Center for Preventive Medicine, funded by a $1.456 million grant from the late oilman's foundation.[23] A 1981 review of Chez Eddy in the *Houston Business Journal* titled "Chez Eddy: A Hearty Dose of First-Class Hospital Food" described the dining experience in the following fashion:

> The founding principle at Chez Eddy, a French and very gourmet restaurant in Scurlock Tower is the firm conviction that the way to man's heart is through his stomach. What else could be expected when the restaurant is an integral part of Methodist Hospital's Institute for Preventative Medicine? Cholesterol-laden cream and butter have been banished from the kitchen and table salt all but shipped back to Siberia, and in one recipe calling for a dozen eggs only one will be the real thing. Lest this sound too dismal, evoking gloomy visions of triglycerides and polyunsaturates, reassurance is certainly in order. Think for a minute: would the people who brought you terrific open-heart surgery ask you to face the like of low-cal mayonnaise? Certainly not. Those who live for butterfat will find the kitchen has quite a knack for transubstantiation. Replacing this and decreasing that is accomplished so skillfully the diner is unlikely to notice, much less fell [*sic*] martyred.[24]

The review went on to describe the "smooth oak accents" and "salmon linens" which made up the décor, and the topflight waitstaff who expertly helped with wine pairing and other services.[25] How much revenue these businesses brought in is not clear. However, they cemented a perception of The Methodist Hospital as a brand, and of preventative services as a critical component that helped to build a reputation for the institution and the physicians affiliated with it in an increasingly crowded marketplace. Healthy lifestyle branding went beyond creating physical spaces like the Total Health Care Center and also seeped into popular culture. In 1984, DeBakey and his surgical colleague Dr. Antonio Gotto were able to add a line to their curriculum vitae that they (along with two others) were now cookbook authors. In 1991, now with Gotto as the primary author, the book was briefly retitled *The Chez Eddy Living Heart Cookbook*.[26]

Mathis also focused on providing all patients with high levels of customer service as a way to differentiate The Methodist Hospital. Drawing from Scandinavian Airlines, Methodist taught employees to treat each patient interaction as a "moment of truth" in which nothing less than the entire reputation of the hospital was on the line. Describing the philosophy for the Texas attorney general's office, Mathis claimed, "When a nurse comes up to the bedside and takes a patient's hand, that's a moment of truth; and if the transaction is a good one, then the patient will go away with a feeling that this is some person, and therefore, an institution that cares for them and serves them well."[27] Mathis and his team also started to offer other downscaled luxury amenities, including valet parking and concierge service, with the staff assigned to these duties euphemistically termed "luggage assistance personnel" by the hospital.[28] As Mark Wallace, the senior vice president for the patient services division at Methodist told the *Houston Business Journal* in 1985, "Patients go to Methodist Hospital not because it's a good hospital, but because of basic human services. . . . We're doing this from the business point of view that it pays to enhance your services because they can be the deciding factor for the patient." Wallace continued, "The patient is paying for everything we do, but there is no quantifiable way of measuring dollar-wise how this had really helped us. We're relying on word of mouth."[29]

A key question that the leadership team at Methodist had to address was how to justify the cost of these new amenities and services at a time when private health care costs were rising, and corporations were rapidly transitioning away from traditional indemnity insurance to managed care. Methodist's solution was simple. Instead of competing primarily on volume, they decided to target those who retained the much more lucrative indemnity insurance. The advantages of refusing most managed care products were clear—when negotiating with traditional indemnity insurers, the hospital and physicians had more flexibility over reimbursement rates and covered services. This meant that Methodist could offer the types of high-end services demanded by affluent patients with expensive and extensive insurance coverage without much fear of losing money.[30] In 1985, the *Houston Chronicle* reported that Methodist, over the course of the prior year, had earned a surplus of $47 million. By 1987, the hospital reported "$272.5 million in cash and savings."[31] While all of these decisions might have been good business, they contributed to a public perception that "Methodist and its high-powered board" were "running a country club-style hospital for the rich while profiting from tax exemptions reserved for charitable organizations."[32]

Concern over not-for-profit health care institutions abusing charitable protections was at the tip of everybody's tongue, thanks to a settlement negotiated by Attorney General Jim Mattox to a ballooning scandal at Hermann Hospital and the Hermann Estate Trust. This scandal involved the misappropriation of funds and eventually led to the criminal conviction of the hospital's executive director and civil liability for two Hermann Estate trustees.[33] But its impact went beyond this fairly straightforward wrongdoing. Over the course of a very public discussion of its lurid details, the cozy relationship among board members, their employers, and the hospital became visible, and it revealed an ugly web of family connections and overlapping business interests that seemed to have enriched themselves at the expense of low-income Houstonians.[34] While there was no hint of the same self-dealing at Methodist, it, too, had plenty of overlapping connections between its board and its business relationships, including a very close relationship to the major Houston law firm of Vinson and Elkins, in which partners held seats on the hospital's board while the firm provided legal work for the hospital.[35] Initially, Mattox was interested in investigating this practice, but concerns over private enrichment were quickly forgotten when it became clear that these arrangements were common throughout the medical center. Mattox then turned his attention to the allegation raised by KHOU—that the hospital had failed to provide sufficient charity care.

Jim Mattox saw the KHOU allegations as a political opportunity. Mattox was born in Dallas in 1943 to a waitress and a union sheet-metal worker. After his father abandoned his family and his mother's death at the relatively young age of fifty-two, he was forced to care for his younger siblings while putting himself through law school. Before being elected attorney general, Mattox served in the Texas legislature and the United States Congress. While in office, he cultivated a reputation as a fierce populist. Once called a "junkyard dog" by a political opponent, Mattox seized on this label, claiming, according to the *Chronicle*, that "he would act like one to protect the children, the elderly, and other powerless Texans."[36] Once elected attorney general, he took on entrenched interest groups like big oil and big agriculture. By the time that the KHOU report broke, Mattox had already built a reputation as a crusader and the Hermann scandal showed him that he could also buoy his reputation by going after "big medicine."

Despite Mattox's aggressive posturing, when the KHOU report first ran in November 1985, Texas law did not require not-for-profit hospitals to provide a specific percentage of indigent care to qualify for a tax exemption. Unlike religious organizations or universities, not-for-profit hospitals have never been recognized as a separate category of public charity by the U.S. tax code.[37] Traditionally, not-for-profit hospitals qualified for their tax exemptions under the presumption that they existed to serve a charitable mission. Prior to 1969, federal tax exemption for not-for-profit hospitals was bound by a narrow interpretation of "charity" that used direct patient care as the standard for how hospital's tax exemptions should be judged. In the wake of the enactment of Medicare and Medicaid, this metric seemed outmoded and failed to capture the full range of benefits that hospitals provided to the communities. In loosening how the contribution of not-for-profit hospitals was measured, the IRS claimed that "the promotion of health, like the relief of poverty and the advancement of education and religion . . . is deemed beneficial to the community as a whole."[38] This new interpretation, known today as the community benefit standard, assumed that Medicare and Medicaid would replace not-for-profit-hospital-provided charity care.[39] Looser federal tax exemption standards didn't necessarily percolate down to the local and the state levels, where separate taxing bodies retained their ability to determine their own criteria that not-for-profit hospitals needed to meet to be exempt from a variety of property, sales, and use taxes.

This resulted in uneven attempts to clarify what, exactly, was a community benefit. One of the most active occurred in Pennsylvania, where the debate over the meaning of "a purely public charity" resulted in a formula for determining charitable contribution known as the HUP test, after the organization, the Hospital Utilization Project, that had spurred the legal action. The HUP test will be discussed in more detail later, since it has not been widely applied outside of Pennsylvania. In Texas, the critical legal precedent for helping to shape the thinking of elected officials like Mattox about the contribution of hospitals like Methodist came from a case in Utah called *Utah County v. Intermountain Health Care Inc.*[40] This lack of clarity meant that issues of how to measure a community benefit were dealt with on an ad hoc basis.

The day after the first KHOU report, Pete Brewton at the *Houston Post* ran an article that he pieced together from "the hospital's income tax returns and statements by hospital officials," which showed that, in 1983, Methodist had returned a "profit" of $27 million and only spent $1 million on charity care. Brewton then contacted the Charitable Trust Division at the attorney general's office for comment. This inquiry was the first hint in the press that the state of Texas might be interested in further investigating Methodist.[41] Later that day, Brewton also made a formal request in writing to Methodist for three years of financial records.[42] A refusal to release the hospital's financial records by Bishop Ben Oliphant only added fuel to the speculations that the allegations against the hospital had merit.

The Methodist Hospital Tries to Redefine Charity in the Medical Metropolis

On November 25, 1985, Larry Mathis and A. Frank Smith Jr., the chairman of the hospital's Board of Trustees, agreed to meet with Jim Mattox to discuss the situation.[43] The following Friday, Methodist's board met and prepared a statement that laid out the basic strategy that the hospital employed throughout the debate over charity care. Important points included an assertion that the hospital was not founded as a charitable hospital, thus it was not required to provide free care, and that "profits" were not that at all—rather, they were surpluses, which by the very nature of Methodist's nonprofit organization were to be reinvested in the hospital to provide financial stability and to fuel further growth. Methodist officials truly believed that using direct patient care was a misleading and highly inappropriate measure of a not-for-profit hospital's commitment to its community.[44]

In front of a friendly audience at the United Methodist Church's Texas Annual Conference, Mathis claimed that the hospital provided "$16 million in unpaid free service in 1985" and "that the hospital is conducted ethically, in full compliance with the law and with the great Christian spirit you would expect from this conference."[45] To demonstrate this commitment, each delegate was handed a report that explained the hospital's position on its charity care obligations in more detail. "In response to the media's misleading effort to equate a hospital having a charitable, non-profit charter with an obligation to provide free care to indigents," the report argued, "Methodist has stated that it is not and never has been a 'free care, charity hospital.'" The report also shed more light on the $16 million figure provided by Mathis. Only $2 million was spent by the hospital on "free care"—the remaining $14 million was for discounted care and uncollectible accounts.[46] The report illustrated a critical tension. With no formal definition of charity care, figures could vary widely. Methodist used a broad definition of charity care that included the value of care provided for free to those unable to pay, coming to a figure of $100 million in 1989 alone.[47] Recognizing that the fight was resulting in adverse publicity, the hospital took a page from corporate America and hired a public relations firm, Burson-Marsteller, which had represented Johnson and Johnson during the Tylenol poisoning case in 1982 and, perhaps more ominously, also represented Union Carbide after the 1984 Bhopal gas disaster, to manage the bad press.[48]

A potential compromise emerged in July 1988 when Mattox created the Task Force to Study Not-for-Profit Hospitals and Unsponsored Charity Care in Texas. The task force was co-chaired by two hospital CEOs from Dallas and included elected officials, academics, attorneys, and representatives from public and private not-for-profit hospitals throughout the state. The task force not only proposed a reasonably broad definition of charity care that attempted to balance issues of unpaid bills, or bad debts, with Medicaid reimbursements, and even to balance the genuine inability of some Texans to pay their hospital bills with the needs of the state of Texas and local communities for free or reduced care for their residents. The state's "miserly Medicaid program" drew particular criticism from the task force.[49] While there was general agreement with the main thrust of the task force's recommendations, various regions did offer their own suggestions. The Houston area was part of "Region Four," which also took in the University of Texas Medical Branch at Galveston. Methodist was represented by Jim Henderson, who was a senior vice president and one of Larry Mathis's close confidants. This region did have some important differences with the overall recommendations. A central one was the desire to allow more flexibility for cost overruns for patients who did not meet the task force's definition of medical indigence. This included care for patients who found themselves unable to pay for a higher-than-expected hospital bill, even if they were not means-tested prior to a procedure, or they were given an emergency procedure and later found unable to pay, thus allowing hospitals to write off what could be classified as "bad debt" (which was not covered under the main task force's definition) as charity care. Another was a warning against counting "non-revenue charitable servies that are quantifiable" services provided "without charges to patients and without expectations of payment" as uncompensated charity care.[50] As the copies of the report were distributed to hospitals around the state, many not-for profit hospitals, including Methodist, took it as a victory, since it provided much more leeway (including not setting a care threshold) than the suggestion by Mattox's office that the state apply the *Intermountain* test in Texas.[51] In the long term, the failure of the task force to satisfy both sides would be its undoing. Rather than providing a compromise, it only temporarily held Mattox back from continuing his attacks on the not-for-profit hospital sector.

Shortly after the task force issued its final report, Ann Kitchen, the assistant attorney general, who was now leading the Methodist investigation, sent a letter to Jim Henderson asking for a copy of the hospital's mission statement. In the letter, Kitchen claimed that the attorney general's office was interested in resetting its relationship with the hospital.[52] Kitchen's pleas for a new relationship didn't mean that Mattox was planning to leave Methodist alone; for the next several months, the attorney general's office kept pushing the hospital to provide more information about how much charity care it really provided. Part of what was driving the continued pressure was the fact that Mattox was locked in a bitter primary campaign for the Democratic nomination for governor. In April, Mattox lost the primary and became what Mathis later called "a lame-duck Attorney General. An angry, lame-duck Attorney General."[53]

On June 22, 1990, Mattox hosted a meeting between representatives from Methodist, including John Bookout, then the CEO of Shell Oil and the new chairman of Methodist's board, Mathis, and Bishop Oliphant. According to Mathis, Mattox stood at the head of a long conference table, squarely between the U.S. flag and the Texas state flag, and demanded that the hospital start immediately allocating 10 percent of its gross revenue to charity care. Furthermore, Mathis claimed, Mattox specifically said that medical education and research costs could not be counted in this 10 percent figure. Finally, Mattox let the men know that Methodist, because of its size and stature, was to be made an example.[54] Despite the posturing during the meeting, it became clear that Mattox was still reluctant to file a formal lawsuit and instead fully intended to use the power of the press to bend Methodist's actions to his will.

Where to draw the line about what was charity care and what was bad debt had real financial ramifications. For example, Methodist claimed that under the task force's definition of charity care, it had provided $48 million of charity care in 1988. It projected that number would rise to nearly $70 million in 1990. At the heart of this argument was a cost disparity of seventeen cents per dollar between what another federal program for the aged, Medicare, reimbursed, and what Methodist spent on these patients. Mathis counted Medicare shortfalls as charity care. However, Mattox and Kitchen claimed that, since Medicare was not needs based, Methodist was simply out of luck and shouldn't get credit for providing charity care for spending more than they were paid for a program not specifically designed to provide for indigent patients.[55]

In July 1990, Methodist's Policy Council, the organization's strategic-planning body, issued a policy paper spelling out the hospital's position as it related to Mattox's claims. First, the Policy Council reiterated Mathis's contention that Methodist was not founded as a charity hospital. Thus, while it had no formal responsibility to care for indigent Houstonians, the directors recognized that "all non-profit organizations . . . receive significant benefit from the government in the form of tax exemptions" and therefore had an obligation to serve the community in the manner in which it was chartered, which in the case of Methodist, the board believed, was by providing general patient care, education experience for medical residents, and cutting edge medical research.[56] The position paper stated:

> The Methodist Hospital believes that all of its activities are part of fulfilling its Charter to operate as a private, non-profit hospital. . . .
> Those activities include everything from the clinical researcher who investigates sleep disorders in infants, to the nurse who monitors the condition of a patient in the intensive care unit; from being one of only twelve hospitals in the nation to participate in the pioneering studies that conclusively linked cholesterol with diet, to being one the leading hospitals in coronary artery bypass surgeries and organ

transplants of all kinds. From admission to discharge, Methodist endeavors to fulfill its mission to provide the best care and service anywhere.[57]

The paper then went on to slam Mattox, claiming that he had backed away from recommendations of his own task force and created his own new definition of charity care. As a final barb, Methodist suggested that the work of the task force continue so they could work cooperatively to "seek meaningful solutions supported by everybody involved in the health care issue" that would "address the areas of access, cost, and quality of health care for *all* Texans."[58] To make sure that Mattox got the message, Mathis provided copies to the *Houston Post* and *Chronicle* and did a round of interviews for all of the major Houston TV stations.[59]

On November 26, just as he was leaving office, Mattox filed suit against The Methodist Hospital and its directors for failure to provide enough charity care to merit its state tax exemption. In his statement to the media, Mattox claimed: "A wealthy, non-profit hospital like Methodist—particularly in light of the hospital's stated charitable purpose in its charter—must do more if it continues to receive the benefits of tax exemption."[60] While Mattox seemed restrained in the pages of the *Houston Post*, that same day his populist streak showed through in an interview with Ruth SoRelle from the *Houston Chronicle*. "Methodist might as well hang out a sign on the front door that says poor people are not welcome here unless they happen to have insurance or are on some kind of government program," he said.[61] Faced with a lawsuit they didn't want, and a lame-duck adversary who had the luxury of taking shots on his way out the door, how did the Methodist directors respond? At first, they bided their time to see how the new attorney general, Dan Morales, would respond. When it became clear that Morales intended to continue the lawsuit, Methodist began to hit back.

For every story the attorney general's office presented of someone denied admission, the hospital could present a countervailing story about the highly technical and specialized care that it provided its patients.[62] Beyond appealing to heartstrings, Mathis and the board decided to stand on principle. They claimed repeatedly that their mission was clear—indigent care was not their responsibility. Moreover, Mathis and the board pointed out that Methodist was located only a stone's throw from both a public hospital (Ben Taub) and a private hospital (Hermann) that were founded with an explicit mission to care for poor Houstonians. Hospital officials also worked to cast the lawsuit as an attempt by the state of Texas to make up for Medicaid shortfalls on the cheap.[63]

Mathis's most controversial statement came in November 1992 while he was being deposed by the attorney general's office. Early in the deposition, Ann Kitchen attempted to back Mathis into a corner by making the point that Methodist appeared to argue that any care (even if it was paid for in the fee-for-service model) seemed to be considered charitable by the hospital. Mathis was undeterred and responded to her in the affirmative, saying, "it is my view that the provision of medical care to the sick and injured people is a charitable purpose that is correct." Kitchen then proceeded to test this idea by bringing up Methodist's relationship to preventative care, alluding to the Institute for Preventative Medicine and the Total Health Care Center, where Chez Eddy was located:

Q: What about the provision of preventative care to those who aren't sick or injured, is that charitable.

A: I believe that is a charitable purpose, one of many charitable purposes.

Q: And that would be so regardless of the income level or socioeconomic status of those provided the care; is that right?

A: I'm not sure what you—would you rephrase the question?

Q: Sure. Taking what you just said, that is, the provision of medical care to the sick and injured as well as providing preventative care is a charitable purpose, that holds true regardless of the income level of those provided that care in your view; is that correct?

A: In my view, it is a charitable purpose to provide care to a rich man or a poor man.

Q: Is one more charitable than another in your view?

A: Not in my view.[64]

It is easy to argue that Methodist was protecting its bottom line at the expense of the community, but in an editorial supporting Methodist's position, Episcopal bishop Maurice Benitez reminded readers that charity care was not really free care. "Every non-profit hospital, even while offering some charitable care to indigents, has a limitation on the amount that can be offered," claimed Benitez, "for the simple reason that virtually the only source of income the hospital has is that which private patients (or insurance companies) pay for their health care. In other words, every dollar in charitable care to the indigent that a hospital offers is a subsidy charged against the paying patients of the hospital."[65] To break the stalemate, both sides agreed to mediation, which ultimately failed.[66]

Had the Methodist story ended when all the parties walked out of the courtroom, then the national outcome for not-for-profit hospitals might have been very different. The Methodist case represented an anomaly—a hospital that fought the system and won. The biggest change that the case sparked was that it finally encouraged the state legislature to address the issue of hospital tax exemption and charity care. In February of 1993, one state senator and one state representative introduced two different bills designed to force nonprofit hospitals to increase the amount of charity care they provided. Representative Glen Maxey claimed that his bill, while "not a direct result of the Methodist suit," was nonetheless informed by the hospital's "arrogant" and "offensive" attitude. In the same *Houston Chronicle* article where Maxey explained his bill, the writer noted that he called the hospital "a shining example' of what happens when non-profit hospitals are not held publicly accountable for their tax breaks."[67]

In June 1993, Texas became the first state to require hospitals to provide a state-mandated level of charity care. In the final bill signed by the governor, Texas not-for-profit hospitals were given a test for exemption that required them to meet one of three standards: providing charity care or Medicaid shortfalls equal to 5 percent of "net patient revenues," with Medicaid shortfalls equaling 3 percent of this total 5 percent; providing charity care and Medicaid shortfalls equal to the "tax-exempt benefits, excluding federal income tax"; or "charity care and Medicaid shortfalls must equal an amount that is 'reasonable in relation to community needs.'"[68] The law went on to define who qualified as a charity patient and what types of care counted (for example, the 1993 law did not allow hospitals to claim bad debts; this was amended in 1995).[69] Shortly after the passage of the new law, Methodist and "the tax man" finally made peace.[70] Since the summary judgment, Morales's office had been threatening to appeal. As part of a settlement between the two parties, Methodist acknowledged it was bound by the new law and that it would provide an endowment funded by a onetime gift of $5 million. The hospital also donated $250,000 to the Harris County Hospital District's foundation "to help expand indigent-care programs."[71] Reflecting on the case in later years, Mathis claimed that the case taught him "the dragon slayers don't go after the small dragons, they want the big guys. If they can kill the largest dragon in the forest, they can easily mop up the little ones."[72]

What the Methodist case reveals are some of the limits of activists and elected officials to shape outcomes in the medical metropolis. Even when the locational-asset model was ascendant, there was always tension between communities and not-for-profits over how much charity care to provide as a reflection of their commitment to community health. But the decision by Mathis and Methodist to try to redefine charity as the broader contributions of patient care and medical education rather than an explicit amount of service to the poor shows how a more market-based vision of the hospital-civic relationship encouraged not-for-profit hospitals to push back against requests, often grounded in an older language of contribution and obligation, that they felt threatened their bottom line. Not all hospitals in the medical metropolis had the financial resources of The Methodist Hospital, or the support of their administrators and boards of trustees to challenge requests by state and local government that they thought were unduly coercive or unfairly affected their competitive position. For those that did, there were real financial consequences, as the story of UPMC and the fight over payments-in-lieu-of-taxes will show.

PILOTs, UPMC, and Not-for-Profit "Taxation" in Pittsburgh

Around the same time that the fight in Texas over charity care was under way, hospitals in Pittsburgh were gearing up for their own fight over tax exemption. Western Pennsylvania had numerous hospitals of all shapes and sizes (even if they were rapidly being merged into large health systems), but Allegheny County lacked a public hospital. This meant that there was not the same level of concern about how much charity care not-for-profit hospitals provided as there was in Houston. Instead, in Pittsburgh, the fight over how hospitals would contribute to the economy of the medical metropolis was deeply tied to the consequences of postindustrialism. As the region's population declined and as significant employers left, communities across the region were facing significant budget shortfalls. The growing size and wealth of health care not-for-profits, especially when combined with the fact that they were significant property holders, raised questions about if they had a special obligation to help offset the shrinking municipal revenue streams that were a consequence of decades of for-profit industry rusting away. The solution that emerged was multiyear payments-in-lieu-of-taxes, or PILOTs, which many not-for-profit hospitals in the region agreed to pay as a way to fend off further challenges.

While most contemporary media accounts of PILOTs begin in 1985, to understand fully the roots of the confrontation over these payments, it is essential to go back to 1968, when municipal authorities in Pittsburgh first attempted to force not-for-profit enterprises (including area hospitals) to pay additional fees.[73] In 1968, the city of Pittsburgh faced two intersecting problems—a budget shortfall for fiscal year 1969 and lack of taxable property from which to generate revenue. In fact, according to local press accounts, nearly half of the real property in the city was exempt from taxation. Thus, the same churches, universities, and hospitals that had brought migrants to the city and provided a solid foundation for its growth now appeared to be undermining its fiscal future.[74] The biggest increase in tax-exempt properties was in the city's cultural and educational center of Oakland, "reflecting," according to the *Pittsburgh Post-Gazette*, "the University of Pittsburgh's and the medical center's expansion programs." However, the newspaper was quick to note that, even if not-for-profit tax exemptions were simply eliminated, returning these properties to the tax rolls would not, in the words of the City Planning Department, be a "panacea . . . to improving real estate returns and solving the City's revenue problems," since many were under-assessed and their return would only provide about "2.1 million more a year" in additional revenue.[75]

Pittsburgh mayor Joseph Barr's solution to the budget gap was deceptively simple—he knew he could not mount a frontal attack on the tax-exempt status of the city's powerful not-for-profit institutions. Instead, why not ask them to contribute a small amount of their overall revenue as a reflection of their charitable roots and to demonstrate their civic pride? The formula Barr created to structure their contributions was a 6-mill tax on gross receipts. This tax was estimated to provide up to $2.25 million in additional revenue annually, which, while only slightly more than returning tax exempt property to the tax rolls, would still have been enough to close the budget gap. Detractors quickly dubbed this idea the "sick tax."[76]

The "sick tax" reflected both the changed political realities in Pittsburgh and the growing willingness of these actors to challenge actions that they felt were not in their best interests. Instead of agreeing to accept Barr's tax, a number of not-for-profits, including the Hospital Council of Western

Pennsylvania, the University of Pittsburgh, Carnegie Mellon University, and even the exclusive Duquesne Club, responded to the mayor's suggestion by filing lawsuits questioning the city's ability to impose a tax on not-for-profit institutions.[77] The fight also set off a discussion within the halls of government over what role the not-for-profit sector should play in the city. City Council finance chair Philip Baskin emerged as a particularly vocal critic of the hospitals, laying personal blame on the "very bad, irresponsible citizens . . . who are in charge of about 12 hospitals in the City." Baskin believed that high hospital rates obligated not-for-profits to provide more service to the community. "If they can charge $90 a day for a room, why can't they pay 54 cents of that money for all the services they demand from the City?" he asked.[78] The Allegheny County Court of Common Pleas, however, disagreed with Baskin's reasoning and ruled, "merely because these (fees) are charged by the hospitals, they do not forfeit their charitable status."[79] The Pennsylvania Supreme Court, hearing the case on appeal, agreed with the lower courts and held that the tax should not apply to transactions that support a charitable purpose by institutions of purely public charity. By early 1971, the city was giving refunds to the few that had paid the tax.[80] The failure of the Institution Service and Privilege Tax seemed to put not-for-profit institutions out of bounds as potential sources of new revenue.[81]

The fight over not-for-profit tax exemption in Pennsylvania was already brewing as the *Intermountain* case wound its way through the courts. In 1980, a small not-for-profit health organization based in Pittsburgh named the Hospital Utilization Project (HUP) asked the Commonwealth of Pennsylvania for a sales and use tax refund.[82] When HUP's petition was denied, it took the case to court, appealing all the way to the Pennsylvania Supreme Court. In the world of not-for-profit health care, HUP was neither fish nor fowl. It emerged in 1963 as a multihospital solution to the problem of uneven and time-consuming separate utilization projects. The organization provided participating hospitals with discharge abstracts, which allowed them to track the numbers and types of diagnoses, as well as physician resource use. All of these metrics, when taken together, illuminated potential areas to grow revenues and to hold down costs.[83] Before the passage of Medicare and Medicaid, most of HUP's funding came from other not-for-profit organizations like the Allegheny County Medical Society and the Hospital Council of Western Pennsylvania, with Blue Cross providing an in-kind donation of data processing services. Medicare changed HUP's funding stream and allowed the organization to transition to a funding model whereby they collected a fee for every discharge abstract sold to a participating hospital.[84] By 1982, the organization had reported at least three consecutive fiscal years at a profit, and it was steadily building cash reserves. HUP's fee-for-service revenue stream became the linchpin on which the case turned and, in 1985, the Pennsylvania Supreme Court found that HUP, largely because it served other not-for-profits only, and billed for its services at a profit, was not an institution of "purely public charity" and therefore was unworthy of its tax refund.

Why was this decision so important? After all, HUP was only one small organization within the larger health care nexus. The answer is that the court used its opinion as an opportunity to clarify the murky definition of an institution of purely public charity by setting five criteria that all charitable not-for-profits needed to comply with to qualify for the privilege of tax exemption. According to these new criteria, which became known as the HUP test, a not-for profit organization:

a. Advances a charitable purpose;
b. Donates or renders gratuitously a substantial portion of its services;
c. Benefits a substantial and indefinite class of persons who are legitimate subjects of charity;
d. Relieves the government of some of its burden; and
e. Operates entirely free from private profit motive.[85]

By taking the opportunity to define clearly and tighten significantly the criteria to which a not-for-profit organization needed to conform to qualify for charitable status, the court opened the door for cash-strapped cities to challenge wealthy not-for-profit organizations like hospitals and universities. The first major challenge brought under the new standard occurred north of Pittsburgh, in Erie, Pennsylvania, where Hamot Medical Center was stripped of its tax exemption after years of engaging in aggressive property acquisition and debt collection policies.[86] Hamot's story became a cautionary tale for many hospitals about how vulnerable they were to outside pressures under the court's new reading of tax exemption laws.

Despite Erie's success at challenging Hamot's tax exemption, aggressive attacks on not-for-profit hospitals were typically considered as a last resort. In Pittsburgh, civic leaders used an appeal to civic good, and if that failed, the threat of a hearing before the Board of Property Assessment, Appeals, and Review, to push for negotiated settlements with hospitals. This was likely the case in 1988 when Presbyterian University Hospital wanted to enlarge its facilities as part of the "Partnership for Medical Renaissance," which included construction of a new biomedical research tower on the hospital's Oakland campus. The city saw an opportunity with the new construction to encourage the hospital to expand its financial contribution. In an editorial titled "A Tax by Any Other Name," the *Pittsburgh Post-Gazette* opined:

> Presbyterian University Hospital emphasizes that its agreement to pay $11.1 million over 10 years to the city is not "a payment in lieu of taxes," or even a fee for services. There was no formula devised to determine the amount of the donation. It was developed instead from "a general sense of what we felt we could afford and what the city expressed as its needs for a project [the new $250 million partnership for Medical Renaissance] of this size," according to a hospital official. In other words, the hospital's intention in making this payment was to show social responsibility and indicate that it is a unique resource with a national mission attempting to minimize the burden of its activities on the taxpayers of Pittsburgh. This explanation will be readily accepted—and also recognized as a deft semantic operation.[87]

A deft operation it was. The not-a-PILOT payment that the hospital agreed to set an important precedent. The paper noted in the same editorial, "This payment to the city deals with most of the issues surrounding the medical-care and research complex's exemption from local property taxes in a very constructive manner. It is also forward-looking in being tied to the construction of a new facility. Thus, it avoids messy arguments over the need to bring existing tax-exempt property onto the tax roll."[88] The problem with this strategy was that it lacked uniformity, and smaller hospitals, especially those with fewer financial resources than Presbyterian University Hospital, resisted efforts to come to an accommodation with the city.

Join You in Partnership or See You in Court: Pittsburgh's Mayors Escalate the Fight

During her 1990 budget address, Mayor Sophie Masloff fired a warning shot across the bow of the city's not-for-profit community, which she felt had not been making adequate financial contributions relative to its income.[89] Masloff was an unlikely hero for those concerned about the emergence of a new economy in Western Pennsylvania. She was in her seventies, barely over five feet tall, often wore unique pins with a local flavor that she paired with garish sweaters, and made cringe-inducing verbal gaffes, like referring to rock and roll legend Bruce Springsteen as "Bruce Bedspring" during a news conference welcoming the musician to the city. She also worked to cultivate an image of herself as the city's "best-loved Jewish grandmother."[90] After a long career as a civil servant, Masloff was elected to the city council until she was elevated to the mayor's office by the untimely death of Richard Caliguiri in 1988. When Masloff took office, most Pittsburghers expected that she heralded a return to the days of the Democratic machine—which was an era of retail ward politics punctuated by a surprisingly productive relationship between city hall and local business elites. Seen in this light, Masloff's 1990 budget address is all the more important. It represented a significant shift away from a haphazard approach to PILOTs toward one that was marked by a growing consensus between city hall and large not-for-profits that nobody was safe, and that a more comprehensive strategy to assess the actual costs of the city's growing knowledge economy was needed. Thus, the statement "We will gladly join you in partnership in Harrisburg or we will see you in court," signaled a determination to right Pittsburgh's fiscal ship by seeking new sources of revenue from all of the major institutions that taxed the city's resources.[91] The not-for-profit community viewed this threat as "almost blackmail," but most were concerned, given the strong language contained in the HUP test, that they had little choice but to pay up, either by negotiating a PILOT agreement or by returning property with questionable uses back to the tax rolls.[92] Hospitals drew special ire from Masloff's tax department. Ira Weiss, the county's deputy solicitor, echoed the administration's position when he told the press that hospitals "do not operate as charities. [They are] cash cows, which generate and pump tax-free dollars into other profit-making ventures."[93] City finance director Ben Hayllar offered a slightly less charged assessment when he told the *Pittsburgh Press* that the city had an obligation to challenge the entrepreneurial not-for-profits because "you can't ignore the growth of institutions that aren't the Little Sisters of the Poor anymore."[94]

In 1990, the Hospital Council of Western Pennsylvania sued to prevent the city and the county from demanding additional PILOTs from member hospitals. The Hospital Council based its argument on the claim that the entire concept of PILOTs for exempt organizations was a power beyond that of local government and should be decided by the legislature. Under this reasoning, the HUP test was invalid, since the supreme court, rather than the legislature, had unilaterally modified the tax law.[95] Furthermore, as Jack Robinette, the Hospital Council's executive director, argued, "Quite simply payments in lieu of taxes will be passed on to patients. This in effect is a sick tax and eventually, everybody will be paying this hidden tax."[96] Taking the city to court proved both costly and ineffective: as the suit wound its way through the federal court system, the pressure was mounting for plaintiffs to pay up. Hospitals and other large not-for-profits tried a new strategy—if they could not overturn the HUP test in court, they would try to rewrite the law in the state house.

Even though city officials "consistently fantasized about the nonprofits as a revenue source," PILOT revenue continued to drop throughout the mid-1990s as existing agreements expired.[97] Working through advocacy organizations, large not-for-profits and lobbyists for the hospital industry created what became the Institutions of Purely Public Charity Act, or Act 55, which was passed in 1997.[98] Act 55 retained the same five criteria that stood at the heart of the HUP test, but it loosened the requirements to meet them successfully by creating a new three-part test to determine eligibility for tax exemption.

The first test retained the HUP test's language that "the institution must donate or render gratuitously a substantial portion of its services," but it allowed not-for-profits several ways of measuring this contribution, including the provision of "uncompensated goods or services at least equal to 75 percent of the institution's net operating income but not less than 3 percent of the institution's total operating expenses; . . . a written policy and a written schedule of fees based on individual or family income" (or the satisfaction of several other percentage-based formulas tied to the provision of goods or services). The second test was more straightforward—the institution merely had to prove it operated free from private benefit and that its officers, employees, or directors did not receive benefits or compensation packages based on the organization's fiscal performance. The final test was a government service test. To qualify, a not-for-profit needed to demonstrate that it relieved government of a burden that it would have borne if the institution did not exist or existed in a different form, provided a service that government had provided, or directly or indirectly reduced dependence on government programs.[99] For Pittsburgh's not-for-profit hospitals, meeting this test was easy—with no public hospital, these were the only places where indigent patients could seek care.

Act 55 had major revenue consequences for the city. By 2000, it was receiving less than $2 million a year in PILOT revenue.[100] The pleading of city officials like Controller Tom Flaherty for not-for-profits to contribute more fell on deaf ears. That year, Flaherty told the *Pittsburgh Tribune-Review*: "We have been more than accommodating, allowing these big institutions to expand and grow unfettered. . . . But now we have reached a stage where we are hurting. . . . We're at a breaking point, certainly in the city of Pittsburgh."[101]

Representatives from not-for-profit hospitals dismissed remarks like Flaherty's as grandstanding. They consistently reminded Pittsburghers that they were the sole providers of charity care for the region. They also started to deploy a new narrative for justifying their community benefit by pointing out how not-for-profit hospitals were the region's major employers and the foundation of the new "eds and meds" economy that had brought the city back from the brink of economic collapse in the immediate post-steel era. UPMC's associate counsel Stephen Nimo provided an example of this shift when, in the words of writer Marisol Bello, he told the *Tribune-Review*'s readers that "the health system makes annual payments totaling $2.5 million to the city, county, and school district" and that this contribution was "fair." Nimo went on to extol the value brought by UPMC's ancillary services, like sports medicine, as drivers of economic growth. Finally, he stated, "Clearly, we don't feel we are a drain on the city. We're creating programs and increasing revenues and jobs."[102]

Act 55 also had substantial policy implications. According to Ira Weiss, the broader exemption criteria codified by the legislation "put a bulletproof vest" around large not-for-profits.[103] By making exemptions harder to challenge, it shifted the power dynamic within the hospital-civic relationship back in favor of the hospitals and, as a result, public shaming, rather than aggressive legal tactics, became the primary way that local government could attempt to extract new concessions on revenue issues. Regardless of who was right or wrong, the city still was having problems paying its bills, resulting in the layoff of nearly 450 municipal employees, including nearly 100 police officers, in 2003.[104] Adding an exclamation point to the layoffs was that, due to years of population decline and a corresponding decline in revenue from property taxes, the city's expenses due to pensions and debt service were projected to outstrip revenue and lead to a projected budget deficit of $115 million by 2009.[105] Hoping to avoid this fate, Pittsburgh filed for distressed municipality status under Act 47 in 2004. This act allowed the city to restructure debt and collect additional wage taxes from for-profit employers.

Were not-for-profits really to blame for the city's fiscal woes, as many citizens and some elected officials seemed to imply? Certainly, the legislature's refusal to consider revenue sharing meant that cities with large amounts of nontaxable properties had a tough road going forward. It is important to remember that these large not-for-profits were not getting a totally free pass with the passage of Act 55. They still were liable for some wage taxes, sales taxes on some items, and real estate taxes on buildings not used for a charitable purpose. Moreover, as a consequence of Act 55 and Act 47, a Pittsburgh Public Service Fund was created. This fund allowed not-for-profit institutions to contribute to the city without labeling their contribution as a formal PILOT. The Pittsburgh Public Service Fund collected almost $14 million between 2005 and 2007. The fund was revived again from 2010 to 2013.[106] Finally, outside of contributing to municipal coffers, not-for-profits like UPMC routinely made financial and in-kind contributions to a range of charitable organizations, community empowerment programs, and public education. Even though Western Pennsylvania health systems grew in scope from the 1990s onward, unlike many other cities, there was not a tremendous growth in their geographic footprint within the city This meant that even though there was a high percentage of nontaxable property in the city, estimated at about 33 percent, the total amount of assessable property owned by hospitals remained consistent at about 1 percent, or roughly 13 percent of nontaxable value—far behind the city's colleges and universities and city government that held properties accounting for 24 and 20 percent of taxable value, respectively, in 2000.[107]

Act 55 seemed to have provided some degree of calm in the relationship between these two parties; however, this calm was shattered in April 2012, when the Pennsylvania Supreme Court once again waded into the issue of not-for-profit tax exemption, upholding a lower court ruling that applied the more stringent HUP test, rather than Act 55, to a case where the Pike County Board of Assessment denied the Mesivtah Eitz Chaim of Bobov Inc.'s summer camp a tax exception for its property in Eastern Pennsylvania.[108] In its majority opinion, the supreme court argued that even though Act 55 was a good faith attempt by the legislature to rationalize the system of not-for-profit tax exemption in the state, "good intentions do not excuse noncompliance with the Constitution" and that the judicial, rather than the legislative, branch was the ultimate arbiter of the constitutionality of tax exemption.[109] Thus, the court argued, Act 55 was invalid and the HUP test should determine exemption criteria. In the wake of this decision, the door was opened for a new round of tax-exempt challenges.

On March 20, 2013, Mayor Luke Ravenstahl walked through this newly opened door and announced that the city of Pittsburgh had filed suit against UPMC. Ravenstahl and the city of Pittsburgh asked the Allegheny County Court of Common Pleas to find that the health care giant was not an Institution of Purely Public Charity and should, therefore, be liable for local payroll taxes. Moreover, the city also asked UPMC to pay six prior years of payroll taxes in full (as if they were a for-profit corporation) plus interest. The crux of the city's argument was that, given the value of the health care enterprise's assets, which UPMC estimated to have increased from just under $2 billion to just under $10 billion a year (an average annual increase in revenue of 13 percent a year between 1997 and 2012), that it donated an insufficient amount of charitable care; used its revenue over expenses to support its for-profit business, including its massive insurance business; provided unreasonable executive compensation packages and perks (the current CEO was paid about $6 million a year in 2011 and at least twenty other employees made in excess of $1 million annually); and had intentionally closed hospitals in poor and underserved communities only to open new hospitals in affluent, and medically well-served, suburban communities and overseas.[110]

The lawsuit galvanized strong public opinions on both sides. UPMC spokesman Paul Wood argued that "the challenge to UPMC's tax-exempt status appears to be based on the mistaken impression that a nonprofit organization must conduct its affairs in a way that pleases certain labor unions, certain favored businesses or particular political constituencies—in other words, the way that some local governments are also run. . . . If UPMC ran its affairs as poorly as some of our local governments, it would not have become the internationally known, world-class health care institution it is today."[111] Subsequent comments by Wood and UPMC suggested that the lawsuit was a politically motivated attempt by the mayor to "divert attention from scandalous public reports of his [Ravenstahl's] precarious legal predicament [the Federal Bureau of Investigation was conducting an investigation of the mayor and the Bureau of Police] and to curry favor with parties intent on harming UPMC and capable of cushioning his political fall."[112]

In April 2013, UPMC filed its own suit against the city and the mayor, alleging that the organization was specifically targeted by public officials in violation of its civil rights.[113] By the summer of 2014, both lawsuits had run their course when the city, soon after the election of a new mayor, William Peduto, declined to appeal an adverse ruling, and UPMC agreed to drop its countersuit. Unlike Ravenstahl, Peduto pledged a more cooperative tone—since his election in the fall of 2013, he had been meeting with UPMC to try to come to an amicable settlement over the not-for-profit's contribution to the city.[114] However, a growing acrimony between UPMC and its not-for-profit rival, the Allegheny Health Network (a product of a takeover of the financially troubled West Penn Allegheny Health System by Highmark Blue Cross and Blue Shield), has kept the debate over not-for-profit responsibility alive while also helping to shift its focus into new areas beyond questions of not-for-profit contributions to the city's tax rolls.

Like the fight over charity care, the back-and-forth over PILOTs showed the power of not-for-profits to help set the terms in which they defined the meaning of civic contribution. It also showed how the more commercialized understanding of the hospital-civic relationship helped to push these institutions to more strongly consider not just their overall financial health but their competitive position within the regional, national, and international health care markets, when thinking about how they related to their local communities.

*   *   *

The contest over revenue versus responsibility revealed some critical limitations in the market-based model of the hospital-civic relationship. Critics of large not-for-profit hospital systems often argue that these institutions use their privileged position to become profitable charities rather than charitable not-for-profits—and that they do so on the backs of poorly paid workers and insufficiently cared for citizens. Not-for-profit hospitals often argue that this criticism is both unjustified and ill-informed. Yet, it is hard to gauge how much either side is really winning in the court of public opinion.. The complexities of tax exemption and the emotional appeal to perceptions of the hospital-civic relationship often means that the public, as opposed to not-for-profit leaders or elected officials, stand on the sidelines as these critical issues that shape the future of the medical metropolis are debated.

What is clear is that the public boundaries of the hospital–civic relationship have dramatically changed. Even though a more market-oriented understanding of health care had been under way for decades, alongside the ongoing corporatization of not-for-profit health care administration, the fights over charity care and PILOTs made it clear that not only were not-for-profits like The Methodist Hospital and UPMC interpreting their position in the hospital-civic relationship as the primary actor, they were willing to aggressively challenge states and cities that sought to reset the relationship in their favor. Certainly, leaders at these institutions, such as Mathis and Romoff, worried that the burdens imposed by the massive social programs of the late 1960s, including Medicaid, would devolve upon their shoulders, and believed that the best way to manage unexpected costs was to generate large surpluses and new ways to build strength in the private pay or managed care market as a necessary hedge against a changing and uncertain marketplace. In Texas, defining "charity care" became an exercise in official zeal for both parties, while thousands of indigent Texans, left out in the cold by the state's miserly Medicaid program, suffered the consequences. But the most aggressive statement of not-for-profit power came in Pittsburgh, where UPMC aggressively pushed back against several mayoral administrations and fought long campaigns to demonstrate that the civic value of not-for-profit health care went beyond financial contributions to offset declining municipal coffers.

Both fights, and others like them across the United States, have created a relationship between cities and large not-for-profits that is both extraordinarily codependent and periodically ridden with strife. It has also reinforced a public perception in both cities that not-for-profit hospitals have become the master and cities the supplicant. This perception is, of course, corrosive to the civic fabric, because neither side can move forward or advance plans for a new future without opening itself up to charges of insider dealing and special treatment, and it shortchanges the real challenges for balancing the future of the eds and meds economy with issues of social and economic justice.[115]

Epilogue

The Future of the Medical Metropolis

President Donald Trump put the postindustrial transformation of Pittsburgh back into the national conversation in the summer of 2017. While he was announcing the withdrawal of the United States from the Paris climate change agreement, he devoted substantial time to defending the ability of the United States to grow legacy industries and be freed from "so called" burdensome international regulations. To punctuate this point, he noted that he "was elected to represent the citizens of Pittsburgh, not Paris."[1] The response to Trump's comments was swift and unsparing; Pittsburgh's mayor, William Peduto, took to Twitter, the president's favorite medium, as well as the traditional media, to counter Trump's declaration by reminding America that Pittsburgh had embraced the new postindustrial economy. Peduto told the *Pittsburgh Post-Gazette*, "In his speechwriter's mind, Pittsburgh is this dirty old town that relies upon big coal and big steel to survive." He continued, saying that Trump's speech "ignores the sacrifices that we made over thirty years in order to get back up on our feet, in order to be creating a new economy, in order to make the sacrifices to clean our air and clean our water."[2]

Peduto's use of the term "sacrifices" highlights one of the challenges with the popular narrative of building the medical metropolis. It is either presumed to be a happy accident or a plucky story of civic determination in the face of overwhelming collapse from the 1980s onward. The medical metropolis is neither. It is first and foremost an intentional creation. It is the result of a set of decisions by civic elites, not-for-profit health care executives, and ordinary citizens over the course of more than seventy years. Since it is an intentional creation, there is hope that we can reshape it for the next generation.

It seems, to paraphrase the famous misquotation of General Motors' Charles Wilson, that we have too often accepted the idea that what has been good for health care has been good for cities. This interdependence will continue as the health care sector expands over the next several decades. In 2015, health care accounted for 17.8 percent of gross domestic product, or more than $10,000 per person. By 2027, it will be 19.4 percent of GDP.[3] But we need to look beyond the percentage of GDP to understand why health care matters for urban change. Unlike steel or petroleum, health care will, at least in the short run, continue to grow. In fact, since 1990, "health care and social assistance" employment has replaced manufacturing and retail as the largest employer in thirty-three states, and by 2024, health care should add more than nine million new jobs, or a 6.5 percent increase, and will beat out government and the service sector as the largest area of employment. Manufacturing jobs are expected to decline by more than 5 percent during the same period.[4] This is driven by an aging population. Almost a decade ago, the Pew Research Center noted that ten thousand Americans per day turn sixty-five—and that number will continue to rise over the next three decades.[5] In theory, this should make for heady times for the medical metropolis. With more patients and more revenue, not-for-profits like Memorial Hermann, The Methodist Hospital, and UPMC should be hiring and expanding their operations. This additional hiring may even help to offset job losses in other parts of the service economy, like higher education.[6]

Theory is one thing, but practice is another. Despite the projected growth, health care as an industry and the cities built around it face some substantial challenges. One of the most important is the current debate over cost control and access to care. Both of these factors have led to powerful changes, including efforts in the 1960s to reach out to underserved communities and the clawing back of these efforts in the 1970s and 1980s to focus on attracting well-insured patients whose dollars helped fuel the transition to health systems in the 1990s. With the passage of the Patient Protection and Affordable Care Act (ACA) in 2010, the health care system is poised for one of the most comprehensive transitions in generations. Unlike the failed efforts at health care reform in the 1990s, which encouraged health care not-for-profits to pursue increased revenue at the expense of patient access, if the ACA remains the law of the land, the focus will be on increasing access for all patients, improving quality metrics, and lowering costs.[7]

One creation of the ACA is a system of health insurance exchanges, whereby those left outside of the private market can purchase affordable health insurance.[8] Since the early 1980s, the rate of nonelderly Americans without health insurance coverage has been between 16 and 18 percent. Those without access to health insurance coverage, including Medicaid, created substantial challenges for health care institutions and cities alike. Exchanges, along with expanded Medicaid in some states, helped to drive the uninsured rate down to slightly over 10 percent of nonelderly Americans since the ACA has been implemented and opened up the possibility of a new vision of the hospital-civic relationship that bridges the social justice-oriented model with a more market-based one.[9]

When managed right, exchange plans can improve the health of the medical metropolis. UPMC provides a good example. In 2017, the not-for-profit controlled about 87 percent of the market share for exchange plans in Western Pennsylvania.[10] While ACA plans are not making UPMC much money (in 2015, the not-for-profit reported breaking even), they are providing access to care for many people who otherwise would have been forced to do without.[11] UPMC plans, however, cost more than those offered by Highmark, which, according to the *Pittsburgh Post-Gazette*, lost more than $800 million on exchange plans up to 2016, with $500 million of this loss due to promised federal reimbursement that failed to materialize.[12] This is the Achilles' heel of this new potential hybrid version of the hospital-civic relationship. Health care institutions cannot sustain massive losses to keep the medical metropolis healthy, yet without their willingness to assume some risk, as with ACA exchange plans, they are unable to fulfill their civic role as protectors of urban health for all residents. While fiscal probity was always important, even in a locational asset model, the expansion of the federal state as a health care backstop raised expectations for the responsibilities of these institutions.

This is clearest in one of the most acrimonious fights over ACA implementation—Medicaid expansion. Part of the strategy to fill the gap between the private market and the public insurance plans was to create a national standard, rather than state-specific guidelines, to expand Medicaid eligibility to 138 percent of the federal poverty line. The federal government planned to fund 100 percent of the cost of expanded Medicaid until 2020, when federal funding would drop to 90 percent. However, the Supreme Court held in *National Federation of Independent Businesses v. Sebelius* (2012) that the way the expansion was written was unduly coercive and, thus, the decision to expand Medicaid coverage should be left up to the individual states. Pennsylvania chose to expand

Medicaid. Texas did not. The difference for Pittsburgh and Houston has been striking.[13]

Expanded Medicaid in Pennsylvania covers more than 700,000 people and has driven down costs for the commonwealth's general hospitals by $92 million in the first year of expansion.[14] This is critical for the medical metropolis. For UPMC, Medicaid pays for "77 percent of care in the ten neighborhoods within Allegheny County with the highest unemployment rates." Moreover, UPMC's "market share for Medicaid patients exceeds those of other provider systems."[15] Outside of the UPMC system, expanded Medicaid has also helped to firm up the bottom line of nonprofit community health centers, helping to continue the goal of expanding ambulatory care that was put into practice by groups like the Neighborhood Committee on Health Care in the 1970s. Finally, expanded Medicaid has also helped to increase access to community mental health and addiction services.[16]

By contrast, "Texas already leads the nation with more than 4 million uninsured, with Harris County topping the state at about 740,000."[17] In 2015, this cost Texas hospitals around $5.5 billion in uncompensated care.[18] One of the hardest-hit health systems in Houston was the public Harris Health System (the renamed and expanded Harris County Hospital District). That same year, the health system started to push its patients toward the exchange market as a way to cut losses, projected at over $50 million for the year. What was particularly telling was that, had Texas expanded Medicaid, it was possible that the "deficit would disappear completely. . . . Harris Heath could then move 70,000 uninsured patients to Medicaid, netting $87 million in new revenue."[19]

Access to care isn't the only way the medical metropolis is facing challenges. The hopes of the leaders in the 1960s and 1970s who saw health care employment as a potential path for greater social mobility and economic equity have also faded. In March 2016, UPMC committed to raising starting wages "for entry-level positions at most Pittsburgh facilities to $15/hour by January 2021" and by 2019 "for average worker pay." The health system also noted that its "average compensation is $64,000 annually, not including benefits," and "UPMC employs nearly 25,000 people with an annual salary of over $50,000, more than any other employer in the region."[20] This includes, one assumes, the physicians and other health care administrators making six- and seven-figure salaries. UPMC's point, as well as the workers protesting it, is that the not-for-profit plays a major role in setting regional wages.[21]

Issues of economic equity and the power of not-for-profits to shape communities was put in the news in the summer of 2018, when Fair Share Pittsburgh pushed to halt part of UPMC's plan to build three new specialty hospitals in the region. Activists and concerned citizens flooded a city council hearing, demanding that the health system put a community health benefits agreement in place that not only addressed issues of wages but also called for collective bargaining rights, access to facilities for all Pittsburghers, and attention to health disparities and mental health. Despite their lobbying, the Pittsburgh City Council approved UPMC's expansion request without substantially requiring the not-for-profit to create this agreement. Instead, UPMC promised to support the more general strategy to solicit not-for-profit contributions, the "One Pittsburgh Initiative" proposed by the Peduto administration, which attempts to address a broad range of issues affecting the Pittsburgh region and not just economic comparativeness and workforce readiness. UPMC also agreed to create an addiction clinic and "grow workforce training programs." This set of solutions left activists feeling that the heart of their critique, which is that the inequality of the industrial economy has been replaced by the inequity of the service economy, was left unaddressed in a meaningful fashion.[22]

These activists appeared to receive some support from the Commonwealth of Pennsylvania when, in February 2019, attorney general Josh Shapiro filed a sweeping seventy-three-page legal action against UPMC. Shapiro's petition was seemingly grounded in the inability of UPMC and Highmark (Allegheny Health Network) to agree on the terms of the consent decrees that shaped the separation of the two health systems. It contained four counts:

1. "Modification of the Consent Decrees is Necessary to Ensure Compliance with Charities Laws";
2. "UPMC's Violation of the Solicitation of Funds for Charitable Purposes Act";
3. "UPMC's Breach of its Fiduciary Duties of Loyalty and Care Owed to its Constituent Health Care Providers and Public-at-Large";
4. "UPMC's Violations of the Unfair Trade Practices and Consumer Protection Law."[23]

While each of these counts generally echoed ideas about the responsibility of not-for-profit health systems that had been voiced by several generations

of elected officials and community activists, there are ways that this petition, depending on how it is adjudicated, might introduce new ways of
rethinking how the hospital-civic relationship has evolved for the twenty-
first century.

One was Shapiro's implication that the intent of private donors should
be considered as to how to assess a not-for-profit's community responsibility.
While measuring private support had long been essential to the claim that
not-for-profit hospitals represented a locational asset, trying to divine their
intent as it related to who could access their faculties is different. Using the
example of the Hillman family interests, who donated more than $70 million
to UPMC (or what later became UPMC facilities and interests) as well as
donations made by Highmark to Children's Hospital, Children's Hospital
Foundation, and other health systems which were subsequently acquired by
UPMC such as the Jameson Health System, Shapiro claimed that these donations represented a form of public financial support and by restricting access
to only certain groups of insured patients, UPMC, having accepted these
donated funds, was subverting the intent of these donors. When this was
combined with favorable tax exemptions for not-for-profit health systems, it
created a situation where "thousands of those tax payers who built UPMC
are now being shut out of the very care they helped pay for."[24]

Another was to focus on the way that the health system marketed itself
in Pennsylvania. While health care marketing was an essential part of the
locational asset model, Shapiro argued it had appeared to have evolved in
a fashion that confused and disempowered the public. This assertion was
at the heart of Count 4. And, while the complaint chastised both UPMC
and Highmark for their "aggressive and often misleading marketing campaigns which caused widespread public confusion and uncertainty as to the
cost and access of Highmark subscribers to their UPMC physicians," it also
focused heavily on how UPMC informed existing and potential Medicare
Advantage customers about their plans to force Highmark subscribers of
these products to prepay for services in UPMC facilities (since they would
be out of network).[25] The petition claimed: "UPMC has presented conflicting messages to the public generally, and to its patients in particular, that
it will treat all patients regardless of the source of their payment, but it has
refused treatment to its patients with Highmark insurance and will no
longer contract with Highmark for any of its commercial or Medicare
Advantage insurance products after June 30, 2019, which will significantly
increase the costs of care for all of Highmark's subscribers."[26]

UPMC has argued that the consent decrees provided adequate time for patients and hospitals to decide which providers they wished to utilize moving forward and that the fracturing of the health care market has been good for consumers overall. In a statement published in the *Tribune-Review,* UPMC stated:

> During that period, [the five-year window between the issuances and expiration of the consent decrees] the region's insurance marketplace transformed from one of the nation's most highly concentrated and least competitive to one of the most competitive and pro-consumer markets in the nation with some of the lowest cost health plans available anywhere. Consumers have greatly benefitted from the heightened competition. Nearly all businesses now offer alternative, affordable plans so their employees can choose insurance products that allow them full, unfettered in-network access to the UPMC hospitals and physicians they desire.[27]

At the time this book went to press, the outcome of this legal action is unknown, nor is it clear if this case will encourage elected officials to more specifically define the limits of not-for-profit health care charitability and, in doing so, attempt to provide some additional clarity as to the boundaries of the hospital-civic relationship in the future.

One of the most pressing questions about the future of the medical metropolis goes beyond debates over access to care, the vicissitudes of health care reimbursement, or questions about charitable contribution by not-for-profits, and asks how sustainable it will be for the long-term future of both Pittsburgh and Houston.[28] While the short-term outlook appears bright, even with potential health care reform, longer-term population trends are worrying. Pittsburgh's population of adults aged sixty-five and older is more than three percentage points above the national average and will continue to increase for the next several decades.[29] However, this elderly population will eventually decline, increasing competition between hospitals for patients, creating a glut in the labor market for those currently rushing to become health care providers, and leaving communities that rely on health care jobs searching for new ways to reinvent themselves. We have been here before with the collapse of the industrial economy—and if we are not careful, the medical metropolis can follow in the footsteps of the steel city.

Houston may be better insulated than Pittsburgh. The city is still rapidly growing and is a much younger city.[30] The high rates of uninsured patients and tepid support for public health care by the state of Texas threaten to restrict care options due to high costs and may force more hospital system consolidations, further changing the dynamics of the city's medical market-place. While Houston might not have the empty hospital beds that Pitts-burgh could have by virtue of its aging population, it is not clear how many residents of the Bayou City will be able to afford to use them.

Long-term planning has never been a strength of the medical metropo-lis. The future is typically only a five- to fifteen-year window, and the past is much shorter. Much of this likely has to do with the immediate nature of health care and the uncertain regulatory environment, which changes with each new Congress and presidential administration. It also has to do with the narrative of change and innovation, and the desire to disrupt old norms and build anew. Whether it was promoting biotechnology or creat-ing massive horizontally and vertically integrated health systems, this Schumpeterian creative destruction has largely paid off. Health care has come to define modern Pittsburgh and Houston as havens for the middle-class health professionals, as world-class destinations for advanced specialty care, and as cities where people want to live. This is a far cry from the dark days of the 1980s, when each struggled to think about the future. It is, however, worthwhile to pause and consider what sort of city we want the medical metropolis to be. Working together, we can draw from the words of a famous Texan named Lyndon Johnson and build a vision of the medi-cal metropolis "where the city of man serves not only the needs of the body and the demands of commerce but the desire for beauty and the hunger for community."[31]

Notes

Introduction

1. Dan Fitzpatrick, "UPMC Logo May Top Off U.S. Steel Tower," *Pittsburgh Post-Gazette*, April 11, 2007; Dan Fitzpatrick, "Top of the Triangle: UPMC Getting Ready to Put Its Name on U.S. Steel Tower," *Pittsburgh Post-Gazette*, April 25, 2008; UPMC Facts and Stats, http://www.upmc.com/about/facts/pages/default.aspx; Steve Hamm, "UPMC: The New Steel in Pittsburgh," *Businessweek*, September 17, 2009. For a historical overview of Pittsburgh's recessions, see Christopher Briem, "Recessions and Pittsburgh," *Pittsburgh Economic Quarterly*, December 2008. For a general overview of the increasing importance of the not-for-profit sector in Pittsburgh, see Sabina Deitrick and Christopher Briem, "More Than Support and Services: The Nonprofit Sector as an Economic Asset," *Pittsburgh Economic Quarterly*, March 2009. Pittsburgh's Amazon HQ2 video, "Future Forged for All," https://www.youtube.com/watch?v = XEw2Ky5XxDM.

2. Joshua Zumbrun, "America's Recession-Proof Cities," *Forbes.com*, April 29, 2008.

3. Matt Hudgins, "A Boom in Houston Is Led by the Energy Industry," *New York Times*, December 4, 2012; Kurt Badenhausen, "While Rest of U.S. Economy Plods, Houston Gets Hot," *Forbes*, July 16, 2012.

4. Greater Houston Partnership, "Houston Economic Highlights," December 8, 2017, 12; Texas Medical Center Facts and Figures, http://www.tmc.edu/about-tmc/facts-and-figures/; Houston's video to attract Amazon's HQ2 not only shows historical images of famous cardiovascular surgeon Dr. Michael E. DeBakey and references the creation of the artificial heart (see Chapter 3), but also highlights the Texas Medical Center, among other technically focused assets. Houston's Amazon HQ2 video, "Houston's Innovation Corridor," https://vimeo.com/242960450.

5. Richard L. Florida, *The Rise of the Creative Class: And How It's Transforming Work, Leisure, Community and Everyday Life* (New York: Basic Books, 2002).

6. PBS NewsHour, "Revisiting Evansville, Two Years After Whirlpool's Move South," October 28, 2011; Mohammed Khayum, "Evansville Forecast 2018," *Indiana Business Review* 92, no. 4 (Winter 2017); John Martin, "Ground Broken for 'Transformative' Downtown IU Med School," *Evansville Courier and Press*, October 23, 2015; Lloyd Winnecke, "Giving Thanks for Evansville's Many Blessings," *Evansville Courier and Press*, November 23, 2017.

7. Michael E. Porter, "Inner-City Economic Development: Learnings from 20 Years of Research and Practice," *Economic Development Quarterly* 30, no. 2 (2016), 105–116. Porter is typically credited with creating the term "anchor institution." There are many different places to see versions of the Pittsburgh comeback story. A few recent examples include the City of

Pittsburgh's Amazon HQ2 video; Dennis B. Roddy, "Pittsburgh: A City Transformed," *Pittsburgh Magazine*, January 22, 2015; Bruce Katz and Jeremy Nowak, "How the Once-Struggling Pittsburgh Is Reinventing Itself as an Innovation Hub," www.nextcity.org, January 15, 2018; and "Pittsburgh: The Comeback," *Time*, www.time.com/pittsburgh.

8. For an overview of the historiography of health care and the American city, see Jared N. Day, "Health Care and Urban Revitalization," *Journal of Urban History* 42, no. 2 (2016), 237–258. Both Catherine Conner and Guian McKee explore the relationship between hospitals and physical change in their work in this same special journal edition. Catherine A. Conner, "'The University That Ate Birmingham': The Healthcare Industry, Urban Development, and Neoliberalism," *Journal of Urban History* 42, no. 2 (2016), 284–305, and Catherine A. Conner, "Building Moderate Progress: Citizenship, Race, and Power in Downtown Birmingham, 1940–1992" (PhD diss., University of North Carolina, 2012); Guian A. McKee, "The Hospital City in an Ethnic Enclave: Tufts–New England Medical Center, Boston's Chinatown, and the Urban Political Economy of Health Care," *Journal of Urban History* 42, no. 2 (2016), 259–283. For a critique of the ways that historians of medicine have explored the relationship of hospitals to cities, see Joel D. Howell, *Technology in the Hospital: Transforming Patient Care in the Early Twentieth Century* (Baltimore: Johns Hopkins University Press, 1995), 10–11. For a more general overview of the relationship between universities and cities, see Margaret Pugh O'Mara, *Cities of Knowledge: Cold War Science and the Search for the Next Silicon Valley* (Princeton: Princeton University Press, 2005); Judith Rodin, *The University and Urban Revival: Out of the Ivory Tower and into the* Streets (Philadelphia: University of Pennsylvania Press, 2007); LaDale C. Winling, *Building the Ivory Tower: Universities and Metropolitan Development in the Twentieth Century* (Philadelphia: University of Pennsylvania Press, 2017); Stephen J. Diner, *Universities and Their Cities: Urban Higher Education in America* (Baltimore: Johns Hopkins University Press, 2017).

9. Daniel M. Fox, *Health Policies, Health Politics: The British and American Experience, 1911–1965* (Princeton: Princeton University Press, 1986); Daniel M. Fox, *Power and Illness: The Failure and Future of American Health Policy* (Berkeley: University of California Press, 1993); Paul Starr, *The Social Transformation of American Medicine: The Rise of a Sovereign Profession and the Making of a Vast Industry* (New York: Basic Books, 1982); and Rosemary Stevens, *The Public-Private Health Care State* (New Brunswick: Transaction Publishers, 2007) provide an excellent overview of the creation of the American health care system and health policy. Christy Ford Chapin, *Ensuring America's Health: The Public Creation of the Corporate Health Care System* (New York: Cambridge University Press, 2015); Jill S. Quadagno, *One Nation, Uninsured: Why the U.S. Has No National Health Insurance* (New York: Oxford University Press, 2005); Jonathan Engel, *Unaffordable: American Health Care from Johnson to Trump* (Madison: University of Wisconsin Press, 2018). For specific aspects of American health care, see Robert Cunningham III and Robert M. Cunningham Jr., *The Blues: A History of the Blue Cross and Blue Shield System* (DeKalb: Northern Illinois University Press, 1997); Betty Leyerle, *The Private Regulation of American Healthcare* (Armonk, N.Y.: M. E. Sharpe, 1994); Theda Skocpol, *Boomerang: Health Care Reform and the Turn Against Government* (New York: W. W. Norton, 1996); Julian Zelizer, *Taxing America: Wilbur Mills, Congress, and the State, 1945–1975* (New York: Cambridge University Press, 1999).

10. Charles T. Clofelter and Thomas Ehrlich, eds., *Philanthropy and the Nonprofit Sector in a Changing America* (Bloomington: Indiana University Press, 1999), which includes a chapter by Bradford Grey, "The Changing Face of Health Care"; Oliver Zunz, *Philanthropy in*

America: A History (Princeton: Princeton University Press, 2012), esp. chap. 8. For a critique of the growing size of the not-for-profit sector and its impact, see John Hawks, *For a Good Cause: How Charitable Institutions Became Powerful Economic Bullies* (Secaucus, N.J.: Carol Publishing Group, 1997). Another approach has been to argue that the not-for-profit sector and capitalism have become too intertwined, creating the "non-profit industrial complex," see INCITE, *The Revolution Will Not Be Funded: Beyond the Non-Profit Industrial Complex* (Cambridge: South End Press, 2007), in particular the contributions of Christine E. Ahn and Andrea Smith. Foundation-specific publications and the popular press have also critiqued the size and wealth of not-for-profits in recent years. Some examples include Josh Freedman, "Are Universities Charities? Why the 'Nonprofit Sector' Needs to Go," *Forbes.com*, December 10, 2013; Joe Mont, "10 Nonprofits That Act Like For-Profits," *thestreet.com*, May 7, 2011.

11. David Rosner, *A Once Charitable Enterprise: Hospital and Health Care in Brooklyn and New York, 1885–1915* (Princeton: Princeton University Press, 1982). For scholarship about issues of tax status, including tax exemption and not-for-profit obligation, see Alan Blankley and Dana Forgione, "Ethical Issues Facing Private, Not-For-Profit Hospitals in the United States: The Case of the Methodist Hospital System," in Aman Khan and W. Bartley Hildreth, eds., *Case Studies in Public Budgeting and Financial Management*, 2nd ed., rev. and expanded (New York: Marcel Dekker, 2003); Evelyn Brody, ed., *Property Tax Exemption for Charities* (Washington, D.C.: Urban Institute Press, 2002).

12. The history of the American hospital is dominated by two synthetic overviews: Charles E. Rosenberg, *The Care of Strangers* (New York: Basic Books, 1987), and Rosemary Stevens, *In Sickness and in Wealth* (New York: Basic Books,1989). Other important books on the development of the hospital include Morris J. Vogel, *The Invention of the Modern Hospital, Boston, 1870–1930* (Chicago: University of Chicago Press, 1980); Rosner, *A Once Charitable Enterprise*; Guenter B. Risse, *Mending Bodies, Saving Souls: A History of Hospitals* (New York: Oxford University Press, 1999); Dana Elizabeth Long and Janet Golden, eds., *The American General Hospital: Communities and Contexts* (Ithaca: Cornell University Press, 1989), 157–169. For more on American medical education, see Kenneth M. Ludmerer, *Learning to Heal: The Development of American Medical Education* (New York: Basic Books, 1985); Kenneth M. Ludmerer, *Time to Heal: American Medical Education from the Turn of the Century to the Era of Managed Care* (New York: Oxford University Press, 1999); Kenneth M. Ludmerer, *Let Me Heal: The Opportunity to Preserve Excellence in American Medical Education* (New York: Oxford University Press, 2016).

13. Alice Sardell, *The U.S. Experiment in Social Medicine: The Community Health Center Program* (Pittsburgh: University of Pittsburgh Press, 1988); William Shonick, *Government and Health Services: Government's Role in the Development of U.S. Health Services, 1930–1980* (New York: Oxford University Press, 1995). More recent work has examined the social justice angle of community medicine and its linkage to ideas of rights, including Beatrix Hoffman, *Health Care for Some: Rights and Rationing in the United States Since 1930* (Chicago: University of Chicago Press, 2012); Jenna Loyd, *Health Rights Are Civil Rights: Peace and Justice Activism in Los Angeles, 1963–1978* (Minneapolis: University of Minnesota Press, 2014).

14. Metro Atlanta Chamber of Commerce, "Top 10 Employers," https://www.metroat-lantachamber.com/assets/metro_atlanta_top_employers_2016_final_02_7JROX36.pdf; Balti-more County Government, "Top Employers," https://www.baltimorecountymd.gov/Agencies/economicdev/meet-baltimore-county/stats-and-figures/top-employers.html; Angie

Stewart, "These Are Chicago's Top 25 Largest Employers," *Crain's Chicago Business*, January 12, 2018, http://www.chicagobusiness.com/article/20180112/ISSUE01/180119954/these-are -chicago-s-25-largest-employers; Ohio Development Services Agency, "Ohio Major Employers," 5, 2018, https://development.ohio.gov/files/research/B2001.pdf.

15. American Iron and Steel Institute, "History of the Steelers Logo," https://www.steel .org/about-aisi/history/steelers-logo.

16. The Rust Belt/Sun Belt literature is an important area of urban history. Examples include Steven High, *Industrial Sunset: The Making of North America's Rust Belt, 1969–1984* (Toronto: University of Toronto Press, 2003); Jon Teaford, *The Metropolitan Revolution: The Rise of Post-Industrial America* (New York: Columbia University Press, 2006); Howard Gillette, *Camden After the Fall: Decline and Renewal in a Post-Industrial City* (Philadelphia: University of Pennsylvania Press, 2006); Jefferson Cowie and Joseph Heathcott, eds., *Beyond the Ruins: The Meanings of Deindustrialization* (Ithaca: Cornell University Press, 2003); Chloe E. Taft, *From Steel to Slots: Casino Capitalism in the Post-Industrial City* (Cambridge: Harvard University Press, 2016); David Goldfield, *Cotton Fields and Skyscrapers: Southern City and Region* (Baton Rouge: Louisiana State University Press, 1982); Bruce Shulman, *From Cotton Belt to Sunbelt: Federal Policy, Economic Development, and the Transformation of the American South, 1938–1980* (Durham: Duke University Press, 1994); Elizabeth Tandy Shermer, *Sunbelt Capitalism: Phoenix and the Transformation of American Politics* (Philadelphia: University of Pennsylvania Press, 2012).

17. This book also speaks to well-developed local history in both communities. In Houston, some important overviews include David G. McComb, *Houston: The Bayou City* (Austin: University of Texas, 1969); Joe R. Feagin, *Free Enterprise City: Houston in Political and Economic Perspective* (New Brunswick: Rutgers University Press, 1988); Marguerite Johnson, *Houston: The Unknown City, 1836–1946* (College Station: Texas A&M University Press, 1991); and Martin V. Melosi and Joseph Pratt, *Energy Metropolis: An Environmental History of Houston and the Gulf Coast* (Pittsburgh: University of Pittsburgh Press, 2007); Gavin Benke, *Risk and Ruin: Enron and the Culture of American Capitalism* (Philadelphia: University of Pennsylvania Press, 2018); Betsy Beasley, "At Your Service: Houston and the Preservation of U.S. Global Power, 1945–2008" (PhD diss., Yale, 2016).

Specific books on the development of health care in Houston include Bryant Boutwell and John P. McGovern, *Conversation with a Medical School: The University of Texas-Houston Medical School, 1970–2000* (Houston: University of Texas-Houston Health Science Center, 1999); Bryant Boutwell, *John P. McGovern, MD: A Lifetime of Stories* (College Station: Texas A&M University Press, 2014); William T. Butler and Diane Ware, *Arming for Battle Against Disease Through Education, Research, and Patient Care at Baylor College of Medicine* (Houston: Baylor College of Medicine), vols. 1–4; N. Don Macon in association with Thomas Dunaway Anderson, *Monroe Dunaway Anderson, His Legacy: A History of the Texas Medical Center 50th Anniversary Edition* (Houston: Texas Medical Center, 1994); and Frederick C. Elliott, *The Birth of the Texas Medical Center: A Personal Account*, ed. with an introduction by William Henry Kellar (College Station: Texas A&M University Press, 2004); Denton A. Cooley, *100,000 Hearts: A Surgeon's Memoir* (Austin: University of Texas Press, 2012); Kenneth L. Mattox, ed., *The History of Surgery in Houston* (Austin: Eakin Press, 1998); Harry Minetree, *Cooley: The Career of a Great Heart Surgeon* (New York: Harper's Magazine Press, 1973); James S. Olson, *Making Cancer History: Disease and Discovery at the University of Texas M.D. Anderson Cancer*

Center (Baltimore: Johns Hopkins University Press, 2009); Ruth SoRelle, *The Quest for Excellence: Baylor College of Medicine, 1900–2000* (Houston: Baylor College of Medicine, 2000); Thomas Thompson, *Hearts: Of Surgeons and Transplants, Miracles and Disasters Along the Cardiac Frontier* (New York: McCall, 1971); Betsy Parrish, *Legacy: 50 Years of Loving Care: Texas Children's Hospital, 1954–2004* (Houston: Elisha Freeman, 2006); Marilyn McAdams Sibley, *The Methodist Hospital of Houston: Serving the World* (Austin: Texas State Historical Association, 1989); and Ted Francis and Carole McFarland, *The Memorial Hospital System: The First Seventy-Five Years* (Houston: Larksdale, 1982); William L. Winters Jr. and Betsy Parish, *Houston Hearts: A History of Cardiovascular Surgery and Medicine and the Methodist-DeBakey Heart and Vascular Center Houston Methodist Hospital* (Houston: Elisha Freeman, 2014).

In Pittsburgh, some important community overviews include Joe W. Trotter and Jared N. Day, *Race and Renaissance: African Americans in Pittsburgh Since World War II* (Pittsburgh: University of Pittsburgh Press, 2010); John F. Bauman and Edward K. Muller, *Before Renaissance: Planning in Pittsburgh, 1889–1943* (Pittsburgh: University of Pittsburgh Press, 2006); Stefan Lorant, *Pittsburgh: The Story of an American City*, 5th ed. (Pittsburgh: Esselmont Books, 1999); Roy Lubove, *Twentieth-Century Pittsburgh* (New York: John Wiley and Sons, 1969); Roy Lubove, *Twentieth-Century Pittsburgh: The Post-Steel Era*, vol. 2 (Pittsburgh: University of Pittsburgh Press, 1996); Shelby Stewman and Joel A. Tarr, "Four Decades of Public-Private Partnerships in Pittsburgh," in R. Scott Foster and Renee A. Berger, eds., *Public-Private Partnerships in American Cities* (Lanham: Lexington Books, 1982). Specific books about the development of health care in Pittsburgh include Margaret Albert, *A Practical Vision: The Story of Blue Cross of Western Pennsylvania* (Pittsburgh: Blue Cross of Western Pennsylvania, 1987); Robert C. Alberts, *Pitt: The Story of the University of Pittsburgh, 1787–1987* (Pittsburgh: University of Pittsburgh Press, 1986); Carol Stein Bleier, Lu Donnelly, and Samuel P. Granowitz, *L'Chaim, to Good Health and Life: A History of Montefiore Hospital of Pittsburgh, Pennsylvania, 1898–1990* (Pittsburgh: Chas. M. Henry, 1997); Mary Brignano, *Beyond the Bounds: A History of UPMC* (Pittsburgh: Dorrance, 2009); Lawton R. Burns et al., "The Fall of the House of AHERF: The Allegheny Bankruptcy, a Chronicle of the Hows and the Whys of the Nation's Largest Non-Profit Healthcare Failure," *Health Affairs* 19, no. 1 (2000). An alternate version of this article was published by Lawton R. Burns and Alexandra P. Burns, titled "Policy Implications of Hospital System Failures: The Allegheny Bankruptcy," as a chapter in Rosemary Stevens, Charles E. Rosenberg, and Lawton R. Burns, eds., *History and Health Policy in the United States: Putting the Past Back In, Critical Issues in Health and Medicine* (New Brunswick: Rutgers University Press, 2006); Barbara I. Paull, *A Century of Medical Excellence: The History of the University of Pittsburgh School of Medicine* (Pittsburgh: University of Pittsburgh Medical Alumni Association, 1986); Georgine Scarpino, *The Rise and Fall of Faith-Based Hospitals: The Allegheny County Story* (Bloomington: AuthorHouse, 2013); Judith P. Swazey, *Merger Games: The Medical College of Pennsylvania, Hahnemann University, and the Rise and Fall of the Allegheny Health Care System* (Philadelphia: Temple University Press, 2012). The *Pittsburgh Post-Gazette* has also been very helpful, especially the work of Steve Levin in 2005.

18. There is an emerging literature on the decline of industrial and rise of postindustrial economies in American cities. Many of these works also draw an explicit connection between postindustrial transformations and neoliberalism. See Barry Bluestone and Bennett Harrison, *The Deindustrialization of America: Plant Closings, Community Abandonment, and the Dismantling of Basic Industry* (New York: Basic Books, 1982). There are also two excellent new books

which examine Pittsburgh: Allen Dieterich-Ward, *Beyond Rust: Metropolitan Pittsburgh and the Fate of Urban America* (Philadelphia: University of Pennsylvania Press, 2016); Tracy Neumann, *Remaking the Rust Belt: The Post-Industrial Transformation of Urban America* (Philadelphia: University of Pennsylvania Press, 2016); Patrick Vitale, "The Atomic Capital of the World: Technoscience, Suburbanization, and the Remaking of Pittsburgh During the Cold War" (PhD diss., University of Toronto, 2013). For the effect of the rise of postindustrial economies on urban areas, see William J. Wilson, *The Truly Disadvantaged: The Inner City, the Underclass, and Public Policy* (Chicago: University of Chicago Press, 1987); William J. Wilson, *When Work Disappears: The World of the New Urban Poor* (New York: Vintage Books, 1997); Michael B. Katz, ed., *The "Underclass" Debate: Views from History* (Princeton: Princeton University Press, 1993); Thomas J. Sugrue, *The Origins of the Urban Crisis: Race and Inequality in Postwar Detroit* (Princeton: Princeton University Press, 1996); Heather Ann Thompson, *Whose Detroit? Politics, Labor, and Race in a Modern American City* (Ithaca: Cornell University Press, 2001); Robert O. Self, *American Babylon: Race and the Struggle for Postwar Oakland* (Princeton: Princeton University Press, 2003); Matthew D. Lassiter, *The Silent Majority: Suburban Politics in the Sunbelt South* (Princeton: Princeton University Press, 2006); and Matthew Countryman, *Up South: Civil Rights and Black Power in Philadelphia* (Philadelphia: University of Pennsylvania Press, 2006). For more general overviews of the larger economic transition during the postwar years, see Jefferson Cowie, *Stayin' Alive: The 1970s and the Last Days of the Working Class* (New York: New Press, 2010); Jennifer Light, *From Warfare to Welfare: Defense Intellectuals and Urban Problems in Cold War* America (Baltimore: Johns Hopkins University Press, 2003); Judith Stein, *Pivotal Decade: How the United States Traded Factories for Finance in the Seventies* (New Haven: Yale University Press, 2010).

19. Because of all the rapid additions of papers to local archives, I have kept the citations in the form in which I encountered them. However, some papers cited in this book, like Peter Safar's, Evan Stoddard's, and Denton Cooley's, have been formally donated to the University of Pittsburgh, the Heinz History Center, and the John P. McGovern Historical Collections and Research Center, respectively. Others, like the Memorial Hermann papers, are currently undergoing formal processing. Interested parties should contact the archivists at these institutions to get a better understanding of the contents and any new access requirements related to these papers.

20. This book builds on a tradition in urban environmental history and the history of public health to explore how contemporary actors equated physical health with urban progress. For some examples of how historians have explored this link, see Martin V. Melosi, *The Sanitary City: Environmental Services in Urban America from Colonial Times to the Present*, abridged ed. (Pittsburgh: University of Pittsburgh Press, 2008); Joel A. Tarr, *The Search for the Ultimate Sink: Urban Pollution in Historical Perspective*, 1st ed. (Akron, Ohio: University of Akron Press, 1996); Judith Walzer Leavitt, *The Healthiest City: Milwaukee and the Politics of Health Reform* (Princeton: Princeton University Press, 1982).

21. Historian Guian McKee has argued that one way to think about the intersection is that health policy has become urban policy, especially around issues of land management and employment. Guian McKee, "Health-Care Policy as Urban Policy: Hospitals and Community Development in the Post-Industrial City," Working Paper for the Federal Reserve Bank of San Francisco, December 2010. Historian Jared Day has echoed McKee's arguments about the role of hospitals in both areas in his introduction to a special section on health care and cities

in the *Journal of Urban History*, published in March 2016. Day has also drawn a crucial connection to the way that health care has reshaped the power structure of the postindustrial city by asking if the actions of health care leaders in Pittsburgh "echo those of industrial titans of the late nineteenth century." This book engaged with both arguments throughout; however, it focuses less on overall health care employment and instead examines how institutions sought to promote specific types of health care employment—often tied to specialty medicine or advanced research. Doing so allows me to examine some of the more aspirational aspects of the changing business of medicine, which I argue were essential for building the concept of the medical metropolis. The day-to-day working environment of hospital floors and other health care is an important story that requires more attention and is, fortunately, receiving attention by scholars like Gabriel Winant in his dissertation "Crucible of Care: Economic Change and Inequality in Postwar Pittsburgh, 1955–1995" (PhD diss., Yale University, 2018). This book also largely eschews telling a story of hospitals and urban renewal (see note 10 for scholars telling this story). The physical expansion of medical centers helped build the medical metropolis; however, unlike in Boston or Birmingham, urban renewal politics never played a central role in the critique of the medical metropolis in Pittsburgh or Houston.

Chapter 1

1. Hospital Council of Western Pennsylvania, *Pittsburgh's Fortresses of Health*, 1959, 3. In Houston, boosters referred to the Texas Medical Center as a "citadel of health." U.S. Information Agency Publication, "The Citadel of Health," 1964, RLC, Box 331, Folder 10.

2. "RX Eternal Triangle: Research, Education, Treatment," *Houston Magazine*, August 1955 TMCI, Series 3 Box 20, FF, News from Outside Sources, Brochures and Clippings. This relationship has also been described as a three-legged stool.

3. Fox, *Health Policies, Health Politics*, 123–131; Shonick, *Government and Health Services*, 357–366; Stevens, *In Sickness and in Wealth*, 216–219.

4. Allegheny County website, "Authorities, Boards, Committees . . . Hospital Development Authority." This was established in 1971. http://apps.alleghenycounty.us/website/boards.asp?Board = 158.

5. Robert Cook-Deegan and Michael McGeary, "The Jewel in the Federal Crown? History, Politics, and the National Institutes of Health," in Stevens, Rosenberg, and Burns, *History and Health Policy in the United States*, 176–201; Keith Wailoo, *Dying in the City of the Blues: Sickle Cell Anemia and the Politics of Race and Health* (Chapel Hill: University of North Carolina Press, 2000); Barron H. Lerner, *The Breast Cancer Wars: Hope, Fear and the Pursuit of a Cure in Twentieth-Century America* (New York: Oxford University Press, 2003).

6. One of the critical ways that philanthropy intersected with public policy was in helping to raise matching funds to unlock Hill-Burton funding. Memorandum from E. R. McCluskey to Lawrence L. Monnett Jr., "Advance Foundation Pledges for Health Center Building Fund," April 27, 1961, EHL, Box 60, Folder 520; letter from E. R. McCluskey to Ira J. Mills, RE: Letter of Intent, 1963 Hill Burton, EHL, Box 60, Folder 520; and "A Report of the University Health Center and the Proposed Capital Improvement Plan," March 1, 1961, UHC, Box 1, FF 5, 18. For a secondary source overview, including a history of the $21.5 million Fund for Health Center Hospitals campaign launched in the early 1960s, see Andrew T. Simpson, "Private Dollars for a Healthier Public," chapter under preparation for Kathy Buechel, ed., *Reflections on Philanthropy in Pittsburgh*, sponsored by the Pittsburgh Philanthropy Project, University of Pittsburgh Graduate School of Public and International Affairs. For a general

overview of philanthropy and its relationship to the state in the twentieth century, see Zunz, *Philanthropy in America*. For more about the growth of hospitals and the geographic distribution of health care resources, see Fox, *Health Policies, Health Politics*, 16–20; Rosenberg, *The Care of Strangers*; Stevens, *In Sickness and in Wealth*; Risse, *Mending Bodies, Saving Souls*.

7. Rosenberg, *The Care of Strangers*, esp. chap. 13.

8. Elizabeth Popp Berman, *Creating the Market University: How Academic Science Became an Economic Engine* (Princeton: Princeton University Press, 2012), 31.

9. Howell, *Technology in the Hospital*; David Rosner, "Doing Well or Doing Good: The Ambivalent Focus of Hospital Administration," in Long and Golden, *The American General Hospital*, 157–169.

10. Edward K. Muller, "Metropolis and Region: A Framework for Enquiry into Western Pennsylvania," in Hays, *City at the Point* (Pittsburgh: University of Pittsburgh Press, 1989), 181–211.

11. Oscar Handlin, "The City Grows," in Lorant, *Pittsburgh*, 88.

12. Kenneth Warren, *Triumphant Capitalism: Henry Clay Frick and the Industrial Transformation of America* (Pittsburgh: University of Pittsburgh Press, 1996), 15, 22; John P. Hoerr, *And the Wolf Finally Came: The Decline of the American Steel Industry* (Pittsburgh: University of Pittsburgh Press, 1988), 86.

13. Hoerr, *And the Wolf Finally Came*, 90–93.

14. Stevens, *In Sickness and in Wealth*, 61–62; Starr, *The Social Transformation of American Medicine*, 112–123; Ludmerer, *Learning to Heal*, 166–190.

15. The Flexner Report had hailed the University of Pittsburgh's medical school as a strong example of how cooperation with a university could improve a school's physical condition and teaching standards. In 1913, the school was given an A+ ranking by the American Medical Association's Council on Medical Education. Evidently, in the subsequent years, funding for the school proved insufficient to maintain this ranking. "History of the University of Pittsburgh School of Medicine," online at http://www.medschool.pitt.edu/about/history; Paull, *A Century of Medical Excellence*, 67–69, 90–91.

16. Alberts, *Pitt*, 118; also noted by R. R. Huggins in "The Advance of Medicine in Pittsburgh," *Pittsburgh Record*, October–November 1931, JGB, Box 6, FF 50.

17. Alberts, *Pitt*, 79–80.

18. Paull, *A Century of Medical Excellence*, 94–98, 118–123. Paull calls Bowman "sympathetic but detached in regard to the medical school, and its needs stood second to those of the university," which was facing substantial financial distress (119).

19. Simpson, "Private Dollars for a Healthier Public"; Paull, *A Century of Medical Excellence*, 95. Quotations from "The Logic of a Medical Center: Views of American Leaders in Medicine on Pittsburgh's Proposed Coalition of Hospitals," ca. 1920s/1930s, UHC, 90/43 A, Box 1, Folder 771.

20. Paull, *A Century of Medical Excellence*, 132–139; Arlene Lowenstein, "A Historical Study of the Development of the Falk Clinic as Part of the University of Pittsburgh Medical Center," UHC, 90/43/3 Publications, Falk Clinic, Box 1, Folder; Paull, *A Century of Medical Excellence*, 138; Agnes Lynch Starrett, *The Maurice and Laura Falk Foundation: A Private Fortune—A Public Trust* (Pittsburgh: Historical Society of Western Pennsylvania, 1966), 8–9, 180–181; Pohla Smith, "Magee-Womens Hospital Turns 100," *Pittsburgh Post-Gazette*, January 19, 2011, http://www.post-gazette.com/life/lifestyle/2011/01/19/Magee-Womens-Hospital-turns-100/stories/201101190146.

21. The Hospital Council of Western Pennsylvania, "General Hospitals in Southwestern Pennsylvania: A Survey and Report on Facilities, Utilization, Personnel, Finance, and Construction," July 1958, individual county percentages on page 19, overall growth rate on page 1. For information about the county's Catholic hospital growth, see Scarpino, *The Rise and Fall of Faith-Based Hospitals*; Carson, *Healing Body, Mind, and Spirit: The History of the St. Francis Medical Center* (Pittsburgh: Carnegie Mellon University Press, 1995). For other area hospital histories, see Ruth C. Maszkiewicz, *The Presbyterian Hospital of Pittsburgh: From Its Foundation to Affiliation with the University of Pittsburgh* (Pittsburgh: Presbyterian-University Hospital, 1978); Bleier, Donnelly, and Granowitz, *L'Chaim*. Mary Brignano, through her individual hospital histories, has also helped to excavate this story. Mary Brignano, *The Story of St. Margaret* (Pittsburgh: UPMC St. Margaret, 1998); *Inheritors of a Glorious Reality: The History of the People of Shadyside Hospital* (Pittsburgh: Shadyside Hospital, 1991); *Strength to Strength: A History of Montefiore Hospital and Jewish Health Care in Pittsburgh* (Pittsburgh: Jewish Healthcare Foundation, 1992).

22. David Lawrence, "Rebirth," in Lorant, *Pittsburgh*, 373–448; Tarr and Stewman, "Four Decades of Public-Private Partnerships in Pittsburgh," 59–127. Jon Teaford notes that private business-oriented coalitions as urban renewal initiators were not abnormal for this period. Jon Teaford, *The Rough Road to Renaissance: Urban Revitalization in America, 1940–1985* (Baltimore: Johns Hopkins University Press, 1990), 45–54; Sherie R. Mershon, "Corporate Social Responsibility and Urban Revitalization: The Allegheny Conference on Community Development, 1943–1968" (PhD diss., Carnegie Mellon University, 2000). The Mellon family were particularly generous donors to the University of Pittsburgh and its health center. A 1964 estimate of the family's giving to the health professions calculated it at $54,653,062. This is discussed in Simpson, "Private Dollars for a Healthier Public." Funding numbers come from "Up to Date Review of the Health Center University of Pittsburgh," November 23, 1964, UHC, Box 1, Folder 3, V.

23. Ralph Reichold, "A Cartoonist Looks at Pittsburgh," 1949, ACCD, Box 21, Folder 61.

24. "Look to the New Pittsburgh," UHC, 90/43, Box 1, Folder 1.

25. Herbert K. Abrams, "A Short History of Occupational Health," *Journal of Public Health Policy* 22, no. 1 (2001), 34–80; Michael Gouchfield, "Occupational Medicine Practice in the United States Since the Industrial Revolution," *Journal of Occupational and Environmental Medicine* 47, no. 2 (February 2005), 115–131; Christopher Sellers, *Hazards of the Job: From Industrial Disease to Environmental Health Science* (Chapel Hill: University of North Carolina Press, 1997).

26. Paull, *A Century of Medical Excellence*, 147–148.

27. *Stretching Your Vision: The University of Pittsburgh Medical Center* (Pittsburgh: Ketchum Incorporated, 1952), 15. The Industrial Hygiene Foundation was founded in 1935 at the Mellon Institute in Pittsburgh as the Air Hygiene Foundation. Industrial air pollution, especially silicosis, was an early area of concern. It became the Industrial Hygiene Foundation in 1941. Industrial Hygiene Foundation, *History of Industrial Hygiene Foundation: A Research Association of Industries for Advancing Industrial Health and Improving Working Conditions* (Pittsburgh: Mellon Institute, 1956), 10; David Rosner and Gerald Markowitz, "Workers, Industry, and the Control of Information: Silicosis and the Industrial Hygiene Foundation," *Journal of Public Health Policy* 16, no. 1 (Spring 1995), 29–58.

28. Andrew T. Simpson, "Transporting Lazarus: Physicians, the State, and the Creation of the Modern Paramedic and Ambulance, 1955–1973," *Journal of the History of Medicine and*

Allied Sciences 68, no. 2 (2013), 163–197; Anne K. Merritt, "The Rise of Emergency Medicine in the Sixties: Paving a New Entrance to the House of Medicine," *Journal of the History of Medicine and Allied Sciences* 69, no. 2 (2014), 251–293; Allegheny General Hospital Annual Report, 1961–1962, EHL, Box 65, FF 548, 9–10. Beatrix Hoffman, "Emergency Rooms: The Reluctant Safety Net," in Stevens, Rosenberg, and Burns, *History and Health Policy in the United States*, 250–272; "Magee Third Largest 'Baby Port' in Nation and Busiest in State," *Pittsburgh Post*, August 19, 1959, UHC, health center clippings file, 1956 to 1959, Box 1, Folder 3.

29. Wailoo, *Dying in the City of the Blues*.

30. University of Pittsburgh Medical Center, "War on Polio: A Progress Report of the University of Pittsburgh Medical Center," September 1952, UHC, 90/43-A, University Health Center Memorabilia, Box 1, Folder 1.

31. Stephen E. Mawdsley, *Selling Science: Polio and the Promise of Gamma Globulin* (New Brunswick: Rutgers University Press, 2016); Jeffrey Kluger, *Splendid Solution: Jonas Salk and the Conquest of Polio* (New York: G. P. Putnam's Sons, 2005); David M. Oshinsky, *Polio: An American Story* (New York: Oxford, 2005); John Troan, *Passport to Adventure: Or, How a Typewriter from Santa Led to an Exciting Lifetime Journey* (Pittsburgh: Geyer Printing Co., 2000), 180–245. For a brief overview of the power of research as a definer of community identity, also see Simpson, "Private Dollars for A Healthier Public," and Andrew T. Simpson, "Health and Renaissance," *Journal of Urban History* 41, no. 1 (2014), 19–27. See University of Pittsburgh Medical Center, "Behind the Scenes of Medical Research," program from a dinner, May 12, 1952, UHC, 90/43-A, UHC Memorabilia, Box 1, Folder 1; Lorant, *Pittsburgh*, 408, 445, 714; University of Pittsburgh "Defeat of an Enemy: Chancellor Mark A. Nordenberg reports on the 50th Anniversary Celebration of the Triumph of the Pitt Polio Vaccine," http://www.chancellor-emeritus.pitt.edu/sites/default/pdfs/defeat_enemy.pdf.

32. Stevens, *In Sickness and in Wealth*, 260; Chapin, *Ensuring America's Health*; Cunningham and Cunningham, *The Blues*.

33. Chapin, *Ensuring America's Health*; Quadagno, *One Nation, Uninsured*, 48–76.

34. Albert, *A Practical Vision*, 62.

35. Blue Cross of Western Pennsylvania, "Blue Cross of Western Pennsylvania Plan History," Revised Version April 1974, 10–14, 20; courtesy of Highmark.

36. Albert, *A Practical Vision*, 75. For more about the development of smaller wards and semiprivate rooms in a more general context, see Stevens, *In Sickness and in Wealth*, 111–114.

37. Abraham Oseroff, "A Program for Hospitals of the Pittsburgh Area," sponsored by the Hospital Council of Western Pennsylvania, April 1947 28. "State-aided hospitals" were hospitals that received some money from the state to offset the cost of indigent care; quote on 27–28.

38. Elliott, *The Birth of the Texas Medical Center*, 61.

39. Ibid., 63.

40. Johnson, *Houston: The Unknown City*, 3–12.

41. Yellow fever was an important concern and hit Houston with epidemics in 1839, 1844, 1848, 1854, 1855, 1858, 1859, 1862, and 1867. McComb, *Houston*, 88–91, 88.

42. Igor Vojnovic, "Governance in Houston: Growth Theories and Urban Pressures," *Journal of Urban Affairs* 25, no. 5 (2003), 606; Feagin, *Free Enterprise City*, 60–61.

43. For a wide range of sources on the history of the oil industry in Texas, see the University of Houston Center for Public History's bibliography of Houston-area sources. For

a more general history of the oil industry, see Daniel Yergin, *The Prize: The Epic Quest for Oil, Money, and Power* (New York: Simon & Schuster, 1991).

44. Feagin, *Free Enterprise City*, 76–148.

45. Macon, *Monroe Dunaway Anderson*, 25.

46. Ibid., 64–65.

47. Ibid., 71.

48. Macon, *Monroe Dunaway Anderson*, 85, and *The Texas Medical Center—Its Origins*, 11. *The Texas Medical Center—Its Origins* is located on noncirculating research shelves at TMC.

49. Macon, *Monroe Dunaway Anderson*, 139; Olson, *Making Cancer History*, 34.

50. Alex Orlando, "Building a City of Medicine," *TMC News*, August 19, 2014.

51. *An Historical Resume of the University of Texas Postgraduate School of Medicine*, 1958. Located on noncirculating research shelves at TMC.

52. SoRelle, *The Quest for Excellence*, 1–18. Prior to 1969, when it separated from Baylor University, the formal name of the institution was Baylor University College of Medicine.

53. *The Texas Medical Center—Its Origins*, 40–43.

54. SoRelle, *The Quest for Excellence*, 45.

55. James A. Tinsley, *The Texas Medical Center: A History of the Founding Years, 1941–1980*, unpublished manuscript, TMCI, chap. 3, 3. The hospital was transferred to the Veterans Administration in 1949.

56. Joseph Pratt, "8F and Many More: Business and Civic Leadership in Modern Houston," *Houston Review of History and Culture* 1, no. 2 (2004), 2–8, 31–44; Feagin, *Free Enterprise City*, 120–121; Benke, *Risk and Ruin*, 17–19.

57. Feagin, *Free Enterprise City*, 126.

58. Jim Abercrombie, for example, gave the seed money for Texas Children's Hospital. Gus Wortham was a member of the board at Texas Children's; James Elkins Sr. was on the board at Methodist; and Leon Jaworski served on the boards of M. D. Anderson and Baylor College of Medicine, and as president of the TMC Inc. board. Other 8F members were also involved, either as board members or contributors to TMC institutions.

59. Feagin, *Free Enterprise City*, 134.

60. Elliott, *The Birth of the Texas Medical Center*, 147.

61. Tinsley, *The Texas Medical Center*, chap. 5, 3.

62. Sibley, *The Methodist Hospital of Houston*, 9–12, 119.

63. "The New Methodist Hospital," *Modern Hospital*. Reprinted from a special section on the Texas Medical Center, November 1952, in Brochures 1950s, TMCI, no. 2, Series 3, Box 15, TMC; Sibley, *The Methodist Hospital of Houston*, 168, 143, 146–148.

64. See Parrish, *Legacy*, 3, 11, 15–18; and Tinsley, *The Texas Medical Center*, chap. 5, 23–25.

65. Tinsley, *Texas Medical Center*, chap. 6, 12–14.

66. "Hospital of Ideas," *Architectural Forum*, February 1952, 116–124. For more recent efforts to link M. D. Anderson's research and community development, see Research Milestones: Making Cancer History, MDA, Box 66, Miscellaneous, TMC; "Houston's Science-Research-Medical-Community Securing Our Future," *Houston Magazine*, November 1967, 68–70, HMRC, H-Medical Center–1960–1969.

67. Louis Blackburn, "Baylor's Research Put Houston in Forefront in War on Disease," *Houston Press*, May 9, 1961, 2, HMRC, H-Medical Center–1960–1969.

68. "Industry Meets the Challenge: A Progress Report of the University of Pittsburgh Medical Center," ca. 1953, UHC, 90/43-A Box 1 Memorabilia, Folder 1.

69. Arnold A. Rivin, "Your Hospital: A Center for Community Health Services," Chicago: Blue Cross Commission, 1960, 21.

70. Ibid.

71. Rosemary A. Stevens, "Times Past, Times Present," in Long and Golden, *The American General Hospital*, 191–206. Other work in health policy has also explored the relationship between business and health care, notably Paul Starr in *The Social Transformation of American Medicine*. Another interesting attempt to use history to understand the (then current) health care systems is William D. White, "The Corporatization of U.S. Hospitals: What Can We Learn from the Nineteenth Century Industrial Experience?" in J. Warren Salmon, ed., *The Corporate Transformation of Health Care: Perspectives and Implications*, vol. 2 (Amityville, N.Y.: Baywood Publishing, 1994), 33–62.

72. According to Evan Melhado, "The Hill Burton Act paid lip service to a planned, regionalized system, but provided no means to achieve it; the sponsoring coalition had downplayed hierarchy to avoid opposition." Thus, for urban areas, especially in Pittsburgh, he argues that corporate and philanthropic interests played a much more important role in promoting hospital planning interests. E. M. Melhado, "Health Planning in the United States and the Decline of Public-Interest Policy Making," *Millbank Quarterly* 84, no. 2 (June 2006), 359–440; "New Group Plans Hospital Fund Program," *Pittsburgh Press*, October 30, 1959, 2; "A Proposal for Organization and Methods of Operation: The Hospital Planning Association of Allegheny County," HPA. For a critique of the corporate origins of voluntary health planning, see Louis Tannen, "Health Planning as a Regulatory Strategy," in J. Warren Salmon, ed., *The Corporate Transformation of Health Care: Issues and Directions*, vol. 1 (Amityville, N.Y.: Baywood Publishing, 1990), 19–36.

73. HPA, bound volumes 1959–1964, 1965–1969, 1968–1969. National-level voluntary planning efforts, including the work of Michael DeBakey through the President's Commission on Heart Disease, Cancer, and Stroke, is discussed by Stevens, *In Sickness and in Wealth*, 275–281.

74. History of UPMC Mercy, at http://www.upmc.com/locations/hospitals/mercy/about/Pages/history.aspx.

75. Letter from George Schein to John Schneider, December 16, 1968, HPA, Box 1, FF 1. See loose documents in Folder 1 for admission numbers.

76. UHCP, "University Health Center of Pittsburgh is Proposed Corporation," press release, August 21, 1965, UHC, 90/43/1, Box 1 Folder 2. For more on the study committee that preceded the creation of UHCP, see "Report of the Special Study Committee of the Health Center," July 21, 1958, UHC, Box 1, Folder 12.

77. The Hospital Council of Western Pennsylvania, "General Hospitals in Southwestern Pennsylvania." The report noted that this $76 million figure translated into $22 per resident (4).

78. Edward Litchfield, untitled note/typed, "Contributions to Allegheny County Residents for 1962–1963," EHL, Box 31, Folder 246; Simpson, "Health and Renaissance," 21.

79. Ludmerer, *Time to Heal*, 172; Dominique Tobbell, "Plow, Town, and Gown: The Politics of Family Practice in 1960s America," *Bulletin of the History of Medicine* 87, no. 4 (Winter 2013), 648–680.

80. American Medical Association, "Summary of Survey of University of Pittsburgh School of Medicine," December 9–12, 1957, with agenda items for meeting of February 7–8, 1958, Executive Council Meetings and Agendas, Association of American Medical Colleges, as quoted in Ludmerer, *Time to Heal*, 172, chap. 9, n. 59. See 117–118 for a more general discussion of the town-gown relationship in other communities with academic medical centers. For accusations of empire building, see Henry W. Pierce, "Medical School Charged with Empire Building," *Pittsburgh Post-Gazette*, March 19, 1966. For larger regional issues after World War II, see R. E. Gregory, George Schein, Ralph Outten to Edmund McCluskey RE: Intern Matching Complaints, September 12, 1960, EHL, Vice Chancellor of Health Professions Files, Box 62, Folder 521; and Edmund McCluskey to R. E. Gregory RE: Response to Intern Matching Complaints, September 16, 1960, EHL, Vice Chancellor for Health Professions Files, Box 62, Folder 521. For more on the history of physician practices prior to World War II and their relationship to communities, see James A. Schafer, *The Business of Private Medical Practice: Doctors, Specialization, and Urban Change in Philadelphia, 1900–1940* (New Brunswick: Rutgers University Press, 2014).

81. Pittsburgh Commission on Human Relations, "Racial Practices in Pittsburgh Hospitals," January 1959 in University of Pittsburgh Public Service Administration Reports and Studies Collection, University of Pittsburgh Archives, 8.

82. Appendix tables in Trotter and Day, *Race and Renaissance*, 212–214.

83. This term comes from Leon Fink and Brian Greenberg, *Upheaval in the Quiet Zone: 1199SEIU and the Politics of Health Care Unionism* (Chicago: University of Chicago Press, 1989), 1–128.

84. Ibid., 161–164.

85. 1199P, "Help Us Avoid a Hospital Crisis," n.d., 1199, Box 33, Folder 78. Emphasis in original.

86. Edward Norian to Elliott Godoff, December 18, 1969, 1199, Box 33, Folder 109.

87. Edward Norian to all employees, October 28, 1969, 1199, Box 73, Folder 78. The minutes of Presbyterian-University Hospital's Board of Directors also discuss unionization; WWB, Box 8 Folder 142 and Box 8 Folder 158.

88. "End Dictatorship at Presby," 1199, Box 33, Folder 2, ca. 1970.

89. "A Brief History of 1199SEIU United Healthcare Workers East," https://www.1199 seiu.org/history; Adam Parker, "Local Hospital Workers' Courage Changed Workplaces Forever," *Charleston Post and Courier*, September 30, 2013; Jonna McCone and Sheilah Kast, "Coretta Scott King's Visit to Baltimore for Economic Justice," WYPR Public Radio, January 19, 2015; Victor Reisel, "Inside Labor: Mrs. King Leads the Drive," *Indiana Gazette*, December 23, 1969, 4.

90. Quotations in Associated Press, "1199P Hits Pittsburgh," *Uniontown Evening Standard*, March 20, 1970, 6, and crowd numbers in "Coretta Scott King Help in Pgh. Hosp. Dispute," *Pittsburgh New Courier*, April 4, 1970, 3.

91. Fink and Greenberg, *Upheaval in the Quiet Zone*, 161–163.

92. Charter and Restrictions Governing the Texas Medical Center, Houston, Texas, 1945.

93. Elliott, *The Birth of the Texas Medical Center*, 87–88. As early as 1946, the TMC Inc. publicity machine was encouraging the Chamber of Commerce to use a $100 million projected cost figure; "Vision of Yesterday Creates $100,000,000 Medical Center," *Houston Magazine*, April 1946, HMRC, H-Medical Center-Up to 1949. This number and the role of private

philanthropy was also picked up by the popular press. Margaret Davis, "Houston Boasts One of World's Greatest Medical Projects Without Much Federal Help," *Houston Press*, June 20, 1949, HMRC, H-Medical Center-Up to 1949.

94. Elliott, *The Birth of the Texas Medical Center*, 96; James Hamilton and Associates, A Study for the Texas Medical Center Houston, 1946, Section III.

95. R. Lee Clark to Ernst Bertner, May 6, 1948, RLC, Series VIII, Box 331, Folder 5.

96. Tinsley, *The Texas Medical Center*, chap. 4, 7; and Elliott, *The Birth of the Texas Medical Center*, 106. Tinsley, *The Texas Medical Center*, chap. 4, 26; TMC Inc., "Texas Medical Center Annual Report, 1963," TMC Inc. Annual Reports, 13–17.

97. "The Texas Medical Center, the First Five Years," online at Planned Parenthood Gulf Coast website, http://pph.convio.net/site/DocServer/TexasMedCtr1946_1951FirstFive Years.pdf?docID = 2661. Other TMC Inc. trustees included a who's who of Houston, including Leyland Anderson (M. D. Anderson's nephew and president of Clayton, Anderson), Jim Abercrombie, Hines Baker (of Baker Botts, the prominent Houston law firm), Roy Cullen, Mayor Oscar Holcombe, Elliot, Burtner, Bates, and Freeman. Oveta Hobby left the board to become the secretary of the Federal Security Agency. She stepped down in 1955 in the wake of the Cutter polio vaccine controversy.

98. HMRC, H-Medical Center-Brochures and Up to 49; HMRC, H-Medical Center–1950–1959; Brochures 1950s, TMCI, Series 3, Box 15.

99. Mari L. Nicholson-Preuss, "Down and Out in the Old J.D.: Urban Public Hospitals, Institutional Stigma and Medical Indigence in the Twentieth Century" (PhD diss., Department of History, University of Houston, 2010), 303–319. She attributes this conflict to a growing gulf between medical specialists, as exemplified by the medical school and the general practice medical community that dominated the Harris County medical society.

100. Zarko Franks, "Tax Fund Paid by Baylor College Not Unique," *Houston Chronicle*, September 1966, HCHD Scrapbook, 1942–1968.

101. Tinsley, *The Texas Medical Center*, chap. 6, 14–15. Baylor College of Medicine would not formally separate from the Baptist Convention until 1968.

102. Sibley, *The Methodist Hospital of Houston*, 143–144, Tinsley, *The Texas Medical Center*, chap. 5, 15–16.

103. "Houston's Symbol of Hope," *Houston Magazine*, August 1957, 30, HMRC, H-Medical Center–1950–1959. This did not include the figures for those employed in medical construction, which was a sizable percentage of the total workers employed in the construction trade during these years. *Houston Magazine* was a PR arm for the Chamber of Commerce.

104. Houston's Hospitals: The Focus of a Nation's Eyes," *Houston Magazine*, July 1964, FCE, Series IV, Box 9, Folder "News Clippings About TMC," TMC.

105. Southwest Research Institute, Item 7 Total Employment Texas Medical Center, RLC, Series VIII, Box 331, Folder 10, 1, TMC. It is not clear what institutions reported.

106. Southwest Research Institute, Item 7 Male Employment Statistics for Persons Earning Under $600. RLC, Series VIII, Box 331, Folder 10, 4.

107. Southwest Research Institute, Item 7 Female Employment Statistics for Persons Earning Under $600 per Month. RLC, Series VIII, Box 331, Folder 10, 5.

108. Texas Medical Center Council of Directors and Administrators Meeting Minutes, May 29, 1964. RLC, Series VIII, Box 331, Folder 10, 5.

109. Ruth Allen, George N. Green, and James V. Reese, "Labor Organizations," Handbook of Texas Online, online at https://tshaonline.org/handbook/online/articles/oml01; Richard B. Freeman, "Unionism Comes to the Public Sector," *Journal of Economic Literature* 24 (March 1986), 41–48, see table 13.

110. Mary Jane Schier, "More Ben Taub Workers Off Job," *Houston Post*, August 17, 1968; Mary Jane Schier, "Most JD Nurse 'Sickouts' Agree to Return to Work," *Houston Post*, June 29, 1971, HCHD Scrapbook.

111. "Houston's Symbol of Hope," *Houston Magazine*, August 1957; Moselle Boland, "In Three Short Decades Medical Center Earns Renown," *Houston Chronicle*, February 16, 1964, HMRC, H-Vertical File, TMC 1950–1960; "Texas Medical Center," *Modern Hospital*, November 1952; Texas Medical Center Assorted Brochures in TMCI 2, Series 3, Box 15 Brochures.

112. Figures in "Medical Center in the Midst of Construction Boom with More to Come," *Houston Post*, November 21, 1974. See also Mary Jane Schier, "Medical Center Growth in '76 Largest Since Founding," *Houston Post*, January 2, 1977, in H-Medical Center 1970–1979, HRMC Vertical File Collection; Kevin B. Blackstone, "Medical Center Helping Cure Houston's Slump," *Dallas Morning News*, December 26, 1987; "Medical Center Helps Ailing Economy," *Houston Post*, January 5, 1987, HMRC, H-Medical Center–1980s; Sandy Lutz, "Healthcare's Building Up in Houston," *Modern Health Care*, July 31, 1987, HMRC, H-Medical. For more on medical construction and economic impact in the 1990s and 2000s, see TMCI, Mary Schiflett Files, Box 4, TMC Economic Impact 2000-UH Clear Lake Material; TMC Inc., MSF, Box 4, Federal Reserve Article; TMC Inc., MSF Box 5, TMC Facts and Figures 1990s–2000s.

113. Franklin D. Murphy, "Report of the Chairman of the Committee on Public Information," American Association of Medical Colleges, Minutes of the Sixty-First Annual Meeting, October 23, 24, and 25, 1950, Lake Placid, NY, 36–38; quotations on 37; Alan C. Davis, "Medical School Public Relations: Whose Responsibility," *Journal of Medical Education* 39 (May 1964), 470–475; C. Lincoln Williston, "The Medical School and Public Relations," *Journal of Medical Education* 28, no. 5 (May 1953), 33–37.

114. Baylor—A Catalyst for Houston's Growth," *Inside Baylor Medicine*, BCM Box, Inside Baylor Medicine 1967–1980, Folder 1960s. The question of physician distribution and retention had important public policy implications and was the subject of a range of studies throughout the 1960s and 1970s. One of the earliest, and most influential, was "Trends in Medical Practice: An Analysis of the Distribution and Characteristics of Medical College Graduates, 1915–1950." This study did find that at least by 1950, many Baylor graduates remained in the same state and community as their prior residence (assuming that they came from Texas). Moreover, Baylor graduates from the class of 1950 practiced in communities of various sizes across the state. Herman G. Weiskotten, Walter S. Wiggins, Marion E Altenderfer, Marjorie Gooch, Anne Tipner, "An Analysis of the Distribution and Characteristics of Medical College Graduates, 1915–1950," *Journal of Medical Education* 35, no. 12 (December 1960), 1017–1121, see esp. 1111–1114. This work was followed up on several times, including by Lawrence E. Schwartz and James R. Cantwell, "Weiskotten Survey, Class of 1960," *Journal of Medical Education* 51, no. 7 (July 1976), 533–540. This survey did not provide as much detail about individual schools as the 1960 survey, but it did note that physicians were increasingly migrating away from rural communities and that increasing specialization was having

an impact on the size of the community in which physicians were choosing to locate their practice. For another detailed study of physician location, see Philip J. Held, "The Migration of the 1955–1965 Graduates of American Medical Schools," Paper P–35, Ford Foundation, January 1973.

Chapter 2

1. Jeff Krieger, "A Time for Mercy Hospital," *Pittsburgher Magazine*, Winter 1972, NCHC, Box 2, Folder 14, 23.

2. Since the middle of the 1960s, there has been a debate over the emergence of an urban "underclass" and what this means for the present and future of American society. For an overview, see Michael Katz, "The Urban 'Underclass' as a Metaphor of Social Transformation," in Katz, *The "Underclass" Debate*; Kenneth Kusmer and Joe W. Trotter, "Introduction," in Kenneth Kusmer and Joe W. Trotter, eds., *African American Urban History Since World War II* (Chicago: University of Chicago Press, 2009), 2–3; William Julius Wilson, *The Truly Disadvantaged: The Inner City, The Underclass, and Public Policy* (Chicago: University of Chicago Press, 1987). For the classic study of postwar urban change, see Sugrue, *The Origins of the Urban Crisis*.

3. Stevens, *In Sickness and in Wealth*, 268–275. For more on efforts to redefine health as part of a larger package of human rights in the 1960s and beyond, see Jonathan Engel, *Poor People's Medicine: Medicaid and American Charity Care Since 1965* (Durham: Duke University Press, 2006), 93–98, Engel, *Unaffordable*, 16–24; Porter, "Inner-City Economic Development." For the theory of the creative class and urban transformation, see Florida, *The Rise of the Creative Class*. The phrase "No margin, no mission" is typically attributed to Sister Irene Krauss, the founding CEO of the Daughters of Charity Health System.

4. For an overview of health care in the early 1960s, including citations for important primary sources, see Rosemary A. Stevens, "Health Care in the Early 1960s," *Health Care Financing Review* 18, no. 2 (Winter 1996), 11–22.

5. "Some Facts About 'Free' Service Provided by Non-Profit Hospitals in Allegheny County," EHL, Box 62, Folder 520; Minutes of Meeting to Discuss "Free" Hospital Care Financing May 2, 1962, EHL, Box 65, Folder 548.

6. Minutes of Meeting to Discuss "Free" Hospital Care Financing May 2, 1962, EHL, Box 65, Folder 548, 2.

7. Stevens and Stevens, *Welfare Medicine in America*, 61–65.

8. "Anatomy of a Dilemma," in Stevens, *The Public-Private Health Care State*, 124.

9. The story of passing both programs has been studied extensively. Theodore R. Marmor and Jan S. Marmor, *The Politics of Medicare* (Chicago: Aldine, 1973); Zelizer, *Taxing America*, 212–254. See also Eric Patashnik and Julian Zelizer, "Paying for Medicare: Benefits, Budgets, and Wilbur Mills's Policy Legacy," *Journal of the Health Politics, Policy, and Law* 26, no. 1 (2001), 7–36.

10. Ludmerer, *Time to Heal*, 221–236.

11. Diane Perry, "Relentless War on Rats Now Being Waged in Pittsburgh," *New Pittsburgh Courier*, March 29, 1971, 29. For a general overview of urban renewal, see Jon C. Teaford, *The Rough Road to Renaissance: Urban Revitalization in America, 1940–1985* (Baltimore: Johns Hopkins University Press, 1990). For Pittsburgh, see Trotter and Day, *Race and Renaissance*.

12. McKee, "The Hospital City in an Ethnic Enclave," 259–283; and Conner, "The University That Ate Birmingham," 284–305.

13. Simpson, "Private Dollars for a Healthier Public"; Allegheny County Mental Health/Mental Retardation Program Drug Abuse Proposal to National Institute of Mental Health Narcotic Addiction Rehabilitation Branch, March 29, 1971, MFMF, Box 20, Folder 10, 1. Briefing on Drug Treatment Programs, November 3, 1970, MFMF, Box 20, Folder 9.

14. City of Pittsburgh Model City Agency, Comprehensive Demonstration Program Application Part I, April 30, 1969, ACCD, Box 231, Folder 1, 8–3, 8–4, 8–7.

15. For health disparities in Pittsburgh, see "Housing Is Blamed for Tot Mortality," *Pittsburgh Courier,* October 5, 1946, 1; "N.S. Has Highest Death Rate Here," *Pittsburgh Courier,* January 7, 1958. For national issues of health disparities, see "Dr. Ferebee Deplores High Death Rate," *Pittsburgh Courier,* February 10, 1940, 8; W. Montague Cobb, "50 Years of Progress in Health," *Pittsburgh Courier,* April 22, 1950, 8; Carolyn Leonard Carson, "And the Results Showed Promise: Physicians, Childbirth, and Southern Black Migrant Women, 1916–1930; Pittsburgh as a Case Study," *Journal of American Ethnic History* 14, no. 1 (Fall 1994), 32–64; Lubove, *Twentieth-Century Pittsburgh,* vol. 1, 59–86; Laurence Glasco, "The Double Burden: The Black Experience in Pittsburgh," in Hays, ed., *City at the Point,* 69–110; Joel A. Tarr and Terry Yousie, "Critical Decisions in Pittsburgh Water and Wastewater Treatment," in Joel A. Tarr, ed., *Devastation and Renewal: An Environmental History of Pittsburgh and its Region* (Pittsburgh: University of Pittsburgh Press, 2003), 64–88. For a look at health disparities in other cities, see Brett Williams, "Deadly Inequalities: Race, Illness, and Poverty in Washington, D.C., Since 1945," in Kusmer and Trotter, *African American Urban History Since World War II,* 142–159. For more general readings in postwar urban health and health inequalities, see Brandon Ward, "Detroit Wild: Race, Labor, and Postwar Urban Environmentalism" (PhD diss., Purdue University, 2014); David Whiteis, "Unhealthy Cities: Corporate Medicine, Community Economic Underdevelopment, and Public Health," *International Journal of Health Services* 27, no. 2 (1997), 227–242. For an overview of the distrust between urban residents and medical centers, see Rebecca Skloot, *The Immortal Life of Henrietta Lacks* (New York: Crown, 2010); Engel, *Poor People's Medicine,* esp. chap. 4. In the late 1950s, seven Pittsburgh hospitals were accused of discriminating in employment and inpatient admissions. Pittsburgh Commission on Human Relations, "Racial Practices in Pittsburgh Hospitals," January 1959.

16. For a more general look at the relationship between health care and social change, see David McBride, *Integrating the City of Medicine: Blacks in Philadelphia Health Care, 1910–1965* (Philadelphia: Temple University Press, 1989); Susan L. Smith, *Sick and Tired of Being Sick and Tired: Black Women's Health Activism in America, 1890–1950* (Philadelphia: University of Pennsylvania Press, 1995); John Dittmer, *The Good Doctors: The Medical Committee on Human Rights and the Struggle for Social Justice in Health Care* (London: Bloomsbury Press, 2011); Beatrix Hoffman, "Don't Scream Alone: The Health Care Activism of Poor Americans in the 1970s," in Beatrix Hoffman, Nancy Tomes, Rachel Grob, and Mark Schlesinger, eds., *Patients as Policy Actors* (New Brunswick: Rutgers University Press, 2011); Alondra Nelson, *Body and Soul: The Black Panther Party and the Fight Against Medical Discrimination* (Minneapolis: University of Minnesota Press, 2011); Loyd, *Health Rights Are Civil Rights.*

17. Diane Perry, "The Making of A Black Militant," *New Pittsburgh Courier,* October 9, 1971, 2; Earl B. Smith, "Racism in Medicine Poses Threat to Negroes," *Pittsburgh Courier,* May 4, 1963, 13.

18. Alyssa Ribeiro, "A Period of Turmoil: Pittsburgh's April 1968 Riots and Their After-math," *Journal of Urban History* 39, no. 2 (2013), 147–171; Trotter and Day, *Race and Renaissance* 103–108; Neighborhood Committee on Health Care Ten Year Anniversary Dinner Brochure, NCHC, Container 2, Folder 16; Kathleen M. Washy, "A Woman, a Commitment: Sister M. Ferdinand Clark and Urban Renewal," *Gathered Fragments* 25 (2015), 11–17.

19. Mercy Hospital Public Relations Office Reprint of Sister M. Ferdinand Clark, "A Hospital for the Black Ghetto," *Hospital Progress*, February 1969, NCHC, Box 2, Folder 14.

20. Ibid.

21. Neighborhood Advisory Committee on Health Care of Mercy Hospital, Purpose, Membership, Organization and Operating Procedures, April 1968, NCHC, bound volumes 1968–1973, 1; "Neighborhood Committee Bridges Gap Between Hospital and Community," *Mercy People*, June 18, 1975, NCHC, bound volumes 1974–1976. The NCHC also hosted dinners and brought in speakers on a range of topics, like Chauncy Eskridge, the Pittsburgh-born former aide to Martin Luther King, who spoke to the community on "Dr. King and the Law" in 1969, "Ex-Pittsburgh, King Aide, Speaks Here in April," *New Pittsburgh Courier*, March 22, 1969, 1.

22. "The Qualities of Mercy, Draft Presentation for the A. W. Mellon Foundation," February 10, 1972, NCHC, Box 2, Folder 13, 8–9.

23. Ibid., 7. The NCHC was involved with emergency triage planning on the hospital's campus. Neighborhood Committee on Health Care, "Highlights of Nine Years of Progress" (1977), NCHC, Box 2, Folder 17.

24. *Mercy Bulletin*, October 1970, NCHC, bound volumes 1968–1973.

25. Letter to Sara Stanley from Reverend J. Van Alfred Winsett, November 5, 1976, NCHC, bound volumes 1974–1976.

26. Montefiore did not formally affiliate with UHCP until 1969 but, because of its proximate location to the health center, shared some physical plant items and offered staff privileges for physicians affiliated with the medical school. Bleier, Donnelly, and Granowitz, *L'Chaim*, 175–177, 194–195.

27. Ibid., 144–145 and 167; cost figures on 145. See also the extensive scrapbooks of press clippings compiled by Montefiore Hospital and now held by the Heinz History Center. Montefiore Hospital Records, MSS# 286, Rauh Jewish Archives, Heinz History Center (hereafter cited as Montefiore Scrapbook).

28. "Low-Income Dental Program for Hill Opens at Hospital," *Pittsburgh New Courier*, March 13, 1971, and "Dr. Wilvor C. Waller Appointed to Head Montefiore-Model Cites Dental Program in Pittsburgh," *Pennsylvania Dental Journal* 38, no. 4 (May 1971), Montefiore Scrapbook.

29. See Health Center Opens Issue, *HazelGreenGlen Herald*, October 1971, Montefiore Scrapbook 1971; Franklin Toker, *Pittsburgh: An Urban Portrait* (University Park: Pennsylvania State University Press, 1986), 268–270.

30. Presbyterian-University Hospital Minutes of the Board of Trustees, September 10, 1970, WWB, Box 8, Folder 156, 4.

31. "Health Chiefs Laud 'Model' Med Center," *Pittsburgh New Courier*, July 8, 1967. This article, plus a detailed history of controversies, can be found in CLP, PGH, Hospitals, Homewood-Brushton Neighborhood Health Center. See also, Refunding Application 1972–1973, Homewood-Brushton Neighborhood Health Center, HSASWP Box 93. One final area

where university physicians were active was the Pittsburgh Free Clinic, founded in 1970. This clinic targeted a young adult clientele and was located in the basement of the East End Christian Church. For more details about the clinic, see Pittsburgh Free Clinic, Inc., HSASWP, Box 93.

32. Nicholson-Preuss, "Down and Out in the Old J.D.," 303–314; David G. McComb, *Houston: The Bayou City* (Austin: University of Texas, 1969), 244–245; J. R. Gonzales, "The Hospital," *Handbook of Texas Online.*

33. Roger Widmeyer, "Quentin Mease and the Establishment of the Harris County Hospital District," *Houston Review of History and Culture* 2, no. 1 (Fall 2004), 38–39; Jan De Hartog, *The Hospital* (New York: Atheneum, 1964).

34. Jane Culpepper, "The Community in Community Medicine," in HCHD, Scrapbook Collection, Folder Scrapbooks 1972, 1 of 2.

35. Author telephone interview with Carlos Vallbona, June 4, 2011. The Houston Medical Forum was the professional organization for African American doctors equivalent to the Harris County Medical Society. In an interview with the author, Carlos Vallbona noted that Baylor's refusal also angered the Houston Medical Forum. Widmeyer, "Quentin Mease and the Establishment of the Harris County Hospital District," 53.

36. Annual Report of the Department of Community Medicine, Baylor College of Medicine, 1969–1970, 3; courtesy of Dr. Carlos Vallbona; Wendy Haskell Meyer, "Marcus Welby Is an Establishment Quack," *Texas Monthly*, May 1973, 45–51.

37. Annual Report of the Department of Community Medicine, Baylor College of Medicine, 1969–1970.15.

38. Ibid., 1.

39. *The Office of Economic Opportunity During the Administration of President Lyndon B. Johnson*, volume 1, *November 1963–January 1969*, National Archives and Records Administration 1–7; Engel, *Poor People's Medicine*, 98–106, 135–138.

40. Maximum feasible participation had its roots in an earlier program, called the "grey areas" program, administered by the Ford Foundation in the early 1960s. This test program's premise was the idea that "poverty was the product of related economic, social, and psychological problems" and had, in the words of an early OEO history, "provided the work of community action as a way to attack poverty at its source." *The Office of Economic Opportunity During the Administration of President Lyndon B. Johnson*, 8. Alondra Nelson shows how the Black Panthers drew from similar principles of community empowerment to create their own People's Free Medical Clinics. While these clinics were often privately funded, some did accept OEO and other government monies. Nelson, *Body and Soul*, esp. chap. 4.

41. Michael Millenson, "Medicare, Fair Pair, and the AMA: The Forgotten History," *Health Affairs Blog*, September 19, 2015, https://www.healthaffairs.org/do/10.1377/hblog20150910.050461/full; Stevens and Stevens, *Welfare Medicine in America*, 156–182.

42. Shonick, *Government and Health Services*, 339–342; Sardell, *The U.S. Experiment in Social Medicine*, 29–44.

43. Carlos Vallbona interview.

44. *The Office of Economic Opportunity During the Administration of President Lyndon B. Johnson*, 186–187; Shonick, *Government and Health Services*, 345. In Houston, a range of newspapers advertised elections, including the black-operated *Voice of Hope*. "What's Going On? Settegast Health Council Election," *Voice of Hope*, September 23, 1972, 9.

45. Ruth SoRelle, "A Half Century of Love," *Solutions*, Baylor College of Medicine, 3, no. 1, Spring 2007.

46. Mary Jane Schier, "Health Clinics for Poor Rising from Long Co-operation," *Houston Post*, n.d., 1969, HCHD, Scrapbooks 1942–1968.

47. Ibid.; Department of Community Medicine Annual Report, 1969–1970, 17.

48. Jane Culpepper, "The Community in Community Medicine," HCHD Scrapbook 1972. Culpepper was the wife of a Baylor College of Medicine student.

49. Carlos Vallbona interview.

50. Baylor College of Medicine Department of Community Medicine Annual Report, 1969–1970, 14.

51. Baylor College of Medicine Department of Community Medicine Annual Report, 1970–1971, 22–23; courtesy of Carlos Vallbona. The same report noted that the department was well under way to helping many of these centers expand their service lines to provide comprehensive care (1). One of the problems with the term "neighborhood health centers" is that there was no precise definition of what constituted one versus a clinic, but it appears in Houston that the ability to provide "comprehensive" services (here again, not fully defined) was how Baylor differentiated between the two.

52. Baylor College of Medicine Department of Community Medicine Annual Report, 1972–1973. JR Box 4, Folder 23; "What's Going On? Harris County Hospital District Satellite Clinic," *Voice of Hope*, June 3, 1972, 9; "Despite Setbacks, Health Clinic Now Open," *Voice of Hope*, September 1, 1972, 2.

53. Department of Community Medicine Annual Report, 1972–1973, 4.

54. Carlos Vallbona interview.

55. Letter from Carlos Vallbona to Julius Rivera, March 30, 1973, JR, Box 4, Folder 16. Evidently, this was dramatically scaled down from an earlier proposal for $600,000 per year for five years. Annual Report to the Commonwealth Fund and the Robert Wood Johnson Foundation, July 1, 1973–June 31, 1974, JR, Box 5, Folder 1, 1.

56. Sociocultural Factors in Health Care Phase I-Estimative Pilot, The Case of Casa De Amigos (Progress Report 1), JR Box 4, Folder 22, 6.

57. Ibid., 7.

58. Ibid., 7–11.

59. Department of Community Medicine Annual Report, 1972–1973, 28, 10–16.

60. Julius Rivera, "Training Young Chicano Mothers in Para-mental Health," JR, Box 4, Folder 18, 2.

61. Department of Community Medicine Annual Report, 1972–1973, 30–31.

62. Letter from Carlos Vallbona to Julius Rivera, September 20, 1974, JR Box 4, Folder 16.

63. Questionnaires from Box 5, Various Folders, JR. Includes numbers 111, 53, 74, 31, 75, 6, 22, 108, 57, 99, 105, 110, 97, 40, 59; 60 and 90 were also reviewed, but since respondents did not visit the clinic, they were not added to the generalizations. Names were redacted by the University of Texas at El Paso.

64. Sociocultural Factors in Health Care Phase I-Estimative Pilot, The Case of Casa De Amigos, Progress Report 1, 3–4.

65. Ibid., 4.

66. Department of Community Medicine Annual Report, 1972–1973, 9. An assumption echoed by Rivera and Baylor at large was that neighborhood clinics were a major way to

incorporate Mexican Americans into society. See also "Casa de Amigos: Clinic as Medicine, Clinic as Home," *Inside Baylor Medicine*, May–June 1974, BCM, Box Inside Baylor Medicine 1967–1980.

67. Questionnaires from Box 5, Various Folders, JR.

68. University Health Center of Pittsburgh, "Development of a Health Maintenance Organization by the University of Pittsburgh," HSASWP, Box 92.

69. Bradford H. Grey, "The Rise and Decline of the HMO: A Chapter in U.S. Health-Policy History," in Stevens, Rosenberg, and Burns, *History and Health Policy in the United States*, 318.

70. University Health Center of Pittsburgh, "Development of a Health Maintenance Organization by the University of Pittsburgh," HSASWP Box 92, 4. Also, see Table 3 in the same document.

71. University Health Center of Pittsburgh, "Offer to Plan and Develop an HMO," HSASWP, Box 92, 3.

72. Memorandum for the Record Re: Meeting with Dr. Cheever to Discuss HMO Development, Hospital Planning Association of Allegheny County, March 2, 1972, HSASWP, Box 92.

73. Letter from Francis Cheever to Steven Sieverts, February 22, 1972, HSASWP, Box 92.

74. Central Medical Brochure, Women in the Urban Crisis Collection, University of Pittsburgh Archives, Box 1, Folder 141.

75. Summary of Proposal #32, Central Medical Pavilion, HSASWP, Box 91.

76. For more on Rice's community organizing and life, see Patrick J. McGeever, *Rev. Charles Owen Rice: Apostle of Contradiction* (Pittsburgh: Duquesne University Press, 1989).

77. "SPECIAL NOTE TO NEWS EDITORS, TOMORROW MORNING (TUESDAY APRIL 10) AT 10 AM CHARLES OWEN RICE WILL PRESENT A DOCUMENTED DENUNCIATION OF THE PROPOSED PROFIT BASE HOSPITAL IN THE LOWER HILL," Charles Own Rice Papers, University of Pittsburgh Archives, Box 3, Folder 30.

78. Gene Reid, "New Hospital to Open in Hill," *New Pittsburgh Courier*, February 2, 1974, 1; Tom Stokes, "Doubt Proposed Hospital Can Serve Needs," *New Pittsburgh Courier*, June 10, 1972, ; Diane Perry, "Diane's Den Questions Lower Hill Hospital," *New Pittsburgh Courier*, March 20, 1971, 11. Huff was employed by Central Medical Pavilion in Community Relations. "Ex-Boxer, Political Activist and Community Organizer, Clarence 'Larry' Huff, Dies at 86," *New Pittsburgh Courier*, June 6, 2014. For more on concerns about the nature of black hospital employment in Pittsburgh, see Diane Perry, "Blacks Hold 'Dead End' Hospital Jobs," *New Pittsburgh Courier*, February 7, 1970, 22.

79. "Pittsburghers Speak Out," *New Pittsburgh Courier*, March 27, 1971, 4; Perry, "Diane's Den Questions Lower Hill Hospital," 11.

80. "New Private Hospital for Hill District Scored," *New Pittsburgh Courier*, January 23, 1971, 1.

81. For examples of the rancor, see the Health Systems Agency hearing transcripts for approval contained in the Health Systems Agency Central Medical Pavilion File, HSASWP, Box 91.

82. Joseph Taylor, "Dick Construction Firm Is Charged with Racism," *New Pittsburgh Courier,* August 4, 1973, 1.

83. Memorandum Mark Marchetti to Jim Robinson, Central Medical Health Services-New Facility-Prepaid Group Practice (HMO) Program-Evaluation of Fifth Annual Report—

CHPA #32, November 22, 1977, HSASWP, Box 91. Folder Comprehensive Health Planning Agency #32 CMP (Central Medical Pavilion) New Facility—Prepaid Group Practice (HMO) Program—Fifth Annual Report—1977.

84. Given the overlapping membership of hospital boards of directors and elite development organizations, however, one is never sure how much health care jobs were talked about informally as part of larger discussions about changing regional economies. Periodically, the press would also become interested in who the hospital trustees were and their connections to the city's corporate infrastructure. The *New Pittsburgh Courier* ran a series in 1979 about this titled "Who Runs Allegheny County's Hospitals?" Chapter 1 of this book discusses the interlocking relationship between Houston's hospital trustees and that city's civic development organizations.

85. Rosemary Stevens, *American Medicine and the Public Interest* (New Haven: Yale University Press, 1971), 364; Ludmerer, *Time to Heal*, 210–211.

86. Ludmerer, *Time to Heal*, 211–212.

87. Ludmerer notes that under the Health Professions Educational Assistance Act of 1963, existing schools were provided with matching funds to build new educational facilities "provided they increase the size of their entering class by 5 percent or five students, whatever was greater." New medical schools were provided money on a two to one match rate. The bill also, for the first time, made federal student loans available to medical students. By 1971, the schools were paid a flat rate per student. Furthermore, "capitation payments were attractive to schools because they could be used for operating expenses, not just construction costs," Ludmerer, *Time to Heal*, 211–212; Engel, *Unaffordable*, 24–30. Foreign medical graduates were also recruited to address the perceived manpower shortage. Engel, *Unaffordable*, 27–28, and Ludmerer, *Time to Heal*, 185.

88. For two examples of the ways that various universities and academic medical institutions tried to illustrate their urban impact, see "To Meet City Problems: Ivy Walls Tumbling," *Pitt Magazine*, Winter 1969, and "Office of Education Report for the Conference of the University of Texas System and Urban Affairs," RLC, Box 210, Folder Urban Affairs Program.

89. Some of these programs predated the Great Society. For example, in 1960, thirty-eight high school students (the majority from the suburban North Hills High School) spent time over the summer working with faculty from the University of Pittsburgh Medical School's Addison H. Gibson Laboratory to learn about basic research. William Gill, "Accent on Research," *Pittsburgh Press*, August 14, 1960, UHC, 90/43 E- Clippings, Box 1, Folder 4, 1960–1962.90. The link between poverty and employment was given a further boost after the March 1968 publication of the Report of the National Advisory Commission on Civil Disorders, or the Kerner Commission. This report, which came out only weeks before the widespread rioting in 1968 touched off by the King assassination, famously claimed America was "moving toward two societies, one black, one white—both separate and unequal." It laid the blame for this division at the feet of economic injustice driven by segregation and racism. Report of the National Advisory Commission on Civil Disorders (Washington, D.C.: Government Printing Office, 1968), 1.

91. Freedom House Ambulance Service, *Pitt Magazine*, Winter 1970. 13; "Freedom House Ambulance Service an Assessment of Program Activities," prepared by Health and Welfare Planning Association of Allegheny County, October 1971, HWPA, Box 135, Folder 4, Heinz History Center; Trotter and Day, *Race and Renaissance*, 127–128.

92. "Begin OEO Program for Ambulance Drivers," *Pittsburgh New Courier*, March 8, 1969, FH Clipping Book Table 1, "Freedom House Ambulance Service an Assessment of Program Activities," prepared by Health and Welfare Planning Association of Allegheny County October 1971, HWPA Box 135, Folder 4, 20. See also Dale McFeatters, "'Super' Ambulances Make Debut Here," *Pittsburgh Press*, April 8, 1969, in FH Clippings book; Richard F. Long, "Ambulance Service Comes to the Inner City," OEO Publication, June 1971, in PS, FH Clippings Book.

93. Don M. Benson et al., "Mobile Intensive Care by 'Unemployable' Blacks Trained as Emergency Medical Technical (EMT's) in 1967–69," *Journal of Trauma* 12, no. 5 (1972), 408. A comprehensive source for newspaper coverage of Freedom House can be found in the clipping book assembled for the thirtieth anniversary of Freedom House in November 1997. For more information, see FH, Freedom House Meeting, November 1997.

94. Peter Safar, *From Vienna to Pittsburgh*, Careers in Anesthesiology, vol. 5 (Park Ridge, IL: Wood Library-Museum of Anesthesiology, 2000), 234; George Cheever, "Freedom House Ambulance Service: Revolution in Emergency Medical Care," *University Times*, April 23, 1970, FH Clippings Book. Cheever noted that, of the initial class of twenty-five, twenty completed the training program, and most without high school diplomas were able to secure GEDs, with some moving on to college or even graduate school.

95. "Freedom House Ambulance Service an Assessment of Program Activities," 49.

96. Benson et al., "Mobile Intensive Care by 'Unemployable' Blacks Trained as Emergency Medical Technical (EMT's) in 1967–69," 415.

97. "Freedom House Ambulance Service an Assessment of Program Activities," 52.

98. Pittsburgh Model Cities Grant III, 3–4, ACCD, Box 213, Folder 3. This application notes the expected role of the medical center as a potential hub for health professions training for the residents of model neighborhoods.

99. For more on this, see Andrew T. Simpson, "Transporting Lazarus: Physicians, the State, and the Creation of the Modern Paramedic and Ambulance, 1955–1973," *Journal of the History of Medicine and Allied Sciences* 68, no. 2 (2013), 163–197; Ryan Corbett Bell, *The Ambulance: A History* (Jefferson, N.C.: McFarland, 2009), 255–277.

100. "A Departing Mitchell Brown Looks Back," *University Times*, January 24, 1980, UHC, Center for Emergency Medicine, School of Medicine Files, Box 9, Folder, Center for Emergency Medicine.

101. Papers of Peter Safar, Letters from Patients, FH, Letter sent January 1974 and letter sent June 29, 1971.

102. Raymond L. Hayes, "Report of the Director: Medical Career Orientation Program," June–August 1968, MFMF, 207, Box 38, Folder 5, 10; Sheila A. Douglas, "Report of the Director: Medical Career Orientation Program," November 1968–August 1969, MFMF, Box 38, Folder 9, 4; Harvey Kantor and Barbara Brenzel, "Urban Education and the 'Truly Disadvantaged': The Historical Roots of the Contemporary Crisis," in Katz, *The "Underclass" Debate*, 366–402.

103. Hayes, "Report of the Director: Medical Career Orientation Program," June–August 1968, 10–21; quotation on 11.

104. Ibid., i.

105. Francis Cheever to Philip Hallen, June 21, 1968, MFMF, Box 38, Folder 5; Maurice Falk Medical Fund, Grant Resolution Slip MCOP, June 26, 1969, MFMF, Box 38, Folder 5.

"The University School of Medicine Begins Program for Black Students," *Pitt News*, June 30, 1968, MFMF, Box 38, Folder 5. More details of the role of the foundation community can be found in Simpson, "Private Dollars for a Healthier Public."

106. Hayes, "Report of the Director: Medical Career Orientation Program," 24. Scaife Hall is the major building housing the University of Pittsburgh's Medical School.

107. Neighborhood Advisory Committee on Health Care, Meeting Minutes June 6, 1968, in NCHC, bound volume 1968–1973. 1.

108. Letter from Regis Bobonis and Jacob H. Williams to Lorenzo Hill, September 12, 1968, NCHC, bound volumes 1968–1973.

109. Neighborhood Advisory Committee on Health Care, Meeting Minutes October 2, 1969, NCHC, bound volumes 1968–1973, 3–4.

110. On the shorter course at Baylor, see "Three-Year Plan Draws Many Freshman to Baylor," *Inside Baylor Medicine*, August 1971, BCM, Box Inside Baylor Medicine 1967–1980. For more on the establishment of the University of Texas Medical School, see "Allied Health Center Physician Assistants Begin Training," *Inside Baylor Medicine*, October 1971, BCM, Box Inside Baylor Medicine 1967–1980, 1, 14.

111. Bryant Boutwell and John P. McGovern, *Conversation with a Medical School: The University of Texas-Houston Medical School, 1970–2000* (Houston: University of Texas-Houston Health Science Center, 1999); Texas Medical Center, Inc. Annual Report, 1973, 97–98.

112. In Pittsburgh, Mercy Hospital utilized a similar concept called "health care expediters." A health care expediter was "a person indigenous to the community, employed by Mercy to provide a liaison between the primary service area and the Hospital." They were supervised by Margaret Washington, the director of Community Programs, and engaged in a range of health-related tasks, including appointment scheduling and follow-up, attending community meetings, and providing information about Mercy and other health care facilities. "Qualities of Mercy," 10, and Minutes of the Neighborhood Committee on Health Care Meeting, November 19, 1970, NCHC, bound volumes 1968–1973.

113. Carlos Vallbona interview.

114. Ibid.

115. Nelson, *Body and Soul*, 78–94.

116. Butler and Ware, *Arming for Battle Against Disease Through Education, Research, and Patient Care at Baylor College of Medicine* (Houston: Baylor College of Medicine, 2011), vol. 2, 642. In his quote, Butler uses BUCM, which is short for Baylor University College of Medicine. See Chapter 1, note 39, for a discussion of the relationship between Baylor University and Baylor College of Medicine.

117. Butler notes that the initial approach came in 1970 from Leonel J. Castillo of the Catholic Council on Community Relations. According to Butler, "Castillo expressed concern for improved education of the expanding work force in the Houston area, particularly for minority students." Ibid., 642.

118. Ibid., 643. In 1974, the name was changed to Health Services Careers Program. Gerald D. Williams, "Health Services Career Program: 1966–1974, Descriptive Profile and Program Evaluation," Report to Office of Health Manpower Studies, School of Health Services, Johns Hopkins University, August 1975, 1.

119. Butler and Ware, *Arming for Battle Against Disease Through Education, Research, and Patient Care at Baylor College of Medicine*, 643. Williams, "Health Services Career Program," 2–3.

120. Butler and Ware, *Arming for Battle Against Disease Through Education, Research, and Patient Care at Baylor College of Medicine*, 644–646.

121. Reports of the size of the incoming class vary. A 1973 Department of Community Medicine Report puts the number at forty-two, but drawing from a later report, Butler cites forty-five students in the initial class. Department of Community Medicine Annual Report, 1972–1973, 26, and Butler and Ware, *Arming for Battle Against Disease Through Education, Research and, Patient Care at Baylor College of Medicine*, 642, 644.

122. Baylor College of Medicine Center for Educational Outreach online at https://www.aamc.org/initiatives/nmso/proven/326448/baylorcollegeofmedicinearticle.htm, and http://www.ccitonline.org/ceo/content.cfm?menu_id = 139. Author interview with William Butler, July 31, 2015; author telephone interview with William A. Thomson, August 5, 2015.

123. Shonick, *Government and Health Services*, 405–407; Kim Phillips-Fein, *Invisible Hands: The Businessman's Crusade Against the New Deal* (New York: W. W. Norton, 2009), 166–212.

124. Safar, *From Vienna to Pittsburgh*, 234–235; Trotter and Day, *Race and Renaissance*, 128; Chuck Staresinic, "Send Freedom House!" *PittMed*, February 2004. See also the papers of Peter Safar, Pittsburgh Ambulance Dilemma Scrapbooks, FHE.

125. Maurice Falk Medical Fund, "1960–1980," MFMF Box 1, 26–28. For more on ongoing efforts by the University of Pittsburgh to address issues of minority health, see "A Decade of Minority Health," *Public Health*, Fall 2004, 8–10; Trotter and Day, *Race and Renaissance*. 160, 182–183.

126. Washy, "A Woman, A Commitment: Sister M. Ferdinand Clark and Urban Renewal," 16.

127. John D. Harden, "Houston Opens $67 Million DeBakey High School for Medical Careers," *Houston Chronicle*, June 2, 2017.

128. Harris Hospital System Primary Care locations, https://www.harrishealth.org/locations/primary-care; Primary Care Health Services, Inc., www.pchspitt.org.

Chapter 3

1. Shelley McKellar, *Artificial Hearts: The Allure and Ambivalence of a Controversial Medical Technology* (Baltimore: Johns Hopkins University Press, 2018) provides an excellent overview of the relationship between Cooley and DeBakey, the history of cardiac transplantation, and development and use of the artificial heart; Denton A. Cooley, *100,000 Hearts: A Surgeon's Memoir* (Austin: Dolph Briscoe Center for American History, 2012); Harry A. Minetree, *Cooley: The Career of a Great Heart Surgeon* (New York: Harper's Magazine Press, 1973); Thomas Thompson, *Hearts: Of Surgeons and Transplants, Miracles and Disasters Along the Cardiac Frontier* (New York: McCall, 1971).

2. Kris Mamula, "How Dr. Starzl Helped Breathe Life into Pittsburgh's Economy," *Pittsburgh Post-Gazette*, March 10, 2017; Thomas Starzl Personal File, University of Pittsburgh Archives; Lee Gutkind, *Many Sleepless Nights: The World of Organ Transplantation* (Pittsburgh: University of Pittsburgh Press, 1988).

3. The history of medical specialization is an area of ongoing interest for historians of medicine. While the literature is vast, for examples, see George Rosen's *The Specialization of Medicine with Particular Reference to Ophthalmology* (New York: Froben Press, 1944); Rosemary Stevens, *American Medicine and the Public Interest: A History of Specialization* (New Haven: Yale University Press, 1971), updated in 1998 with a helpful bibliography of works;

Starr, *The Social Transformation of American Medicine*, 220–225, 355–359; George Weisz, *Divide and Conquer: A Comparative History of Medical Specialization* (New York: Oxford University Press, 2006); Ludmerer, *Let Me Heal*. This last book examines the rise of medical residency.

4. Starr, *The Social Transformation of American Medicine*, 428–430; Since the 1990s, there has been a robust discussion of the perception of a growing corporatization of American health care. For some examples, see Salmon, *The Corporate Transformation of Health Care*, vols. 1 and 2; Gregory C. Pope and John E. Schneider, "Trends in Physician Income," *Health Affairs* 11, no. 1 (Spring 1992), 181–193; Michael A. Morrisey, "Competition in Hospital and Health Insurance Markets: A Review and Research Agenda," *Health Services Research* 36, no. 1 (April 2001), 191–221, 198; Engel, *Unaffordable*, 47–48. Engel provides some cost for cardiovascular surgery.

5. Howard S. Berliner and Carol Regan, "Multinational Operations of US for-Profit Hospital Chains: Trends and Implications," *American Journal of Public Health* 77, no. 10 (October 1987), 1280–1284; Mary Wagner, "More Hospitals Vie for Foreign Patients," *Modern Healthcare*, June 7, 1993, 30–31; John J. Hutchins, "Bringing International Patients to American Hospitals: The Johns Hopkins Perspectives," *Managed Care Quarterly* 6, no. 3 (Summer 1998), 22–27; Olivia F. Lee and Tim R. V. Davis, "International Patients: A Lucrative Market for U.S. Hospitals," *Health Marketing* Quarterly 22, no. 1 (2004), 41–56; Mona Al-Amin et al., "Hospital Ability to Attract International Patients: A Conceptual Framework," *International Journal of Pharmaceutical and Health Care Marketing* 5 no. 3 (2011), 205–221. For a brief overview of some of the ways the Texas Medical Center developed a global reputation around specialty and other types of clinical and research services, see Rosanne Clark, "Texas Medical Center: Making a World of Difference in Health Care," *TMC News*, March 1, 1996, in MED, Box 5, Folder 5, as well as other assorted publications in this folder about the historical development of specialty medicine at the facility. For a brief discussion on the creation of facilities overseas by not-for-profit hospitals, see "Crossing Borders: Searching for a New Line of Business to Boost Revenue, Some Providers Look Overseas," *Hospitals and Health Networks Magazine*, June 2002, 26, 28.

6. The relationship between elected officials and hospital expansion is discussed in more detail in Chapter 1.

7. For example, Mercy Hospital in Pittsburgh and Hermann Hospital in Houston developed expertise in burn care. Hermann also built a strong liver transplantation program and a strong reputation in emergency medical services. Pittsburgh's Allegheny General Hospital attempted to build its own transplantation program (which is discussed in note 103), invested in building an air ambulance service, and strengthened its own cardiovascular surgical program.

8. McKellar, *Artificial Hearts*, 62–63; MED, Box 5, Folder 45; Baylor College of Medicine, "In Memoriam: Michael E. DeBakey," *BCM Family Newsletter*, June 2008, in Subject File, Michael E. DeBakey, John P. McGovern Historical Collections and Research Center, Texas Medical Center Library, Houston, TX. DeBakey also worked to make innovative procedures routine, such as carotid endarterectomy, which involves opening the carotid artery in the neck, removing the blockage that is obstructing blood flow to the brain, and then closing the artery. For more on Dacron, see Michael DeBakey, "Developments in Cardiovascular Surgery," *Baylor Cardiovascular Research Center Bulletin*, July–September 1980, BCM, Box Cardiovascular Research Center Bulletin, vols. 1–20; Stephen Westaby and Cecil Bosher,

Landmarks in Cardiac Surgery (London: Oxford, 1997), 236; McKellar, *Artificial Hearts*, 64–65; National Library of Medicine, Michael E. DeBakey, Profiles in Science"From Tulane School of Medicine to the U.S. Army, 1928–1946," and "Building Baylor College of Medicine and Expanding Surgical Frontiers, 1948–1963," online at https://profiles.nlm.nih.gov/FJ/.

9. For more on DeBakey's reputation as a medical statements see MED Box 2 and National Library of Medicine, Michael E. DeBakey, Profiles in Science, "DeBakey as a Medical Statesman," online at https://profiles.nlm.nih.gov/ps/retrieve/Narrative/FJ/p-nid/333/. For information on the Duke of Windsor's surgery see Sibley, *The Methodist Hospital of Houston*, 3–5; quotation on 4.

10. As a young man, DeBakey invented the mechanical roller pump, which would later play a key role in heart-lung machines. National Library of Medicine, Michael E. DeBakey Profiles in Science, From Tulane School of Medicine to the U.S. Army, 1928–1946," online at https://profiles.nlm.nih.gov/ps/retrieve/Narrative/FJ/p-nid/329; Steven L. Johnson, *The History of Cardiac Surgery, 1895–1955* (Baltimore: Johns Hopkins University Press, 1970), 150–158; W. Bruce Fye, *Caring for the Heart: Mayo Clinic and the Rise of Specialization* (New York: Oxford University Press, 2015), 211–219; David K. C. Cooper, *Open Heart: The Radical Surgeons Who Revolutionized Medicine* (New York: Kaplan, 2010), 145–167, 178–214; David S. Jones, *Broken Hearts: The Tangled History of Cardiac Care* (Baltimore: Johns Hopkins University Press, 2013), 113–124.

11. Cooley, *100,000 Hearts*, 100–105.

12. Ibid., 106.

13. Winters and Parish, *Houston Hearts*, 133.

14. In fact, by the late 1950s, the Methodist Hospital (where DeBakey operated) was expanding its presence in cardiovascular surgery. McKellar, *Artificial Hearts*, 62; Sibley, *The Methodist Hospital of Houston*, 146–149.

15. Cooley, *100,000 Hearts*, 115–117; McKellar, *Artificial Hearts*, 64–65. For more on Herring and the Fish Foundation, see Cooley, *100,000 Hearts*, 118–119. The Houston Natural Gas Company later became known as Enron. During the 1960s and 1970s, Herring was widely regarded as a major player in Texas politics. His wife, Joanne, was also Houston's best-known socialite during these years. She went on to achieve national fame through her work with Texas congressman Charlie Wilson and his efforts to arm the mujahideen in Afghanistan against the Soviet Union during the 1980s. For more on the Herrings, see Paul Burka, "Power," *Texas Monthly*, December 1987, and Kent Demaret and Tom Scott, "Let Them Eat Caviar: Joanne King Herring Is the Social Queen of Houston," *People*, October 25, 1976. For a profile of Herring and Wilson, see Philip Sherwell, "How Joanne Herring Won Charlie Wilson's War," *London Telegraph*, December 2, 2007.

16. Westaby and Bosher, *Landmarks in Cardiac Surgery*, 260.

17. Ibid., 265; McKellar, *Artificial Hearts*, 66–72; Stanford Medical School, "Norman Shumway, Heart Transplant Pioneer, Dies at 83," press release February 10, 2006; Jeremy Pierce, "Richard Lower Dies at 78, Transplanted Human and Animal Hearts," *New York Times*, May 31, 2008.

18. Cooley, *100,000 Hearts*, 126–127; "Heart Transplants," Handbook of Texas Online, http://www.tshaonline.org/handbook/online/articles/sdh01.

19. Cooley, *100,000 Hearts*, 130–131. Also, see the list of transplants in Thompson, *Hearts*.

20. DeBakey, Profiles in Science; Eric Berger, "Dr. Denton Colley, Famed Houston Heart Surgeon, Dead at 96," *Houston Chronicle*, November 18, 2016; McKellar, *Artificial Hearts*, 72.

21. Thompson, *Hearts*, Appendix, "Summary of Heart Transplants as of March 1, 1971," 276; McKellar, *Artificial Hearts*, 73.

22. McKellar, *Artificial Hearts*, 74–76. This book provides a very comprehensive and balanced overview of the process of creating the artificial heart and its use in Haskell Karp. Cooley, *100,000 Hearts*, 137–138.

23. Cooley, *100,000 Hearts*, 140–144; McKellar, *Artificial Hearts*, 76–79.

24. Detailed files on the controversy from DeBakey's perspective are available at the National Library of Medicine, MED, Box 36; McKellar, *Artificial Hearts*, 80–86.

25. See Louis Blackburn, "Medical Center World-Famed for Research and Treatment on Three Greatest Problems," *Houston Press*, May 9, 1961; Louis Blackburn, "Baylor's Research Put Houston in Forefront in War on Disease," *Houston Press*, May 9, 1961; "Heart of the Healing Art," *Houston Magazine*, November 1968; Miriam Kass, "They Come to Houston . . . Because the Care Is Here," *Houston Post*, December 1, 1970, HMRC, H-Medical Center, 1960–1969.

26. Cooley, *100,000 Hearts*, Appendix C and D; Michael E. DeBakey, Curriculum Vitae, September 13, 2002, MED, Box 1, Folder 3.

27. Joseph S. Coselli and Ourania Preventza, "In Memoriam: Edward B. Diethrich, MD (1935–2017), *Texas Heart Institute Journal* 44, no. 3 (June 2017), 164–166; Arizona Heart Institute, MED, Box 6, Folder 19.

28. National Heart, Lung, and Blood Institute, "What Is Coronary Artery Bypass Grafting?" online at http://www.nhlbi.nih.gov/health/health-topics/topics/cabg/.

29. David S. Jones, "How Much CABG Is Good for Us?" *The Lancet* 380, no. 2 (2012), 557–558; quote from David S. Jones, "CABG at 50 (or 107)—The Complex Course of Therapeutic Innovation," *New England Journal of Medicine* 36, no. 19 (May 11, 2017), 1809–1811, 1809; Baylor College of Medicine, "In Memoriam Michael E. DeBakey, M.D.," 3. (See earlier note, 8, for full cite.

30. Cooley, *100,000 Hearts*, 152.

31. Julia Wallace and *Dallas Time Herald*, "Dr. Denton Cooley—Star of the 'Heart Surgery Factory," *Washington Post*, July 29, 1980; Bryant Boutwell, who worked for the THI doing public relations in the 1980s, first told me about the monitors, although they were confirmed from examining a photograph of Cooley's office in *100,000 Hearts*. For general information about the arrangement of space within the operating room and efforts to bring scientific management to surgical disciplines over the course of the twentieth century, see Howell, *Technology in the Hospital*, 57–68, and Stevens, *In Sickness and in Wealth*, 75–79.

32. Allen R. Myerson, "It's a Business. No, It's a Religion," *New York Times*, February 13, 1994; J. Michael Kennedy, "Cooley in Bankruptcy: King of Hearts on the Road to Recovery," *Los Angeles Times*, March 10, 1988; Tom Curtis, "Lifestyles of the Rich and Bankrupt," *Texas Monthly*, March 1988, 86.

33. Frits Gonggrijp, "Dutch Export Heart Patients to Houston," prepared for Texas Heart Institute News Release, June 25, 1976, 2; courtesy of Dr. Denton Cooley and the Texas Heart Institute.

34. For more on the estimated backlog, see ibid. For costs, see Denton A. Cooley, "The Dutch Airlift: A Twelve-Month Surgical Experience," *Texas Heart Institute Bulletin* 4, no. 3

(1977), 335–342; Stuart Auerbach, "Texas Heart-Surgery Airlift Set Up for Dutch Patients," *International Herald Tribune,* June 28, 1976; "Heartline Houston Cuts Holland's Surgery Queue," *To the Point International* 2, no. 16, August 9, 1976; Denton A. Cooley to Mrs. Henk Fievet, letter of condolence, February 21, 1977; courtesy of Dr. Denton A. Cooley and the Texas Heart Institute.

35. "Dutch Airlift Brings Heart Patients to THI," *Texas Heart Institute Newsletter,* October 1976, 3; courtesy of Dr. Denton A. Cooley and the Texas Heart Institute.

36. Cooley, "The Dutch Airlift: A Twelve-Month Surgical Experience"; Cooley, "A Brief History of the Texas Heart Institute" *Texas Heart Institute Journal,* 35, no. 3 (2008), 235–239. The 1,500 number and quotation is from the latter, 238; "Heartline Houston Cuts Holland's Surgery Queue," 45. It is not clear how big the patient groups were; it appears they were around twenty to thirty patients per month.

37. Cooley, "The Dutch Airlift: A Twelve-Month Surgical Experience."

38. Undated fact sheet ca. 1979–1980 titled "Heart Patients Do Best in Houston"; courtesy of Dr. Denton A. Cooley and the Texas Heart Institute.

39. Shirley Kowitz, "The Saudi Arabian Connection: A Sheikdom Grows in Houston," *Houston Business Journal,* August 17, 1981, HMRC, H-Business-Foreign Investment.

40. Policies varied by hospital. In the mid-1970s, M. D. Anderson required all non-Texas residents to make either a $500 or $1,000 deposit when they registered, which would be applied to the final bill. If they did not have "adequate insurance to cover the anticipated costs of treatment," then they were required to make an additional deposit to cover the anticipated gap. Collecting this additional deposit was "especially true for foreign nationals." The memorandum went on to note of the decision to collect these deposits, "This is not being mercenary, just a fact of life." Memorandum to Staff Physicians, Fellows & Residents from Robert C. Hinkey RE: Out-of-State Deposit and Registration or Admission of Out-of-State and Foreign National on Weekend or After Working Hours, December 8, 1976, MDA, Box 64, Folder MDA Archival 1976–1977.

41. Darrin Schlegel, "Luring Latins: Houston Hospitals Expand Medical Marketing Efforts Below Border," *Houston Business Journal,* September 6, 1993, HMRC, II-Foreign Trade Zone. In a graphic accompanying the article, it notes that Hermann, the Methodist Hospital, St. Luke's, and Texas Children's all had some type of international program.

42. For a sampling of what these services looked like, see M. D. Anderson International Services Brochure, ca. 1990s/2000s, MDA, Box 66 Misc.

43. This program was part of the Methodist Hospital's broader networking strategies, which are discussed in more detail in Chapter 5. Kathryn Tesar, "Global Warmth," in *The Journal: Magazine of the Methodist Hospital System* 34, no. 1, 1995, MED, Box 2, FF 6, 20–21.

44. Russell Scott Jr., "Description of the King Faisal Specialist Hospital and Research Center, Riyadh, Saudi Arabia, July 11, 1975," RLC, Series II, Box 27, Folder Saudi Arabia, 1.

45. American Hospital Association, Kim M. Garber, ed., "Interview with Thomas F. Frist Jr.," January 17, 2013. American Hospital Association Hospital Administration Oral History Collection; Sandy Lutz and E. Preston Gee, *Columbia/HCA: Health Care on Overdrive* (New York: McGraw-Hill, 1998), 14–15. Note: the Frist interview was online at the time I reviewed it, it appears to no longer be available online. https://www.aha.org/oral-history-project/2006-01-13-hospital-administration-oral-history-collection.

46. Thomas Frist Jr. interview, 6.

47. Lutz and Gee, *Columbia/HCA: Health Care on Overdrive,* 15.; Jeffrey L. Rodengen, *The Legend of HCA* (Ft. Lauderdale: Write Stuff Enterprises, 2003), 14.

48. Newspaper Advertisement for Modernization Plans Overview, Kingdom of Saudi Arabia, n.d., n.p., RLC, Series II, Box 27, Folder Saudi Arabia; M. Almalki, G. Fitzgerald, and M. Clark, "Health Care System in Saudi Arabia: An Overview," *Eastern Mediterranean Health Journal* 17, no. 10, 2011, 784–793. Hospital Corporation of America, "A Unique Adventure Living and Working at the King Faisal Specialist Hospital and Research Centre," 1976, and Special Section on King Faisal Specialty Hospital and Research Centre, *Aramco World Magazine*, July–August 1979, RLC, Series II, Box 27, Folder Saudi Arabia.

49. King Faisal Hospital and Research Center, Recommendations of a Conference of Consultants, January 26–27, 1976, in the papers, RLC, Series II, Box 27, Folder Saudi Arabia. This meeting seems to have built on a smaller meeting in Denver in August 1975. "Research for Saudi Arabia," meeting August 14, 1975. See the same set of folders for correspondence laying out the longer history of contacts between M. D. Anderson and parties concerned with the King Faisal project.

50. "Baylor Medical School to Set Up Heart Surgery Program in Saudi Arabia," *American Medical News* 20 (33), August 22, 1977, MED, Box 5, Folder 45.

51. Michael E. DeBakey, Arthur C. Beall Jr., Nizar Feteih, Mohammed Mardini, Gene A. Guinn, and Kenneth L. Mattox, "King Faisal Specialist Hospital and Research Centre Cardiovascular Surgery Unit: First Year," *Cardiovascular Research Center Bulletin*, October–December 1979, 1–20, BCM, Box Cardiovascular Research Center Bulletin, 41, 43–44. The program was designed to last five years.

52. Michael E. DeBakey, Arthur C. Beall Jr., Nizar Feteih, Gene A. Guinn, Kenneth L. Mattox, Gerald M. Lawrie, Hartwell H. Whisennand, Mohammed Mardini, Mohammed Fawsy, Jacques Heibig, Rashid Tabba, and Laurens R. Pickard, "King Faisal Specialist Hospital and Research Centre Cardiovascular Surgery Unit: Progress Report After Two Years," *Cardiovascular Research Center Bulletin*, January–March 1980, BCM, Box Cardiovascular Research Center Bulletin, 1–20, 59–60.

53. HCA founder and former CEO Thomas Frist Jr. noted, "We managed the King Faisal Specialist Hospital for 20 years and were handsomely paid for our efforts. We kept the money received offshore rather than repatriating and paying taxes." Thomas F. Frist Jr. Interview, 30–31, quotation on 31. Howard S. Berliner and Carol Regan, "Multi-National Operations of U.S. For-Profit Hospital Chains: Trends and Implications," in Salmon, *The Corporate Transformation of Health Care* vol. 1, 155–165.

54. "Baylor Medical School to Set Up Heart Surgery Program in Saudi Arabia."

55. Claudia Feldman, "Baylor Heart Surgery Program in Saudi Arabia Cited as Success," *Houston Chronicle*, October 14, 1978, MED, Clippings. In 1980, efforts were made to create a linkage between the Saudi government, Baylor, and the University of Texas to build out Saudi allied health capacity. However, this program was never realized due to confusion with the University of Texas about the clarity and scope of the proposed program. Robert Roush to Fred Taylor, RE: Summary of Discussions Held on 9 July 1980 with the Saudi Representatives From the University of Riyadh, June 15, 1980; William T. Butler to Mansour Al-Turki, April 28, 1981; Draft Memorandum from Robert Roush to Ibrahim A. Al-Sowaygh and Isaac Al-Khawashki, RE: Baylor College of Medicine's Participation with the University of Riyadh's College of the Allied Medical Sciences, April 20, 1981 (not clear if it was sent in a final form); Charles C. Sprague to William T. Butler, RE Affiliation Agreement, April 30, 1981, BCM, Office of the President Central Files, Box 1, Folder 33. In an interview with the author, Butler

noted that this program was funded through contracts, which meant that BCM was not making a significant financial expenditure. Dr. William T. Butler interview with author, July 31, 2015.

56. William T. Butler to Michael E. DeBakey, RE King Faisal Contract, June 20, 1983 (includes cost breakdown for FY 1982); Alfus O. Johnson to William T. Butler, RE: Financial Report King Faisal Project, February 15, 1984 (includes cost breakdown for FY 1983); William T. Butler to Gibson Gayle, May 11, 1984, BCM, Office of the President Central Files, Box 1, Folder 33.

57. For primary source newspaper accounts of the lawsuit, see "Doctors Sue Baylor College of Medicine," *Longview News-Journal*, February 25, 1982, and "Baylor Illegally Kept Jews Off Saudi Hospital Team," *Los Angeles Times*, December 8, 1986. Issues of compensation are addressed in *Abrams v. Baylor College of Medicine*, 581 F. Supp. 1570 (S.D. Tex. 1984), U.S. District Court for the Southern District of Texas, March 5, 1984. A secondary source dealing with the mechanics of the case is Michael A. Olivas, *Suing Alma Matter: Higher Education and the Courts* (Baltimore: Johns Hopkins University Press, 2013), 91–97.

58. C. R. Richardson to Alfus O. Johnson, October 31, 1984, BCM, Office of the President Central Files, Box 44, Folder King Faisal Hospital II, 1884–1985; William T. Butler interview. Butler also discussed several other efforts by BCM to create overseas partnerships for specialty care or medical education, including in Costa Rica and Trinidad, which was another cardiac surgical program.

59. This is discussed in more detail in Andrew Simpson, "The Power of a Name: Michael DeBakey and the Changing Business of American Medicine," National Library of Medicine, Circulating Now, April 9, 2018, https://circulatingnow.nlm.nih.gov/2018/04/19/the-power-of -a-name-michael-debakey-and-the-changing-business-of-american-medicine.

60. DeBakey Consulting Group Promotional Materials, "Introduction and Background," MED, Box 10, Folder 14.

61. Ibid., "Experiences and Capabilities."

62. DeBakey-Pechersky Partners LLC, Company Profile, MED, Box 6, Folder 39; DeBakey-Pechersky Partners LLC, Proposal for the Government of Georgia, Cardiovascular Center, MED, Box 6, Folder 39.

63. Denton A. Cooley, "Lecture for Jager Club of Wichita, Kansas," January 2013, video recording courtesy of Dr. Gerald Nelson, M.D., and the University of Kansas School of Medicine, Wichita; Cooley, "A Brief History of the Texas Heart Institute," 238.

64. Cooley, "Lecture for Jager Club of Wichita, Kansas"; Cooley, "A Brief History of the Texas Heart Institute," 238; telephone interview with John Adams and Tobin Lassen from the Texas Heart Institute, August 18, 2015; Grady L. Hallman and Charles Edmonds, "Integrated Cardiac Care," *Annals of Thoracic Surgery* 60 (1995), 1486–1489; Charles Edmonds and Grady L. Hallman, "CardioVascular Care Providers: A Pioneer in Shared Risk, and Single Payment," *CardioVascular Care Providers* 22, no. 1 (1995); Denton A. Cooley and John W. Adams Jr., "Package Pricing at the Texas Heart Institute," in Regina E. Herzlinger, ed., *Consumer-Driven Health Care: Implications for Providers, Payers, and Policy Makers* (San Francisco: Jossey-Bass, 2004), 612–619. Reprints courtesy of John Adams and the Texas Heart Institute. Cooley, *Brief History of the Texas Heart Institute*, 238.

65. Cooley and Adams, "Package Pricing at the Texas Heart Institute"; Edmonds and Hallman, "CardioVascular Care Providers," 73.

66. Edmonds and Hallman, "CardioVascular Care Providers" 73–74; quotation on 74.

67. Ibid., 74.

68. Cooley, "A Brief History of the Texas Heart Institute," 238.

69. Myerson, "It's a Business. No, It's a Religion."

70. Edmonds and Hallman, "CardioVascular Care Providers," 72. Original quote in Health Policy Forum in *Texas Medical Center News*, March 1, 1994; Cooley, *100,000 Hearts*, 1–2, 171.

71. Myerson, "Its a Business. No, It's a Religion."

72. Cooley, "A Brief History of the Texas Heart Institute," 238; Cooley, *100,000 Hearts*, 169–170.

73. Pittsburgh's early transplant history is referenced in several places. The program was eventually limited to kidney transplantations, which were conducted under the supervision of Dr. Thomas Hakala, who saw this program as a way to establish a new Department of Urology separate from the Department of Surgery. Thomas E. Starzl, *The Puzzle People: Memoirs of a Transplant Surgeon* (Pittsburgh: University of Pittsburgh Press, 1992), 225; Chuck Staresinic, "Only Starzl Dared To," *PittMed*, May 2006, 17; "The House That Hank Built," *PittMed*, October 2002; Henry Bahnson, "Transplantation of the Heart: Reminiscences of the Past and Inklings of the Future," *Annals of Thoracic Surgery* 64 (1997). See also Henry W. Pierce, "Transplant Pioneer Retires from Presby," *Pittsburgh Post-Gazette*, June 2, 1987. For overviews of transplantation medicine see Renée C. Fox and Judith P. Swazey, *The Courage to Fail: A Social View of Organ Transplants and Dialysis*, 2nd ed. (New Brunswick: Transaction Publishers, 2002); Susan E. Lederer, *Flesh and Blood: Organ Transplantation and Blood Transfusion in Twentieth-Century America* (New York: Oxford University Press, 2008); David Hamilton, *A History of Organ Transplantation: Ancient Legends to Modern Practice* (Pittsburgh: University of Pittsburgh Press, 2012).

74. Starzl, *The Puzzle People*, 126.

75. University of Pittsburgh Library System, "The Dog Liver Models," Online at http://www.starzl.pitt.edu/transplantation/dog_liver_models.html.

76. Ibid.

77. Starzl, *The Puzzle People*, 98–105; University of Pittsburgh Library System "Transplanted Organs: The Liver," Online at http://starzl.pitt.edu/transplantation/organs/liver.html.

78. Author interview with Dr. Thomas Starzl, April 14, 2012; Hamilton, *A History of Organ* Transplantation, 303–304. For a history of ESRD see Richard A. Rettig, "Special Treatment—the Story of Medicare's ESRD Entitlement," *New England Journal of Medicine* 346, no. 7 (2011). I am also grateful for the opportunity to chat with Dr. Rettig over the telephone during my interview with Dr. Starzl and for his helpful suggestions over e-mail about the history of ESRD and transplantation medicine more generally.

79. Starzl, *The Puzzle People*, 206–209.

80. Jean F. Borel, "The History of Cyclosporin A and Its Significance," in D. J. G. White, ed., *Cyclosporine A: Proceedings of an International Conference on Cyclosporine A* (Cambridge: Elsevier Biomedical, 1982), 5.

81. University of Pittsburgh Library System, Drug Immunosuppression, online at http://www.starzl.pitt.edu/transplantation/immunology/drug.html; Starzl, *The Puzzle People*, 209–214.

82. Starzl, *The Puzzle People*, 214, Cooley, *100,000 Hearts*, 133.

83. Liz Marshall, "The Commander' Spurs Researchers in Development of FK-506," *The Scientist*, February 5, 1990; Thomas E. Starzl et al., "FK 506 for Liver, Kidney, and Pancreas Transplantation," *The Lancet* 334, issue 8760, 1989, 1000–1004.

84. Thomas Starzl Curriculum Vite, TS.

85. Starzl, *The Puzzle People*, 243–244.

86. Ibid., 261.

87. Lindsey Gruson, "Center for Transplants Aids Pittsburgh Ascent," *New York Times*, September 16, 1985; Anita Srikameswaran, "Surgeon's Health the Price of His Career," *Pittsburgh Post-Gazette*, June 2, 2000.

88. "Background Information and Recommendations Concerning Organ Transplantation in Foreign Nationals at the University Health Center of Pittsburgh," HB, Box 4, Folder 4, 7.

89. Thomas Starzl to Surgeon General C. Everett Koop, January 13, 1982, TS, Box 3, Folder Bahnson, Henry T., 1982–1984, 4.

90. Thomas Starzl interview; Thomas Starzl to Henry Bahnson, June 11, 1983, TS, Box 3, Folder Bahnson, Henry T., 1982–1984. For more about negotiations with Blue Cross, see Thomas Starzl to Susan Kanus, Blue Cross and Blue Shield of Wisconsin, May 9, 1984. For insurance denial challenges, see Thomas Starzl letter to Dorothy Knight, UHCP Billing Office and Blue Shield of Michigan Patient Denial, May 10, 1984. Both are in TS, Box 4, Folder BCBS 1984–1991. Pitt was one of six academic medical centers asked to participate in the Health Care Financing Administration's National Heart Transplantation study, which helped to set reimbursement rates for this procedure. For more on this, see Henry Bahnson to Daniel Stickler, Administrator Presbyterian-University, April 22, 1982, and Richard H. Husk, Director Division of Health Service Studies, (Health Care Financing Administration) HCFA, April 13, 1982, TS, Box 3, Folder Bahnson, Henry T., 1982–1984.

91. Draft letter from Henry Bahnson to Thomas Detre, ca 1, 1987. This letter was likely never sent, as there is a note from Starzl accompanying it, saying, "Personally, I would not send this letter unless it has been requested. It will not change anything and will only cause hard feelings." TS, Box 3, Folder Bahnson, Henry T., 1987.

92. For an example of the complaints being raised by others about the transplantation program dominating hospital resources, like operating room space, see Peter Winter to Henry Bahnson, June 30, 1983, TS, Box 3, Folder Bahnson, Henry T., 1982–1984; Thomas Starzl interview.

93. Andrew Schneider and Mary Pat Flaherty, "Favoritism Shrouds Presby Transplants," *Pittsburgh Press*, May 12, 1985, TS, Box 23, Folder Public Relations, 1985–1988.

94. Henry W. Pierce, "U.S. Patients Get Most Livers," *Pittsburgh Post-Gazette*, May 18, 1985, TS, Box 23, Folder Public Relations, 1985–1988. This incident is also discussed in Renée C. Fox and Judith P. Swazey, *Spare Parts: Organ Replacement in American Society* (New York: Oxford University Press, 1992), 79–81; Jed Adam Gross, "Playing with Matches Without Getting Burned: Public Confidence in Organ Transplantation," in Keith Wailoo, Julie Livingston, and Peter Guarnaccia, eds., *A Death Retold: Jesica Santillan, the Bungled Transplant, and the Paradoxes of Medical Citizenship* (Chapel Hill: University of North Carolina Press, 2006), 194–197.

95. Andrew Schneider and Mary Pat Flaherty, "Foreigners Get Damaged Kidneys, Starzl Says," *Pittsburgh Press*, June 7, 1985; Andrew Schneider and Mary Pat Flaherty, "Woman

Passed over After 3-Year Wait," *Pittsburgh Press*, May 12, 1985; Andrew Schneider, "Presbyterian to Revise Policy on Transplanting Kidneys," *Pittsburgh Press*, May 20, 1985, TS, Box 23, Folder Public Relations, 1985–1988; editorial, "Transplant Line-Jumping," *Pittsburgh Press*, May 19, 1985, TS, Box 23, Folder Public Relations, 1985–1988.

96. Schneider, "Presbyterian to Revise Policy on Transplanting Kidneys."

97. "Background Information and Recommendations Concerning Organ Transplantation in Foreign Nationals at the University Health Center of Pittsburgh," 7. Fox and Swazey note that this was released to the press. Fox and Swazey, *Spare Parts*, 80.

98. "Background Information and Recommendations Concerning Organ Transplantation in Foreign Nationals at the University Health Center of Pittsburgh," 2.

99. Ibid., 3–5, 9–10; Mary Pat Flaherty, "Prestige Lures Glut of Hospitals to Seek Transplant Status," *Pittsburgh Press*, June 16, 1985, TS Box 23, Folder Public Relations, 1985–1988.

100. Schneider and Flaherty, "Foreigners Paid Extra for Kidney Transplants."

101. "Background Information and Recommendations Concerning Organ Transplantation in Foreign Nationals at the University Health Center of Pittsburgh," 2, 7, 10. The document also addressed the allegations that once the *Press* had raised questions about organ allocation, the program had started to provide foreign nationals with inferior quality organs compared to those transplanted into American patients. Bahnson noted that there was a clinical reason for using these organs on foreign patients. Citing the same example used by the *Press* in which an eleven-year-old Egyptian boy was given a kidney over a sixty-year-old local woman, the document noted that because the boy had "not been exposed to dialysis or blood transfusion," his risks, should this "flawed" kidney fail, would be much lower than for the older women, because he could still undergo the type of therapeutic intervention, i.e., dialysis, that the woman had already benefited from. Thus, the decision to transplant suboptimal organs was about choosing the most appropriate course of therapeutic action, rather than any nefarious plan on the part of the transplant program to allocate damaged organs to foreign nationals.

102. For more on the relationship between Pittsburgh University Hospital and Allegheny General regarding transplant programs, see Henry Bahnson to Thomas Detre, April 2, 1986, TS, Box 3, Folder Bahnson, Henry T., 1986 (2).

103. Starzl, *The Puzzle People*, 205–206.

104. Göran B. Klintmalm, "The History of Organ Transplantation in the Baylor Health Care System," *BUMC Proceedings* 17 (2004), 23–34, 24; Thomas Starzl to Jefferson Pennington, February 4, 1986, TS, Box 67, Folder Pennington, Jefferson.

105. "Agreement Between Baylor University Medical Center and the University of Pittsburgh in Establishing and Operating a Human Organ Transplantation Program at the Baylor University Medical Center," TS, Box 3, Folder Baylor University, 1984–1985.

106. Thomas Starzl to Jefferson Pennington, February 4, 1986, 2. Starzl noted that not only did transplant surgeons at both programs agree to limit their incomes, there were no additional fees paid to any of the affiliation's principles as a reward for setting up the arrangement.

107. Thomas Starzl to Henry Bahnson, July 25, 1985, TS, Box 3, Folder Bahnson, Henry T., 1985, 2; Klintmalm, "The History of Organ Transplantation in the Baylor Health Care System," 23–34; unsigned affiliation agreement between University of Pittsburgh Transplant Program and George University Medical Center, HB, Box 3, Folder Bahnson, Henry T., 1986 (2).

108. Hospital Corporation of America, "Statement on Centers of Excellence," n.d., TS, Box 67, Folder Pennington, Jefferson.

109. In a letter to Starzl dated June 31, 1986, Pennington noted that the fear of "HCA's reputation in taking over hospitals (interest & familiarity_joint venture_often purchasing_ management assistance_management control_ownership)" led Dan Stickler, the administrator at Presbyterian-University, to withhold transplant revenue figures from HCA. Jefferson Pennington to Thomas Starzl, June 31, 1986, TS, Box 67, Folder Pennington, Jefferson.

110. "Possible Agreement with Hospital Corporation of America for Development of Multiple Organ Transplantation Services," TS, Box 12, Folder Hospital Corporation of America, 1986–1987.

111. Part of what may have fueled HCA's interest in transplantation medicine was that its competitor, American Medical International, had created a thriving international transplant business at its British hospitals using unwanted American organs. See Andrew Schneider and Mary Pat Flaherty, "Exploiting Trust: Neglect and Greed Infect Transplant System," *Pittsburgh Press*, November 3, 1985, and Andrew Schneider and Mary Pat Flaherty, "Common Market in U.S. Kidneys," *Pittsburgh Post*, November 6, 1985, TS, Box 23, Folder Public Relations, 1985–1988.

112. Jefferson Pennington to Thomas Starzl, January 10, 1986, TS, Box 67, Folder Pennington, Jefferson.

113. Thomas Detre to Jefferson Pennington, April 8, 1986, TS, Box 67, Folder Pennington, Jefferson, 2.

114. Ibid., 3.

115. Ibid., 3, 4. The 20 percent estimate was based on an interview with Brian Boznick, the director of the Pittsburgh Transplant Foundation.

116. Starzl, *The Puzzle People*, 267–280. Another of Starzl's significant contributions to transplantation was his work helping to rationalize the organ procurement process, which is discussed in more detail in *The Puzzle People*. See also Memorandum from Alexander J. Ciocca to George A. Huber RE: Legal Research Regarding Organ Procurement and Transplantation Services, January 30, 1987, TS, Box 12, Folder Hospital Corporation of America, 1986–1987.

117. Memorandum Ciocca to Huber RE: Legal Research Regarding Organ Procurement and Transplantation Services, 3.

118. Richard McCaskill to Jeffrey Romoff, June 5, 1986, TS, Box 67, Folder Jefferson Pennington. While Starzl didn't leave, HCA did manage to recruit away Leonard Makowka from Pitt. See Thomas Starzl to Jefferson Pennington, November 20, 1987, TS, Box 67, Folder Pennington, Jefferson.

119. Thomas Starzl to Jefferson Pennington, February 4, 1986, 3. Both DeBakey and Starzl did receive substantial salaries from their medical practice. In 1991, Starzl's name appeared in the *University Times* as one of the five highest paid faculty members with a salary for FY 1990 of $350,000, which was more than Chancellor Wesley W. Posvar and Detre. The following year, the *New York Times* noted that "Dr. Starzl's salary of $300,00 is not the highest among surgeons at the University of Pittsburgh. It is also less than a third of what is earned by some of his pupils, who are liver transplant surgeons elsewhere." Laurence K. Altman, "A Transplant Surgeon Who Fears Surgery," *New York Times*, July 7, 1992. The *New York Times* described DeBakey's relationship with salary in the following way: "Comfortable on a substantial income that, he says, has never approached $1 million, he gives 75 percent of his fees to

Baylor, and insists others on the faculty contribute too. 'In the academic world, you don't have time to use all that excess money,' he said. 'You're interested in providing the best teaching and care. Your leisure time is your work.'" Myerson, "It's a Business, No, It's A Religion."

120. Thomas Starzl to Henry Bahnson, July 25, 1985, TS, Box 3, Folder Bahnson, Henry T., 1985.

121. Thomas Detre to Abdul Mohsin Al Tuwaijri, Director General of Modernization & Training Services Kingdom of Saudi Arabia, July 6, 1989; Thomas Detre to Representative Bill Coyne, November 15, 1989; Thomas Detre to Representative Doug Walgren, November 5, 1989. TS, Box 19, Folder Detre, Thomas P., 1988–1989.

122. Draft "Memorandum of Understanding for Scientific and Educational Cooperation Among The Kingdom of Saudi Arabia and The Medical and Health Care Division of the University of Pittsburgh and Presbyterian-University Hospital of Pittsburgh," TS Box 73, Folder Romoff, Jeffrey A., 1989–1990. During these same years, UPMC did consult on other areas of strength, including work in psychiatry undertaken in Saudi Arabia and on cardiac surgical capacity in Egypt. Brignano, *Beyond the Bounds*, 171–172.

123. Brignano, *Beyond the Bounds*, 172.

124. The history of ISMETT is discussed in several sources, including Brignano, *Beyond the Bounds*; UPMC International, "Building a Leading Transplant Center in Sicily, Italy: Cross-Continental Partnership Meets Local Needs and Drives Economic Growth," Case Study 2015 online at https://upmcinternational.com/wp-content/uploads/2014/02/UPMC051 -IsmettCaseStudy-v9-1-1.pdf where the number of patients with liver disease comes from page 1; and Sean Hamill, "UPMC's Overseas Operations Blossomed in 14 Years," *Pittsburgh Post-Gazette*, May 30, 2010.

125. Brignano, *Beyond the Bounds*, 177.

126. Ibid., 177, 182–185.

127. UPMC International, "Building a Leading Transplant Center in Sicily, Italy: Cross-Continental Partnership Meets Local Needs and Drives Economic Growth," 11; Brignano, *Beyond the Bounds*, 185.

128. Brignano, *Beyond the Bounds*, 187; UPMC International, "Bringing World-Class Cancer Treatment to Patients in Southeast Ireland: A Unique Public-Private Partnership with UPMC Provides Care Closer to Home," Case Study, 2015 online at https://upmcinternational .com/wp-content/uploads/2015/05/UPMC-Whitfield-CaseStudy.pdf1.

129. Kris B. Mamula, "Irish Export," *Pittsburgh Business Times*, June 6, 2005.

130. Kris B. Mamula, "Doctors Pleased with Telemedicine Care," *Pittsburgh Business Times*, June 24, 2014; Kris B. Mamula, "Use of Telemedicine Surges at UPMC," *Pittsburgh Business Times*, May 23, 2014. Author interview with Harun Rashid, November 10, 2016.

131. UPMC International, "Improving Emergency Medical Care for Patients in Qatar: UPMC Partners with Hamad Medical Corporation to Establish a Trauma Center of Excellence," Case Study 2015; UPMC International, "Meeting the Challenges of Health Care Reform in Singapore: Asian American Medical Group Partners with UPMC to Deliver Quality Organ Transplantation," Case Study 2015; UPMC International, "Providing World-Class Cancer Care to Patients in Italy: UPMC Partners with San Pietro Fatebenefratelli Hospital to Develop and Advanced Radiotherapy Center of Excellence," Case Study 2015; UPMC International Kazakhstan: Oncology Center Consults, and "UPMC Partners with Bon Secours to Open Advanced Radiation Treatment Center in Ireland," at www.upmc.com.

132. Jeffrey Romoff quoted in Hamill, "UPMC's Overseas Operations Blossomed in 14 Years." This language of export is also echoed by Romoff in Brignano, *Beyond the Bounds*, 189. September 11th showed another upside to exporting medical care. In a 2008 interview for *Pittsburgh Magazine*, Charles Bogosta noted, "I wish I could say we had the foresight of how things would change in the way in which patients could travel . . . but we basically took the philosophy that it was better to keep these patients in their home country and treat them there. And it was profitable enough that we could bring back the revenue and invest that in our Western Pennsylvania health care system." Charles Bogosta quoted in Jeffery Fraser, "The Jet Set: UPMC Exports Its Brand and Services Across Continents," *Pittsburgh Quarterly*, Winter 2008.

133. Kris Mamula, "UPMC Pulls Out of Beacon Hospital in Ireland," *Pittsburgh Business Times*, April 8, 2014; Sean D. Hamill, "A Tale of Two Hospital Closures: Braddock and East Cleveland," *Pittsburgh Post-Gazette*, July 27, 2014.

134. *Life Magazine*, "A Bitter Feud," April 10, 1970. For details of their reconciliation, see Cooley, *100,000 Hearts*, 193–198.

135. Arnold S. Relman, "The New Medical-Industrial Complex," *New England Journal of Medicine* 303, no. 17 (1980), 963–970.

Chapter 4

1. Jane Blotzer, "When the Fire Dies," *Pittsburgh Post-Gazette*, December 30, 1985, ACCD, Box 174, Folder 6, 32.

2. Hoerr, *And the Wolf Finally Came*.

3. Lisa Belkin, "Now, It's Remember the Oil Bust," *New York Times*, August 22, 1989.

4. "100 Years: Oil Bust, Space Tragedy and Chronicle Sale," *Houston Chronicle*, October 14, 2001.

5. Belkin, "Now, It's Remember the Oil Bust." "Astroworld" quotation reprinted from a supplement to the *Houston Post* called "Boom."

6. Dieterich-Ward, *Beyond Rust*; Neumann, *Remaking the Rust Belt*; also see *Journal of Urban History* 41, no. 1, "Forum on Pittsburgh's Renaissance Revisited," January 2015.

7. Florida, *The Rise of the Creative Class*. Several economic bloggers and traditional print journalists have seized on parts of Florida's argument to offer prescriptive solutions to urban decline, such as the ongoing "what Detroit can learn from Pittsburgh" dialog that has achieved a life of its own on the Internet. For examples of this discussion, see WXYZ-TV, Detroit—Detroit 2020 Project, "Learning from Pittsburgh," January 6, 2011, http://detroit2020.com/2011/01/06/learning-from-pittsburgh/; Randi Kaye, Anderson Cooper 360, "Can Pittsburgh Save Detroit?" March 18, 2009, http://ac360.blogs.cnn.com/2009/03/18/can-pittsburgh-save-detroit/; Kate Phillips, "Why Pittsburgh?," *New York Times*, Caucus Blog, September 24, 2009, http://thecaucus.blogs.nytimes.com/2009/09/24/why-pittsburgh/; Mike Householder, "Pittsburgh, Detroit Can Learn Much from Each Other," *USA Today*, June 6, 2009.

8. Posvar as quoted in Tom Barnes, "Out of Rubble, Robotics: Pitt's, CMU's High-Tech Adventure Underway," *Pittsburgh Post-Gazette*, October 11, 1986, 4; Lubove, *Twentieth-Century Pittsburgh*, vol. 2, 24–116; Dieterich-Ward, *Beyond Rust*, 205–230; Neumann, *Remaking the Rust Belt*, 45–106.

9. Berman, *Creating the Market University*, 5.

10. Bluestone and Harrison, *The Deindustrialization of America*; High, *Industrial Sunset*.

11. Dieterich-Ward, *Beyond Rust*, esp. chap. 8; Lubove, *Twentieth-Century Pittsburgh*, vol. 2, esp. chap. 3.

12. Stephen Karlinchak, interview with William J. Ceriani, "Employer Outlook: Work-Force Changes Evolving and Continuing," *Pittsburgh Post-Gazette*, May 20, 1995.

13. Josie Carey and Marty Wolfson, "This Is Pittsburgh and Southwestern Pennsylvania: We Live Here . . . We Like It," ACCD, Box 217, Folder 25.

14. Neumann, *Remaking the Rust Belt*, 188–201; Aaron Cowan, *A Nice Place to Visit: Tourism and Urban Revitalization in the Postwar Rustbelt* (Philadelphia: Temple University Press, 2016). See also the Allegheny Conference Collection, which features several mid–1980s articles highlighting the city's changing economy, esp. ACCD, Box 12. Within the economics of biotechnology, there has been some discussion about how biotechnology companies grow. One theory is that communities with scientific "stars" help to build regional interest and beget more scientific stars. This idea reflects the marketing campaigns of the 1950s and 1960s, which also focused on demonstrating the contribution of key individuals to the community's scientific identity. Lynne G. Zucker, Michael R. Darby, and Marilynn B. Brewer, "Intellectual Human Capital and the Birth of U.S. Biotechnology Enterprises," *American Economic Review* 88, no. 1 (March 1998), 209–306; Simpson, "Private Dollars for a Healthier Public," discusses this in Pittsburgh. For an archival example, see "Behind the Scenes of Medical Research," program from a dinner, May 12, 1952, UHCP, 90/43-A Memorabilia Box 1, Folder 1.

15. "A Time When They Were All Happy," *Pittsburgh Post-Gazette*, in "When the Fire Dies," December 30, 1985, 34. Likely Jane Blotzer, but a box within a larger article.

16. Jane Blotzer, "Moving On When Hope Runs Out," *Pittsburgh Post-Gazette*, in "When the Fire Dies," December 30, 1985, 40.

17. For example, the Community College of Allegheny County offered the Dislocated Workers Educational Training Program, the federal government offered job training assistance through the Job Training Partnership Act, and U.S. Steel provided a $1 million grant to retrain displaced workers. "Aid for Those Who Retrain," *Pittsburgh Post-Gazette*, in "When the Fire Dies," December 30, 1985, 38. Also a box within a larger article by Eleanor Bergholz.

18. Eleanor Bergholz, "Some Retrain for New Careers," *Pittsburgh Post-Gazette*, in "When the Fire Dies," December 30, 1985, 37.

19. Ibid.

20. The question of why the American economy changed from industrial to postindustrial has fascinated social scientists, historians, and economists for nearly four decades. In one telling, organized labor is the villain, whose demands for high wages and workplace safety helped to create inflexible rules and damaging regulations that squandered America's legacy of manufacturing and served up decay. A more middle-of-the-road critique softens the focus on labor's failures and refocuses blame on corporate ineptitude, highlighting, for example, U.S. Steel's purchase of Marathon Oil or American automakers' lackluster focus on quality and consumer demand, as reasons why the industrial might of the United States declined. A third critique lays primary blame for deindustrialization at the foot of the federal and local states and argues that deregulation, structural racism, and Cold War foreign policy that encouraged and subsidized the movement of manufacturing overseas and undercut America's self-interest at home. Nelson Lichtenstein and Elizabeth Tandy Shermer, eds., *The Right and Labor in America* (Philadelphia: University of Pennsylvania Press, 2012); Stein, *Pivotal Decade*; Cowie, *Stayin' Alive*; Sugrue, *The Origins of the Urban Crisis*.

21. In addition to "When the Fire Dies," see stories like Michael Schroeder, "As Smoke Clears, High-Tech's Allure Grows"; Michael Schroeder, "Boston Finds Fortune in Rings of High-Tech"; Lorna Doubet, "It's No Silicon Valley, but R&D Intense Here"; Jennifer Lin, "Few Signs of a Boom in the 'Robot Valley,'" *Pittsburgh Post-Gazette*, January 24, 1983.

22. Dieterich-Ward, *Beyond Rust*, 206–209.

23. Edward H. Litchfield, "Research: The Key to Pittsburgh's Economic Growth," n.d., EHL, Box 154, Folder 1308, 1. This is discussed in Andrew T. Simpson, "Health and Renaissance: Academic Medicine and the Remaking of Modern Pittsburgh," *Journal of Urban History* 41, no. 1 (January 2015), 19–27.

24. Alberts, *Pitt,* 249–250.

25. Ibid., 311. Litchfield, "Research: The Key to Pittsburgh's Economic Growth," 1–7. For more on the model of research and development pioneered in Silicon Valley and Boston, see O'Mara, *Cities of Knowledge*; John W. Servos, "Changing Partners: The Mellon Institute, Private Industry, and the Federal Patron," *Technology and Culture* 35, no. 2 (April 1994), 221–257; Pittsburgh Regional Planning Association, "The Oakland Study: Preliminary Report Linkages," December 1960. Carnegie Tech became Carnegie Mellon in 1967 when it merged with the Mellon Institute of Science.

26. Oakland Development Corporation, "This Is an Urban Area," n.d., EHL, Box 155, Folder 1309, 1.

27. Ibid., 23; Edward Litchfield, Draft Memorandum "Organizing for Spin-Off," September 26, 1962, EHL, Box 155, Folder 1309.

28. Alberts, *Pitt,* 311–312.

29. Vitale, "Decline Is Renewal," 34–39.

30. Berman, *Creating the Market University*, 62–64.

31. Martin Kenney, *Biotechnology: The University-Industrial Complex* (New Haven: Yale University Press, 1986), 23–27; Paul Berg and Maxine Singer, "The Recombinant DNA Controversy: Twenty Years Later," *Proceedings of the National Academy of Sciences* 92 (September 1995), 9011–9013; Robert Olby, *The Path to the Double Helix* (Seattle: University of Washington Press, 1974). For more on the general development of American biology, see Keith R. Benson, Jane Maienschein, Ronald Rainger, eds., *The Expansion of American Biology* (New Brunswick: Rutgers University Press, 1991).

32. Nathaniel Comfort, *The Science of Human Perfection: How Genes Became the Heart of American Medicine* (New Haven: Yale University Press, 2012); Barton Childs, *Genetic Medicine: A Logic of Disease* (Baltimore: Johns Hopkins University Press, 2003); Evelyn Fox Keller, *The Century of the Gene* (Cambridge: Harvard University Press, 2000); "UPMC Fosters 'Personalized Medicine' with $100 Million Investment in Sophisticated Data Warehouse and Analytics," UPMC press release, October 1, 2012.

33. William S. Dietrich II, "Against the Odds: Thomas Detre and the Birth of UPMC," *Pittsburgh Quarterly*, Summer 2009. There is a substantial literature on the ways that Cold War science, government funding, and local development intersected. Shulman, *From Cotton Belt to Sunbelt,* esp. chap. 6; Light, *From Warfare to Welfare*; O'Mara, *Cities of Knowledge*; Neil M. Maher, *Apollo in the Age of Aquarius* (Cambridge: Harvard University Press, 2017), esp. chap. 1.

34. "Understanding Indirect Costs," *Funding News*, National Institute of Allergy and Infectious Diseases, National Institutes of Health, https://www.niaid.nih.gov/grants-contracts/understanding-indirect-costs-0.

35. For a relatively contemporaneous view of the potential of spin-offs to help the financial bottom line of academic medical centers, see David Blumenthal and Gregg S. Meyer, "Academic Health Centers in a Changing Environment," *Health Affairs* 15, no. 2 (1996), 200–215, 209–210.

36. David C. Mowery et al., *Ivory Tower and Industrial Innovation: University-Industry Technology Transfer Before and After the Bayh-Dole Act in the United States* (Stanford: Stanford Business Books, 2004).

37. Berman, *Creating the Market University*, 16, 81–85, 108–109.

38. Ibid., 99. Berman notes that one of the reasons why venture capital funds were appealing to large pension funds was that the inflation of the mid to late 1970s had cut into the returns on blue-chip stocks, making them less attractive investments. She also notes that venture capital funds allowed pension funds to diversify their investment mixes quickly. Ibid., 73–76. For more on the history of changes to the capital gains tax, see United States Senate, Joint Economic Committee Report, "Cutting Capital Gains Tax Rates: The Right Policy for the 21st Century," Prepared by Lawrence Whitman (Washington, DC: Government Printing Office, 1999), 5; Christopher Briem and Vijai Singh, "The Role of Universities in the Evolution of Technology-Based Economic Development Policies in the United States," in Ulrich Hilpert, ed., *Routledge Handbook of Politics and Technology* (New York: Routledge, 2016), 132–143. There is a debate over how much access to venture capital really matters for incentivizing the growth of start-ups. However, it is clear that the perception that it mattered drove actions in both Pittsburgh and Houston. Mark L. Burton and Michael J. Hicks, "Do University Based Biotechnology Centres Impact Regional Biotechnology (Commercial) Employment?" *International Journal of Technology Transfer and Commercialization* 5, no. 4 (2006), 360–400, 394. This is also mentioned by Zucker, Darby, and Brewer, "Intellectual Human Capital and the Birth of U.S. Biotechnology Enterprises," 298.

39. Berman, *Creating the Market University*, 72.

40. Anne Watzman, "Medrad/Intec, Inc—Thriving on Affairs of the Heart," *Pittsburgh's New Dimension in Advanced Technology*, RIDC, in ACCD, Box 221, Folder 20; and Medrad corporate history online at http://www.medrad.com/en-us/aboutmedrad/Pages/History.aspx; "Redrawing the Economic Landscape: Technology-Based Economic Development in Pittsburgh, 1978–2005," Carnegie Mellon Department of History Senior History and Policy Project Class Report, December 14, 2005, 100–103; "Eli Lilly Agrees to Pay About $45 Million to Acquire Medrad/Intec, Inc's Implantable Defibrillator Business," *Wall Street Journal*, March 26, 1985, 56.

41. Watzman, "Thriving on Affairs of the Heart."

42. Urban Redevelopment Authority of Pittsburgh, Economic Development Department, "Advance Briefing Book Pittsburgh Industrial Park," prepared for the Urban Land Institute Panel, November 11–16, 1984, 2–1; courtesy of Evan Stoddard.

43. Ibid., 5–11.

44. URA, "Advance Briefing Book," 2–2, 2–3.

45. PRMS Documentation for New Feature Plan for Creation of a Subsidiary Corporation for the Conduct of Technological Innovation, January 6, 1982, UPIF, Foundation for Applied Science and Technology, 3–5.

46. Ibid., Appendix A, "Proposal for the Creation of an Industrial Research Institute at the University of Pittsburgh, 10 December 1980," 2.

47. PRMS Documentation, 7–8; quotation on 7.

48. FAST promotional materials, especially "Business and Higher Education: Partners in Progress," UPIF.

49. PRMS Documentation, 2.

50. Diane Lefkowitz, "Board OKs Creation of Foundation," *Pitt News*, October 22, 1982, UPIF.

51. Mike Crawmer, "Trustees Consider Research Proposal," *University Times*, 15 no. 4, October 21, 1982, UPIF.

52. Henry Hillman, press statement about Penn's Southwest, November 15, 1971, ACCD, Box 124, Folder 5, 4; Neumann, *Remaking the Rust Belt*, 183.

53. Hillman, press statement, 4; Angel Jordan, interview with the author, October 5, 2011.

54. Peter K. Eisinger, *The Rise of the Entrepreneurial State: State and Local Economic Development Policy in the United States* (Madison: University of Wisconsin Press, 1988). In this model, local political subdivisions and state-level actors worked to allow the public sector to assist with the creation of new sources of venture capital, promote a vision of high-tech economic development, and helped to push for state-specific export primacy.

55. Susan B. Hansen, "State Governments and Industrial Policy in the United States: The Case of Pennsylvania" in Joachim Jens Hesse, ed., *Regional Structural Change and Industrial Policy in International Perspective: United States, Great Britain, France, Federal Republic of Germany* (Baden-Baden: Nomos, 1988), 104–105. See also Morton Coleman, "Public-Private Cooperative Response Patterns to Regional Structural Change in the Pittsburgh Area," in Hesse, *Regional Structural Change and Industrial Policy*, 123–160. Neumann, *Remaking the Rust Belt*, 87–88.

56. Hansen, "State Governments and Industrial Policy in the United States," 105, and National Council for Economic Development, "The Ben Franklin Partnership Linking Higher Education, Government & Business for Economic Growth," Information Service, November 1985, Richard Thornburgh Papers (RT) Box 277, Folder 10.

57. Allegheny Conference on Community Development, *A Strategy for Growth*, vol. 1, 8.

58. Ibid.

59. City of Pittsburgh, the County of Allegheny, the University of Pittsburgh, Carnegie-Mellon University, *Strategy 21: A Proposal to the Commonwealth of Pennsylvania*, June 1985, 5E, 5D; Roger S. Ahlbrandt Jr. and Clyde Weaver, "Public-Private Institutions and Advanced Technology Development in Southwestern Pennsylvania," *Journal of the American Planning Association* 53, no. 4 (1987), 449–458.

60. Letter to Robert Pease from Alfred W. Wishart and Douglas D. Danforth, September 8, 1987, ACCD, Box 246, Folder 1. Pease was unable to attend the meeting.

61. Biomedical Research Meeting Attendee List sent to Robert Pease from Dana Phillips, Pittsburgh Foundation, October 20, 1987, ACCD, Box 246, Folder 1. Some attendees included Jerome Schultz, Thomas Detre, Wesley Posvar, Robert Gleeson and Timothy Parks from the Pittsburgh High Technology Council, John Thorne from the Pittsburgh Seed Fund, and Sherif Abdelhak from Allegheny Health Services, which was a competitor health system to UPMC based out of Allegheny General Hospital. This would later become known as Allegheny Health, Education, and Research Foundation, or AHERF. By the 2000s, after a major bankruptcy and other numerous changes, the Allegheny Health Network emerged as the health system serving this hospital. This transition is discussed more in Chapters 5 and 6.

62. Remarks by Vincent Sarni, "Meeting Notes Biomedical Research Activities October 6, 1987," as sent to Robert Pease, ACCD, Box 246, Folder 1.

63. Charles Rial and Associates and Arthur Young & Co., "Interim Status Report and Program Direction Strategy for Biotechnology Commercialization," for the Urban Redevelopment Authority and Western Pennsylvania Advanced Technology Center, January 19, 1988, ACCD, Box 246, Folder 1, 1–2. Rial was an attendee of the October 6 meeting.

64. Ibid., 2–6.

65. Shorebank Advisory Services, Arthur Young & Co, J. Katy Noel & Associates, "Developing Pittsburgh's Biotechnology Assets: A Strategy for Growth," Report to the Urban Redevelopment Association and the Western Pennsylvania Hightechnology Council, July 1988; courtesy of Evan Stoddard.

66. The creation of the Pittsburgh Biomedical Development Corporation was announced on July 13, 1988. Letter from Howard M. Love to Robert B. Pease, July 8, 1988, ACCD, Box 246, Folder 1; Pittsburgh High Technology Council, "Pittsburgh Biomedical Development Corporation Launched," press release, July 13, 1988; courtesy of Evan Stoddard. Evan Stoddard, "Local Government's Efforts to Promote High-Technology Industries in Pittsburgh," paper presented at the International Symposium on Regional Restructuring and Advanced Industry Development, Osaka, Japan, November 8, 1989, 2; courtesy of Evan Stoddard.

67. Ahlbrandt and Weaver, "Public-Private Institutions and Advanced Technology Development in Southwestern Pennsylvania," 450–452; quotation on 452.

68. Dennis Yablonsky interview with author.

69. Economic Development Department, Urban Redevelopment Authority of Pittsburgh, "Pittsburgh Economic Development Strategy," Draft Report, December 4, 1987, 2–21; courtesy of Evan Stoddard.

70. Stoddard, "Local Government's Efforts to Promote High-Technology Industries in Pittsburgh."

71. Evan Stoddard interview with author, February 21, 2014.

72. RIDC, *Pittsburgh's New Dimension in Advanced Technology*, 5. For a broader history of the venture capital industry, including an explanation of the important changes in the 1980s and 1990s similar to what Hillman describes, see Paul Gompers and Josh Lerner, "The Venture Capital Revolution," *Journal of Economic Perspectives* 15, no. 2 (2001).

73. The Enterprise Corporation of Pittsburgh, *A Survey of Venture Capital in Pittsburgh, 1989*, sponsored by Ben Franklin Technology Center of Western Pennsylvania, Mellon Bank, Pittsburgh High Technology Council, Price Waterhouse, Reed Smith Shaw & McClay, 1.

74. For a detailed history of URA actions and the site's environmental challenges, see Evan Stoddard, *Transformed: Reinventing Pittsburgh's Industrial Sites for a New Century, 1975–1995* (Pittsburgh: Harmony Street Publishers, 2016), esp. chap. 2; Dieterich-Ward, *Beyond Rust*, 219–221; Neumann, *Remaking the Rust Belt*, 152–153.

75. Lubove, *Twentieth-Century Pittsburgh*, vol. 2, 48; Fact Sheet, Center for Biotechnology and Bioengineering, ACCD, Box 246, Folder 1.

76. Dennis Yablonsky was appointed founding CEO of the Pittsburgh Life Sciences Greenhouse near the end of 2001. Yablonsky described much of his job as "a contact sport," saying, "I just spend a lot of my time meeting with the leadership of government, academia, industry, and economic development." From 2009 to 2018, Yablonsky was the CEO of the Allegheny Conference. Quotation from Christopher Davis, "Yablonsky Will Focus on the

'Details' in Leading Life Sciences Greenhouse," *Pittsburgh Business Times*, December 7–13, 2001, 10–11; quotation on 11. Additional information comes from author interview with Dennis Yablonsky, October 17, 2011; "Redrawing the Economic Landscape," 119–131.

77. "Recycling Slums," *U.S. News and World Report*, Special Section "Big Cities," April 5, 1976, HMRC, H-Growth and Development General, 62.

78. "Can a Transplanted New Yorker Find Happiness in Houston?" *Houston Magazine*, May 1976, HMRC, H-Growth and Development General.

79. Robert Reinhold, "2 Years After Energy Bust, City Comes to Grips with Future," *New York Times*, September 8, 1984, HMRC, H-Growth and Development 1983–1985.

80. Peter Bishop as quoted in the *Houston Business Journal*, January 20, 1983, HMRC, H-Growth and Development 1983–1985.

81. Johnson, *Houston: The Unknown City*; Feagin, *Free Enterprise City*; Bryan Burrough, *The Big Rich: The Rise and Fall of the Greatest Texas Oil Fortunes* (New York: Penguin Press, 2009). Pratt, "8F and Many More," 31.

82. Loyd S. Swenson Jr., James M. Grimwood, Charles C. Alexander, *This New Ocean: A History of Project Mercury*, NASA-SP4201, 1989, chap. 12–3, "Space Task Group Gets A New Home and Name" online at https://www.hq.nasa.gov/pao/History/SP–4201/toc.htm. Not only did NASA help to bring dollars and industries to communities, "southern leaders saw the space program as a conduit to a 'New South' of science and technology-based enterprise." Schulman, *From Cotton Belt to Sunbelt*, 148. This was later renamed the Johnson Space Center after former president Lyndon Johnson.

83. Jessica A. Cannon, "Owls in Space: Rice University's Connection to the NASA Johnson Space Center," *Houston History* 6, no. 1 (Fall 2008), 32–35; Eric Berger, "A Worthy Endeavor: How Albert Thomas Won Houston NASA's Flagship Center: Money and Political Power Landed Johnson Space Center Here and Rocketed Houston into Prominence," *Houston Chronicle*, September 14, 2013.

84. Pratt, "8F and Many More," 38.

85. Kevin M. Brady, "NASA Launches Houston into Orbit: The Political, Economic, and Social Impact of the Space Agency on Southeast Texas, 1961–1969," in Steven J. Dick and Roger D. Launius, eds., *Societal Impact of Spaceflight* (Washington, D.C.: National Aeronautics and Space Agency, 2007), 451–466; Shelly Henley Kelley, "Mutually Beneficial: The University of Houston-Clear Lake and NASA Johnson Space Center," *Houston History* 6, no. 1 (Fall 2008), 36–41.

86. Texas Medical Center Inc., *Annual Report 1963*, TMCI, 9.

87. Texas Medical Center Inc., *Annual Report 1965*, TMCI, 10.

88. Houston Chamber of Commerce, "Houston's Growing R&D Capability," May 1965, HMRC, H-Growth and Development–1960s.

89. Steven Chapman, "The Great Texas Oil Bust," *Chicago Tribune*, May 19, 1983, 18.

90. Notes of Meeting Human Resources Council, October 26, 1983, CAL, Series 1A, Box SG5/1, Memberships HCC Human Resources Council 1983–1984. For more on Bishop's path to Houston and preparation to deal with national issues of technology and urban development, see Neumann, *Rethinking the Rust Belt*, 78.

91. Houston Chamber of Commerce Committee on Economic Diversification Planning. "Houston's Blueprint for Economic Diversification," May 2, 1984, CAL, Series 1A, Box SG5/1, HCC Economic Diversification Committee 1983–1984, 2.

92. Bill Schadewald, "Smooth and Stormy Memories of Schnitzer," *Houston Business Journal*, November 7, 1999.

93. Barbara Eaves, "Creation of the Greater Houston Partnership," *Houston Review of History and Culture* 1, no. 2 (2004), 43–44. Contemporary media accounts note that the HEDC was paying $11,000 per month to rent space from the Chamber. That same article claimed the HEDC operated through the Chamber, but noted that the funding came from outside sources. See Bob Sablatura, "Where the $6 Million Went," *Houston Business Journal*, August 11, 1986, 1, 5.

94. Charles A. LeMaistre to Richard Wainerdi, October 17, 1984, CAL, Series 1A, Box SG5/1, HCC Economic Development Committee, 1984–1985.

95. HEDC, "The Houston Economic Development Council—Building from Strength, to Strength, for the Houston Region," n.d., HMRC, H-Economic Development Council.

96. Sablatura, "Where the $6 Million Went."

97. Daniel Yergin, *The Quest: Energy, Security and the Remaking of the Modern World* (New York: Penguin Press), 325–328.

98. For more details about The Woodlands and its contribution to American city and regional planning, see George T. Morgan and John O. King, *The Woodlands: New Community Development, 1964–1983* (College Station: Texas A&M University Press, 1987); Ann Forsyth, *Reforming Suburbia: The Planned Communities of Irvine, Columbia, and The Woodlands* (Berkeley: University of California Press, 2005), 161–207.

99. "The Business of Biotech," *Houston Post*, September 7, 1986, HMRC, H-Business-Medical, 3E. "Baylor's Biotechnology Laboratories Under Construction at The Woodlands," *Houston Post*, September 7, 1986, HMRC, H-Business-Medical; interview with William Butler by author, July 31, 2015.

100. Brian Levinson, "Biotechnical Firms Find Financing from Venture Capitalists," *Houston Chronicle*, May 14, 1986, HMRC, H-Business-Medical; "Baylor's biotechnology laboratories under construction at the Woodlands" 3E.

101. Jeanne Lang Jones, "Biotechnology: Houston-Area Industry Positioned for Long-Term Growth," *Houston Post*, July 24, 1994, HMRC, H-Business-Biotech.

102. "The Business of Biotech." Another idea that was floated was that of creating a biotechnology or life science triangle south of the city from the TMC, taking in NASA at Clear Lake, and extending down toward the University of Texas Medical Branch in Galveston. Liz Doyle, "South Corridor Triangle: A Biotech Gold Mine," HMRC, H-Growth and Development 1986. For more on HARC, see Kristen Hays, "George Mitchell Still Pushes Energy Conservation," *Houston Chronicle*, August 2, 2008, http://www.chron.com/business/energy/article/George-Mitchell-still-pushes-energy-conservation–1678366.php and http://www.harc.edu/AboutHARC/tabid/54/Default.aspx.

103. Houston Chamber of Commerce Committee on Economic Diversification, "Medical Services Project Group Report'83–84, CAL, Series 1A, Box SG5/1, HCC Economic Development Committee, 1984–1985; emphasis in original. For a more detailed description of what a proposed TMC Research Institute would look like, see "Discussion Notes for Medical Service Project Group," CAL, Series 1A, Box SG5/1, HCC Economic Development Committee, 1984–1985.

104. Houston Chamber of Commerce Committee on Economic Diversification, "Medical Services Project Group Report," 83–84.

105. HEDC Economic Diversification Committee, "Draft Final Report 1984–1985," CAL, Office of the President, Series 1A, Box SG5/1, HCC Economic Development Committee, 1984–1985, 4.

106. Arthur D. Little, untitled report, in CAL, Series 1A, Box SG5/1, HCC Economic Development Committee, 1984–1985, 1.5.

107. Ibid., 1.6.

108. Butler and Ware, *Arming for Battle Against Disease Through Education, Research, and Patient Care at Baylor College of Medicine*, vol. 4, 1139–1143.

109. Ibid., 1143–1147.

110. Ibid., 1149.

111. Discussion Group D, Resources for the Future, Materials Prepared for Executive Faculty Retreat, April 22, 1994, MED, Box 7, Folder 23.

112. Kate Thomas, "Baylor's Biotech Mission Ready to Deliver," *Houston Post*, June 22, 1993, HMRC, H-Business-Biotech. Quote in Joe Hart, "A Budding Boom in Biotechnology," *Houston Business Journal*, June 7, 1986, HMRC, H-Business-Medicine. Thomas reports the date of BCM Technologies founding as 1984. Baylor sources report it as 1983. The roughly $4 million figure also comes from Thomas. However, financial sheets provided by BCM Technologies to the Baylor Faculty Executive Committee show gross patent royalty income between 1988 and November 1993 as slightly over $6 million. It is not clear where Thomas's numbers came from. For BCM Technology–provided numbers, see Materials Prepared for Executive Faculty Retreat, Addendum II, MED, Box 7, Folder 23. See also "Pioneers in Technology Transfer in Baylor College of Medicine 1987–1988," Annual Report BCM, Baylor Miscellaneous—1980s.

113. Brian Levinson, "Emerging Biotechnology Company: Firm Will Create 200 Jobs Here, Plans to Move into New Structure," *Houston Chronicle*, May 8, 1986, HMRC, H-Business-Biotechnology. In 1996, Houston Biotechnology merged with the New Jersey–based firm Medarex. "Medarex, Houston Biotechnology Finalize Merger Deal," *Houston Business Journal*, December 24, 1996.

114. Memorandum from Eugene M. McKelvey to Charles A. LeMaistre, RE: Andetech Proposal, February 29, 1984, CAL, SG5/1D, Unfilmed Records, Andetech, 1983–1984, 1.

115. Memorandum to the File, RE: Andetech, July 23, 1986, CAL, SG5/1D, Unfilmed Records, Andetech, 1984–1986.

116. Eileen O' Grady, "Japan Trade Mission Will Spotlight City's Growing Biotechnology Base," *Houston Post*, March 16, 1988, HMRC, H-Growth and Development 1987–1988.

117. Robert A. Viehweger, "Houston's Most Promising New Business Partner," March 1, 1987, *Houston Chronicle* in HMRC H-Foreign Trade Zone.

118. William Tucker, "As Health Reform Looms, the Biotech Industry Cringes," *Insight on the News*, July 8, 1994, 6.

119. Ronald Ozio, "Baylor College of Medicine Named Site for Human Genome Research Center," *TMC News* 13, no. 3, March 1991, TMCI, Series 2, Box 7, John P. McGovern Historical Research Center, Texas Medical Center Library, Houston, 1, 20.

120. Baylor College of Medicine, "Research 2000: Summary Report to the W. M. Keck Foundation," Confidential Report, BCM, Baylor Miscellaneous—1980s. This report called for recruitment of "a nationally recognized leader" to help the school make genetic sequencing a research priority (16).

121. National Aeronautics and Space Administration, "NASA, Baylor College of Medicine, Sign Agreement to Establish a National Space Biomedical Research Institute," press release issued May 29, 1997.

122. Charles A. LeMaistre to Charles B. Mullins, April 26, 1994, Re: RGene; Charles A. LeMaistre to Charles B. Mullins, April 26, 1994, Re: Intron, CAL, SG5/12, Unfilmed Records, Technology Development Office, 1993–1994.

123. Vicki Brower, "Biotech Aims High in the Lone Star State," *Genetic Engineering and Biotechnology News* 27, no. 21, December 1, 2007. The relationship between Mendelson, the drug, and clinical trials of it at M. D. Anderson generated controversy. Justin Gillis, "A Hospital's Conflict of Interest," *Washington Post*, June 30, 2002.

124. Brower, "Biotech Aims High in the Lone Star State."

125. Greater Houston Partnership, "Meeting Medical Challenges: Houston: 'Third Coast' in Bioscience," March 2000, HMRC, H-Business-Biotech.

126. Ibid.

127. Council on Science and Biotechnology Development, "Biotechnology and the Life Sciences: Building on Our Strengths, Sustaining Our Competitiveness," 2002–2003 Report to the Governor, March 2003.

128. State of Texas Biotechnology and Life Science Cluster, "State of Texas Biotechnology and Life Science Cluster Report," August 2005, 4. A 2007 investment by the state of Texas and the Cancer Prevention and Research Institute of Texas faced questions about its use of public resources, including allocation of research funds and commercializing contracts, which led to resignations and litigation. Robert T. Garrett, "Texas Cancer-Research Agency Survived a Scandal. Now, It Hopes to Prove That It's Working," *Dallasnews.com (Dallas Morning News)*, September 2015; Edgar Walters, Alana Rocha, and Justin Dehn, "Revamped Cancer Agency Faces New Questions," *Texas Tribune*, February 26, 2015.

In 2018, the Texas Medical Center announced plans to build a collaborative biomedical science facility, and other plans are in place to build an innovation district. Pittsburgh also has the Keystone Innovation District, which takes in many of the major universities and hospitals. Council on Science and Biotechnology Development, Rice Alliance, http://alliance.rice.edu/about/; the University of Houston's Center for Life Sciences Technology, www.texas biotech.org; and the GHP's list of Technology Transfer Organizations in Houston at http://www.houston.org/economic-development/business-resources/tech-transfer/index.aspx; Greater Houston Partnership, Houston Innovation Corridor, https://www.houston.org/innovationcorridor/; Scott Andes, Mitch Horowitz, Ryan Helwig, and Bruce Katz, *Capturing the Next Economy: Pittsburgh's Rise as a Global Innovation City* (Washington, D.C.: Brookings Institution, 2017), 21.

129. Kris B. Mamula, "Pennsylvania Seeing Shift in Biotechnology Industry," *Pittsburgh Post-Gazette*, June 7, 2016.

130. Greater Houston Partnership Fact Sheet, https://www.houston.org/business/industry-sectors.html.

131. Sheryl Silver, "In Demand: Growth Industries Need Engineering Specialists," *Pittsburgh Post-Gazette*, November 23, 1986; Joyce Gannon, "Hi-Tech Salaries Advance," *Pittsburgh Post-Gazette*, November 20, 1991; Pittsburgh biotechnology salaries, Indeed.com, https://www.indeed.com/salaries/Biotechnology-Salaries,-Pittsburgh-PA.

132. Bergholz, "Some Retrain for New Careers." Pittsburgh rap artist Jasiri X has put out an excellent YouTube video titled "America's Most Livable City," which makes the point that

although Pittsburgh was named "America's Most Livable City" by several publications in recent years, the city still leads the nation in black poverty. A poignant line is "How we gonna get a job in biotechnology if all we ever learn is survival physiology / Why we so poor if you' all revived the economy/but we ain't getting nothing besides an apology." This is superimposed over a backdrop of masked men with guns and the demolition of a public housing tower in the city's East Liberty neighborhood.

133. Jim Barlow, "Biotech Industry Lags in Houston," December 20, 1987, HMRC, H-Business-Biotech.

Chapter 5

1. Katharine R. Levit et al., "National Health Expenditures, 1993," *Health Care Financing Review* 16, no. 1 (Fall 1994), 247–294.

2. Larry Mathis, "Larry L. Mathis: Health Care Reform Requires Tough Choices," *Texas Medical Center News*, March 1993.

3. "Chart 1, Total Nonfarm and Health Care Indexes of Employment, Seasonally Adjusted, 1990–2010"; "Chart 3, Employment Index for Selected Components of Health Care Industry, Seasonally Adjusted, 1990–2010," in Catherine A. Wood, "Employment in Health Care: A Crutch for the Ailing Economy During the 2007–2009 Recession," *Monthly Labor Review*, April 2011, 13–18.

4. Stevens, *In Sickness and in Wealth*, 302. Between the 1980s and 2000s, the creation and potential success or failure of integrated delivery systems generated a great deal of interest in the health policy literature, as did the role of for-profit firms in shaping competition. For examples, see Jeffrey A. Alexander et al., "Acquisition Strategies of Multihospital Systems," *Health Affairs* 4, no. 3 (Fall 1985), 49–66; Steven M. Shortell, "The Evolution of Hospital Systems: Unfilled Promises and Self-Fulfilling Prophesies," *Medical Care Review* 45, no. 2 (Fall 1988), 177–214; Steven M. Shortell, Robin R. Gillies, and David A. Anderson, "The New World of Managed Care: Creating Organized Delivery Systems," *Health Affairs* 13, no. 5 (Winter 1994), 46–64; Katherine Saenz Duke, "Hospitals in a Changing Health Care System," *Health Affairs* 15, no. 2 (Summer 1996), 49–61; Gloria J. Bazzoli et al., "A Taxonomy of Health Networks and Systems: Bringing Order out of Chaos," *Health Services Research* 33, no. 6 (February 1999), 1863–1717; Gloria J. Bazzoli et al., "Tracking the Changing Provider Landscape: Implications for Health Policy and Practice" *Health Affairs* 20, no. 6 (2001), 188–196; Gloria J. Bazzoli et al., "Hospital Reorganization and Restructuring Achieved Through Merger," *Health Care Management Review* 27, no. 1 (2002), 7–20; Lawton R. Burns and Mark V. Pauley, "Integrated Delivery Networks: A Detour on the Road to Integrated Health Care?," *Health Affairs* 21, no. 4 (July–August 2002), 128–143; Paul B. Ginsberg, "Competition in Health Care: Its Evolution over the Past Decade," *Health Affairs* 24, no. 6 (November–December 2002), 1512–1522; Roice D. Luke, "Taxonomy of Health Networks and Systems: A Reassessment," *Health Services Research* 41, no. 3 (June 2006), 618–628.

5. Chapin, *Ensuring America's Health*, 37–193; Quadagno, *One Nation, Uninsured*, 49–52; Christopher P. Thompkins, Stuart H. Altman, and Efrat Eilat, "The Precarious Pricing System for Hospital Services," *Health Affairs* 25, no. 1 (2006), 45–56.

6. Center for Medicare and Medicaid Services, National Health Expenditure Data, online at https://www.cms.gov/research-statistics-data-and-systems/statistics-trends-and-reports/nationalhealthexpenddata/nationalhealthaccountshistorical.html. Quadagno, *One Nation, Uninsured*, 140.

7. Quadagno, *One Nation, Uninsured*, 159–168; Leyerle, *The Private Regulation of American Health Care*, 99–128.

8. Stevens, *In Sickness and in Wealth*, 281–293; Quadagno, *One Nation, Uninsured*, 96–99.

9. Stevens, *In Sickness and in Wealth*, 322–327; Leyerle, *The Private Regulation of American Health*, 59–66, and "Financing for Health Care," in Anthony R. Kovner and Jame R. Knickman, eds., *Jonas and Kovner's Health Care Delivery in the United States*, 8th ed. (New York: Springer, 2005), 76; Rick Mayes, "Causal Chains and Cost Shifting: How Medicare's Rescue Inadvertently Triggered the Managed-Care Revolution," *Journal of Policy History* 16, no. 2 (2004), 144–174; Rick Mayes and Robert A. Berenson, *Medicare Prospective Payment and the Shaping of U.S. Health Care* (Baltimore: Johns Hopkins University Press, 2008); Engel, *Unaffordable*, 81–101.

10. Thomas Frist Jr. interview, 10; Lutz and Gee, *Columbia/HCA*, 16; Fox, *Power and Illness*, 50.

11. Thomas Frist Jr. interview, 7; Engel, *Unaffordable*, 68–75.

12. Lutz and Gee, *Columbia/HCA*, 20–22; "A Campus Grows in Wichita," *KU History* online at http://kuhistory.com/articles/a-campus-grows-in-wichita/; Rodengen, *The Legend of HCA*, 24–25, 58–61; Gordon H. Berg and John M. Tucker, "Techniques for Arranging Hospital Financing," *Financial Management* 1, no. 1 (Spring 1972), 48–57. HCA made aggressive moves into the managed care insurance market. Rodengen, *The Legend of HCA*, 63–67; Thomas Frist Jr. interview, 19; Lutz and Gee, *Columbia/HCA*, 16–43; Howard S. Berliner and Robb K. Burlage, "Propriety Hospital Chains and Academic Medical Centers," in Salmon, *The Corporate Transformation of Health Care*, vol. 1, 97–116.

13. Skocpol, *Boomerang*, 25–26; 48–73. For more on the long history of health care reform, see Beatrix Hoffman, *The Wages of Sickness: The Politics of Health Insurance in Progressive America* (Chapel Hill: University of North Carolina Press, 2001); Quadagno, *One Nation, Uninsured*, 48–93; Fox, *Health Policies, Health Politics*, 149–168, 197; Engel, *Unaffordable*, 102–123.

14. Stevens, *In Sickness and in Wealth*, 335; Engel, *Unaffordable*, 136–144, Starr, *The Social Transformation of American Medicine*, 430–439.

15. "TMH's Corporate Organization," *Happenings*, May 1982, TMH, *Happenings* 1988–1994, 1. The article notes that, as of 1982, affiliations included at least one hospital in Mexico and several outside of the Houston-Sugar Land-Baytown MSA. The organization has gone through several name changes, and today it is known as the Methodist Hospital System. This new entity, abbreviated as HCS, offered "four types of clinical and managerial relationships." The first was an affiliation agreement whereby the goal was to create a clear pathway for referrals between community hospitals and the Methodist Hospital's facility in the TMC. HCS also offered management contracts whereby ownership remained with the local hospital but responsibility for its day-to-day management fell to HCS. The final two models, leasing and "acquisition/merger," involved the transfer of ownership from the individual hospital to the system. Colleen Fox, "The Wave of the Future," *Methodist Hospital Journal*, Special Issue, 20, no. 10 (1982), TMH, No. 20, The Methodist Hospital History Project, 8. Larry L. Mathis, *The Mathis Maxims: Lessons in Leadership* (Houston: Leadership Press, 2001), 41–47; John J. Verber, "The Methodist Hospital Health Care System, Giant in the Making" (MA thesis, University of Texas Health Science Center at Houston, School of Public Health, 1982), 14–27.

16. For the push to remain primarily a fee-for-service institution, telephone interview with former Methodist CFO and CEO Ron Girotto by author, July 8, 2011.

17. Larry L. Mathis, "A Stronger Network," TMH, *Happenings* 8, no. 3 (April 1988), 2.

18. Larry Mathis, telephone interview with author, July 1, 2011.

19. Megan Seaholm, "Hermann Hospital," *Handbook of Texas Online* (Austin: Texas State Historical Association), quotation; Claudia Feldman, "George Hermann: Houston's Eccentric Philanthropist," *Houston Chronicle*, May 19, 2016; Bryant Boutwell, *I'm Dr. Red Duke* (College Station: Texas A&M University Press, 2018).

20. Gary D. McHenry and John G. Self, "The Business of Good Health: Herman's Multihospital System" *Fall 1981*, in HH, 4–5. Eileen O'Grady, "Hermann Trust to Sell Division," *Houston Post*, June 3, 1987 in H-Business-Medical, HMRC. Memorial later bought the remains of Hermann Affiliated Systems in 1989. See John Barnett, "Memorial Care Seeks More Hospitals," *Houston Chronicle*, February 17, 1989 in H-Hospitals-Memorial, HMRC Vertical File Collection.

21. V. R. Gleason, "OneCare/Hermann Hospital Relationship and the Board Committee Approval Process," February 22, 1995, HHC, BOT Box 7, Folder One Care (unprocessed).

22. Starr, *The Social Transformation of American Medicine*, 161–169; quote on 166.

23. Gerald Tresslar Curriculum Vitae, HHC, BOT Box 7, Folder One Care; OneCare Fact Sheet 95; and "Satterwhite Named CEO of OneCare," *Houston Chronicle*, September 28, 1996, 95, HHC, BOT Box 7, Folder One Care (unprocessed).

24. OneCare Description Sheet, December 7, 1993, HHC, BOT Box 7 (unprocessed).

25. Numbers from "Operations Report to the Board of Trustees," March 17, 1994, HHC, BOT Box 7 (unprocessed). For a national level view of these type of organizations, see Michael A. Morrisey et al., "Managed Care and Physician/Hospital Integration," *Health Affairs* 15, no. 4 (Winter 1996), 62–73.

26. A $250,000 loan from the hospital, which was soon converted into an equity stake, provided initial funding. Hermann Hospital, "Minutes of the Audit, Finance, and Compensation Committee Meeting," December 9, 1993, HHC, BOT Box 7 (unprocessed); Hermann Hospital, "OneCare Health Industries, Inc.," HHC, BOT Box 7 (unprocessed); letter from Terry Satterwhite to Melinda Perrin and David Page, RE: Problems with OneCare and Peak, June 23, 1996, HHC, BOT Box 7, 2 (unprocessed); memorandum from Keith A. Bolton, Terry K. Satterwhite, Roland Goertz to All One Care Specialist Providers, RE: Specialist time sharing—One Care clinic locations, May 9, 1995, HHC, BOT Box 7 (unprocessed).

27. William H. Frey, "Population Growth in Metro America Since 1980: Putting the Volatile 2000's in Perspective," Brookings Institution paper, 3. Online at https://www.brookings.edu/research/population-growth-in-metro-america-since–1980-putting-the-volatile–2000s-in-perspective/.

28. Author interview with Osama Mikhail, June 6, 2011.

29. "Hermann Estate Names Trustees," *Baytown Sun*, June 19, 1985, 11-A.

30. Dan Wilford quoted in Jeanne Lang Jones, "High Stakes Health Care," *Texas Business*, January/February 1996, in TMCI, MSF, 52.

31. Problems with Columbia stemmed from a Medicare billing fraud investigation and eventually caused the company to revert to the HCA name in 2000. Lucette Lagnado, "Columbia/HCA Changes Its Name in Attempt to Return to Its Roots," *Wall Street Journal*, May 26, 2000; Hermann Hospital, "NewSys Business Plan Draft," April 25, 1996, HHC, Executive Summary 1.

32. St. Luke's and Columbia HCA were attempting to create a management service organization to manage joint hospital and physician governance, an ambulatory services network

that would be a 50/50 ownership split of non-TMC-based outpatient services and physician practices, and a managed care organization that would be responsible for administering managed care contracts for both organizations. "Exhibit B Summary of Proposed Transaction Between St. Luke's Episcopal Hospital and Columbia/HCA Health Care Corporation," 1–7, and "Outline of Proposed Healthcare System Between St. Luke's Episcopal Health System and Columbia/HCA Corporation," supplementary materials to *Texas Medical Center v. St. Luke's Episcopal Hospital*, August 1996, TMCI, Series 3, Box 7, Folder TMC v. St. Luke's 2; Osama Mikhail interview.

33. "Notes from Conference Call," January 10, 1997, HHC, BOT Box 12, Creating the Successful System binder, 1, 3–4 (unprocessed).

34. See assorted correspondence and notes, HHC, BOT Box 12 (unprocessed).

35. Executive Summary of the Compelling Case for Consolidation of Hermann and SCH SETX," HHC, BOT Box 12 (unprocessed). The statement used by Hermann, and boldfaced in the executive summary, was "Hermann and SCH SETX offer a unique alternative to the Houston market as mission driven providers. If either did not exist, mission driven care, particularly the focus on the poor and the support of education, would be seriously compromised. Conversely, if Hermann and SCH SETX combine, their ability to ensure this focus would be significantly enhanced."

36. Ibid.

37. "Info from Melinda Perrin following the meeting she and DRP (David R. Page) had 11/5 at the Villa with Sisters Christina and Elizabeth Ann," HHC, BOT Box 12 (unprocessed).

38. "Ethical and Religious Directives Discussion," January 9, 1997, HHC, BOT Box 12, Binder "Capturing the Vision" (unprocessed).

39. "Agenda Key Constituents Meeting," February 4, 1997, HHC, BOT Box 12, Binder "Capturing the Vision" (unprocessed).

40. "Notes from Conference Call," January 10, 1997.

41. Ted Francis and Carole McFarland, *The Memorial Hospital System: The First Seventy-Five Years* (Houston: Larksdale, 1982), 18, 24, 142–146.

42. National Health Advisors, "Summary of Strategic Planning Meeting-Draft," January 16, 1997, HHC, Box 12, 5 (unprocessed). For a list of participants, see page 8.

43. "Draft Affiliation Letter," January 23, 1997, HHC, BOT Box 12 (unprocessed).

44. A memorandum of understanding was finally signed on June 30, 1997, HHC, BOT Box 12, White Binder (unprocessed).

45. "Agreement and Plan of Merger Draft," October 16, 1997, HHC, BOT Box 12, White Binder (unprocessed).

46. Prior to the passage of the Balanced Budget Act, when hospitals merged or were sold they were allowed to file depreciation claims on assets used to treat Medicare patients such as equipment and buildings; if the sales price of the deal exceeded the book value of the assets, hospitals would have to pay the difference back to Medicare; but if the book value of the depreciating assets was greater than the sales price, then Medicare would reimburse hospitals the difference. The Balanced Budget Act ended the practice of the Health Care Financing Administration reimbursing hospitals for below-book-value sales. See Bill Mintz, "Hermann Eager to Complete Merger," *Houston Chronicle*, August 8, 1997, and Bruce Japsen, "Beat the Clock: Balanced-Budget Law May Speed Hospital Mergers," *Modern Healthcare*, August 18, 1997, HHC, BOT Box 12 (unprocessed).

47. Currently, the Allegheny Health Network does have medical education opportunities in the Pittsburgh region through an affiliate site, Temple University School of Medicine, and clinical campuses for the Lake Erie College of Osteopathic Medicine and the Drexel University College of Medicine. For more, see https://www.ahn.org/education/undergraduate-medical-education; https://www.ahn.org/education/graduate-medical-education.

48. Brignano, *Beyond the Bounds*, quotations on 23, 33, 56. The Dracula metaphor also appeared in the *Pittsburgh Post-Gazette* in 1989, in David Guo and Christina Rouvalis, "Detre Transforms Pitt Medical Complex," *Pittsburgh Post-Gazette*, October 4, 1989; William S. Dietrich II, "Against the Odds: Thomas Detre and the Birth of UPMC," *Pittsburgh Quarterly*, Summer 2009. Romoff would later reflect on their shared reputation in "The Transformation of the Academic Medical Center" when he noted, "We have always been regarded historically as the 800-pound gorilla, and the characterization of even the personalities of Dr. Detre and I have been synchronous with this image. This has been an image that has engendered fear and distance in the community." Jeffrey Romoff, "The Transformation of the Academic Medical Center," November 15, 1995, video recording in author's possession.

49. Ludmerer, *Time to Heal*, 282–287.

50. This model did face some internal opposition. In a letter to Detre dated April 10, 1985, Department of Surgery chairman Henry "Hank" Bahnson warned that "in the hue and cry over research, often by those who are not great investigators, sight is lost of what a health center and the clinical facility of a medical school are about, namely taking care of patients and using this as a laboratory in order to improve the care we give today and tomorrow and to teach others to do likewise." Letter from Henry Bahnson to Thomas Detre, April 10, 1985, HB, Box 1, FF 47, 4. In another letter sent on July 3, Bahnson raised the same concern again, saying, "Like everybody else I aspire to a great research center, but the goal of the University and the Medical School, primus inter pares, is to educate and prepare students for the future. Have we gotten too far away from this and too far into the research lab?" Letter from Henry Bahnson to Thomas Detre, July 3, 1985, HB, Box 1, Folder 47.

51. Brignano, *Beyond the Bounds*, 36–38; quotation on 36.

52. Ibid., 37.

53. Ibid., 48.

54. Ibid., 48–50, 54.

55. Brignano, *Beyond the Bounds*, 80; Arthur D. Little, "Future Directions: University Health Center of Pittsburgh," UHC, 90/43-A, UHC Memorabilia, Box 1, Folder 3; Organizational Chart, ibid., 13.

In a speech given on November 19, 1990, at the Board Retreat for Presbyterian University Hospital, Detre made this argument clear when he outlined the history of efforts to create MHCD. Detre claimed, "In 1971 the Arthur D. Little Company was commissioned to look at the situation and make recommendations. Their report stressed that the center had great potential but required more coordination and planning that would transcend the individual interests of each institution. These recommendations were accepted but never acted upon." Thomas Detre, "Transcript of Presentation at the Board Retreat of Presbyterian University Hospital and Montefiore University Hospital," November 19, 1990. Sent to Chancellor Wesley W. Posvar, January 4, 1991, WP, 2/10 1982–83, Box 3, Folder 3.4.5.

56. "An Outline for Corporate Restructuring Presbyterian University Hospital March 1982," in WP, 2/10 1982–83, Box 3, Folder 3.4.5E.

57. "Dinners to Benefit Transplant Program," *North Hills News Record*, September 13, 1983, 19; Henry W. Pierce, "Hospital to Open Profit-Restaurant," *Pittsburgh-Post Gazette*, January 24, 1984, A1; "Hotel, Office Building Sold," *Pittsburgh Press*, June 21, 1989, C8; Lawrence Walsh, "Judge Says Nephew's Work for Mosque Buyer Not Conflict," *Pittsburgh Press*, June 29, 1991, C1.

58. Memorandum from Thomas Detre to Nathan Stark and Edison Montgomery, October 14, 1982, WP, 2/10 1982–83, Box 3, Folder 3.4.5E, 1–3, 5–6.

59. Wesley Posvar, "Memorandum to the Faculty," March 28, 1983, WP, 2/10 1982–83, Box 3, Folder 3.4.5, 1.

60. Ibid., 80–85. Evidently, Detre once remarked to J. Wray Connolly, a member of Eye and Ear's board, that "my enemy's enemy is my friend," in reference to Eye and Ear's relationship with Presbyterian-University. Quotation from Brignano, *Beyond the Bounds*, 84.

61. Brignano, *Beyond the Bounds*, 82.

62. Presbyterian-University Concept Paper, June 25, 1986, HB, Box 3, Folder 1,14–15. Quotation from Brignano, *Beyond the Bounds*, 90.

63. Brignano, *Beyond the Bounds*, 92, 90; See also Steve Levin's series on the history of UPMC, which ran in the *Pittsburgh Post-Gazette* on December 25–29, 2005.

64. Brignano, *Beyond the Bounds*, 64.

65. Ibid., 63.

66. Ibid., 95.

67. Background Paper Resolution to Change Designation of Medical and Health Care Division to University of Pittsburgh Medical Center, n.d., WP, 2/10 1990–1991, Box 55, 2. This idea of retaining the balance of leadership was one that would continue to shadow the new organization as Posvar prepared to retire. In a twelve-page memorandum sent to Thomas Detre by Posvar, but widely copied throughout health centers and the university leadership, the Chancellor (who had retitled himself President) reminded Detre that "the prime consideration of governance is that the University itself, though the President who is responsible to the Board of Trustees, bears the ultimate responsibility and liability for the management, operations, and performance of the University of Pittsburgh medical center. . . . It follows, therefore, that the President of the University, functioning with his staff the University Executive, must be in charge that the officers of the UPMC, though the Senior Vice President for the Health Sciences who is the President of the UPMC, report unambiguously to the President of the University. It is vitally important, as I shall emphasize in the following that the various officers of the UPMC, whatever their relations with affiliated organizations, have an unequivocal legal commitment and loyalty to the University, unconfused by their roles as executives of hospitals, clinics, or other affiliates." Wesley Posvar to Thomas Detre, RE: Governance of the University of Pittsburgh Medical Center within the University, April 19, 1991, WP, 2/10 1990–1991, Box 55, Folder 908.0, 2.

68. Brignano, *Beyond the Bounds*, 107; Dietrich, "Against the Odds: Thomas Detre and the Birth of UPMC."

69. Brignano, *Beyond the Bounds*, 107. The *University Times*, a faculty and staff-oriented publication at the University of Pittsburgh, ran several articles about the search, including Heather Gahres, "Faculty Assembly Call for Investigation," September 9, 1992; "Assembly Looking into Naming of Romoff to Post sans Search," n.d., Personal File, Jeffrey Romoff, University of Pittsburgh Archives.

70. Brignano, *Beyond the Bounds*, 38.

71. Ibid., 38–51.

72. Romoff, "The Transformation of the Academic Medical Center," November 15, 1995, video recording in author's possession. In this speech, he noted that 1995 was an important transitional year between the old model of medicine as a social good and the new model of medicine as a commodity. He called it falling off a cliff of the old world into a "chasm" of a new world. Apparently, this recording was widely circulated within UPMC at the time.

73. Ibid.

74. Romoff made it clear that this new outlook was not commercialization simply for commercialization's sake. He noted that, without a healthy infusion of cash, around $100 million per year, the School of Medicine would be left to rely on tuition (about $5 million a year) and an appropriation from the Commonwealth of Pennsylvania (about $6 million a year). Thus, he argued that the drive for more revenue was to protect the mission of academic medicine, because UPMC giving back was "the right thing to do in an academic medical center. Also," continued Romoff, "because at least in the past good science has also been good business and that is our mission." Ibid.

75. "Update on Shadyside Hospital/University of Pittsburgh Medical Center Merger Discussions," March 25, 1996, sent to Elsie Hillman via facsimile transmission from Jeffrey Romoff, March 27, 1996, EH Box 68, Folder 2.

76. Ibid.; letter to Charles F. Lewis from Ketchum Inc., March 25, 1929 BF, Box 12, Folder 2; quotations on 1 and 2.

77. Romoff, "Transformation of the Academic Medical Center."

78. Ibid.

79. Ibid. Romoff also noted that, as inpatient length of stay declined, UPMC also lost revenue from ancillary services.

80. Romoff asked the assembled crowd: "If the University of Pittsburgh Medical Center in this context is to maintain its market share, its critical mass essential to support everything from the biomedical science tower, to the new medical research facility, all the way up to the recruitment of a new surgeon, that we are talking about the necessity to be in serious competition, particularly with our tertiary hospitals, particularly in Pittsburgh. After all, if you were to rationalize what to do in a system like this that was so overbedded you would say 'Do you need an Altoona hospital? Well, it is the only hospital in Altoona. And Passavant is up in the Ross Township area, and South Hills is down there [pointing to the floor] and it serves a community and it serves an interest. But do you in fact need an Allegheny General, a Mercy, a Shadyside, West Penn, St. Francis, UPMC, Children's, and Magee, all within spitting distance of one another, all the most expensive, all teaching residents, and training what we will soon see is a surplus of physicians? So this will be quite a competitive situation." Ibid.

81. Bleier, Donnelly, and Granowitz, *L'Chaim: To Good Health and Life*, 253–256. Brignano, *Beyond the Bounds*, 93–95; Steve Levin, "Empire Building: Consolidation and Controversy at UPMC," *Pittsburgh Post-Gazette*, December 27, 2005; Steve Levin, "Empire Building: Clash of the Titans," *Pittsburgh Post-Gazette*, December 28, 2005.

82. For more on these companies, see "Hospital Networks Plan Strategy for Coming Year," *Pittsburgh Business Times*, January 13, 1997; "Hospitals Engage in Mating Game," *Pittsburgh Business Times*, February 10, 1997; "Doctor-Led Providers Prepare Region's Fourth Health Network," *Pittsburgh Business Times*, May 12, 1997; "Health Care Ltd.," *Pittsburgh*

Business Times, June 2, 1997; "Hospital Network Falls Apart," *Pittsburgh Business Times*, August 2, 1997; and "Unmanaged Care: One Network's Fall," *Pittsburgh Business Times*, August 18, 1997; quotation from "Health Care Ltd."

83. Arthur Levine, Thomas Detre, Margaret McDonalds, Loren Roth, George Huber, Mary Brignano, Sandra Danoff, David Farner, Jeffrey Masnick, Jeffrey Romoff, "The Relationship between the University of Pittsburgh School of Medicine and the University of Pittsburgh Medical Center—A Profile in Synergy" *Academic Medicine* Vol. 831 No., September 2008, 816–826, 820. This ownership versus management distinction would become important in how the system approached labor policy. In response to a 2012 NLRB action, UPMC argued that since its hospitals had separate governing boards (with shared overlap with the system board) and, prior to 2006, filed individual tax returns, it could not be included on the NLRB claim since it was a holding company and thus had no employees. Charles Deitch, "No Help Wanted," *Pittsburgh City Paper*, January 2013.

84. Levine et al., "The Relationship Between the University of Pittsburgh School of Medicine and the University of Pittsburgh Medical Center—a Profile in Synergy," 821.

85. Romoff, "The Transformation of the Academic Medical Center."

86. For more on UPMC satellite efforts, see Romoff, "The Transformation of the Academic Medical Center"; Pamela Gaynor, "If You Build It, Will They Come?" *Pittsburgh Post-Gazette*, March 1, 1996, B9; Pamela Gaynor, "Pitt Flexes Medical Muscles: Health Care Competitors Angry About the Purchase of Monroeville Center," *Pittsburgh Post-Gazette*, February 24, 1996, A1. The Broudy quotation is in the latter article.

87. Ibid.

88. Burns et al., "The Fall of the House of AHERF"; Burns and Burns, "Policy Implications of Hospital System Failures: The Allegheny Bankruptcy," in Stevens, Rosenberg, and Burns, *History and Health Policy in the United States*, 273–308; *Pittsburgh Post-Gazette*, "Lifeline for an Institution," a timeline of AHERF, Special Report, Anatomy of a Bankruptcy, n.d.

89. Steve Massey, "Part 3: Full Steam Ahead," *Pittsburgh Post-Gazette*, January 20, 1999, Special Report, Anatomy of a Bankruptcy. While billed as a "merger," it was, in the words of one Allegheny General Hospital executive, "an acquisition. We tried everything we could to make it feel like a merger, but with obvious changes in the upper management, reporting arrangements, and decision-making processes the faculty quickly became disillusioned, comparing the changes to the fall of the Alamo." Swazey, *Merger Games*, 40.

90. Ibid., 53–73. For more on AHERF's acquisitions, see "Lifeline for an Institution," a timeline of AHERF, in Anatomy of a Bankruptcy.

91. At one time, Abdelhak faced "more than 1500 criminal charges" related to AHERF, but eventually pleaded to a single misdemeanor of "misusing charitable funds." Jim McKinnon, "Former AHERF Chief Pleads No Contest," *Pittsburgh Post-Gazette*, August 30, 2002.

92. Gertha Coffee, "Prudential Attempts to Lower Area's Blue Cross 'Fever,'" *Pittsburgh Press*, July 3, 1988, D14, CLP, PGH, Hospitals HMOs (Health Maintenance Organizations) 1980–1989.

93. Blue Cross of Western Pennsylvania, "Asserting Competitiveness: The 1985 Plan," Box P65163, BCWP Corporate Plans, 1979–1995, 5; courtesy of Highmark.

94. Blue Cross of Western Pennsylvania, 1985 Annual Report, Box P65153, Folder 1985 Annual Report, 1; courtesy of Highmark.

95. The year 1987 marked the first rate increase in nearly four years for Blue Cross after underwriting losses exceeded $40 million. Blue Cross of Western Pennsylvania, "A Constant

Strength in a Changing Arena, 1987 Annual Report," Box P65153, Folder BCWP 1987 Annual Report, 3; courtesy of Highmark. For more on the national environment for the Blues, including changes to the organization's federal tax exemption, see Robert Cunningham III and Robert M. Cunningham Jr., *The Blues: A History of the Blue Cross and Blue Shield System* (DeKalb: Northern Illinois University Press, 1997), 204–216. New subsidiaries included Healthcare Affiliated Services, which provided computer-based analytic support to major employers to manage health costs; Pen-Wel Inc., which provided third-party benefits administration for self-insured companies; market and health system research services through the nonprofit Pittsburgh Research Institute (which replaced an in-house research department); and the Standard Property Company, which managed Blue Cross properties. Blue Cross of Western Pennsylvania, "Innovating for Tomorrow, 1986 Annual Report," Box P65153, Folder BCWP 1986 Annual Report; courtesy of Highmark.

96. Blue Cross of Western Pennsylvania/Veritus Inc., "A Time for Choices, 1991 Annual Report," Box P65153, Folder 1991 Annual Report (Short Version), 4; courtesy of Highmark. See also Blue Cross of Western Pennsylvania, "Dedication to Total Quality, 1991 Corporate Plan," Box P65163; courtesy of Highmark.

97. Blue Cross of Western Pennsylvania/Veritus Inc., "Health Care Management, 1993 Annual Report," Box P65153, Folder 1993 Annual Report, 6; courtesy of Highmark.

98. Promotional Materials for Primary Care Centers, Box P65133, Folder PCC Open House; courtesy of Highmark. The term "private physicians" is used throughout the promotional materials.

99. The 1996 Annual Report for the merged company called it "a watershed in the region's health care history." Highmark, "Positioning for the Future," Box P65153, Folder 1996 Annual Report, 2; courtesy of Highmark.

100. This money bought about 324 physicians. "A Defensive Blunder," *Pittsburgh Business Times*, April 20, 1998.

101. "Highmark Physician Unit Loses $40 Million," *Pittsburgh Business Times*, January 18, 1999; and "Highmark Sells Greentree Road Building for $2 Million," *Pittsburgh Business Times*, December 13, 2006.

102. "Highmark Shifts Center Strategy," *Pittsburgh Business Times*, June 11, 2001.

103. "Highmark Sells Greentree Road Building" and "Highmark Shifts Health Center Strategy."

104. "A Defensive Blunder"; and Pamela Gaynor, "Physician Practice Acquisitions Going Sour," *Pittsburgh Post-Gazette*, November 4, 1998, E1.

105. Romoff, "The Transformation of the Academic Medical Center."

106. "A Widening Highmark, UPMC Rift," *Pittsburgh Business Times*, April 20, 1998. The thinking here was that since primary care physicians drove specialist and hospitalization referrals in the Security Blue program, ownership would give UPMC an edge for capturing Security Blue patient referrals. For more on Security Blue, see "Security Blue: The Health Coverage Designed for You," video recording ca. 1995; courtesy of Highmark.

107. "A Widening Highmark, UPMC Rift."

108. "Clash of the Health Care Titans," *Pittsburgh Business Times*, September 21, 1998.

109. Brignano, *Beyond the Bounds*, 141–143; and Pamela Gaynor, "County Picks Mental Health Services Concern," *Pittsburgh Post-Gazette*, October 10, 1997, D1.

110. Because UPMC hospitals were usually academically affiliated hospitals, they treated, on average, a sicker patient population, which increased inpatient costs. For example, in 1993

the average cost for a non-cancer patient at Presbyterian-University was $21,215 and $16,399 at Montefiore, while the regional average was $8,218 per non-cancer patient. On a regional level, cancer patients cost more than non-cancer patients at $11,134 per patient. Within the UPMC system, the cost to treat cancer patients was highest at Montefiore ($17,300) followed by Presbyterian-University ($17,220). St. Francis Central Hospital (the old Central Medical Pavilion) came in third at $17,194 per cancer patient. See Nick Jesdanun, "Pitt Hospital Fees Tops in That Area," *Harrisburg Patriot*, June 2, 1993, CLP, PGH, Hospitals, University of Pittsburgh Medical Center (UPMC) 1990–1999.

111. Bill Toland, "Health Insurer Grew Stronger in 2007," *Pittsburgh Post-Gazette*, April 3, 2008, CLP, PGH, Hospitals, Blue Cross, 1998-.

112. Pamela Gaynor, "UPMC Plan Adds Clients at Expense of Highmark," *Pittsburgh Post-Gazette*, October 11, 1997, CLP, PGH, Hospitals, University of Pittsburgh Medical Center (UPMC) 1990–1999.

113. "Ticket-scalping" quotation from Brignano, *Beyond the Bounds*, 144. UPMC also irked Highmark by poaching several top Highmark executives to run its health plan. See Pamela Gaynor, "UPMC Health Plan Fills Top Posts from Old Rivals," *Pittsburgh Post-Gazette*, May 13, 1999, CLP, PGH, Hospitals, University of Pittsburgh Medical Center (UPMC) 1990–1999.

114. Romoff, "The Transformation of the Academic Medical Center."

115. Pamela Gaynor, "Health Insurance Debated," *Pittsburgh Post-Gazette*, December 10, 1998, CLP, PGH, Hospitals, University of Pittsburgh Medical Center (UPMC) 1990–1999.

116. Pamela Gaynor, "UPMC's Insurance Arm Lands U.S. Airways, Heritage Valley," *Pittsburgh Post-Gazette*, October 6, 1999, CLP, PGH, Hospitals, University of Pittsburgh Medical Center (UPMC) 1990–1999. In 1998, UPMC and the University of Pittsburgh legally separated, although the relationship between the two has remained somewhat murky even to the present, especially since the two have retained overlapping board appointments. Brignano, *Beyond the Bounds*, 145–147.

117. Pamela Gaynor, "UPMC Steps Up Merger Attack," *Pittsburgh Post-Gazette*, April 16, 1999, CLP, PGH, Hospitals, University of Pittsburgh Medical Center (UPMC) 1990–1999.

118. Neumann, *Remaking the Rust Belt*, and Dieterich-Ward, *Beyond Rust*, describe these larger efforts in more detail.

Chapter 6

1. This is discussed in the Introduction; Fitzpatrick, "Top of the Triangle: UPMC Getting Ready to Put Its Name on U.S. Steel Tower."

2. U.S. Steel Corporate Headquarters online at https://www.ussteel.com. Romoff quotation from "U.S. Steel Tower Will Become UPMC's New Corporate Headquarters," UPMC news release, April 10, 2007. Since the demolition of the Civic (Mellon) Arena, the Pittsburgh Penguins had been committed to redeveloping parts of the Lower Hill District.

3. For example, according to UPMC spokesman Paul Wood, "Fewer than 8 percent of our employees make less than $12 an hour. The average wage of UPMC workers is $30 an hour. And with benefits the wage of that $12 an hour worker jumps to more than $21 an hour. The benefits at McDonald's and many other employers in this region can't come close to matching ours." Quote in Ann Belser, "Unions Here Focusing on UPMC's Low Wages,

Not Pay at McDonald's," *Pittsburgh Post-Gazette*, August 30, 2013. UPMC also announced in 2016 that it planned to raise starting wages to $15 an hour "at most UPMC facilities." UPMC, "$15/Hour by 2019," press release, March 29, 2016. Health care workers in Houston are more limited in their fight for $15/hour since Texas law prohibits the city of Houston from passing an ordinance to raise minimum wages above the federal level. This leaves it up to each institution in the medical center to act on its own to raise starting wages. *Houston Chronicle* editorial, "Minimum Wage," April 6, 2016.

4. For more about hospital rate setting and the distribution of charity care resources, see Thompkins, Altman, and Eliat, "The Precarious Pricing System for Hospital Services"; Allen Dobson, Joan DaVanzo, and Namrata Sen, "The Cost-Shift Payment 'Hydraulic': Foundation, History, and Implications," *Health Affairs* 25, no. 1 (2006), 22–33. The most comprehensive way to track regional variation in costs and rates is through the Dartmouth Atlas of Health Care, online at www.dartmouthatlas.org.

5. Special Task Force to Study Not-for-Profit Hospitals and Unsponsored Charity Care, "Final Report," Office of the Texas Attorney General (1989), Executive Summary, 4.

6. General Accounting Office, "Report to the Honorable Ronald D. Coleman, House of Representatives, Medicaid: The Texas Disproportionate Share Program Favors Public Hospitals," March 1993, 2.

7. The history of EMTALA is discussed by Beatrix Hoffman in two related works: Hoffman, *Health Care for Some*, 169–175, and Hoffman, "Emergency Rooms," 264–265; Centers for Medicare and Medicaid Services' guide on EMTALA at CMS.gov.

8. Hoffman, *Health Care for Some*, 176–181; Jonathan Bell, "Rethinking the 'Straight State': Welfare Politics, Health Care and Public Policy in the Shadow of AIDS," *Journal of American History* 104, no. 4 (March 2018), 931–952; Engel, *Unaffordable*, 74–75. For more details on AIDS in Houston, see Andrew T. Simpson, "Making the Medical Metropolis: Academic Medical Centers and Urban Change in Houston 1945–2010"; Molly Ellen Bundschuh, "Cowboys, 'Queers,' and Community: The AIDS Crisis in Houston and Dallas, 1981–1996" (MA thesis, University of North Texas, 2014); Jonathan C. Heath, "Strength in Numbers: Houston's Gay Community and the Aids Crisis, 1977–1989" (MA thesis, University of Houston, 2006); Bruce Remington, "Twelve Fighting Years: Homosexuals in Houston, 1969–1981" (MA thesis, University of Houston, 1983). For primary sources on AIDS in Houston, see AIDS-Houston: Montrose Clinic, Center for AIDS, RITA, Institutional Collection No. 72, John P. McGovern Historical Collections and Research Center, Texas Medical Center Library, Houston, TX; HMRC Vertical File Collection, H-Diseases-AIDS.

9. "Houston Has 6th Highest Level of AIDS," *Houston Post*, January 27, 1984, HMRC, H-Diseases-AIDS-1984.

10. Leslie Loddeke, "Nursing Homes Turning Away AIDS Victims," *Houston Post*, July 29, 1984, HMRC, H-Diseases-AIDS-1984; Patrick Wallis, "Debating a Duty to Treat: AIDS and the Professional Ethics of American Medicine," *Bulletin of the History of Medicine* 58, no. 4 (2011), 620–649; Dion A. Sullivan, "ERISA, the ADA, and AIDS: Fixing Self-Insured Plans with Carparts," *Maryland Journal of Contemporary Legal Issues* 7, no. 2 (1996); Peter Mansell and Sue Cooper, Mansell/Cooper Interview, Making Cancer History Voices Oral History Project, M. D. Anderson Research Medical Library, Houston, TX; Olson, *Making Cancer History*, 189–191.

11. Randy Ormsby, "A Conversation with Larry Mathis," *TMC News*, January 1986, TMC News 1986–1987, TMCI Series 2, Box 4.

12. This story has been related in several places, including Olson, *Making Cancer History*; Simpson, "Making the Medical Metropolis"; Bundschuh, "Cowboys, 'Queers,' and Community"; Heath, "Strength in Numbers." For primary sources, see CAL, Series 12, Box SG5/4, American Medical International Inc. (AMI), various.

13. Pete Brewton, "Contrasting Standards for 2 Hospital Patients," *Houston Post*, November 3, 1988, HMRC, H-Hospitals-Methodist.

14. Mathis, *Mathis Maxims*, 228.

15. Sibley, *The Methodist Hospital of Houston*, 170–171. Ella Fondren was a critical figure in the hospital's history. Born in Hazel, Kentucky, in 1880, young Ella Cochrum was forced to quit school in 1895 to help care for her six siblings after the death of her father. She seemed consigned to help run the family boarding house in Corsicana, Texas, until she met her future husband, Walter Fondren. Walter Fondren had even less formal education than his wife, but together they built one of the great Houston fortunes. After his death in 1939, she embarked on a long career as a philanthropist. The Methodist Hospital became an important project until she died at 101 in 1982, "having lived the last eight years of her life in a suite" at the hospital. Betty T. Chapman, "Ella Fondren Played a Pivotal Role in City's Progress," *Houston Business Journal*, August 3, 2008.

16. Leigh Hopper, "High-Profile Patients a Boost for Hospitals," *Houston Chronicle*, October 7, 2002; Christine Hall, "Hospital Suites Across the Texas Medical Center Offer Patients a Hotel-Like Experience," *TMC News*, September 6, 2016.

17. Stevens, *In Sickness and in Wealth*, 112.

18. Kelly J. Deavers et al., "Changes in Hospital Competitive Strategy: A New Medical Arms Race?," *Health Services Research* 38, no. 1(2003). 447–469. This article provides a helpful overview of not-for-profit behavior in general, although the findings are not necessarily fully applicable to The Methodist Hospital.

19. 5 West Jones Brochure, HHC, Box 7, Public Affairs Brochures.

20. Regional Medical Programs, Profiles in Science, National Library of Medicine, https://profiles.nlm.nih.gov/RM/.

21. Nancy Milo, "The Profitization of Health Promotion," in Salmon, *The Corporate Transformation of Health Care*, vol. 2, 75–89.

22. Charter and Restrictions Governing the Texas Medical Center, Houston, Texas, 1945.

23. Ibid., 183–189.

24. HBJ Gourmet, "Chez Eddy: A Hearty Dose of First-Class Hospital Food," *Houston Business Journal*, June 27, 1981, 4–5.

25. Ibid.; "Methodist Total Health Care Center," advertisement in *Houston Chronicle*, HMRC, H-Hospitals-Methodist; Texas Medical Center Covenant Compliance Committee Policy Guidelines, TMCI Series 3, Box 7, TMC vs. St. Luke's, 1996, Folder TMC vs. St. Luke's #6, 2.

26. Michael DeBakey et al., *The Living Heart Cookbook* (New York: Simon and Schuster, 1984); Antonio Gotto et al., *The Chez Eddy Living Heart Cookbook* (New York: Simon and Schuster, 1991).

27. Deposition of Larry Lee Mathis in *State of Texas vs. The Methodist Hospital et al.*, November 23, 1992, TAG, Box 4, page 64.

28. Ruth SoRelle and Rad Sallee, "Non-Profit Hospital Role Changes Vastly," *Houston Chronicle*, November 10, 1985, HMRC, H-Hospitals-Methodist.

29. Susan Allen, "Medical Marketing: Proper Prescription for the 1980s?," *Houston Business Journal*, June 10, 1985; quotation on 13C.

30. In Houston, the overall market penetration was quite low during the early to mid–1980s. For example, in 1983, the *Houston Business Journal* reported that HMOs (largely Pru-Care, but also some competitors like MaxiCare, which came online that year) only had about a 3 percent share of the overall market. By 1986, their market penetration had risen to between 8 and 11 percent. Julie Gilbert, "Health Care Industry Heats Up as New HMOs Enter Insurance Field," *Houston Business Journal*, January 17, 1983, 17A; Eileen O'Grady, "Managed Health Care 'Major Step' in Control of Costs," *Houston Post*, July 13, 1986, HMRC, H-Health Maintenance Organizations; Thompkins, Altman, and Eliat, "The Precarious Pricing System for Hospital Services," 46–48.

31. Numbers for 1985 from Ruth SoRelle, "Methodist Hospital 'Not Charity,'" *Houston Chronicle*, November 17, 1985. Numbers for 1987 from Pete Brewton, "Methodist Surplus Draws Fire," *Houston Post*, November 20, 1988. Both in HMRC, H-Hospitals-Methodist.

32. Tara Parker Pope, "Methodist Hospital defends tax status: Says service to the rich is also charitable" *Houston Chronicle*, February 16, 1993, HMRC, H-Hospitals-Methodist. Pope argues that these accusations came from the Texas attorney general's office.

33. "Ex-Hermann Officer Found Guilty of Theft," *New Braunfels Herald-Zeitung*, January 11, 1986, 3A; "Herman Hospital Case: Convicted Former Trustee of Estate Files for Bankruptcy," *Longview News-Journal*, June 15, 1986, 11-A; "Ex-Hermann Estate Officials to Pay," *Longview News-Journal*, May 10, 1986, 6-D.

34. Harry Hurt III, "A Trust Corrupted, a City Betrayed, Part One," *Texas Monthly*, February 1986; and Harry Hurt III, "A Trust Corrupted, a City Betrayed, Part Two," *Texas Monthly*, March 1986.

35. In the case of Methodist, board members with ties to Vinson and Elkins included A. Frank Smith, "former governor John Connally, William Randolph Smith and Marvin Collie." Glenn Smith and Pete Brewton, "Mattox to Investigate Methodist Hospital," *Houston Post*, November 27, 1985.

36. Janet Elliott, "Former Texas AG Jim Mattox Dies at 65," *Houston Chronicle*, November 20, 2008.

37. Nina J. Crimm, "Evolutionary Forces: Changes in for-Profit and Not-for-Profit Health Care Delivery Structures: A Regeneration of Tax Exemption Standards," *Boston College of Law Review* 37, no. 1 (1995), 7.

38. Daniel M. Fox and Daniel C. Schaeffer, "Tax Administration as Health Policy: Hospitals, the Internal Revenue Service, and the Courts," *Journal of Health Politics, Policy, and Law* 16, no. 2 (1991), 251–279; quotation on 258.

39. Robert Bromberg, the IRS official most responsible for creating the community benefit standard, remembered accepting the claims of hospital administrators that, given the success of these two programs, they "couldn't find any patients to whom to give free care." Furthermore, Bromberg also believed, given the environment of the late 1960s, that it would only be a matter of time before these federal programs were expanded to cover all of the medically indigent. See Robert Bromberg as quoted in ibid., 262.

40. This case had its roots in a 1981 decision by Utah County, Utah, to deny a tax exemption for two of Intermountain Health Care's community hospitals. Unlike previous

cases, where local authorities denied or revoked tax exemption as punishment for hospitals engaging in bad behavior, Utah County assessed property taxes because it believed that hospital tax exemption violated the Utah State Constitution. At the heart of the county's argument, and the decision the court eventually rendered, was a rather limited definition of charity care and an even more circumscribed understanding of how not-for-profit hospitals should function. The court declared that modern not-for-profit hospitals could no longer reasonably be considered a charity, since they relied on patient care revenues, rather than philanthropic support, to fund their operations. The majority opinion claimed, "We are convinced that traditional assumptions bear little relationship to the economics of the medical-industrial complex of the 1980's." Thus, the court found that the majority of not-for-profit hospitals should be considered commercial enterprises rather than public charities. It also held that, despite concerns that Medicare and Medicaid reimbursed at rates lower than costs, accepting patients whose care was paid for by these programs was not a community service but instead constituted a payment for services rendered. Justices disagreed with the IRS's idea that the presence of a hospital that served all patients who were admitted through an emergency room constituted a "community benefit," claiming that this interpretation presupposed that the services provided by a hospital were of a higher order than the services provided by any number of other commercial enterprises. Edward J. Bernert and Christopher J. Swift, "The 'Charity Care' Requirement for Hospital Property Tax Exemptions," in *American Bar Association Section on State and Local Taxation* (2009); quotation on 11; Kevin B. Fischer, "Tax Exemption and the Health Care Industry: Are the Challenges to Tax-Exempt Status Justified," *Vanderbilt Law Review* 49, no. 161 (1996); David A. Hyman, "The Conundrum of Charitability: Reassessing Tax Exemption for Hospitals," *American Journal of Law and Medicine* 16, no. 327 (1990).

41. Pete Brewton, "Methodist Hospital Cleared $27 Million in '83," *Houston Post*, November 5, 1985, HMRC, H-Hospitals-Methodist.

42. *State of Texas vs. The Methodist Hospital* Timeline of Events, Exhibits to the Hearing, February 5 and 6, 1992, TAG, Box 14. Brewton's request was quickly followed up with a similar one by Ruth SoRelle, the medical writer at the *Houston Chronicle.*

43. Mathis, *The Mathis Maxims*, 230.

44. The statement went on to deny a conflict of interest between the hospital and companies the board members represented, as well as refuting the other allegations of financial improprieties. See "Allegations Unjustified, Methodist Hospital Says," *Houston Post*, November 17, 1985, HMRC, H-Hospitals-Methodist.

45. Richard Vara, "Methodists Applaud Defense of Hospital," *Houston Post*, May 28, 1986, HMRC, H-Hospitals-Methodist.

46. Ibid.

47. Mary Lenz, "Mattox Sues Directors of Methodist Hospital," *Houston Post*, November 27, 1990, HMRC, H-Hospitals-Methodist.

48. Pete Brewton, "Methodist Hospital Hires PR Firm to Deal with Bad Publicity," *Houston Post*, November 23, 1985, HMRC, H-Hospitals-Methodist.

49. Special Task Force to Study Not-for-Profit Hospitals and Unsponsored Charity Care, "Final Report," Office of the Texas Attorney General (1989), Executive Summary, 4.

50. Ibid., Region 4, 4.

51. Mathis, *The Mathis Maxims*, 234. Alan Blankley and Dana Forgione, "Ethical Issues Facing Private, Not-for-Profit Hospitals in the United States: The Case of the Methodist

Hospital System," in Aman Khan and W. Barley Hildreth, eds., *Case Studies in Public Budgeting and Financial Management*, 2nd ed., rev. and expanded (New York: Marcel Dekker, 2003), 716.

52. Timeline, 5; and Mathis, *The Mathis Maxims*, 235.

53. Mathis, *The Mathis Maxims*, 235.

54. Ibid., 236. Mattox also directly stated this to the *Houston Post*. Mary Flood and Pete Brewton, "Mattox Wants Methodist to Up Charity Care," *Houston Post*, June 23, 1990, HMRC, H-Hospitals Methodist.

55. D. J. Wilson, "Mattox's Office Refuses to Let Up on Methodist," *Houston Post*, July 31, 1990, HMRC, H-Hospitals-Methodist.

56. "Position Paper of The Methodist Hospital," July 30, 1990, in *State of Texas vs. The Methodist Hospital et al.*, TAG, Box 4, 2.

57. Ibid., 2.

58. Ibid., 3–5; quotation on 5; emphasis in original.

59. Mathis, *The Mathis Maxims*, 237.

60. Mary Lenz, "Mattox Sues Directors of Methodist Hospital," *Houston Post*, November 29, 1990, HMRC, H-Hospitals-Methodist.

61. Quotation by Jim Mattox in Ruth SoRelle, "Methodist Accused of Neglecting Its Charitable Work," *Houston Chronicle*, November 27, 1990, HMRC, H-Hospitals-Methodist.

62. As part of the opposition to the hospital's motion to dismiss the lawsuit on summary judgment in 1993, the attorney general's office produced several affidavits, telling the story of patients whose inability to pay forced a denial of care by Methodist. *State of Texas vs. The Methodist Hospital et al.*, Affidavit of Roberta M. Sherwin, MD; Affidavit of Leticia Balboa; Affidavit of Sue Denosowicz, in TAG, Box 4.

63. Mary Lenz, "Methodist Says Mattox Lawsuit Effort to Remedy Medicaid Woes," *Houston Post*, November 28, 1990, HMRC, H-Hospitals-Methodist.

64. Mathis deposition, 25–26.

65. Maurice M. Benitez, "State of Texas Has No Business Telling Methodist What to Do," *Houston Post*, January 2, 1991, HMRC, H-Hospitals-Methodist.

66. Mathis, *The Mathis Maxims*, 238.

67. Tara Parker Pope, "'Arrogance' Fuels Efforts to Revise Hospital Tax Law," *Houston Chronicle*, February 23, 1993, HMRC, H-Hospitals-Methodist.

68. Sandy Lutz, "Special Report: A Primer on Keeping Tax-Exempt Status at Texas' Private, Not-for-Profit Hospitals," *Modern Healthcare*, May 6, 1996, 42. Lutz notes that the threshold for Medicaid shortfalls was raised to 4 percent in 1995.

69. James E. Tyrell III, "Non-Profits Under Fire: The Effects of Minimal Charity Care Requirements Legislation on Not-for-Profit Hospitals," *Journal of Contemporary Health Law and Policy* 26, no. 2 (2009), 383.

70. "Tax man" from Sandy Lutz, "Methodist Makes Its Peace with the Tax Man in Texas," *Modern Healthcare*, June 7, 1993.

71. Ibid.

72. Mathis, *The Mathis Maxims*, 243.

73. Jonathan D. Silver and Sean D. Hamill, "Hospitals Avoid Taxes with Laws, Voluntary Payments," *Pittsburgh Post-Gazette*, November 21, 2011, A-1, A-5.

74. Joseph P. Browne, "Half of City's Property Tax Free," *Pittsburgh Post-Gazette*, November 18, 1968, CLP, Pittsburgh, Taxation, Exempt Properties. This number was nearly

double the 1949 numbers. See H. J. Cutler, "Fourth of City Real Estate Goes Untaxed," *Pittsburgh Post-Gazette*, May 29, 1949, CLP, Pittsburgh, Taxation, Exempt Properties.

75. Quotation in Browne, "Half of City's Property Tax Free."

76. Gabriel Ireton, "City Appeals Ruling on Institution Levy," *Pittsburgh Post-Gazette*, December 16, 1969, CLP, Pittsburgh, Taxation, Institution and Service Privilege Tax. One mill is equal to $1,000 of taxable value. In this case, it was $6 per $1,000 taxable dollars.

77. "2 Suits Filed Opposing City Institution Tax," January 28, 1969, and "Elite Clubs Bring Suit on 'Sick Tax,'" *Pittsburgh Press*, June 13, 1969, CLP, Pittsburgh, Taxation, Institution and Service Privilege Tax. Only a few not-for-profits choose to pay the tax while it was in court. Lawrence Walsh, "Last Court Test for 'Sick' Tax," *Pittsburgh Press*, March 22, 1970, CLP, Pittsburgh, Taxation, Institution and Service Privilege Tax.

78. Lawrence Walsh, "Baskin Lashes City Hospitals," *Pittsburgh Press*, October 28, 1969, CLP, Pittsburgh, Taxation, Institution and Service Privilege Tax.

79. City Faces Costly Medicine to Replace 'Sick Tax,'" *Pittsburgh Press*, December 11, 1969, CLP, Pittsburgh, Taxation, Institution and Service Privilege Tax.

80. "City Refunds on 'Sick Tax' Trickle Out," *Pittsburgh Press*, March 7, 1971, CLP, Pittsburgh, Taxation, Institution and Service Privilege Tax.

81. The Institution and Service Privilege Tax is still in place in Pittsburgh. The current city code says the following about what not-for-profit institutions the tax applies to: "Any organization, foundation, corporation or unincorporated association operating under a non-profit charter or organized as a nonprofit entity by the Commonwealth including, but not limited to, hospitals, nursing homes, colleges, universities, schools other than elementary and secondary, cemeteries, veterans organizations and all other organizations which provide service to the general public. INSTITUTION does not include any political subdivision, any agency of the federal, Commonwealth or local government, any elementary or secondary school within the City or a truly public charity in respect to transactions directly related to its principal charitable purpose." Pittsburgh City Code Chapter 247, §247, 2001; Charles L. Potter Jr., Shelby D. Bennett, Philip E. Cook, and Sheldon Michaelson, *2009 Guidebook to Pennsylvania Taxes* (Chicago: CCH, 2008), 730.

82. Opinion in *Hospital Utilization Project v. Commonwealth of Pennsylvania*, 507 Pa. 1, 487 A.2d 1306, 1985; hereafter cited as HUP Opinion.

83. Paul E. Lewis, "The Hospital Utilization Project of Pennsylvania," *Public Health Reports* 83, no. 9 (September 1968), 743–750.

84. Ibid., 744–745.

85. HUP Opinion, 11.

86. Silver and Hamill, "Hospitals Avoid Taxes with Laws, Voluntary Payments." In 2011, Hamot was acquired by UPMC and agreed to pay a $1.2 million a year PILOT to the city of Erie as part of that merger.

87. Editorial, "A Tax by Any Other Name," *Pittsburgh Post-Gazette*, March 24, 1988, CLP, Pittsburgh, Taxation, Exempt Properties. For a year-by-year breakdown of what Presbyterian University Hospital paid the city and what other expenses the settlement covered, see City of Pittsburgh and Presbyterian University Hospital Agreement/Supplement Settlement Financial Overview, TM, Box 125, Folder 3.

88. Editorial, "A Tax by Any Other Name."

89. Silver and Hamill, "Hospitals Avoid Taxes with Laws, Voluntary Payments." Masloff's plan was to have hospitals across the commonwealth pay into a single fund and have this fund reimburse cities for the services they provided to hospitals. "Hospitals Show Disapproval of Masloff Plan," *Pittsburgh Post-Gazette*, January 5, 1990, 8.

90. Mary Breasted, "The Eveready Mayor: Pittsburgh's Best Loved Jewish Grandmother Keeps Going, and Going," *Pittsburgh*, July 1992, SM, Box 1; Vince Rause, "Pittsburgh Cleans Up Its Act," *New York Times Magazine*, November 26, 1989.

91. Masloff as quoted in Silver and Hamill, "Hospitals Avoid Taxes with Laws, Voluntary Payments."

92. Quote by Joe Geiger, executive director of Pennsylvania Association of Nonprofit Organizations (PANO), in Andrew Conte, "City Collecting Less Money from Nonprofit Groups," *Pittsburgh Tribune-Review*, October 3, 1992.

93. Silver and Hamill, "Hospitals Avoid Taxes with Laws, Voluntary Payments." The following year, the two largest hospitals in the city, Allegheny General and Presbyterian University, reported revenue over expenses for fiscal year (FY) 1990 of $25 and $28 million, respectively. While it is not fully clear where all of these excess revenues went, they likely went into several processes that played out from the early 1990s forward, including the massive expansion of clinical services, purchase of physician practices, property acquisition in Oakland, the funding of a system-wide expansion of UPMC, and the growth of for-profit divisions. "Progress on Tax-Exempts," *Pittsburgh Press*, January 5, 1991, CLP, Pittsburgh, Taxation, Exempt Properties.

94. Mary Kane, "City, County Challenge Tax-Exempt Properties," *Pittsburgh Press*, January 5, 1990, CLP, Pittsburgh, Taxation, Exempt Properties.

95. Robert Baird, "Hospitals Sue to End Tax Pressure," *Pittsburgh Press*, April 13, 1990, CLP, Pittsburgh, Taxation, Exempt Properties.

96. Ibid.

97. Quote from Rowan Miranda, city budget director for Mayor Thomas Murphy, in Marisol Bello, "Tax Exemptions Wreak Havoc on City Budgets," *Pittsburgh Tribune-Review*, November 26, 2000, CLP, Pittsburgh, Taxation, Exempt Properties.

98. Silver and Hamill, "Hospitals Avoid Taxes with Laws, Voluntary Payments." One major organization leading the push was the Pennsylvania Association of Nonprofit Organizations, which organized the Charities Build Communities Coalition as an umbrella lobbying organization for Act 55. See Statement of Jack Owen to the Pennsylvania Senate Finance Committee, August 30, 2007. https://www.pasenategop.com/committees/finance/2007/083007/Owen.pdf.

99. The Institutions of Purely Public Charity Act, 10 P.S. §371.

100. Bello, "Tax Exemptions Wreak Havoc on City Budgets."

101. Ibid.

102. Ibid.

103. Ibid.

104. "City of Pittsburgh, Pennsylvania Municipalities Financial Recovery Plan," July 11, 2004.

105. Ibid., 5.

106. City of Pittsburgh Act 47 Rescission Report, November 8, 2012, 18; Kimberly Barlow "Nonprofits Finalizing Public Service Pledges," *University Times*, October 25, 2012; Mark

Nootbaar, "Peduto Could Shift Millions in Taxes to Schools," WESA, December 2, 2013; Robert Zullo, "City Negotiating New Pact on Nonprofits' Contributions," *Pittsburgh Post-Gazette*, September 6, 2004.

107. "Municipalities Financial Recovery Final Plan, City of Pittsburgh," May 11, 2004, 207; and Bello, "Tax Exemptions Wreak Havoc on City Budgets."

108. Sean D. Hamill and Jonathan D. Silver, "Ruling 'Game-Changer' for Nonprofit Tax Status," *Pittsburgh Post-Gazette*, May 2, 2012; Jeremy Boren, "Courts Whittle Nonprofits' Tax-Exempt Status," *Pittsburgh Tribune-Review*, March 21, 2013.

109. *Mesivtah Eitz Chaim of Bobov, Inc. v. Pike County Board of Assessment Appeals*, No. J-73–2011, Pennsylvania Supreme Court, April 25, 2012, 8.

110. Revenue figures UPMC Fast Facts 2012, *City of Pittsburgh, Pennsylvania v. UPMC*, No. GD-13-, Court of Common Pleas of Allegheny County, April 20, 2013. The initial complaint was amended as the case worked its way through the course of the system.

111. Jeremy Boren and Alex Nixon, "Ravenstahl to Challenge UPMC's Tax-Exempt Status," *Pittsburgh Tribune-Review*, April 20, 2013.

112. Brian Bowling, "UPMC Claims Ravenstahl Challenged Its Tax Status to Create 'Soft Landing' for Once He Leaves Office," *Pittsburgh Tribune-Review*, June 2, 2013.

113. Rich Lord, "UPMC Sues Pittsburgh, Mayor Luke Ravenstahl," *Pittsburgh Post-Gazette*, April 20, 2013; Forum for Economic Development, http://forumforeconomicdevelopment.blogspot.com/.

114. Robert Zullo, "UPMC, City Drop Legal Fight over Taxes," *Pittsburgh-Post Gazette*, June 29, 2014; Kris B. Mamula, "Peduto Talks About Why City Dropped UPMC Lawsuit—and the Way Forward," *Pittsburgh Business Times*, June 29, 2014.

115. "UPMC Criticized for Tax-Exempt Status," *Pittsburgh Post-Gazette*, June 27, 2012; Len Barcousky, "Wagner: Allegheny County Should Check Tax-Exempt Status Annually," *Pittsburgh Post-Gazette*, June 25, 2012; and Jeremy Boren and Bobby Kerlik, "Ravenstahl: Pittsburgh Sues to Remove UPMC's Tax-Exempt Status," *Pittsburgh Tribune-Review*, March 21, 2013.

Epilogue

1. Donald J. Trump, statement by President Trump on the Paris Climate Accord, June 1, 2017.

2. Adam Smeltz, "Mayor Peduto Slams Trump for Name-Dropping Pittsburgh," *Pittsburgh-Post Gazette*, June 1, 2017, and Twitter, @billpeduto. In an article in *Jacobin*, geographer and Pittsburgh historian Patrick Vitale also noted that the Trump/Peduto exchange missed the larger point of inequality in the postindustrial city. Patrick Vitale, "The Pittsburgh Fairy Tale," *Jacobin Magazine*, June 20, 2017.

3. Centers for Medicare and Medicaid, National Health Expenditures Fact Sheet 2015, online at https://www.cms.gov/research-statistics-data-and-systems/statistics-trends-and-reports/nationalhealthexpenddata/nhe-fact-sheet.html; Ricardo Alonzo-Zaldivar, "$10,345 per Person: U.S. Health Care Reaches New Spending Peak," *Associated Press*, July 13, 2016.

4. For an interactive map of this, see https://www.bls.gov/opub/ted/2016/mobile/major-industries-with-highest-employment-by-state.htm; Bureau of Labor Statistics, Employment Projections-2014–2024, December 8, 2015.

5. Pew Research Center, "Baby Boomers Retire," December 2010, online at http://www.pewresearch.org/fact-tank/2010/12/29/baby-boomers-retire; "General Accounting Office,

"The Nation's Fiscal Health," Report Number GAO = 7–237SP, January 2017, 19; Eric Pianin, "10,000 Boomers Turn 65 Every Day. Can Social Security Handle It?" *Fiscal Times*, May 19, 2017.

6. This boom and crash will be even more profound for rural communities. Robert Siegel and Jessica Cheung, "After Decline of Steel and Coal, Ohio Fears Health Care Jobs Are Next," *National Public Radio*, June 26, 2017.

7. For a comprehensive overview of the ACA, see the Kaiser Family Foundation Summary of the ACA online at http://www.kff.org/health-reform/fact-sheet/summary-of-the -affordable-care-act.

8. Nationally, these exchanges have helped to lower the rate of uninsured patients, although as support for them by the Trump administration dwindles, the uninsured rate is moving up. Sara R. Collins, Munira Z. Gunja, Michelle M. Doty, and Herman K. Bhupal, "First Look at Health Insurance Coverage in 2018 Finds ACA Gains Beginning to Reverse," *To the Point: Quick Takes on Health Care Policy and Practice*, Commonwealth Fund, May 1, 2018.

9. Kaiser Family Foundation, Uninsured Rate Among the Nonelderly Population, online at http://www.kff.org/uninsured/slide/uninsured-rate-among-the-nonelderly-population— 1972-2016.

10. Lydia Nuzum, "UPMC Posts Profit in First Half of Fiscal Year," *Pittsburgh Business Times*, February 28, 2017.

11. Ben Schmitt and Wes Venteicher, "UPMC Health Plan Says It Breaks Even on Obamacare Marketplace," *Pittsburgh Tribune-Review*, November 5, 2015.

12. Steve Twedt, "After Three Years, UPMC Health Plan, Highmark See Reversal in Marketplace Fortunes," *Pittsburgh Post-Gazette*, December 5, 2016. UPMC intentionally priced its plans higher as a way to make sure that it would have less exposure if federal risk corridor payments failed to materialize.

13. Alec MacGillis, "Medicaid's Expansion: The Impact on the States," in *Washington Post, Landmark: The Inside Story of America's New Health Care Law and What It Means for Us All* (New York: Public Affairs, 2010), 164—166; Sara Rosenbaum and Timothy M. Westmore-land, "The Supreme Court's Surprising Decision on Medicaid Expansion: How Will the Federal Government and the States Proceed," *Health Affairs* 31, no. 8 (August 2012), 1663—1672; Kaiser Family Foundation, Pennsylvania Medicaid Expansion Fact Sheet, http://www.kff.org/ medicaid/fact-sheet/medicaid-expansion-in-pennsylvania; Phil Galewitz, "Texas Hospitals Fear Losing $6.2B Medicaid Deal," *Kaiser Health News*, June 12, 2017.

14. Testimony of Leesa Allen, Deputy Secretary, Office of Medical Assistance Programs, Commonwealth of Pennsylvania, before the Pennsylvania General Assembly, House Democratic Policy Committee. March 29, 2017, 3.

15. UPMC Fast Facts and Community Benefits, June 2016.

16. Kristen Wong, "Pittsburgh-Area Community Health Centers Brace for Obamacare Repeal," *PublicSource.org*. February 22, 2017.

17. Jenny Deam, "Obamacare Repeal and Replacement Could Come with Hidden Costs," *Houston Chronicle*, January 24, 2017.

18. Wade Goodwyn, "Texas Loses Billions to Treat the Poor by Not Expanding Medicaid, Advocates Say," *National Public Radio*, May 29, 2015.

19. Carrie Feibel, "Harris Health Will Restrict Financial Aid and Push 15,000 Patients Toward Obamacare," *Houston Public Media*, September 25, 2015. In a follow-up article, Feibel

noted that Harris Health beat revenue projections for the year due to more patient revenue and a program of painful layoffs. Carrie Feibel, "Harris Health System Squeaks Through Fiscal Year, Barely," *Houston Public Media*, April 1, 2016.

20. UPMC press release, "$15/Hour by 2019," May 29, 2016.

21. Richard Florida, Charlotta Mellander, and Kevin Stolarick, "Inside the Black Box of Regional Development: Human Capital, the Creative Class, and Tolerance," Working Paper, the Martin Prosperity Institute, Joseph L. Rotman School of Management, University of Toronto, April 2007, 5, 27, 29. See also Richard Florida, "Why Eds and Meds Alone Can't Revitalize Cities," *Atlantic*, September 18, 2012.

22. UPMC press release, "UPMC Announced $2B Investment to Build 3 Digitally Based Specialty Hospitals Backed by World-Leading Innovative, Translational Science," press release, November 3, 2017; Fair Share Pittsburgh, "What Is a Community Benefits Agreement?" http://www.fairsharepittsburgh.com/community-benefits; Pittsburgh United, "Unhealthy Choices: How UPMC's Low Wages Endanger the Future of Pittsburgh's Middle Class," April 24, 2013, online at http://makeitourupmc.org/2013/08/unhealthy-choices-how-upmcs-low-wages-endanger-the-future-of-pittsburghs-middle-class/; Liz Reid and Kathleen J. Davis, "City Council Approves UPMC Mercy Expansion, Despite Outrage from Community," WESA Public Radio, July 31, 2018.

23. Commonwealth of Pennsylvania, Josh Shapiro, Attorney General, et al; v UPMC, A Nonprofit Corp., et al; No 334 M.D. 2014, February 2, 2019, 37–70, online at https://www.attorneygeneral.gov/upmc/.

24. Ibid., 8—10. Quotation on page 10.

25. Ibid., 13.

26. Ibid., 61.

27. UPMC Statement in Bob Bauder, "AG Shapiro: UPMC's 'corporate greed' hurting patients" *Tribune-Review*, February 7, 2019, online at https://triblive.com/news/pittsburgh-allegheny/ag-josh-shapiro-files-legal-challenge-against-upmc-highmark-dispute/

28. The eds and meds alarm has been sounded most clearly by urban blogger Aaron Renn. See Aaron M. Renn, "The End of the Road for Eds and Meds," *TheNewGeography.com*, September 12, 2012, http://www.newgeography.com/content/003076-the-end-road-eds-and-meds. For the region surrounding Pittsburgh see Vitale, "The Pittsburgh Fairy Tale."

29. University Center for Social and Urban Research, University of Pittsburgh, "The State of Aging in Allegheny County," October 2014, 9, 16, online at https://ucsur.pitt.edu/files/center/soa/2014/State%20of%20Aging%20in%20Allegheny%20County.pdf. In 2014, this meant that 16.8 percent of the population of Allegheny County was sixty-five and older versus 13 percent of the population of the United States.

30. Houston Demographic Data, online at http://www.houstontx.gov/planning/Demographics.

31. Lyndon B. Johnson, "Remarks at the University of Michigan," May 22, 1964. American Presidency Project, University of California Santa Barbara, online at http://presidency.proxied.lsit.ucsb.edu/ws/index.php?pid=26262&st=&st1=.

Archival Collections and Abbreviations

Abbreviations used in the notes appear in parentheses.

Archives of Industrial Society, University of Pittsburgh, Pittsburgh, Pennsylvania
Health Systems Agency of Southwestern Pennsylvania Records, 1971–1987 AIS.1987.02
Dick Thornburgh Papers, 1932– AIS.1998.30.17
Elsie H. Hillman Papers, 1920–2015 AIS.2013.02
Charles Owen Rice Papers, 1894–2005 AIS.1976.11

Baylor College of Medicine Archives
Office of the President Central Files
Department of Community Medicine Files

Carnegie Library of Pittsburgh, Pennsylvania Room, Pittsburgh, Pennsylvania
Carnegie Library Newspaper Vertical File Collection (CLP)

C. L. Sonnichsen Special Collections Department, University of Texas at El Paso, El Paso, Texas
Julius Rivera Papers, MS162 (JR)

Harris County Archives, Houston, Texas
Harris County Hospital District Records, CR028 (HCHD)

Houston Public Library, Houston Metropolitan Research Center, Houston, Texas
Houston Metropolitan Research Center Newspaper Vertical File Collection (HMRC)

John P. McGovern Historical Collections and Research Center, Texas Medical Center Library, Houston, Texas
Baylor College of Medicine, Institutional Collection IC006 (BCM)
Papers of R. Lee Clark, Manuscript Collection No. 70, Series VIII (RLC)
University of Texas M. D. Anderson Cancer Center, Institutional Collection IC014
Michael E. DeBakey Subject File
Papers of Frederick C. Elliott, Manuscript Collection No. 71 (FCE)
Herman Hospital Collection, Publications (HHC)
The Methodist Hospital, Institutional Collection, IC020 (TMH)
Hermann Horizons Bound Volume (HH)
St. Luke's Episcopal Hospital, Institutional Collection: IC021 (SLEH)
Texas Medical Center Inc., Institutional Collection IC002 (TMCI)

Unprocessed at the Time of Review (identified in notes)
Memorial Hermann Merger Files (HHC)

Kheel Center for Labor–Management Documentation and Archives, Catherwood Library, Cornell University, Ithaca, New York
Local 1199 Collection, MS 5206 (1199)

M. D. Anderson Historical Resources Center, Houston, Texas
Charles A. LeMaistre Papers, Office of the President—filmed and unfilmed records (CAL)

Mercy Hospital Archives, Pittsburgh, Pennsylvania
Records of the Neighborhood Committee on Health Care (NCHC)
Records of the Hospital Planning Association, 1958–1973 (HPA)

Office of the Texas Attorney General, Consumer Protection Division, Austin, Texas
State of Texas vs. The Methodist Hospital et al. and related (TAG)

Senator John Heinz History Center, Thomas and Katherine Detre Library and Archives, Pittsburgh, Pennsylvania
Allegheny Conference on Community Development Collection, MSS#285 (ACCD)
Buhl Foundation Records, MSS #187 (BF)

Montefiore Hospital Records, MSS# 286, Rauh Jewish Archives
Papers of Sophie Masloff, MSS #589, Rauh Jewish Archives
Mayor Thomas J. Murphy Administration (Pittsburgh, Pennsylvania), 1974–2005, MSS #499 (TM)
Records of the Maurice Falk Medical Fund, 1960–1994, MSS#207 (MFMF)
Records of the Health and Welfare Planning Association, 1908–1990, MSS#158 (HWPA)

Texas State Archives, Austin, Texas
Report of the Special Task Force to Study Not-For-Profit Hospitals and Unsponsored Charity Care

University of Pittsburgh Archives and Special Collections, Pittsburgh, Pennsylvania
Dr. Henry T. Bahnson Papers, 1943–2002 UA.90.F82 (HB)
John Gabbert Bowman, Administrative Files, 1921–1945 UA.2.10.1921–1945 (JGB)
William Wallace Booth Papers, 1922–1973 AIS.1973.23 (WWB)
Edward H. Litchfield, Administrative Files, 1956–1965 UA.2.10.1956–1965 (EHL)
Wesley W. Posvar, Administrative Files, 1967–1991 UA.2.10.1967–1991 (WP)
Public Administration Reports and Studies (Assorted), 1910–1992 AIS.1996.16
University of Pittsburgh Archives Information Files, c. 1900–present (UA.Info.Files)
Dr. Thomas E. Starzl M.D. Papers, 1908– 2014, UA.90.F68 (TS)
University Health Center Records, UA.90.43 (UHC)

U.S. National Library of Medicine, Bethesda, Maryland
Michael E. DeBakey, MS C 582 (MED)

U.S. National Archives and Records Administration, College Park, Maryland
RG 381, Records of the Community Service Administration

Privately Held Papers at Time of Review
Assorted Baylor College of Medicine Department of Community Medicine Annual Reports, Carlos Vallbona

Records of Blue Cross of Western Pennsylvania/Highmark
CardioVascular Care Providers
Papers of Denton Cooley
Papers of Peter Safar, Freedom House (FH)
Papers of Evan Stoddard

Index

Page numbers followed by *p* indicate photographs

Acknowledgments

Historians often say that ours is a lonely profession—the hours spent alone researching and writing is supposed to lead to the emergence of a fully formed monograph. *The Medical Metropolis*, like all works of historical scholarship, is the product of many contributions from a wide range of people and institutions. It started life at Carnegie Mellon University's History Department and owes much to Joel Tarr and Jay Aronson, as well as to the intellectual influence of Joe W. Trotter, Katherine Lynch, Wendy Goldman, and John Soluri. One could not ask for a better mentor than Caroline Jean Acker, who has constantly pushed me to expand the scope of the project and think critically about how the past and present intersect. I am also grateful to CMU colleagues Amund Tallaksen, Andrew Ramey, John Weigel, Kevin Brown, Avigail Oren, Russell Pryor, Lisa Seibert, Rachel Oppenheimer, and Shera Moxley who provided intellectual encouragement and comradery.

Many of the ideas in this book, including portions of Chapter 1 and Chapter 6, were sharpened by presentations at a variety of academic conferences and in two articles in the *Journal of Urban History*. Portions of these articles are included with the permission of the journal and are cited in this book's endnotes. I would like to especially thank Edward Muller for organizing the forum on "Renaissance Revisited," which grew out of a session at the Society for American City and Regional Planning History in 2013. This section appeared in January 2015, and fellow presenters included Laura Grantmyre, Muriel Issacson, Tracy Neumann, Patrick Vitale, and Allen Dieterich-Ward. Many of the ideas from this conference and article helped to inform Chapter 1. I would also like to thank Jared Day for his work on coordinating the special section on health care and urban revitalization, which appeared in March 2016, and helped to inform Chapter 6, as well as his deep commitment to this book and to Pittsburgh's history. Jared's and Joe Trotter's work has been an important influence on how I approach Pittsburgh's contemporary history. Jeremy Greene's and Gianna

Pomota's generous invitation to Johns Hopkins to present portions of Chapter 2 at the History of Science, Medicine, and Technology Colloquium resulted in a lively discussion that helped me rethink key parts of this chapter's argument. Other scholars whose work has shaped this book include Aaron Cavin; Christy Ford Chapin, who read early drafts and provided feedback; Aaron Cowan; Catherine Conner; Dr. Christopher Crenner; Guian McKee; Todd Michney; Nic Ramos; Elizabeth Tandy Shermer; Jon Teaford; Dominique Tobell; Gabriel Winant; and my two peer reviewers with the University of Pennsylvania Press, James Schafer and Allen Dieterich-Ward, who both provided excellent feedback on the entire manuscript. Allen's thoughtful historical work on Pittsburgh has influenced my own approach to the city's and region's history.

At Duquesne University, I have been surrounded by supportive colleagues, including my History Department colleagues and interdisciplinary research collaborators Cathleen Appelt and Jessica Devido. John Mitcham has read several drafts and offered helpful comments. Thanks also to Frederick Evans and the Center for Interpretative and Qualitative Research where I had the opportunity to speak about Pittsburgh health care and the city's postindustrial development. Several graduate students, including Sarah Greenwald, Lindsay Davenport, Kristin Fagan, and Kerry Jo Green, provided research assistance.

Private and corporate papers formed an important source base. I would like to thank Fran Mistrick and Dr. Patrick Kochanek for once again opening up the papers of Dr. Peter Safar, and Dr. Thomas Starzl, Osama Mikhail, and Evan Stoddard for sharing their papers. Highmark generously pulled records from their storage facility and provided me with office space for document review, and I would like to thank Thomas O'Brien, Aaron Bilger, and Adrienne Londino. I would also like to thank Dr. Denton Cooley for opening up his files on the Dutch Air Bridge.

The remainder of the archival work for *Making the Medical Metropolis* was conducted in publicly available collections, and I owe an important debt to tremendous archival staffs in both cities. In Pittsburgh, I would like to thank Zach Brodt, Edward Galloway, David Grinnell, Marianne Kasica and Miriam Meislik, Wendy Pflug, Debbie Rougeux, and Ashley Taylor at the University of Pittsburgh Archives, Oliva Glofelty-Scheuring at UPMC Mercy Hospital Archives, and C. Art Louderback, formerly of the Heinz History Center. In Houston, I would like to thank Philip Montgomery, Alethea Drexler, and Sandra Yates at the John P. McGovern Historical

Center at the Houston Academy of Medicine-Texas Medical Center Library, JoAnn Pospisil, Carolyn Tabata and the staff at the Baylor College of Medicine Archives, Jose Javier Garza at the M. D Anderson Historical Research Center, Sarah Canby Jackson and Annie Groves, at the Harris County Archives, and the staff at the Houston Metropolitan Research Center at the Houston Public Library. The State of Texas Attorney General's Office also made files and office space available as I reviewed sources for Chapter 6. Anne Allis provided help in El Paso at the C. L. Sonnichsen Special Collections at the University of Texas at El Paso and Melissa Holland and Patrizia Sione helped by sending me electric files from the Kheel Center for Labor Management Documentation and Archives at Cornell University. The expert guidance through Dr. DeBakey's papers by Jeffrey Reznick, Stephen Greenberg, Ken Koyle, John Rees, Susan Speaker, and Rebecca Warlow from the National Library of Medicine's History of Medicine Division contributed substantially to the development of several chapters, but most especially Chapter 3.

Jonathon Erlen and Bryant Boutwell generously opened up their homes, shared their experiences in Pittsburgh and Houston's health care market, and helped connect me to key individuals and institutions. I would also like to thank Dr. Gerald Nelson, of Wichita, Kansas, for including me in that city's history of medicine community, and the University of Kansas School of Medicine-Wichita for providing me the recorded lecture of Dr. Cooley speaking to the Jager Club. Kathy Washy helpfully connected me with UPMC Mercy Hospital's archives. I am deeply thankful to my editor Robert Lockhart, whose helpful suggestions made this a much better book, and Mark Rose, who was an early advocate of the project and continued to provide guidance and support throughout its development. Other friends, too numerous to mention but nevertheless appreciated, have provided small favors from allowing me to stay with them on archival research trips, to dinners, and conversations that have helped remind me of the joy that comes with being a historian.

I would also like to thank everybody who participated in the events described in this book who took time to chat with me in person or over the telephone. These rich personal conversations helped to shape my understanding of the events described within. In Pittsburgh, this included Dr. John Delaney, Angel Jordan, Harun Rashid, Dr. Thomas Starzl, Evan Stoddard, and Dennis Yablonsky. In Houston, I had the privilege of speaking with John Adams and Tobin Lassen, Bryant Boutwell, Dr. William T.

Butler, Larry Mathis, Osama Mikhail, Ron Girotto, Fred Welch, William Thomson, and Dr. Carlos Vallbona.

Funding for this project at all stages was provided by several sources, including the Carnegie Mellon Department of History, the Andrew W. Mellon/American Council of Learned Societies Dissertation Completion Fellowship, the Michael E. DeBakey Fellowship in the History of Medicine through the National Library of Medicine and the Michael E. DeBakey Medical Foundation, the Forum for Economic Development, and the Wimmer Family Foundation. The Duquesne University History Department and Dean James C. Swindal of the McAnulty College and Graduate School of Liberal Arts at Duquesne have also provided financial support.

Finally, my most sincere thanks are for my family. I am fortunate to have two wonderfully supportive parents, Thomas and Nancy Simpson, as well as my sister Sara Gibson, and my nephew Quinn Gibson, who have all encouraged my interests and believed in my dreams. My most heartfelt thanks are for my wife, Amy, who made these interests and dreams possible, and through her own work in the health care field taught me a great deal about the business of medicine. This book is for her and our son Ethan, who arrived just as this project was concluding but who, as a Pittsburgher, will live with the realities of the medical metropolis—both bad and good—for years to come.